BENEFICIAL BOMBING

MARK CLODFELTER

BENEFICIAL BOMBING

The Progressive Foundations of American Air Power, 1917–1945

UNIVERSITY OF NEBRASKA PRESS • LINCOLN & LONDON

Library of Congress Cataloging-in-
Publication Data
Clodfelter, Mark.
Beneficial bombing: the progressive
foundations of American air power,
1917–1945 / Mark Clodfelter.
p. cm.—(Studies in war, society, and
the military)
Includes bibliographical references and
index.
ISBN 978-0-8032-3398-0 (cloth: alk.
paper)
1. Bombing, Aerial—United States—
History—20th century. 2. Air power—
United States—History—20th century.
3. Precision bombing—United States—
History—20th century. 4. World
War, 1914–1918—Aerial operations.
5. World War, 1939–1945—Aerial
operations. 6. Progressivism (United
States politics)—History—20th
century. I. Title.
UG703.C56 2010
358.4'14097309041—dc22
2010021757

Set in Sabon.

CONTENTS

ILLUSTRATIONS

ACKNOWLEDGMENTS

While writing a work based to a substantial degree on historical records may appear to be an individual project, it is not—it requires a tremendous amount of assistance from many other people. Moreover, such an endeavor also requires a substantial amount of time. Accordingly, I must first thank Major General Robert Steel, USAF, and the staff of the National War College for providing me with a sabbatical year that allowed me the necessary time to complete a project that has long occupied my attention.

Archival collections provided many of my sources, and I must make special mention of some of the archivists who gave me invaluable assistance. At the Air Force Historical Research Agency at Maxwell Air Force Base, Alabama, Ms. Lynn O. Gamma, Dr. James H. Kitchens, and Mr. Joseph D. Caver all were tremendously helpful. Joe in particular was wonderful, tracking down answers to questions that I had, and finding many of the photographs used in this book. At the Air Force Office of History at Bolling Air Force Base DC, Dr. Roger Miller and Ms. Mary Lee Jefferson also provided many excellent photographs, several of which I had never before seen. Mr. Jeff Flannery and Ms. Jennifer Brathovde at the U.S. National Archives offered essential guidance as I plowed through manuscript collections. In the Special Collections branch of the U.S. Air Force Academy Library, I received considerable help from the masterful archivist (now retired), Mr. Duane Reed, as well as from Dr. Edward A. Scott, the Director of Academy Libraries. The superb staff at the National Defense University Library, including Ms. Carolyn Turner, Ms. Rosemary Marlowe-Dzuik, and Ms. Kimberley Jordan, graciously and expeditiously responded to my many requests.

I must also thank the "IT gurus" of National War College, Mr. Anthony Muschelli and Mr. Peter Pettigrew, who kept me "logged in" to the National Defense University network throughout my sabbatical. I could not have written this book without their tireless efforts. National War College's Dr. Chris Bassford, who also has a considerable amount of IT expertise (besides being our Clausewitz guru!), graciously gave much of his time to refine many of the photographs that I selected.

For suggestions, advice, and consultation, I am grateful to many people as well. Ms. Heather Lundine and Ms. Bridget Barry at University of Nebraska Press provided me with a multitude of useful tidbits that I would never have considered and made this book much better than it otherwise would have been; I also appreciate the sage advice of Ms. Sarah Steinke, the copy editor. Dr. David Mets, a dear friend and outstanding historian who taught with me at the School of Advanced Air and Space Studies, provided a critique of the first two chapters that I took to heart. Professor Emeritus Gerhard Weinberg—*the* historian of the Second World War—also provided me with an invaluable critique of my chapter drafts. Students from the National War College and Industrial College of the Armed Forces in my "Air Power and Modern War" class during the past decade never failed to challenge my thinking, as did Air Force Colonel Peter Faber—a wonderful air power historian—who twice taught the class with me. Air Force Lieutenant Colonel Rondall Rice, author of the excellent book *The Politics of Air Power: From Confrontation to Cooperation in Army Aviation Civil-Military Relations*, read the manuscript and provided me with sound recommendations. Rondall, a fellow North Carolinian, was one of my advisees when I taught at the Air Force Academy, and his assistance is a classic case of the student instructing the teacher. My next-door neighbor, Dr. (and physicist) Leslie Cohen, gave me many useful insights in frequent discussions. Former students at the University of North Carolina—and current

Air Force officers—Chris Holland, Sheila (Johnson) Baldwin, Jessica Rice, Bob Champion, and Wendy (Williams) Walker provided continued encouragement and advice. Air Force Colonel "BA" Andrews, who has taught at both National War College and the Industrial College of the Armed Forces, provided invaluable suggestions, both in terms of research and structure.

Professor Peter Maslowski, who has served as my mentor since 1982 when I became one of his graduate students at the University of Nebraska, provided continual support and a tremendous critique of an early draft of this work. I never cease to be amazed by his continued drive for excellence and his absolute commitment to making his students better people—in all facets of life. Pete has been my definition of the ideal teacher for as long as I have known him, and he is the example I have tried to emulate throughout my teaching career.

This book would not have occurred without the guidance provided by two key people in my life—my father-in-law and my father. My father-in-law, Dr. David MacIsaac, wrote the definitive study of World War II's U.S. Strategic Bombing Survey, and taught me when I was a senior cadet at the Air Force Academy—long before his daughter Donna caught my eye. He was a rigid disciplinarian when it came to historical scholarship then, and nothing has changed in almost thirty-five years since. He read an early draft of this work and took me to task on many parts of it, and the resulting product is far better than it would have been without his comments. I cannot thank him enough for his help—in this endeavor and many others—and I dedicate this book in part to him.

My dad—Walter Allen Clodfelter Jr.—is a part of America's greatest generation, and served in a control tower on Tinian during the early morning of 6 August 1945 when the *Enola Gay* took off on its fateful mission to Hiroshima. His stories of what it was like in the closing stages of the war—to include talking down a squadron of Mustangs through a solid overcast over

Tinian's runway—planted the seed that got me interested in the Air Force and air power, and I'm sure were instrumental in my decision to attend the Air Force Academy. He also read an early draft of this work and, as the most meticulous proofreader I have ever seen, pointed out errors I would not otherwise have caught, as well as asked me "big picture" questions that I had not considered. He is a continual source of inspiration, and I dedicate this book in part to him.

Despite the considerable advice and assistance that I have received, the responsibility for all that is written is mine alone, and my work does not necessarily represent the views of the National War College or any government agency.

I have already mentioned the role that my father played in helping me craft this work, but I must also mention Mom as well, for together my parents provided an unceasing amount of guidance and support. I also cannot fail to mention Donna, for without her this project would never have happened. She never doubted my instincts, constantly encouraged me through difficult periods, plus gave me that greatest of all commodities—time—and she never laughed too much when I came bursting through the door after a run on the GW Parkway Trail and madly scrambled to find a pen and paper.

Finally, I would be remiss if I did not acknowledge Coach Roy Williams and the National Championship North Carolina basketball team of 2008–9. As a die-hard Tar Heel who will have part of his ashes scattered at the Old Well, I was consistently thrilled and inspired by the exploits of Tyler Hansbrough, Ty Lawson, Wayne Ellington, Danny Green, Deon Thompson, and company as they brought back a fifth NCAA Championship to Chapel Hill. I can't guarantee that it helped the quality of my research and writing, but I'm certain that it didn't hurt.

M. C.
Mount Vernon, Virginia

SOURCE ACKNOWLEDGMENTS

Portions of chapter 2 previously appeared in "Molding Airpower Convictions: Development and Legacy of William Mitchell's Strategic Thought," in *The Paths of Heaven: The Evolution of Airpower Theory*, ed. Philip S. Meilinger, 79–114 (Maxwell Air Force Base AL: Air University Press, 1997).

Portions of chapters 2 and 3 previously appeared in "Pinpointing Devastation: American Air Campaign Planning before Pearl Harbor," *Journal of Military History* 58, no. 1 (1994): 75–102.

Portions of chapter 5 previously appeared in "Aiming to Break Will: America's World War II Bombing of German Morale and Its Ramifications," *Journal of Strategic Studies* 33, no. 3 (June 2010): 401–35.

Portions of chapter 7 previously appeared in "A Strategy Based on Faith: The Enduring Appeal of Progressive American Airpower," *Joint Force Quarterly*, no. 49 (2008): 24–31, 150–60.

BENEFICIAL BOMBING

Introduction

In October 1910, former president Theodore Roosevelt was in St. Louis campaigning for the Republican governor of Missouri, Herbert Hadley. Upon learning of an "International Aeronautic Tournament" outside the city, the energetic and always inquisitive Roosevelt demanded to see it. "TR" and Hadley arrived at Kinloch Field on 10 October by an eighty-automobile motorcade—the largest such procession St. Louis had then seen—just as one of the Wright brothers' six aircraft landed near the grandstand. The pilot of the fragile machine was Arch Hoxsey, a pince-nez-wearing aviator who earlier that year had made America's first recorded night flight, and who had recently set an endurance record of 104 miles by flying non-stop to St. Louis from Springfield, Illinois. Hoxsey jumped out of the Model B biplane and walked to Roosevelt's car through an array of Missouri National Guard troops surrounding the vehicle.

"I was hoping, Colonel, that I might have you for a passenger on one of my trips," Hoxsey said to Roosevelt.[1]

"By George, I believe I will," Roosevelt replied. He accompanied Hoxsey to the Model B and, to the surprise of those who had arrived with him at the air show, sat down in the passenger seat and said, "Let her go!"

After a four-minute spectacle above Kinloch Field that included a series of climbs and dives—punctuated by "oohs" and "ahhs" from the crowd below—Roosevelt became the nation's first president to fly in an airplane. During the flight he pointed to a Signal Corps building close by and had Hoxsey pretend to attack it. "War, army, aeroplane, bomb!" Roosevelt shouted as Hoxsey flew back and forth above the installation. Onlookers mobbed TR once he landed, despite the best efforts of the Missouri guardsmen to keep them away. When the crowd finally parted enough to give him a chance to speak, he triumphantly exclaimed, "By George, it was fine!"[2]

Roosevelt's flight befitted the sense of American adventurism that he embodied, and it also befitted his role as a leader of the progressive movement in the United States. Indeed, as a standardbearer of the progressives, Roosevelt was on the lookout for ways to improve the daily lives of American citizens, and the airplane offered to do just that. The "flying machine" portended revolutions in transportation and communications; commerce and trade would benefit enormously from its continued development. Yet as Roosevelt's comment to Hoxsey above Kinloch Field indicated, the airplane also offered tremendous potential as an instrument of war. A generation of American airmen would view the airplane's military promise in progressive terms—as the key to winning conflicts quickly, cheaply, and efficiently.

For most Americans, though, progressivism had nothing to do with war. The movement, which spanned the nation during the late nineteenth and early twentieth centuries, affected many different groups and encompassed several disparate threads. All focused on progress and reform, and included efforts to reduce inefficiency and waste in manufacturing and business practices, eliminate corruption from government and business, increase the responsiveness of government institutions, promote fairness and equality for all social classes, improve working conditions and protect workers, and enhance the public's general well-being. At its heart, progressivism promised change that was just, rational, positive, and efficient. Roosevelt emerged as a progressive leader of the Republican Party famous for his "trust busting" and would later break away from the Republicans to form his own "Progressive Party" in 1912. Democrat Woodrow Wilson, the winner of the 1912 election, also considered himself a progressive, and worked hard to assure the success of the "individual entrepreneur" against the perceived evils of "big business." The progressive movement's span across political party lines demonstrated its wide national appeal.

The devastation and ugly realism of World War I ended the progressive era for most Americans; the repudiation of the Versailles Treaty and Wilson's League of Nations exemplified the public's postwar rejection of the movement's ideals. Yet for Army Air Service officers like Edgar Gorrell and William "Billy" Mitchell, the carnage and waste that they witnessed on the Western Front sparked the beginning of a progressive effort that was unique—an attempt to reform *war* by relying on its own destructive technology as the instrument of change. They were convinced that the airplane—used as a bombing platform—offered the means to make wars much less lethal than conflicts waged by armies or navies.

The airmen contended that a clash of armies, with its subsequent slaughter, was unnecessary to fight and win future conflicts. Instead, the truly vital ingredients of modern war—the essential industries that produced weapons and fuel, key communications centers, and lines of transportation—were vulnerable to attack from the air. The loss of those installations would not only wreck a nation's ability to fight, it would also sap the will of the populace, because the same facilities needed to wage modern war were also those necessary to sustain normal, day-to-day life. Aircraft would destroy the vital centers through *precision* bombing—sophisticated technology would guarantee that bombs hit only the intended targets, and few lives would be lost in the process. The finite destruction would end wars quickly, without crippling manpower losses—maximum results with a minimum of death—and thus, bombing would actually serve as a beneficial instrument of war.

To assure the success of their ideas, the advocates of "progressive air power" also called for reforming America's defense structure, with the establishment of a separate air force as a new armed service. They set out to convince the nation of that perceived need, and along the way recruited a core of like-minded officers who took their ideas and further refined them. The conviction that the "strategic bombing" of vital centers offered the solution to fighting and winning future wars efficiently blended with the belief that service autonomy was essential to assure the bomber's proper wartime use against industrial targets—not against armies or navies. Ultimately, the two notions became inseparable—the ability of air forces to fight and win wars independently of armies and navies justified an autonomous air force—and an autonomous air force was necessary to assure that air power could efficiently achieve victory on its own.

By the eve of Pearl Harbor, Mitchell disciples like Henry H. "Hap" Arnold and Frank Andrews, and a legion of officers inculcated with Mitchell's notions refined by the Air Corps Tactical School, combined to produce a substantial coterie of airmen who subscribed to a belief in "progressive air power." Most would not have used such a term to describe their convictions; Mitchell himself used the term rarely. Yet they were just as committed to reforming war as the muckrakers had been to reforming industrial working conditions.

Collectively, the airmen subscribed to the following central tenet: air power was a more efficient military instrument than land or sea power because it offered a way to fight and win wars more quickly and less expensively (in terms of lives lost on *both* sides) than did armies or navies. The plan devised by former Tactical School instructors in August 1941 for using American air power in the ongoing European war called for strategic bombing to wreck Germany's war-making ability to such a degree that an invasion of the continent might prove unnecessary. Arnold, by then Commanding General of the Army Air Forces, approved the plan, as did Army Chief of Staff George Marshall and Secretary of War Henry Stimson. The promise of progressive air power had broad appeal.

The reality of war—which revealed that American bombers and their crews were rarely capable of pinpoint destruction during combat conditions, and included an overarching political objective of "unconditional surrender" that allowed unlimited devastation—generated a momentum of its own that undermined several of the progressive notions that had guided American airmen before the conflict. By 1945, "progressive air power" meant quickly ending the war to reduce American casualties. Still, many air commanders continued to believe that the destruction of vital centers—despite the accompanying death and desolation—not only hastened the war's end, but also ultimately saved lives on both sides. As a result, the progressive mindset that guided airmen on the eve of war never really disappeared during its conduct.

The progressive notions of beneficial bombing—germinated in World War I and tested in World War II—became the basis of doctrine for an independent Air Force in the immediate postwar era, and continue to guide Air Force thought today.

1 • Genesis in the Great War

Accurate bombing on a large scale is a new science and requires the entire time and study of
the man who is to shoulder the responsibility for success or failure during the coming year.
• LT. COL. EDGAR S. GORRELL, 2 JANUARY 1918

29 May 1910

On a warm Sunday morning, U.S. Military Academy cadets assembled at Trophy Point to witness a spectacular event. Aviation pioneer Glenn Curtiss had announced that he would pilot
his thirty-foot-long biplane from Albany to New York and claim
the *New York World*'s prize of ten thousand dollars for making
the first flight between the two cities. The initial leg of his journey
had gone well: Curtiss had taken off shortly after 7:00 a.m., had
stopped for fuel at Camelot, and had taken off again at 9:30. Yet
as he approached Storm King Mountain a few minutes later at an
altitude of one thousand feet, violent air currents above the Hudson River plummeted his frail craft to within fifty feet of the water. He struggled with the flight controls to prevent a further loss
of altitude and, as he did so, flew past West Point. His dive hid
the airplane from the cadets' view and caused them to run to Cul-
lum Hall, perched high on a bluff overlooking the Hudson. From
there they could clearly see the tiny craft, the first flying machine
that most of them had ever witnessed. Oblivious to the pilot's difficulty, the cadets tossed their caps into the air and shouted their
favorite football cheer, with a slight modification: "Rah, rah, ray!
Rah, rah, ray! West Point, West Point, Armay! Curtiss! Curtiss!
Curtiss!"[1]

One of those chanting was Edgar Staley Gorrell, a diminutive nineteen-year-old "yearling" from Baltimore. Gorrell's small stature and boyish features had earned him the nickname "Nap" from his classmates, and Nap was mightily impressed by the spectacle. From the day he viewed Curtiss's flight—which arrived in New York City after two hours and forty-six minutes of air travel—Gorrell determined that he too would become an aviator. Assigned to the infantry after graduation, he transferred to the Signal Corps' Aviation Section in 1914 and then completed flight training. Two years later, as one of eleven pilots in the First Aero Squadron, he helped track Pancho Villa's band of outlaws across northern Mexico. He became the first American to fly an aircraft equipped to take automatic photographs, the first to fly an aircraft while conducting radio experiments, the first American Army officer to volunteer for a parachute jump, and one of the first officers to fly at night. He also developed the first plan for an American bomber offensive against an enemy nation.[2]

Early Notions of American Air Power

Gorrell's scheme for attacking Wilhelmine Germany called into question the basic purpose of an air force: whether to support the Army directly through air operations tied to the Army's immediate progress on the front lines or to conduct "independent" operations, such as "strategical" bombing, that would ultimately improve the Army's situation at the front but that also offered the prospect of a rapid, cheap victory by destroying the enemy's war-making capability and will to fight. *If* air power *could* achieve victory independently of ground forces, it implied that the Army's "air" branch might deserve a measure of autonomy. Before World War I, however, such concerns were minimal, even among airmen. When Congressman James Hay proposed a bill in February 1913 to create an "Air Corps" equivalent in stature to the infantry, cavalry, or artillery, aviators were almost unanimous in condemning the proposal. Lieutenants Benjamin D. Foulois and Henry H. "Hap" Arnold testified that the Signal Corps' control of aviation was satisfactory.[3] Captain William "Billy" Mitchell, at that time a non-flyer and the lone Signal Corps representative on the Army's General Staff, argued that aviation was essential to Signal Corps reconnaissance and communication. "The offensive value of this thing has yet to be proved," he stated.[4]

The outbreak of war in Europe heightened interest in the airplane's military potential. That conflict, combined with a growing rift between Signal Corps aviators and their non-flying superiors, spurred Secretary of War Newton D. Baker to launch a General Staff investigation in April 1916 on the appropriateness of severing aviation from Signal Corps control. Many pilots bemoaned the "under 30, bachelor only" restrictions on flying, while many of their non-flying superiors regarded the young aviators as undisciplined. Baker decided that air autonomy was not the answer, but also admitted that combat in Europe had demonstrated that the air arm was more than just an auxiliary service.[5] The next year, on the eve of America's entry into the Great War, a joint Army-Navy panel recommended purchasing "a rigid airship of the zeppelin type" that could bomb an enemy's homeland.[6] Although the dominant focus of America's air power vision remained on supporting the Army, that view did not exclude independent operations.

The failure of American civilian and military leaders to articulate a definitive concept of military aviation likely stemmed from the paucity of military aviation available. When Congress declared war against Germany on 6 April 1917, the Signal Corps' Aviation Section numbered only 65 officers on active duty, of whom 26 were certified pilots, backed by 1,100 enlisted men and 200 civilian personnel. The Army's sole example of applying air

power against an enemy was the use of eight Curtiss JN3 training aircraft in Brigadier General John J. Pershing's expedition to
Mexico, and all had broken down. That fiasco caused Congress
to lavish appropriations of almost thirteen million dollars on the
Aviation Section, but by the end of 1916 the Army possessed only
149 aircraft—mostly trainers and virtually all obsolete—while
another 302 were on order but undelivered. Only twelve companies were capable of building airplanes for the government, and
they produced just 90 aircraft in 1916. In contrast, twenty-seven
British firms built 5,716 airplanes that year. The chairman of the
National Advisory Committee of Aeronautics, the civilian pre-
paredness agency that initially coordinated Army wartime aviation policy with American industry, warned: "Though millions
may be available for a specific purpose in time of great need, no
amount of money will buy time."[7]

Yet time would not be forthcoming. On 23 May 1917, French
Premier Alexandre Ribot, responding to pleas from his generals
for American material as well as men, cabled his ambassador in
Washington DC and requested 4,500 airplanes for the 1918 campaign, along with 2,000 replacements per month. Given the state
of Army aviation, Ribot's request bordered on the fantastic—
multiplied out for just the first half of the year, it totaled 16,500
aircraft! Moreover, the cable failed to mention what *types* of aircraft the United States should produce. With Foulois, now a major, serving as Signal Corps representative, the Joint Army-Navy
Technical Board hurriedly sketched out a program for a 9,000-
aircraft force with a reserve of 3,000 airplanes. Of those totals, the
board slated 1,000 and 333 respectively as bombers; the remainder
would be fighters and observation aircraft. The program's magnitude disheartened many members of the Army's General Staff, who
believed that the emphasis on aviation might limit the nation's capability to manufacture other needs for the service.[8] Their reser-

vations led Brigadier General George O. Squier, the Army's chief signal officer, to present the board's proposal directly to Secretary of War Baker. Baker then took it to Congress, which appropriated a staggering $640 million to fund the entire program. President Woodrow Wilson signed the measure into law on 24 July.

Even before Congress approved the plan, an American mission departed for Europe to obtain information on the best aircraft designs to produce in the United States. Arriving in Liverpool on the twenty-sixth, the mission spent the next five weeks interviewing air officers and industrialists in Britain, France, and Italy. Led by Major Raynal C. Bolling, a former U.S. Steel lawyer who had organized the National Guard's first aviation unit, the group consisted of 105 military and civilian aviation experts. One of them was Captain Nap Gorrell, fresh out of MIT and sporting a master of science degree in aeronautical engineering.

Despite the group's qualifications, Bolling faced a difficult task. Besides the time constraint demanding an immediate start to full-scale American production, the mission suffered from two key problems. First, it would not finish its work before the arrival of General John J. Pershing's American Expeditionary Force (AEF) staff, which would evaluate air requirements from the vantage point of the force that would do the fighting. Bolling's mission reported to General Squier in Washington DC, not Pershing, and the mission's conclusions would not match those of Pershing's officers. Second, the group's departure for Europe almost a month before Congress approved the air arm's structure compelled its members to devise a structure of their own, and doing so required making determinations about air strategy that would dictate aircraft roles and the types needed to fulfill them.[9] Many of their decisions stemmed from the ideas of Allied airmen. For Nap Gorrell, the insights gained would endure, and would form the basis of his plan for a bomber offensive.

Bolling's group spent its first week in Britain meeting with British Director-General of Military Aeronautics and General Officer Commanding the Royal Flying Corps, Sir David Henderson. He suggested that the Americans concentrate exclusively on bomber production and not try to develop a balanced force of fighters, bombers, and observation aircraft.[10] The first attack on London by German Gotha bombers a fortnight before the Bolling mission arrived may have triggered Henderson's recommendation. In two minutes, fourteen Gothas had dropped nearly two tons of bombs, killing 162 people and injuring 432.[11] The bombers attacked in daylight and with impunity; none fell to antiaircraft fire or fighters. Many of London's East End workers, fearing the bombers' return, stayed away from their factories. Meanwhile, British Prime Minister David Lloyd George and his War Cabinet ordered two squadrons of fighters home from France. Britain's leaders also looked to pay the Germans back in kind. Before the Gotha assault, the British had shunned the development of an independent bombing force. In April 1917, their air strength in France consisted of twenty-seven fighter squadrons, twenty-one army support squadrons, and two bomber squadrons. After the Gotha raid, the British government's Air Board recommended developing forty squadrons of long-range bombers.[12]

In France and Italy, Bolling's group also discovered a strong preference for bomber development. The French could not produce enough aircraft to satisfy both the demand for additional air support at the front and the desire for bombers to attack Germany. They hoped that the 4,500 figure mentioned by Premier Ribot could form a strategic force—that intent had been mistakenly omitted from the cable—and they made certain that Bolling's mission understood their wishes.[13] In Italy, the Americans found bombing operations that were more than mere speculation. The Italians had begun a long-range air campaign against targets in

Austria and were, at the time, the only Allied nation conducting "strategic" bombing. Their air offensive, sporting as many as 140 aircraft on a single raid, impressed Bolling's group.[14] The group was also impressed by the man who had molded the Italian bomber force, the designer and theorist Gianni Caproni. Gorrell in particular was inspired by Caproni's vision of air power, which paralleled the thoughts of Giulio Douhet, Caproni's close friend and confidant.[15] Caproni maintained that for bombing to be effective it had to be "systematic, thorough, and consistent."[16] This assertion became a cornerstone of Gorrell's plan.

Submitting his initial report to General Squier on 15 August 1917, Bolling called for the production of training aircraft, aircraft to support American troops in the field, and "aircraft in excess of the tactical requirements of the Army in France."[17] His group had selected four types of Allied aircraft for American production: the British Dehaviland DH-4 for day-bombing and observation; the British Bristol and French SPAD for air-to-air combat, and the Italian Caproni Tri-motor for long-range night bombing. He recommended that the United States build as many of all types as possible. Bolling contended that the number of airplanes needed to support the ground forces depended on the size of the Army and would vary in proportion to it. Combat aircraft in excess of those required for Army support could conduct "independent" air operations, such as night raids on Germany. He further suggested a precise apportionment of aircraft types for this independent force: 37.5 percent of its aircraft should be fighters capable of escorting bombers, 25 percent should be day bombers, and the remainder should be Caproni night bombers.[18] He found the prospects of night bombing especially appealing, and noted that if it were conducted "on a sufficiently great scale and kept up continuously for a sufficient time, there seems good reason to believe that it might determine the whole outcome of military operations."[19] Yet Bolling's "third-place mention of the strategic force was apparently taken to mean that it was third in order of relative importance,"[20] and bombers did not appear in the initial American aircraft manufacturing program.

One individual had no intention of allowing the notion of an American air offensive to wither away—Billy Mitchell. Since opposing an autonomous air service four years earlier, Mitchell had come to believe that air power might hold the secret to winning wars. After finishing his General Staff assignment in June 1916, he became General Squier's deputy in the Signal Corps' Aviation Section and was promoted to major. He then took advantage of a provision in the 1916 National Defense Act lifting the ban on flight training for servicemen over thirty (Mitchell was thirty-six). From September 1916 to January 1917, he paid a dollar a minute for 1,470 minutes of off-duty flying instruction at the Curtiss Aviation School in Newport News, Virginia.[21] His flying "expertise" likely caused the War Department to send him to Europe as an aeronautical observer, and he arrived in Paris four days after America's declaration of war.[22] Two weeks later he spent ten days at the front lines observing French General Robert Nivelle's disastrous offensive and visiting French aviation units. He recalled his thoughts after first viewing trench warfare from the air:

> A very significant thing to me was that we could cross the lines of these contending armies in a few minutes in our airplane, whereas the armies had been locked in the struggle, immovable, powerless to advance, for three years. To even stick one's head over the top of a trench invited death. This whole area over which the Germans and French battled was not more than sixty miles across. It was as though they kept knocking their heads against a stone wall, until their brains were dashed out. They got nowhere, as far as ending the war was concerned.[23]

In May, Mitchell visited the headquarters of Major General Hugh Trenchard, commander in the field of Britain's Royal Flying Corps (RFC). Mitchell arrived abruptly, wearing an extravagant uniform that he designed himself, but his unbridled exuberance persuaded the general who was "decided in manner and very direct in speech" to give him a three-day dose of RFC operations and Trenchard philosophy. Mitchell was particularly impressed by Trenchard's commitment to a single, unified air command that would allow him to "hurl a mass of aviation at any one locality needing attack." For the British air leader, a tightly controlled, continuous aerial offensive was the key to success, and assigning air units to individual ground commanders for defense was a mistake. Trenchard highlighted the RFC's General Headquarters Brigade, a force designed to destroy the German army's means of supply and reinforcement, but which possessed too few aircraft to do so in the spring of 1917. He argued that air power should attack as far as possible into the enemy's country, and noted that the development of new airplanes with greater ranges would make Berlin a viable target. He did not, however, contend during his first encounter with Mitchell that the quickest way to defeat the German army was through an air offensive aimed at the German nation. While others around Trenchard stressed a "radical air strategy" against the German homeland, he remained focused on using air power to defeat the German army on the Western Front. Nonetheless, Mitchell emerged from his initial contact with Trenchard profoundly affected by the general's ideas and convinced that an aerial offensive was a key to winning the war.[24]

As a result of observing Allied operations, Mitchell proposed dividing the American air contingent into categories of "tactical" and "strategical" aviation. He made his proposal to Pershing's chief of staff, who arrived in France with the commanding general in mid-June. Tactical aviation would consist of squadrons attached to divisions, corps, or armies and would operate as any other combat arm. In contrast, strategical aviation "would be bombardment and pursuit formations and would have an independent mission very much as independent cavalry used to have. . . . They would be used to carry the war well into the enemy's country."[25] This mission, he insisted, could have "a greater influence on the ultimate decision of the war than any other arm."[26] Soon after receiving Mitchell's plan, Pershing selected a board of officers to determine the proper composition for AEF aviation. Because Mitchell was the senior American aviator in Europe, the general made him chief of the newly created Air Service, which had replaced the Signal Corps as the Army's air organization in the AEF.[27] Mitchell's appointment did not, however, guarantee his proposal's acceptance. On 11 July, Pershing outlined a comprehensive plan for AEF organization that authorized fifty-nine squadrons of tactical aircraft for service with the field armies. It made no mention of an independent force for "strategical" operations.

A Plan Evolves

Pershing's failure to approve the proposal caused Mitchell to redouble his efforts. In August 1917 he asked the AEF Intelligence branch to provide information on strategic targets in Germany, and later received a list of industrial targets in the Ruhr from the French.[28] He also created a staff to explore the possibilities of bombing Germany in more detail. To direct the Air Service's Technical Section, Mitchell picked the twenty-six-year-old Gorrell, who had just completed his work with the Bolling mission. Gorrell's job for Mitchell would be similar to his former work for Bolling: to determine Air Service requirements, including the various types of aircraft needed. In trying to estimate the correct number of bombers, Gorrell considered the prospects of strategic bombing, and ultimately produced America's first plan for a strategic air campaign. He developed this plan in relative splendor, for Mitchell chose the Chateau de Chamarandes, a magnificent hunting lodge built by Louis XV, as his headquarters. Located within a mile of Pershing's headquarters at Chaumont, the chateau provided both living quarters and office space. It continued to serve as Air Service headquarters after Mitchell left in October to become Air Service Commander in the Zone of the Advance.[29]

Besides Mitchell, a variety of individuals helped Gorrell develop his plan. Gorrell stayed in contact with Bolling, who remarked in early September that the importance of "bombing operations with direct military ends in view" could not be overestimated.[30] In addition, veteran pilots Harold Fowler and Millard F. Harmon, both Air Service majors, assisted Gorrell.[31] Fowler flew with the Royal Flying Corps before America's entry in the war, while Harmon was an Air Service pilot in the Philippines before the conflict. Gorrell also received a large measure of support from three individuals uniquely qualified to help develop an air campaign plan: Wing Commander Spencer Grey of the Royal Naval Air Service (RNAS), Gianni Caproni, and Major Hardinge Goulborn Tiverton, a British Lord and, like Grey, a pilot with the RNAS. Grey was a liaison officer attached to Air Service headquarters and had participated in raids against German inland targets from the RNAS base at Dunkirk, plus he had helped develop a 1,650-pound bomb. Gorrell considered him the "world's greatest authority on questions dealing with aerial bombardment" and relied heavily on his expertise.[32]

Caproni, whose bomber was slated for American production, met frequently with Gorrell in the autumn of 1917. Besides providing Gorrell with a list of Germany's major industrial targets,[33] Caproni also sent him an English-text copy of a new book, *Let Us Kill The War; Let Us Aim at the Heart of the Enemy*, by the Italian journalist Nino Salveneschi. The book was a compilation of Caproni's major thoughts on how air warfare could achieve an independent victory, and Gorrell embraced its message enthusiastically. "I have read with great interest your book entitled 'Let us Kill the War; Let us Aim at the Heart of the Enemy,' which you so kindly gave me," he wrote Caproni on 31 October. "May I ask you to let me have half a dozen copies of this book and I will guarantee to spread the gospel in all directions."[34]

Salveneschi's book—an unabashed endorsement for Caproni's Tri-motor bomber—contained a number of perceptions that reappeared in Gorrell's plan. The Italian argued that victory in the current conflict meant destroying the enemy's army rather than occupying his country, and that the key to destroying his army was to take away its means to fight. The Allies could thus obtain victory in one of two ways: by exceeding the enemy's armament production, or by wrecking the factories that built the weapons.[35] Outproducing Germany's enormous industrial capacity would be difficult, Salveneschi asserted. Air power, however, offered the means to destroy the factories, which were the "heart" of the enemy war effort. Stabbing the heart would in turn kill the war.[36]

Salveneschi warned that the Germans would build up their own bomber force for an offensive against Allied production centers unless the Allies first attacked German industry. He listed the major German factories as those in Essen, Munich, along the Rhine, and in Westphalia. Allied bombers did not have to destroy all of them, however, to achieve success—wrecking other factories closer to the front might produce greater results. "In this war there is, among the factories, as far as the front, a mechanism like a perfect watch-making workshop," Salveneschi wrote. "Enough to destroy a 'specialized' factory to obtain, in a short time, enforced inaction of the enemy."[37] Because the Central Powers were likely to defend their key factories with fighter aircraft, the attacking air fleet needed to be as large as possible and com-

18

posed of sturdy aircraft (like the Tri-motor) so at least part of the bombers could hit their target. The Italian acknowledged that some bombs would miss their aim points and kill civilians, but cautioned that "one must not permit sentimentality to interfere with the destruction of factories. . . . [T]he life of every German labourer at work for the war has less value than one of our boys who is fighting for his country."[38] Yet Salveneschi did not advocate killing civilians to defeat the enemy. Rather, he moved past that question to assert, somewhat antiseptically, that Caproni's dream of an aerial victory could "be converted into [the] reality of figures and *formulae*."[39]

Salveneschi's writings meshed neatly with those of RNAS Major Lord Tiverton, whom Gorrell met in France during the autumn of 1917. While serving as technical liaison officer for the Royal Navy's Air Department in Paris, Tiverton completed his own thorough study of long-range bombing in early September, and his analysis compared favorably to that provided by Salveneschi and Caproni.[40] Gorrell found Tiverton's views particularly compelling—so much so that he used Tiverton's paper, virtually verbatim, for the body of his own plan that he finished in late November.[41] Although Gorrell's plan took into account Grey's expertise and Caproni's images, as well as Mitchell's ideas, gleaned largely from Trenchard, about air power's ability to destroy the German army's means to fight, Tiverton's notions had a telling impact on Gorrell's thoughts. Gorrell added an introduction and conclusion to address strictly American concerns, but most of the remaining words came from Tiverton.[42]

Gorrell began by noting that three and a half years of conflict had produced a stalemate on the ground and at sea, and that only "a new policy of attacking the enemy" would affect the war's conduct.[43] That new policy was "strategical bombing," which he defined as air attacks on commercial centers and lines of communication to stop the flow of enemy supplies to the front. Much like Salveneschi, Gorrell asserted that "there are a few certain indispensable targets without which Germany cannot carry on the war."[44] The German army could be likened to a drill, whose point could continue to bore only if the shank—the German national effort—remained durable. Four target groups were essential to keeping the shank strong: the industries surrounding Dusseldorf, Cologne, Mannheim, and the Saar. If those vital factories and their transportation links were destroyed, the drill would become impotent. "German shells are being fired at Allied troops and positions over a large area of the Front," he observed, "but the manufacture of these shells and bombs is dependent upon the output of a few specific, well-known factories turning out the chemicals for them. . . . If the chemical factories can be blown up, the shell and bomb output will cease, to a greater or lesser degree, dependent upon the damage done these chemical plants."[45] In addition, Germany's main aircraft engine factory and magneto plant were both in Stuttgart, and their destruction would severely hamper Germany's ability to sustain its air power on the Western Front.

The belief that the essence of an enemy nation's war-making capability consisted of certain key components linking together its industrial complex was the crux of Gorrell's proposal—and a conviction that ultimately became a central pillar of the American approach to strategic bombing.

Although destroying German war-making capability was the focus of Gorrell's plan, his scheme presupposed that attacks on industrial targets would also break the morale of the German work force. His rationale stemmed partly from the effects of German air raids on the French factory at Pont-St. Vincent, where workers had been reluctant to return to their duties even though the bombs had missed the mark; he knew as well of the work stoppages resulting from the Gotha offensive against London.[46] Gorrell believed that a concentrated air attack against the four enemy target groups would persuade the German populace to demand an end to the conflict, and called for one hundred bomber squadrons to start the campaign by simultaneously attacking armament works in Mannheim and Ludwigshafen for five continuous hours. "If immediately afterwards, on the next possible day, Frankfurt were attacked in a similar way, judging from the press reports of what has already occurred in Germany," he contended, "it is quite possible that Cologne would create such trouble that the German government might be forced to suggest terms if that town were so attacked."[47]

To Gorrell, a nation's will to fight equated to the population's willingness to endure the conflict. A mass revolution that threatened to dislodge the enemy government—and forced its government to make peace to stay in power—would certainly indicate that bombs had broken enemy morale. Yet a popular revolt was not necessary to break German will. For Gorrell, widespread absenteeism would suffice, and would have the same impact as factories destroyed by bombs. The ultimate goal was to prevent the German army from waging war.

The enemy's capability and will to fight were complementary objectives, and Gorrell's offensive aimed at both. "From both the morale point of view and also that of material damage, concentration of our aerial forces against single targets on the same day is of vital importance since it tends to hamper the defense and also to complete in a thorough manner the work which the bombardment is intended to perform," he observed.[48]

Gorrell estimated that between three thousand and six thousand American bombers were necessary to carry out his plan, provided that the force received adequate logistical support and aircrew training.[49] The armada would fly en masse, and concentrate on destroying a particular set of targets completely before assaulting a different target group. Hearkening to Trenchard, Gorrell stressed continuous, systematic bombing as the key to overwhelming German defenses while unnerving workers and preventing them from making repairs. Yet the Germans, Gorrell warned, also realized the potential of strategic bombing and aimed to launch a similar large-scale effort against the Allies during the next year. Thus, the sooner the American campaign began, the better. "This is not a phantom nor a dream," he wrote to Bolling in October 1917, "but is a huge reality capable of being carried out with success if the United States will only carry on a sufficiently large campaign for next year, and manufacture the types of airplanes that lend themselves to this campaign, instead of building pursuit planes already out of date here in Europe."[50]

Gorrell submitted his plan on 28 November to Brigadier General Benjamin Foulois, who had become Chief of the AEF Air Service the previous day. The two had served together as pilots in the First Aero Squadron during the Mexican punitive expedition and knew each other well. Like Mitchell, Foulois had changed his attitude on the value of independent air operations since his 1913 testimony that Army aviation belonged under Signal Corps' control. He approved Gorrell's plan in December and sent it to General Pershing for his endorsement. Foulois also placed Gorrell— now a lieutenant colonel—in charge of Strategical Aviation in the Zone of the Advance. Persuaded that an independent bombing force would not deprive him of air support for American ground troops, Pershing approved the plan in early January. Gorrell then transferred to Pershing's staff as the Air Service's G-3 (War Plans and Operations) representative to oversee the plan's implementation, but he remained attuned to Pershing's concern that the Air Service might neglect American armies.

To assuage this fear, Gorrell produced a written analysis of his plan's impact on Army aviation for Pershing's staff. Entitled "The Future Role of American Bombardment Aviation," the study borrowed heavily from a report that Trenchard had presented to the British War Cabinet in December 1917, as well as from a recent French bombing plan that American staff officers had translated into English.[51] Yet Gorrell made certain that his paper addressed the Army's anxiety over air support while emphasizing the great benefits of strategic bombing. He pointedly observed in the first paragraph: "The Air Service is an integral part of a homogeneous team, no portion of which, working by itself, can alone decisively defeat the enemy."[52] Gorrell then noted that air power would continue to support ground combat operations by serving as a "long range gun" that could attack the enemy's rear echelons beyond the range of fixed artillery, as well as by attacking the enemy's frontline positions when necessary. Raids would also occur against important road and rail junctions near the front, which would prevent the flow of vital supplies and cause the enemy "grave results." Attacks against enemy industries would pay dividends at the front as well. "To successfully strike at such works, is to injure the source of the current which furnished the combative energy of the enemy," he maintained.[53]

Besides devoting a large amount of attention to "tactical" air power, Gorrell provided ample insights on "strategical bombing," many of them courtesy of Hugh Trenchard. Gorrell stated that such bombing occurred mainly at long distances and was integral to the air offensive on the Western Front. It was not primarily a vehicle for retaliation. Instead, its basic purpose was "to weaken the power of the enemy both directly and indirectly; directly, by interrupting his production, transport, and organization through the infliction of damage on his industrial, railway, and military centers and by compelling him to draw back his [aerial] fighting machines to deal with the enemy's; indirectly, by producing discontent and alarm among the industrial population. In other words, it aims at achieving both a material and a moral effect."[54]

Gorrell reiterated that German war production depended on a

few key links in its industrial complex and that destroying them would grind the German war effort to a halt. Pinpointing those links was the essence of successful bombing. Thus far, the lack of "proper scientific knowledge" and the failure to identify "the real object" of an air offensive had prevented bombing from achieving its potential.[55] Gorrell claimed that the necessary expertise now existed, and he was determined to use it. Aircraft would attack the industrial centers earmarked in his plan, and the bombs that missed would have "the desired moral effect" by depriving the enemy of "the enormous number of man-hours that a single aerial bombardment of necessity always causes."[56] Attacks would occur throughout daylight and darkness, with day bombers flying at high altitude in tight formation to overcome enemy defenses, while night bombers flew with the impunity that he believed allowed them to conduct the most accurate bombing.

Implementation Problems

As Gorrell worked to sell his scheme at AEF headquarters, Lieutenant Colonel Ambrose Monell took over in late January as Chief of Strategical Aviation in the Zone of the Advance. An ex-president of the International Nickel Company, Monell was assisted in his new endeavor by Gorrell's former compatriots Fowler and Grey. Meanwhile, Gorrell helped create an Office of Air Intelligence in the G-2 (Intelligence) Section of the AEF staff. This section contained a "bomb target unit," described by historian Thomas Greer as the "prototype of the organizations which played such an important role in the strategic operations of World War II."[57] The unit produced target maps, antiaircraft defense maps, and maps of key German railroads and industries, all divided into "target folders" for specific installations.

While the Americans geared up to bomb Germany, the British had already launched the assault. In October 1917, in response to the Gotha raids, Prime Minister David Lloyd George had promised London's citizens: "We will give it all back to them and we will give it to them soon. We shall bomb Germany with compound interest."[58] Limited attacks began before the end of the year, and many of them were indiscriminate. Trenchard announced at a meeting with Gorrell and French representatives on 22 December that he aimed to establish a special force for bombing German industry and asked whether the French and Americans would contribute to it. Gorrell stated that the Americans planned to begin a similar effort but that he could not pledge the Air Service to a joint endeavor without Pershing's approval.[59] In contrast to the eagerness for bombing Germany that they had displayed to the Bolling mission, the French were lukewarm now that the idea had become a reality. They stressed Germany's ease of retaliation against French cities, and indeed in January 1918 German bombers attacked Paris for the first time in two and a half years.[60] The British then confined their raids to factories and rail yards, but they did not curb their plans for a separate bombing unit. On 5 June 1918, Trenchard took command of the Independent Air Force (IAF) of the newly created Royal Air Force. The need to devote half his sorties against German airfields, and the small number of aircraft available (his force varied between five and ten squadrons), limited the amount of IAF bombs dropped on Germany to 550 tons, which were spread over fifty towns and cities.[61] Nonetheless, Trenchard claimed that the "moral effect" of his bombing outweighed its material impact by twenty to one.[62]

Because Trenchard took orders only from the British Air Ministry, the IAF effort endeared itself to neither the French nor the Americans. The French were particularly incensed, as their Marshal Ferdinand Foch was Supreme Allied Commander. Trenchard's restricted chain-of-command also led the AEF Chief of Staff, Major General James W. McAndrew, to prohibit American bombing

with the IAF once Air Service bombardment units reached sufficient strength to conduct separate operations. In January 1918
Pershing had agreed that British personnel could organize, train,
and equip the thirty projected American night bombing squadrons, and British flying schools also taught some American day
bombing aircrews. In all, thirty-six Americans attached to the IAF
flew combat "training" missions over Germany, and half of them
were killed, wounded, or captured.[63] Yet just as Pershing prohibited American ground combat units from amalgamating with Allied armies, he would not condone American bombers flying to
achieve British objectives, especially when American ground forces
needed air support. "In making arrangements with the British it
must be thoroughly understood that when our [air] forces reach
a certain importance the regions to be bombed will be designated
by these headquarters and that the selection of targets will de-
pend solely upon their importance with respect to the operations
which we contemplate for our ground forces," McAndrew told
Major General Mason Patrick, who had replaced Foulois as AEF
Air Service chief.[64] The issue of cooperative allied air operations
was a sticky one, however, and Americans would revisit it with
the British in the years to come.

In the end, America's bombing contribution to the Great War
consisted of day bombers raiding targets in France, and that contribution was meager. Eight antiquated Breguet-14 B-2 biplanes of
the Ninety-sixth Aero Squadron flew in the first American bombing raid, a 12 June 1918 attack on the rail yard and warehouses
in Dommary-Baroncourt. Two planes returned to base with engine problems, while three others ran out of gas after dropping
their bombs. Because of the Breguets' feeble engines, it took several minutes for the tiny formation to climb to its bombing altitude of four thousand feet. Still, some of the aircraft hit the target, and they survived attacks by three enemy fighters on the way

home. This first attack typified those occurring for the remainder of the war. In August the Ninety-sixth flew twenty missions and dropped forty-three thousand pounds of bombs against transportation and supply targets; in September and October it teamed with the Eleventh and Twentieth Aero Squadrons to support the American ground offensives at St. Mihiel and the Argonne.[65]

Colonel Billy Mitchell, who directed almost 1,500 allied aircraft at St. Mihiel as Chief of Air Service, First Army, now stressed air power's auxiliary mission rather than its independent one. In February 1918, as Chief of Air Service, First Corps, he had argued that the first mission of offensive air power must be the destruction of the enemy's air force. Thereafter, bombing operations "should be essentially tactical in their nature and directed against active enemy units in the field which will have a direct bearing on operations during this Spring and Summer, rather than a piecemeal attack against large factory sites and things of that nature. The factories, if completely destroyed, would undoubtedly have a very far-reaching effect, but to completely demolish them is a tremendously difficult thing, and, furthermore, even if they were ruined, their effect would not be felt for a long period of time (possibly a year) upon the fighting of their army."[66]

Although after the war Mitchell berated Pershing's staff for "trying to handle aviation as an auxiliary of some of the other branches, instead of an independent fighting arm,"[67] such criticisms during the conflict were infrequent. All his duties after leaving the Chateau de Chamarandes—Air Service Commander in the Zone of the Advance; Chief of Air Service, First Army; Chief of Air Service, First Corps; Chief of Air Service, First Brigade; once again Chief of Air Service, First Army; and finally, Chief of Air Service, Army Group—directly supported American troops at the front. As a result, his focus changed. "The Air Service of an army is one of its offensive arms," he stated after taking command in the Zone of the Advance. "Alone it cannot bring about a decision. It therefore helps the other arms in their appointed missions."[68]

Late in the war, knowing that the Germans could not stop the continued American ground advance, Mitchell's focus returned to the possibilities of strategic bombing. Yet as long as the Army's progress remained uncertain, he devoted his full energies to providing it with immediate air support. Of course, Mitchell's ego had much to do with his pragmatic approach to air power—he craved a combat command, and the only combat air commands available were those attached to Army headquarters. Still, by the summer of 1918, he realized that America's major contribution to the Allied advance would be made by AEF *ground* echelons, and that air support would enhance their impact.

McAndrew and Pershing agreed with Mitchell's emphasis on supporting the ground battle. Besides limiting air operations with the British, in mid-June Pershing's chief of staff had admonished Patrick that his officers who stressed an "independent" air campaign must realize that their views were contrary to the needs of the service. "It is therefore directed that these officers be warned against any idea of independence and that they be taught from the beginning that their efforts must be closely coordinated with those of the remainder of the Air Service and those of the ground army," McAndrew stated.[69] Recent savage fighting by the American Second and Third Divisions at Chateau-Thierry had helped stop the German drive on Paris, and further bloodshed was imminent as Pershing readied his troops to support Foch's counteroffensive. When the assault began, the American commander wanted his soldiers to have maximum backing from their Air Service. The June name-change of the Strategical Aviation branch to the General Headquarters (GHQ) Air Service Reserve reflected this continuing concern.

By the summer of 1918 Gorrell's scheme for a massive American air offensive had atrophied. Colonel Monell had, in Gorrell's words, worked on developing a strategic air force for only "a month or so,"[70] and Major Fowler left Air Service headquarters to command the American air units operating with the British. Discouraged by production deficiencies and convinced that an American strategic bombing campaign would never materialize, Wing Commander Grey returned to a British assignment. Monell succeeded during his tenure as Chief of the Strategical Section/GHQ Reserve only in selecting prospective airfields for his phantom force.[71]

After the war, Gorrell wrote that a major reason American strategic bombing never materialized was that his plans "were not synchronized properly, especially from a mental point of view" with the Army's General Headquarters.[72] General Foulois concurred, declaring in October 1919: "The General Staff of the Army, either through lack of vision, lack of practical knowledge, or deliberate intention to subordinate the Air Service needs to the needs of other combat arms, has utterly failed to appreciate the full military value of this new military weapon, and, in my opinion, has failed to accord it its just place in our military family."[73] Even Mitchell, who had worked tirelessly to support the ground forces with air power, agreed that Army officers—with the sole exception of Major General Hunter Liggett, who had commanded the First Army—did not know what "air power" meant.[74] In July 1918, Mitchell had insisted that the Chief of the Air Service, rather than the Army's General Staff, should direct the Air Service's GHQ Reserve. He based his argument on the need for unity of command, which would allow the Air Service chief to concentrate all available air power in a critical area for maximum impact.[75] His plea went unheeded, even though the GHQ Reserve existed in name only—an American squadron of night bombers did not arrive at the front until 9 November 1918.

29

In his memoirs, Pershing articulated his views regarding the subordination of air power to ground combat. He remarked in his discussion of the Argonne offensive: "The tendency of our air force at first was to attach too much significance to flights beyond the enemy's lines in an endeavor to interrupt his communications. However, this was of secondary importance during the battle, as aviators were then expected to protect and assist our ground troops."[76] To him, the main functions of an air force were to drive off hostile aircraft and provide the infantry and artillery with information on enemy troop movements. Many Army officers agreed. One week before the Armistice, a General Staff analysis noted that the meager number of American bombers at the front (the Air Service had six squadrons of day bombers at the end of the war) and the small number of bombs they carried made their destructive potential "practically the same as long-range artillery." Ignoring the issue of range, the study's authors concluded that it took "two squadrons of bombing planes to equal the work of one 155mm. gun."[77]

In the final analysis, the key reason that the United States never mounted a bomber offensive was indeed the failure to build bombers for it. "Aircraft production [was] the greatest American air headache of World War I," recalled Hap Arnold, who tracked the building of warplanes as a thirty-year-old colonel and assistant to the director of the Signal Corps' Aeronautical Division.[78] Arnold bemoaned the inefficient organization that divided responsibility for developing aircraft between the civilian Bureau of Aircraft Production and the Signal Corps' Production Division. The Bureau, led by the former chief of Hudson Automobiles, Howard Coffin, supervised engineering, supply, and testing, while the Production Division oversaw procurement. Neither organization had an aviator assigned to it on a full-time basis. Arnold remembered that after Coffin boasted forty thousand aircraft would be built by June 1918, he asked the industrialist how many spare parts he had ordered. "What do you need spare parts for?" was Coffin's reply.[79] Competing guidance from Americans in Europe matched the overlapping authority of production agencies in the United States. After the Bolling mission recommended building the Caproni bomber, General Pershing claimed final authority to determine aircraft types, and in November 1917 he recommended production of the British two-engine Handley-Page.[80] Incredibly, despite the difficulties that would stem from building two types of bombers, the Joint Army-Navy Technical Board suggested producing both—and the Secretary of War and the Secretary of the Navy approved the recommendation![81]

European designs compounded American production problems. Most of the materials provided by the French, British, and Italian builders to serve as guidelines for Coffin's manufacturers were incomplete or delayed. American production centered on the machine tools and detailed blueprints of the assembly line, whereas European production stressed skilled craftsmen and individual workmanship.[82] Not until 16 January 1918—almost six months after the Bolling mission's initial selection—did Caproni's representatives arrive in the United States. British designers for the Handley-Page had arrived only two weeks earlier.[83] The combination of differing production philosophies, delayed arrivals, and overlapping authority produced construction programs with wildly fluctuating numbers of projected aircraft. The planned number of Caproni bombers went from 500 on 9 August 1917 to 9,000 a week later, to 2,000 on 24 August, to 50 on 19 February 1918, and to 250 on 3 May.[84] In actuality, the United States built only one Caproni before the Armistice. As for the Handley-Page, plans to assemble 300 bombers in Britain resulted in only the *shipment* of parts for 101 before the war's end, and none were assembled in time to fight.[85] General Patrick's July 1918 proposal of an Air

Service of 202 total squadrons, of which 41 would be bombers, compared to his proposal six weeks earlier for 261 squadrons, of which 101 would be bombers, reflected no loss of faith in the bomber's ability to change the war. Rather, it displayed a realistic appraisal of America's dismal production capability.[86]

That the war ended before American bombers had the chance to bomb German soil proved significant. Production deficiencies had prevented Gorrell's dream of defeating Germany through strategic bombing from becoming a reality, yet the dream endured. Gorrell, Mitchell, and other Air Service officers could speculate about the probable effect that an American bomber offensive might have had on the outcome of the war, and blame the lack of aircraft as a reason why the offensive never materialized. Such difficulties could be overcome. Now air officers were aware of Gorrell's postwar admonition that "money and men could not make an air program over night,"[87] and they would make amends.

Had the war continued into 1919, Mitchell, certain that the German Army could not stop the American ground advance, planned an aerial assault against Germany's interior. "I was sure that if the war lasted, air power would decide it," he wrote after the Armistice.[88] According to his diary, he intended to combine incendiary attacks with poison gas to destroy crops, forests, and livestock. This air offensive, he mused, "would have caused untold sufferings and forced a German surrender."[89] Yet the likelihood of Mitchell's vision becoming reality was remote. President Wilson told Congress in his war message: "We shall, I feel confident, conduct our operations as belligerents without passion and ourselves observe with proud punctilio the principles of right and fair play we profess to be fighting for."[90] Secretary of War Baker reflected those sentiments, telling Army Chief of Staff General Peyton March to notify the Air Service that the United States would not conduct any bombing that "has as its objective, promiscuous bombing upon industry, commerce, or population, in enemy countries disassociated from obvious military needs to be served by such action."[91] Moreover, in early January 1919, Mitchell revealed that his notion of strategic bombing had come to resemble Gorrell's. In a treatise entitled "Tactical Application of Military Aeronautics," he argued that the main value of bombardment would come from "hitting an enemy's great nerve centers at the very beginning of the war so as to paralyze them to the greatest extent possible."[92]

Gorrell's plan, which initially had won Pershing's approval, borrowed heavily from Caproni and Tiverton in stressing attacks against key industrial centers rather than the German populace and its livelihood. By destroying those elements of Germany's industrial complex that were essential components of the army's means to fight, Gorrell aimed to render enemy forces impotent. For him, the key to applying air power successfully was identifying those industries that made the German army tick and then wrecking them through accurate bombing. Such bombing would also terrify the German work force and keep it away from the target factories. "Precision" bombing had proved far from precise, though.[93] Night raids were notoriously inaccurate, despite Gorrell's belief that accuracy increased because of immunity from enemy defenses. American day raids, which relied on formation bombing aided by a primitive bombsight in the lead aircraft,[94] also offered less than pinpoint accuracy. Still, the problem of bombing precisely appeared to be a mechanical one that could be solved through improved equipment, much like production problems could be eliminated through efficient organization.

For both Mitchell and Gorrell, scientifically applied air power offered the prospect of ending a war without the horrendous slaughter of trench warfare. If bombing achieved that objective, the Army's air units might merit status as an independent service—and armies would perhaps become obsolete.

In the aftermath of the Great War, the clamor for air independence would become a roar, with Mitchell howling loudest of all. The Air Service had achieved an enduring measure of autonomy at the end of May 1918, when the Overman Act removed it from Signal Corps' control and created a "Director of Military Aeronautics" directly under the Army's Chief of Staff. Three months later Congress named Jack D. Ryan, who had succeeded Howard Coffin as chief of Aircraft Production, as Second Assistant Secretary of War and Director of Air Service. Yet for Mitchell these steps were not enough. As his cry became increasingly shrill, it welded the bond between air power's independent application and service autonomy until the link was impossible to break.

In October 1918, the twenty-seven-year-old Gorrell became the youngest American colonel since the Civil War. He served as Assistant Chief of the Air Service until the Armistice, and then began writing the Air Service's combat history. In March 1920 he left the military to try his hand as a corporate executive, ultimately becoming director and president of the Stutz Motor Car Company and president of the American Air Transport Association. In the meantime, his plan for bombing Germany, and his 1918 analysis of it, inspired lectures for a future generation of air strategists at Maxwell Field's Air Corps Tactical School. Three days after he died in March 1945, a single Army Air Forces airplane scattered Gorrell's ashes across the plain at West Point, where he had sprinted almost thirty-five years before to catch a glimpse of Glenn Curtiss's flying machine. The tribute befitted the man who laid the cornerstone for vast air campaigns then underway in Europe and the Pacific.

2 • Progressive Prophecy

As air power can hit at a distance, after it controls the air and vanquishes the opposing air power, it will be able to fly anywhere over the hostile country. The menace will be so great that either a state will hesitate to go to war, or, having engaged in war, will make the contest much sharper, more decisive, and more quickly finished. This will result in a diminished loss of life and treasure and will thus be a distinct benefit to civilization.

• BRIG. GEN. WILLIAM MITCHELL, 1925

There is one thing certain: Air power has given to the world a means whereby the heart of a nation can be attacked at once without first having to wage an exhausting war at that nation's frontiers.

• MAJ. HAROLD LEE GEORGE, 1935

---

21 July 1921

For Billy Mitchell, the final attack on a relic of the Kaiser's navy was as important as any he had directed on the Western Front. One by one, the six Martin MB-2 bombers and a single Handley-Page flew past Mitchell's *Osprey*, a blue and white DH-4 with a blue command pennant flapping from the rudder. The dual-engine biplanes formed the essence of the First Provisional Air Brigade, which Mitchell had created ad hoc in January 1921. For the next six months, its thousand men had devoted their full attention to preparing for the task that now awaited the seven bomber crews—sinking the rust-covered German battleship *Ostfriesland*. The Navy had received the dreadnought, along with several smaller warships, for testing as a result of the Versailles Peace Treaty, and Mitchell had convinced influential congressmen that the Air Service should participate in those tests as well. To him, though, only the *Ostfriesland* mattered. His goal was to demonstrate—unequivocally—that bombers could sink the world's mightiest warships. By proving that air power had supplanted the Navy as America's traditional first line of defense, Mitchell believed that he would establish an ironclad rationale for his dream of an independent air force.

The challenge was formidable. The Navy anchored the *Ostfriesland* sixty-five miles off the Virginia Capes, requiring Mitchell's aircraft, based at Langley Field, Virginia, to fly almost one hundred miles before arriving at their destination. Navy rules also limited the number of hits airmen could score against the imposing target. Launched in 1911, the twenty-seven-thousand-ton dreadnought sported a four-layered hull and numerous watertight compartments. It had survived eighteen direct hits and a mine detonation at the Battle of Jutland. And it had withstood earlier attacks that morning and on the previous day by Navy aircraft and Mitchell's Martins. The Martin bombers had scored three hits with 1,100-pound bombs, but Navy inspectors deemed that the ship remained seaworthy. Mitchell agreed; he knew that standard bombs would not suffice to wreck the German behemoth. In his eyes, the previous attacks had been for the Navy's benefit, as they permitted observers to scrutinize the damage inflicted at periodic intervals. After the next bomb run, he aimed to make further inspections superfluous.

Slung beneath the fuselage of each bomber that flew past the *Osprey* was a specially built two-thousand-pound bomb. While those bombs would likely cause substantial damage to the German battleship if they hit it, Mitchell had directed his crews to drop their ordnance in the water near the ship. He planned to take advantage of the Navy's limit on direct hits by relying on the hammer-like pressure of underwater explosions to crush the unarmored hull. The first of the massive bombs exploded one hundred feet off the *Ostfriesland*'s starboard bow, causing the ship to list 15 degrees before righting itself. The second detonated three hundred feet in front of the vessel. The third glanced off her port bow, exploded in the water, and ripped a gaping hole in the hull. The fourth landed off her port beam, and the fifth struck the water twenty-five feet off the port side near the waist gun turret. These last two blows raised the bow, causing the ship to roll from side to side while the stern disappeared below the waves. A sixth bomb landing off the starboard side blasted the stern out of the water. Suddenly, the bow began rising until it reached a height of one hundred feet above the surface, and the stern slid downward. Twenty-one minutes after the first two-thousand-pound bomb fell, the *Ostfriesland* sank.

Mitchell hovered over the battleship during the attack at an altitude of three thousand feet, five hundred feet above his bombers. From among the flotilla of vessels observing the tests he now picked out the *Henderson*, the Navy transport filled with admirals, generals, congressmen, and foreign dignitaries, and dived to within two hundred feet of the craft. Grinning widely, he doffed his goggles and helmet and waved his arms to the cheers of many of those on deck. All did not respond approvingly, however; several admirals wept. For Mitchell the moment was one of supreme triumph. "The problem of the destruction of seacraft by Air Forces has been solved, and is finished," he wrote in his report of the tests. He was certain that his bombers had vindicated his faith in the supremacy of air power and justified the need for an independent air force.[1]

Mitchell and the Foundations of Progressive Air Power

The *Ostfriesland* episode demonstrated much more than simply Mitchell's commitment to Air Service autonomy. It also revealed that the vestiges of progressivism remaining in postwar America had enveloped many airmen, and none more so than Billy Mitchell.[2] Far more ambitious than their muckraker predecessors, Mitchell and the air progressives aimed to reform the most violent of man's activities—war. Rifled artillery, the machine gun, and poison gas had made war an endless nightmare that killed millions, as typified by the unremitting fury of the Western Front. Technology was the demon responsible for the slaughter, but, Mitchell and his cohorts believed, technology was also the key to salvation. The bomber would be their instrument of change. Not only would it prevent a naval force from attacking the United States, it would obviate trench warfare, single-handedly achieving a victory that was quicker, cheaper, and hence more humane than one gained by ground combat. The wartime application of air power would, Mitchell contended, "result in a diminished loss of life and treasure and will thus be a distinct benefit to civilization."[3]

Mitchell's unabashed faith that air power had altered the character of war caused him to demand an air force separate from Army or Navy control to guarantee its proper use. He continually voiced progressive notions in his appeals for service independence, and used the term directly in the foreword to his book *Winged Defense*: "The time has come when aviation must be developed for aviation's sake and not as an auxiliary to other exiting branches [of the service]. Unless the progressive elements in our makeup are availed of, we will fall behind in the world's development."[4] Much like the muckrakers, Mitchell took his case for autonomy straight to the American public. In the aftermath of the "War to End All Wars," however, he found that his message could not persuade a populace beset by isolationism, pacifist tendencies, and, ultimately, the Great Depression.[5] Still, his progressive ideals endured among airmen, and provided the foundations for the bombing doctrine they developed during the interwar years.

Mitchell was an apt choice to serve as the messiah of American air power. With a United States senator for a father and a railroad tycoon grandfather, he possessed ties to leaders in both government and industry. World War I provided him with considerable experience as a combat air commander, and he had excelled at it—most of the pilots who flew in his units adored him. Brimming with confidence in any situation, he could charm most audiences, often by relying on his fluent French or his expert polo. Yet his overwhelming self-assurance did not stem entirely from expertise. Mitchell was a driven man, a man on a mission, a man with little time to waste. He wrote his mother in December 1919 that he "was practically the only one that can bring about a betterment of our national defense at this time" and noted with pride in his diary on Christmas Eve five years later: "Supposed to be a half-holiday, but I worked hard all day in the office nevertheless."[6] Those who interfered with his promotion of air power—or his boundless ego—incurred his wrath. "Mitchell tried to convert his opponents by killing them first," observed British Air Marshal Sir Hugh Trenchard, who served as Mitchell's air power mentor during World War I.[7] During the war, Mitchell's vanity produced bitter clashes with fellow airmen Benjamin Foulois and "Nap" Gorrell, both of whom, he believed, snubbed him after obtaining high Air Service positions.[8]

After the Armistice Mitchell turned his temper toward those who opposed his ideas and his methods of espousing them. His quick tongue and steadfast beliefs prevented him from commanding the Air Service; he had to settle for Assistant Chief, which carried with it a brigadier general's rank. As such, he refused to defer to Major General Charles T. Menoher, a non-flying Air Service chief who had led the Forty-second "Rainbow" Division in World War I. Mitchell published his report of the *Ostfriesland* sinking despite Menoher's warning not to do so. Instead of confronting Mitchell afterward, Menoher resigned his post. His successor, Major General Mason Patrick, was an engineer, the West Point classmate of General John J. Pershing, and the Air Service commander during the last six months of the world war. He learned to fly at age sixty to enhance his image with his subordinates.

Upon replacing Menoher, Patrick stated that he would be chief in deed as well as name in a remark aimed at Mitchell. When Mitchell responded with an offer of resignation, Patrick told him that the offer would be accepted, and Mitchell reconsidered.[9] Patrick realized his deputy's brilliance and even came to share his views on an independent air force, but he did not appreciate Mitchell's unorthodox methods of pursuing his goal. Patrick sent him to inspect European air forces to prevent Mitchell from disrupting the 1922 Washington Naval Conference, and also dispatched him to the Pacific in early 1924. In the end, though, the Air Service chief proved incapable of curbing his deputy's penchant for seeking public support.

Because his ideas conflicted with traditional Army views on the "proper" role of air power in war, Mitchell believed that the Army leadership would never endorse air force autonomy. He understood full well the Army's desire to guarantee that it received adequate air support for its ground forces—he had provided that backing in France during the war, and he did not dismiss the need for it afterward. Yet the auxiliary application of air power offered meager prospects for overcoming the murderous technology of modern land warfare—or for justifying an autonomous air force. As long as ground advance remained the primary means to achieve victory (and Army leaders had little incentive to change that emphasis), the bomber's ability to revamp war remained limited. "Should a War take place on the ground between two industrial nations in the future," Mitchell wrote in 1919, "it can only end in absolute ruin, if the same methods that the ground armies have followed before should be resorted to."[10] In contrast, independently applied air power presented an opportunity to win a war by avoiding stalemate and slaughter.

Mitchell maintained that air power alone could defeat a nation by paralyzing its "vital centers," which included great cities, factories, raw materials, foodstuffs, supplies, and modes of transportation.[11] All were essential to wage modern war, and all were vulnerable to air attack. Moreover, many of the targets were fragile, and wrecking them promised a rapid victory. Mitchell asserted: "Air forces will attack centers of production of all kinds, means of transportation, agricultural areas, ports and shipping; not so much the people themselves. They will destroy the means of making war, because now we cannot cut a limb out of a tree, pick a stone from a hill and make it our principal weapon. Today to make war we must have great metal and chemical factories that have to stay in one place, take months to build, and, if destroyed, cannot be replaced in the usual length of a modern war."[12] Only an air force possessed the means to attack vital centers without first confronting enemy surface forces, and destroying those centers would eliminate the need to advance through enemy territory on the ground. "The influence of air power on the ability of one nation to impress its will on another in an armed conflict will be decisive," he insisted.[13]

Like many Army officers of his time, Mitchell could recite Clausewitz's dictum on the objective of war, and he did so with a parochial twist. Air power would wreck an enemy's will to fight by destroying its capability to resist, and the essence of that capability was not the army or navy, but the nation's industrial and agricultural underpinnings. Eliminating industrial production "would deprive armies, air forces and navies . . . of their means of maintenance."[14] Air power also offered the chance to attack the will to fight directly. Mitchell equated the will of a nation to the will of its populace, but he vacillated about the propriety of bombing civilians. On the one hand, he called for attacks on "the places where people live and carry on their daily lives" to discourage their "desire to renew the combat at a later date," advocated burning Japanese metropolitan areas in the event of a war with Japan, and noted that poison gas could be used to contaminate water supplies and spur evacuations from cities. On the other hand, in a 1922 bombing manual written for Air Service officers, he argued that attacking a factory was ethical only if its workers received "sufficient warning that the center will be destroyed" and that "in rare instances Bombardment aviation will be required to act as an arm of reprisal."[15]

The dominant theme emerging from these discussions was not the desire to attack civilians directly, but rather the desire to sever the populace from the sources of production. "It may be necessary to intimidate the civilian population in a certain area to force them to discontinue something which is having a direct bearing on the outcome of the conflict," Mitchell observed in his bombing manual. Achieving that goal might cause some civilian deaths, but the number would pale compared to the deaths produced by a ground war between industrialized powers. Moreover, once bombed, civilians were unlikely to continue supporting the war effort. "In the future, the mere threat of bombing a town by an air force will cause it to be evacuated and all work in munitions and supply factories to be stopped," he asserted.[16] In Mitchell's eyes, civilian will was exceedingly fragile, and its collapse would cause a corresponding loss in war-making capability. In addition, civilians did not have to be attacked directly to produce a direct impact on an enemy's will to fight.

Although adamant about the fragile nature of civilian will, Mitchell was less than explicit about how breaking it would translate into a rapid peace. He thought that air raids would trigger evacuations of hundreds of thousands of people from urban areas. Those refugees would not be able to obtain adequate food or shelter, and their plight would cause a war to end. "There is only one alternative and that is surrender," he wrote in 1930. "It is a quick way of deciding a war and really much more humane than the present methods of blowing people to bits by cannon projectiles or butchering them with bayonets."[17] Yet Mitchell neglected to say whether "surrender" would occur because the government of the battered nation was sympathetic to the plight of its people, feared overthrow by an irate populace, or had in fact been displaced by a new regime demanding peace.

In many of his futuristic examples, he depicted the United States as the country undergoing air attack, so the presumption was that surrender would stem from a sympathetic government. Mitchell claimed that America's "strategical heart" consisted of the manufacturing complexes within a triangle formed by Chicago, Boston, and the Chesapeake Bay, and that destroying those centers and their transportation links would not only wreck industrial productivity but also lead to widespread starvation if the nation chose not to capitulate.[18] In such projections, war-making capability ceased once bombs destroyed vital industries and agricultural areas, or once civilians left the factories and fields. Mitchell dismissed stockpiles of materiel, especially food, and he also rejected reserves of morale.[19] He bestowed on the governments under attack a degree of rationality that ignored the enemy's war aims and the possibility that the population would willingly suffer to avoid capitulation. His examples intimated that all industrial powers were alike—and that all resembled *his view* of the United States. He thus overlooked crucial distinctions between nations—and the types of wars they fought—that would directly affect bombing's ability to achieve an independent victory, much less a rapid one.

For Mitchell, the key prerequisite for achieving victory through air power mirrored the requirement stipulated by the Italian air theorist Giulio Douhet: gaining control of the sky. Mitchell later stated that he had "frequent conversations" with Douhet during his 1922 visit to Italy; whether those conversations actually occurred, he was well acquainted with Douhet's confidant, Gianni Caproni, and received a synopsis of Douhet's classic book, *The Command of the Air*, in late 1922.[20] Much of Mitchell's and Douhet's writing was remarkably similar.[21] Both agreed that "nothing can stop the attack of aircraft except other aircraft," and that after achieving air supremacy, an enemy's vital centers—a term used by both men—could be wrecked at will.[22] They differed, however, about how best to achieve air control. For Douhet, the best method was to destroy the enemy air force on the ground, either at its bases or before it left factory assembly lines.[23] Mitchell countered that air combat was also a suitable means, and that attacking a critical vital center would compel the hostile air force to rise in defense, whereupon it could be overcome.[24] Both initially thought that escort fighters for bombers were essential to ward off the enemy's fighters, although Douhet would later advocate an air force based on a single type of aircraft, a bomber bristling with machine guns that he dubbed the "battleplane" in his 1926 revision to *Command of the Air*.

Like Mitchell, Douhet argued that an independent air force emphasizing the bomber was the cheapest and most efficient means to defend his nation. Yet unlike his American counterpart, Douhet had to consider that his country was susceptible to air attack.[25] The Italian asserted that a defending air force could not protect all of a nation's vital centers, because the defender could never be certain what centers the attacker would choose to strike.[26] His answer was to attack first, with as much air power as possible, and destroy the enemy's ability to retaliate in kind. Once enemy bombers took to the air against an unknown target, attempting to stop them was probably futile.[27] Mitchell realized that advancing technology would ultimately overcome the limitation on range that protected the United States from air attack by a European or Asiatic power. Under his guidance, Air Service Colonel Townsend F. Dodd prepared an April 1919 study evaluating the need for a separate air force that concluded: "The moment that [an] aircraft reaches that stage of development which will permit one ton of bombs to be carried from the nearest point of a possible enemy's territory to our commercial and industrial centers, and to return to the starting point, then national safety requires the maintenance of an efficient air force adapted for acting against the possible enemy's interior."[28] By the time that trans-oceanic flight had been perfected, Mitchell aimed to make Americans an "air-going people," ready to conduct "war at a distance" through a Department of the Aeronautics equal in status to the Army and Navy Departments in a single Department of National Defense.[29]

Mitchell tried to transform the American populace into air power advocates by emphasizing the progressive notions of order and efficiency. Not only could an autonomous air force protect the United States and achieve an independent victory in war, he insisted that it could do so more cheaply—and more effectively—than either the Army or the Navy. Yet the Air Service could not perform an independent mission, Mitchell argued, as long as the Army controlled it. Because the Army divided air units among its various corps and divisions to assure that they received adequate air support, air units had a meager chance of being massed together for a long-range independent mission in which Army commanders had little interest. "To leave aviation essentially under the dominance and direction of another department is to absolutely strangle its development, because it will be looked on by them merely as an auxiliary and not as a principal thing," he protested in December 1919.[30] Mitchell provoked the Navy's ire with his persistent claims that the sea service provided minimum defense for a maximum price tag. In 1922 he contended that an average battleship cost roughly forty-five million dollars to build and equip, while bombers cost twenty thousand dollars each. Thus, the nation could either build one battleship or two thousand bombers—each of which could sink a battleship![31] Mitchell's argument omitted a great deal, such as the rapid rate of obsolescence of aircraft compared to capital ships, and the high costs of training aircrews and building air bases, but its simplistic logic touched a receptive chord in many Americans.

In December 1924 Representative Julian Lampert, chairman of the House Military Affairs Committee, began hearings in response to Representative John F. Curry's bill for a unified aviation service. Mitchell testified extensively at the hearings, making some of his most inflammatory accusations. "All the organization that we have in this country really now is for the protection of vested interests against aviation," he told the committee. He added that some individuals testifying for the government had showed "a woeful ignorance . . . and in some cases possibly a falsification of evidence, with the evident intent to confuse Congress." When asked by Secretary of War John W. Weeks to elaborate on his testimony in writing, Mitchell declined to provide specifics and added additional charges. He berated the Navy for the conduct of its bombing tests, remarking that it "actually tried to prevent our sinking the *Ostfriesland*."[32] Mitchell had recently angered Secretary Weeks by publishing an explosive series of aviation articles, unreviewed by the War Department, in the *Saturday Evening Post*. The confrontational testimony following on the heels of those articles caused Weeks to deny Mitchell's reappointment as Assistant Chief of the Air Service when it came up for renewal in March 1925.[33] At the end of the month Mitchell reverted to his permanent grade of colonel and was transferred to Fort Sam Houston in San Antonio, Texas, as aviation officer for the Army's Eighth Corps Area.

Mitchell, however, had no intention of remaining dormant in the Texas hinterland. In August 1925 he published *Winged Defense*, which expanded many of the arguments that he had made in the *Saturday Evening Post*. Although stressing the importance of an independent air force built around the bomber, the book continued the attack on Army and Navy leaders opposed to such an organization.[34] It also contained cartoons lampooning Secretary Weeks, who at the time of publication had become seriously ill. Mitchell had been unaware that the cartoons would be published in the book, and on 4 September received a letter from his wife, Elizabeth, who was in Detroit with their infant daughter. Elizabeth was greatly distressed about the appearance of the cartoons and contended that no one would believe that Mitchell had not approved them. "I don't very well see how they can avoid court-martialing you now, my sweet—but I'm sorry it will have to be over something sort of cheap like those cartoons," she lamented.[35] Mitchell's receipt of his wife's letter coincided with the crash of the Navy dirigible *Shenandoah* in an Ohio thunderstorm and perhaps influenced his decision to make the Navy disaster his personal Rubicon. On 5 September he told San Antonio newspapers that the crash resulted from "the incompetency, criminal negligence, and almost treasonable administration of the National Defense by the Navy and War Departments."[36] Two weeks later he was court-martialed.

For Mitchell, the trial and the "Morrow Board" that preceded it were anticlimaxes. An enraged President Calvin Coolidge, who called Mitchell a "God-damned disturbing liar," proffered the court-martial charges himself.[37] Coolidge summoned friend and J.P. Morgan banker Dwight Morrow to conduct a formal investigation of American aviation that would undercut the publicity of Mitchell's trial.[38] The president directed Morrow to produce a report by the end of November, and Morrow's hearing concluded on 15 October, thirteen days before the court-martial started. Mitchell testified for the Morrow Board but chose to read long passages of *Winged Defense* rather than to engage in the verbal sparring at which he excelled. Although he returned to form at his trial, the verdict was a given. Found guilty on 17 December—ironically, the twenty-second anniversary of the Wright brothers' first powered flight at Kitty Hawk—he retired from the service on 1 February 1926 to continue his crusade sans uniform.[39]

While newspapers gave the court-martial proceedings extensive coverage, no outcry for an independent air force erupted following the verdict. The Morrow Board, which had received testimony from an array of civilian and military aviation specialists, had indeed diminished interest in the court-martial. *Winged Defense* sold only 4,500 copies between August 1925 and January 1926 during the peak of sensationalism.[40] Mitchell received many supportive letters in that span, but few individuals were willing to back his cause with a demand for legislation.[41] Future general Henry H. "Hap" Arnold, then an Air Service major and a close personal friend of Mitchell's, later speculated on why the American people failed to act on Mitchell's recommendations: "the public enthusiasm . . . was not for air power—it was for Billy."[42] Flamboyant, intrepid, and cocksure, Mitchell appealed to New Era America. His message, though, struck an uncertain chord. His argument that bombers could now defend the nation more efficiently than battleships seemed to make sense, as did his assertion that bombers could defeat an enemy without the need for a ground invasion. Yet questions remained—defend against *whom*? *Whom* would air power defeat? The Morrow Board's conclusion, "that air power

... has yet demonstrated its value—*certainly not in a country situated as ours*—for independent operations of such a character as to justify the organization of a separate department," reflected concerns held by the bulk of Americans regarding Mitchell's ideas.[43] In 1925, the public realized that no enemy threatened the United States, and airplanes could not cross the Atlantic or Pacific. The mood endured for more than a decade.

Incremental Interwar Developments

The failure of the American public to respond directly to Mitchell's outcry did not mean that the issue of air autonomy disappeared, but it did mean that the steps taken during the interwar years would be incremental. National boards and committees continued to study the issue of how best to organize Army aviation. The Air Corps Act of July 1926 changed the Air Service's name to the Air Corps and provided an Assistant Secretary of War for Air and special representation on the War Department's General Staff. It also authorized an Air Corps of twenty thousand men and 1,800 aircraft, but Congress failed to fund the expansion.

The Great Depression further slowed the Air Corps' growth. From 1927 to 1931 annual budgets ranged from $25–30 million; in 1934 appropriations fell to $12 million; in 1938, $3.5 million.[44] Manpower, which averaged 1,500 officers and 15,000 enlisted men during the first three Depression years, stood at only 1,700 officers and 17,000 enlisted men as late as 1939.[45] Aircraft totaled 1,619 in 1933, of which 442 were obsolete or nonstandard.[46] Still, the recommendation of the 1934 aviation board chaired by former Secretary of War Newton D. Baker led to the creation of a General Headquarters (GHQ) Air Force, containing all Air Corps combat units, in the spring of 1935. Although the air power comprising the GHQ Air Force was never significant—in 1939 it owned just 14 four-engine B-17 bombers—it nevertheless was one step closer toward Mitchell's progressive vision of an autonomous air force capable of achieving an independent victory.

Establishment of the GHQ Air Force did not indicate that either the nation or the Army accepted Mitchell's air power ideology. The Baker Board's final report cautioned: "The ideas that aviation, acting alone, can control the sea lanes, or defend the coast, or produce decisive results in any other general mission contemplated under our policy are all visionary, as is the idea that a very large and independent air force is necessary to defend our country against air attack."[47] The primary bomber assigned to the GHQ Air Force's three air wings at the end of the decade was the Douglas B-18 "Bolo," a dual-engine aircraft designed for short-range interdiction or battlefield support. The War Department ordered 217 B-18s in 1935 over the objections of the Air Corps, which had endorsed the B-17.

To most General Staff officers, "air power" meant preventing enemy aircraft from attacking friendly troops, or using friendly aircraft to attack enemy troops and supplies near the battlefield. It did not mean achieving an independent victory from the sky— a proposition that many Army leaders viewed with thinly veiled scorn. Mitchell's public outcries led many Army officers to reject future proposals for air force autonomy out of hand. Arnold remarked that "they seemed to set their mouths tighter, draw more into their shell, and, if anything, take even a narrower point of view of aviation as an offensive power in warfare."[48] Army Brigadier General Charles E. Kilbourne, chief of the General Staff's War Plans Division, critiqued Mitchell's impact on Army leadership in harsher terms. In 1934, Kilbourne remarked that "for many years the General Staff of the Army has suffered a feeling of disgust amounting at times to nausea over statements publicly made by General William Mitchell and those who followed his lead."[49]

While Mitchell may have repelled many Army officers, most airmen gravitated to his message if not his methodology.[50] The coterie of "believers" who surrounded him during his tenure as Assistant Chief of the Air Service—Hap Arnold, Carl "Tooey" Spaatz, William Sherman, Herbert Dargue, Robert Olds, Kenneth Walker, Harold Lee George, and Ira C. Eaker—were not only many of the Air Corps' future leaders, but also many of its future theorists. Together, they refined Mitchell's notions and conveyed them throughout the close-knit community of the airmen, and they found their audience receptive. Strong ties bonded the small number of aviators—the dangers of flying, even in peacetime, made the Air Service responsible for almost 50 percent of the Army's active duty deaths between 1921 and 1924.[51] Airmen realized as well that advancing in rank was tenuous as long as the Army controlled promotion lists, given that most Army leaders viewed the air weapon as an auxiliary feature of a ground force. After Arnold and Dargue received reprimands in 1926 for sending Congressmen pro-autonomy literature, most airmen adopted a stoic posture that reflected Mitchell's ideas, but they hesitated to speak those thoughts too loudly outside their clan.

Air chiefs also absorbed Mitchell's notions. Mason Patrick, who initially shunned Mitchell's ideas on Air Service autonomy and regarded him as "a spoiled brat,"[52] submitted a study to the War Department in December 1924 advocating "a united air force" that placed "all of the component air units, and possibly all aeronautical development under one responsible and directing head." As for its wartime usage, Patrick asserted that "we should gather our air forces together under one air commander and strike at the strategic points of our enemy—cripple him even before our ground forces come into contact."[53] Patrick's successors as Chief of the Air Corps—James E. Fechet, Benjamin Foulois, Oscar Westover, and Hap Arnold—were equally committed to Mitchell's goal of an independent air force and shared his faith that air power could single-handedly win wars (although Foulois disliked Mitchell personally). Brigadier (later Major) General Frank Andrews, who commanded the GHQ Air Force from 1935–39, was an air power disciple who relentlessly spouted Mitchellese to both the War Department and the public, and like Mitchell was banished to Fort Sam Houston. Aside from Andrews and the outspoken Foulois, however, air leaders restrained their advocacy. Most worked to improve relations with the War Department while securing high visibility peacetime missions that stressed air power's ability to defend the nation.[54] Although Mitchell the prophet remained uppermost in their minds, so too did Mitchell the martyr.

Refining the Ideals: The Air Corps Tactical School

Mitchell's prophecy not only endured among air leaders, it also was the fundamental underpinning of the Air Corps Tactical School (ACTS), the focal point of American air power study during the interwar years.[55] The school provided an intense, nine-month, air power-focused curriculum to the Air Corps' top mid-level officers, and graduated 261 of the 320 generals serving in the Army Air Forces at the end of World War II.[56] Initial classes were small. An average of 22 students attended while the school was located at Langley Field from 1920 to 1931, and they learned "the air tactics and techniques necessary for direction of air units in cooperation with other branches of the armed forces."[57] By 1926 the curriculum's focus had begun to shift to independent air operations, and by 1935 it stressed the bomber as a war-winning weapon.[58]

In concert with the new emphasis, the school moved to Maxwell Field, Alabama, and also acquired more students: the average increased to fifty-nine in 1931, and jumped to one hundred in 1939, when a series of four twelve-week courses began.[59] Mitchell had been instrumental in founding the school, and his bombing

52

manual still served as a textbook in 1939.[60] Many of the school's officer-instructors were his protégés. Sherman, Dargue, George, Olds, and Walker—the latter two had served as Mitchell's aides—filled key positions on the faculty, and all promoted Mitchell's vision of independent air power founded on the bomber.

From the student perspective, the Tactical School opened new vistas in air power thought. Laurence S. Kuter, who left the Forty-ninth Bombardment Squadron at Langley Field to begin school in the class of 1934–35 as a new first lieutenant (and the second youngest member of the class), later commented that "imaginations were released, aroused at Maxwell, when they were dormant at Langley. *I think* I'm speaking for all of my generation at the time. We had our first introduction to any sort of air strategy."[61] Major Ira C. Eaker, a distinguished pilot sporting a Southern California journalism degree who graduated from the Tactical School in 1936, remarked: "If military education may be likened to a bad pill, it is not too much to say that a very satisfactory sugar coating is put on it at Maxwell Field."[62]

Students attended classes Monday through Friday from 0900–1200, with afternoons reserved for flying and Wednesday afternoons off. For much of the 1930s horsemanship was a mandatory course, although most of the curriculum explored more serious subjects. Between 1931 and 1938, courses the first half of the year focused on specific branches of the Army, such as the infantry, cavalry, and artillery, while naval topics also received attention. The study of air power dominated the second half of the curriculum. The Department of Air Tactics and Strategy was responsible for that instruction, and the "Air Force" section was its primary subdivision. Other branches included "Observation," "Attack Aviation," "Pursuit," and "Bombardment," with the most hours devoted to "Bombardment." A faculty and staff consisting of twenty-two officers in 1935 oversaw the school's program. Of that total seventeen were in the Air Corps.[63]

The Air Corps officers serving on the Tactical School faculty played an enormous role in shaping air power convictions. Most students arriving at Maxwell needed little convincing that Air Corps autonomy was a worthwhile goal, although the notion of a separate air force did not receive an overriding emphasis in flying squadrons.[64] Entering students also likely agreed that the independent application of air power was the key to achieving separation from the Army. What the Tactical School—"the only common location of experienced air corps officers who had enough time for creative thinking"[65]—provided them was a distinctive *methodology* for applying air power to achieve victory independently of surface forces, and hence a rationale for service autonomy. The officers who developed the unique approach were an eclectic group, possessing disparate backgrounds and large amounts of flying time. Lieutenant Kenneth Walker, who began teaching the "Bombardment" course in 1929, had developed bomber formation tactics just before his arrival at Maxwell while serving as the Second Bombardment Group's operations officer; Major Donald Wilson, who taught the "Air Force" course from 1931 to 1934, had worked for American railroads before entering the military. Walker and Wilson typified those who passionately believed in an independent air force and who openly debated its merits in the kitchens of student and faculty quarters late at night over mason jars of moonshine. Yet in the classrooms—which contained a smattering of students who were not airmen—the appeal for air autonomy rested on the logic of the school's unique approach to bombing.[66]

No instructor made that pitch better than Major Harold Lee George. Before teaching at the Tactical School, George flew day bombers in World War I, helped Billy Mitchell sink the *Ostfries-*

land and testified at his court-martial, and served as a bomber test pilot at Aberdeen Proving Ground. He directed the school's Bombardment section from 1932 to 1934, and then doubled for two years as the director of Air Tactics and Strategy and its "Air Force" subdivision. The holder of a George Washington University law degree and winner of a national competition in typing and shorthand, he played a major role in structuring the curriculum that formed the basis of America's World War II strategic bombing doctrine. His progressive views on the nature of war and air power paralleled those of Mitchell—with whom he corresponded frequently—and were manifest in his opening lecture for the "Air Force" course. He began by telling his students:

> The question for you to consider from today onward, to have constantly before you as you continue your military careers, is substantially this:
>
> Has the advent of air power brought into existence a method for the prosecution of war which has revolutionized that art and given to air forces a strategical objective of their own, independent of either land or naval forces, the attainment of which might, in itself, accomplish the purpose of war; or has air power merely added another weapon to the waging of war which makes it in fact only an auxiliary of the traditional military forces?[67]

George then outlined the probable answer. "Modern inventions" such as the machine gun and rapid-fire artillery significantly increased the power of defensive land warfare, he asserted, and a conflict similar to the world war "might mean a breakdown of civilization itself." Yet he also argued that achieving victory did not require defeating an enemy's army. Pointing to 1918, he stated that Germany surrendered because its populace lost the will to resist, not because its army had been destroyed. Overcoming hostile will was the true object of war. "The continuous denial

55

of those things which are essential, not only for the prosecution of war but to sustain life itself" compelled the German people to yield. The Allied blockade threatened Germany with starvation, but George did not believe that such drastic measures were necessary to cause national will to collapse. "There is plenty of indication that modern nations are interdependent," he maintained, "not so much for the essentials of life as for those 'non-essentials' needed to conduct their daily lives under the existing standards of living." Because most aspects of modern society were not self-sufficient—for example, many workers in large cities depended on public transportation to get to work, and many factories and homes received electric power from distant locations—eliminating the interdependent features of *normal* life might suffice to crack civilian morale.[68]

Moreover, George insisted, the key elements that sustained normal life were the *same* ones that enabled a nation to wage modern war. Interrupting this economic web would likely defeat a nation, and air power could attack it directly, preventing an exhaustive ground campaign or a time-consuming sea blockade. "It is possible that the moral collapse brought about by the break-up of this closely knit web would be sufficient [to cause defeat]," he postulated, "but connected therewith is the industrial fabric which is absolutely essential for modern war. To continue a war which is hopeless is worse than an undesirable peace, because the latter will come soon or late anyway; but to continue a modern war without machinery is impossible."[69]

Despite his obvious conclusion, George stopped short of saying that air power could win a war single-handedly. He noted that the prospect remained "an academic question," but added: "That the air phase of a future war between major powers will be the decisive phase seems to be accepted as more and more plausible as each year passes."[70]

The belief, widely shared among Tactical School instructors, that the industrial apparatus essential to a state's war-making capability was also necessary to sustain its populace was a fundamental tenet of the school's "industrial web theory." In brief, its main points were: (1) in "modern warfare," the military, political, economic, and social facets of a nation's existence were so "closely and absolutely interdependent" that interruption of this delicate balance could suffice to defeat an enemy state; (2) bombing, precisely aimed at these "vital centers" of an enemy's industrial complex, could wreck the fragile equilibrium and hence destroy the enemy state's war-making capability; and (3) such destruction would also wreck the enemy nation's capacity to sustain normal day-to-day life, which would in turn destroy the will of its populace to fight.[71] Those notions would guide American strategic bombing for the next half century.

Although seemingly straightforward, the industrial web theory stemmed from a hodgepodge of ingredients, and the Tactical School cooks who stirred them together sometimes added more of one item than another. Clausewitzian frameworks and Marxist economics, set against the backdrop of World War I's totality, flavored the instructors' thoughts on war. George's lecture echoed a 1926 school publication that viewed the objective of war as "undermining the enemy's morale, his will to resist,"[72] yet George also noted that destroying the *capability* to fight might be the key to wrecking will. The school attempted to differentiate between the "national" objective of wrecking will and the "military" aim of destroying "the enemy's material and moral means of resistance," but the multi-layered goals overlapped and distinctions between them were subtle—especially when discussing air power that promised victory in one fell swoop.[73]

According to the Tactical School, the capability to fight modern war stemmed from a nation's economic prowess, and economic concerns generated war's impetus. A 1934 lecture asserted that "world conflicts arise over outlets for over-production"; another added that modern wars "are essentially economic wars, caused by the clash of rival production machines."[74] Using air power to destroy those machines would eliminate the motive for conflict—hence removing the will to keep fighting. "Air power is the only means of waging war which has the capability of striking directly at the will to resist of a hostile nation, by paralyzing its economic structure and threatening its very existence," concluded a school text.[75] Instructors further elaborated: "The principal and all important mission of air power, when its equipment permits, is the attack of those vital objectives in a nation's economic structure which will tend to paralyze that nation's ability to wage war and thus contribute directly to the attainment of the ultimate objective of war, namely, the disintegration of the hostile will to resist."[76]

Besides Clausewitz and Marx, the industrial web theory hearkened to Nap Gorrell and Billy Mitchell. In 1935 the mustachioed Lieutenant Kuter, now an instructor in the school's Bombardment section after graduating first in his class, discovered a copy of Gorrell's plan and decided to devote an entire lecture to it. He contacted Gorrell—who had become president of the American Air Transport Association—to verify that the lecture conveyed the essence of the 1917 proposal, and Gorrell invited him to his Chicago office to discuss it. When Kuter arrived he found that the retired colonel had distributed copies of the lecture to many senior officers from the First World War. All expressed satisfaction that it accurately represented the past, as did Gorrell himself.[77] An invigorated Kuter then returned to Maxwell. "No principle or doctrine in the Confidential Air Force text that is being written today was missed in that plan," he proclaimed to his students. "We may return to our steel desks considerably refreshed by the knowledge that our school plans and our theories are not only supported by, but identical with the plans of the level-headed commanders in the field when the grim realities of actual war demanded effective employment."[78]

Like both Gorrell and Mitchell, most Tactical School instructors equated the will of the nation to the will of its populace. They also presumed that civilian will was fragile, and that bombs could crack it without killing large numbers of people. Air power would instead break morale by putting people out of work. "The effects of an attack against the industrial facilities on the social life of a nation can not be overestimated," stated a 1934 text. "The psychological effect caused by idleness is probably more important in its influence upon morale than any other single factor."[79] Unemployment further offered a gauge to determine when civilian will was on the verge of collapse. "The effectiveness of an air offensive against a nation may find its yard stick in the number of people which it will deny work," a 1936 lecture asserted. "Idleness breeds discontent—and discontent destroys morale."[80]

Tactical School instructors considered the prospect of destroying enemy will by attacking the populace directly, but dismissed the idea because they believed it less effective than an attack on key industries. In addition, many thought that such an approach was inhumane. Major Muir S. Fairchild, like George a veteran of World War I day bombers, told students in 1938 that "the direct attack of civilian populations is most repugnant to our humanitarian principles, and certainly it is a method of warfare that we would adopt only with great reluctance and regret. . . . Furthermore, aside from the psychological effects on the workers, this attack does not directly injure the war making capacity of the nation." He also argued that it was difficult to determine the amount of bombs needed to terrorize a population to such a degree that it forced its government to surrender. Thus, Fairchild advocated attacks on the industrial web, which would have "the great virtue of reducing the capacity for war of the hostile nation, and of applying pressure to the population both at the same time and with equal efficiency and effectiveness."[81]

To George, *efficient* bombing was the overriding concern. He rejected the direct attack on populations, "not because of the fact that it might violate some precept of humanity," but because attacking the industrial web promised greater dividends, and promised them sooner, than killing civilians. Railroads, refineries, electric power, and key industries were his targets of choice; "no highly industrialized nation could continue existence" without them. Yet George also provided a caveat that left the door ajar for attacks that did more than just disrupt normal life. He remarked that "any sane nation" would capitulate once the key threads of its industrial web were severed. If surrender did not occur—implying that the enemy was not rational—as a last resort the attacker might destroy the enemy's water supply system. George acknowledged that doing so would have grave implications. "The results and consequences of such an attack are too terrible for any nation to bring about unless it offered probably the only means in which it could be successful in the prosecution of the war," he cautioned.[82]

Much like Mitchell, the Tactical School instructors presumed a uniform code of rationality for both the government and the populace of any modern nation attacked from the air. The government would "sense" the discomfort of its people and would act to end their pain. Accordingly, the attacker should avoid bombing government centers, because "the political establishment must remain intact if the attitude of the people at large is to be rapidly sensed and given appropriate consideration."[83] Instructors expected the attitudes of a beleaguered government and its populace to resemble

those projected for "the greatest industrial nation in the world—
the United States." Major Fairchild observed that America's vulnerability to a well-conceived air offensive mirrored that of other
industrialized powers. He asserted that the key elements of American production were 11,842 "critical" factories, almost half of
which were located in New York, Pennsylvania, and Massachu-
setts. Destroying the factories in those three states, or the transportation or power systems linking them, would "apply tremendous pressure to our civilian population while at the same time
seriously imparing [*sic*] our ability and capacity to wage war."[84]
Tactical School instructors thought that such destruction would
fatally affect American morale. "With life unbearable or perhaps
not even supportable, it seemed that even the sturdiest people in
our own Northeast country with their army and navy could soon
be persuaded to yield to the will of an enemy with effective independent air action," Kuter remembered.[85]

The school devoted much time to determining which particular elements in the industrial web would have the greatest impact
if destroyed. Here too, the United States served as the predom-
inant example for the theorizing. Fairchild noted that without
adequate raw materials and the power to drive machinery, the
American industrial complex could not function. A precarious
balance held the system together even in peacetime; a strike in a
small factory producing door latches for automobiles had halted
production in many automobile factories across the country. The
demands of war strained that balance to the utmost, as could be
seen from the failure of American industry to provide more than
token support to the Allied cause in 1917–18.

"A careful and complete scientific analysis" would identify the
proper targets, Fairchild insisted.[86] The key was to pinpoint basic commodities essential for both public services and war-fighting. Once identified, air power could attack them in a variety of

ways. Factories manufacturing essential commodities were usually found in specific locales, adjacent to raw materials, markets, labor, or lines of communication. They were generally large enough to allow easy identification from the air and too numerous to allow "an efficient local defense."[87] Examples included the steel industry in Pittsburgh and Birmingham, and the brass industry in Connecticut. Besides destroying the factories, air power could eliminate essential commodities by attacking the raw materials needed to produce them. Removing either coal or iron ore would prevent the production of steel. A school text concluded: "Air power could thus defeat a nation by depriving it of just one commodity, [such as] steel, because no nation can successfully wage war without it."[88]

Because Tactical School instructors based the industrial web theory on American projections, they have since been criticized for "mirror-imaging"—substituting America's economic and social make-up for that of all other industrialized nations. Kuter later remarked that they had little choice. A small number of officers (seventeen total) from Britain, Canada, Mexico, Spain, Sweden, and Turkey attended the school, and their presence prevented instructors from focusing their analysis on potential enemies Germany and Japan. "It would have been unthinkable in peacetime to have U.S. Army Air Corps officers estimating the national fabric of an industrial nation, searching for critical and vulnerable elements and concluding how many long range heavy bombers would be required to overcome their will to resist our objectives," Kuter recalled. "Not only would it have been politically unthinkable to assume that another nation was our enemy, but at the ACTS it would have been downright embarrassing."[89] Haywood S. Hansell, a first lieutenant fighter-pilot-turned-bomber-advocate who taught with Kuter in the Bombardment section, remembered that instructors deemed target selection a problem for industrial economists. Since the school had none, it "did the best it could. It reasoned that other great nations were not unlike our own, and that an analysis of American industry would lead to sound conclusions about German industry, or Japanese industry, or any other great power's industry."[90]

Yet in the final analysis, Hansell, Kuter, and their compatriots did *not* project American characteristics onto the socioeconomic infrastructure of their potential enemies. They instead replicated their *perceptions* of the United States, and those perceptions in all likelihood did not conform to reality. Like Billy Mitchell, the instructors *assumed* that the American populace had a low threshold of pain, that it would demand surrender once key industrial centers in the Northeast were destroyed, and that the government would acquiesce to the request. Such assumptions ignored—as had Mitchell—the nature of the enemy and its war aims, and America's own goals in the conflict, which may have been that high-priced survival was preferable to occupation. Those assumptions also underestimated the resilience of industrial complexes and the possibility that dispersal and deception might keep them running in spite of bombs. In short, the enemy state portrayed by the Tactical School was a generic one, stripped of fundamental elements like culture and ideology. Overcoming its "will to resist" became a straightforward goal with quantifiable results.[91]

The instructors realized that their vision of the future rested on theory rather than fact, but countered that the lack of proof for their claims was no certainty that air power could not achieve them.[92] To bolster their convictions they relied on large doses of progressive philosophy. "Air power is the natural enemy of a well-organized state," they asserted in 1935.[93] Technological advance had made the various facets of a modern state interdependent, linked together by strands of a delicate web. Air power was the ideal means to severe those threads quickly. "The more speedily a war is over and the world can revert to its normal peacetime pursuits, the better it is for the entire world," George remarked.[94] Mitchell had said much the same, and so had Douhet, whose translated works were available at Maxwell.[95] Yet neither Mitchell nor Douhet placed the overriding emphasis on *accurate* bombing that came from the Tactical School. Although Mitchell stressed precision attacks against a hostile fleet, he also advocated the development of "aerial torpedoes," self-propelled, remotely controlled bombs accurate enough only to "hit great cities."[96] For Douhet, population centers were legitimate targets, and victory would come from terrorizing the enemy populace into demanding peace. Tactical School instructors believed that such random bombing could not rapidly snip away the key strands of the industrial web.

In 1930, the school shunned night bombing as inefficient; texts stated that daylight was necessary to pinpoint key targets.[97] But attacking in daylight exposed aircrews to enemy defenses, forcing them to attack at high altitudes to avoid anti-aircraft artillery (AAA) and in formation for mutual protection against enemy fighters. High altitude bombing was also inherently more inaccurate than that conducted at lower levels, and in 1930 the Air Corps did not possess a bombsight that assured a reasonable degree of precision. Nor did it possess a bomber that could deliver a substantial bomb load against an enemy's economic web. Nevertheless, Tactical School instructors continued to refine the industrial web theory, confident that air technology would ultimately provide them with a means to implement it without suffering crippling losses.

In the days before radar, air maneuvers appeared to show that even antiquated bombers could attack targets in daylight and emerge relatively unscathed. The defending fighters often failed to locate the bomber formations, and if they did so, it was often too late to intercept them. Major Walter H. Frank, the Tactical School's Assistant Commandant, remarked after watching 1929 air maneuvers in Ohio: "There is considerable doubt among the umpires as to the ability of any air organization to stop a well-organized, well flown air attack."[98] Mitchell's former aide, Lieutenant Kenneth Walker, echoed this sentiment as a Bombardment instructor from 1929 to 1933, and the notion found its way into Tactical School texts. Most instructors believed that the defensive firepower of tight formations would ward off any fighters that happened to intercept a bomber attack. Still, they considered the possibility of an escort fighter that could accompany bombers to target, but dismissed the notion for two reasons: (1) they could not envision an aerodynamic design that successfully melded a fighter's speed and maneuverability with a bomber's range; and (2) money for both fighter and bomber development simply did not exist during the Depression, and fighters were not going to gain the independent victory that would lead to an autonomous air force.[99] Major Claire Chennault, who directed the Tactical School's Pursuit section from 1934 to 1935, adamantly opposed using fighters as escorts—in his mind, their sole mission was air defense.[100] Dogmatic views also prevailed regarding anti-aircraft artillery. Kuter recalled teaching that "anti-aircraft gunfire may be important but should be ignored." He also remembered that in classroom exercises instructors deemed "bombing inaccuracy"—not enemy defenses—the greatest threat to a successful air offensive. "Nothing could stop us," he reflected. "I mean this was a *zealous* crowd."[101]

The confidence displayed by faculty and students at the ACTS would intensify during the decade with the development of the four-engine B-17 "Flying Fortress" and the sophisticated Norden bombsight. Together, those technological marvels seemingly offered the means to validate the industrial web theory. Yet before that theory could be put to the test, the Army's leaders had to endorse it. A difficult challenge loomed for the believers in progressive air power—one that was far more demanding than Mitchell faced in sinking the *Ostfriesland*.

3 · From Prophecy to Plan

To understand Air Power, it must be realized that the airplane is not just another weapon. It is another means, operating in another element, for the same basic purpose as the application of Military Power or Sea Power—the destruction of the enemy's will to fight. The true object of war has never been merely to defeat an army or navy. Such defeat is only a means to an end. That end is the destruction of the enemy's will.

The fundamental difference between Air Power and Military Power is that Air Power can be applied *directly* against the objective sought, without first having to overcome barriers and obstacles such as swamps, rivers, mountains, and enemy surface forces.

• MAJ. GEN. FRANK ANDREWS, 15 OCTOBER 1936

I do not believe that air attacks can be stopped by any means known. . . . The best defense is a strong offense. We must have an air force capable of going out and meeting an enemy before he can get under way.

• MAJ. GEN. FRANK ANDREWS, 20 MAY 1937

---

12 May 1938

Army Air Corps First Lieutenant Curtis LeMay felt his stomach churning as he trudged through a heavy morning downpour toward the B-17 bomber designated "Number 80" and parked at Mitchel Field, Long Island. LeMay was a handpicked member of three B-17 crews who would fly their bombers as "blue force" aircraft in the Army's spring maneuvers against a fictional "black force" invasion fleet bound for the northeastern United States. The Navy, participating in a simultaneous exercise in the Pacific, had been unable to provide any ships for the black fleet. To remedy that problem, the enterprising Lieutenant Colonel Ira Eaker, Chief of Air Corps Information, had devised an intriguing substitute. He learned that the Italian luxury liner *Rex*, traveling from Gibraltar to New York City, would be roughly seven hundred miles east of New York on 12 May, making it a superb double for an enemy aircraft carrier. The Air Corps had received permission from General Malin Craig, the Army Chief of Staff, as well as from the Italian cruise line to intercept the vessel. LeMay, as lead navigator for the mission, was to guarantee that the three B-17s found the *Rex* in the Atlantic Ocean at the appointed time.

The idea of intercepting the *Rex* before its theoretical aircraft would be in range to attack the east coast delighted Major General Frank Andrews. As Commander of the General Headquarters (GHQ) Air Force, the Air Corps branch containing all combat aircraft, Andrews touted the merits of the B-17 as the nation's first line of defense to all who would listen. The *Rex* intercept would emphatically demonstrate the bomber's ability to thwart an invading carrier force far from American shores, and Andrews aimed to assure that it received maximum publicity. The Navy had downplayed the successful results of an "attack" on the battleship *Utah* by seven B-17s during maneuvers the previous August. For the *Rex* mission, an NBC radio crew would ride in "Number 80" and broadcast the event live to millions of listeners across the country, while newspaper reporters, including the *New York Times*'s Hanson Baldwin, would also fly in one of the bombers. In addition, Major George Goddard, the Air Corps' ace photographer, would record the scene using a specially modified Graflex camera.[1]

Shortly after 8:00 a.m. on 12 May, the aircrews and journalists crowded into the three B-17s on Mitchel Field. Sheets of rain cascaded across the runway, and clouds clung just above the frothing Atlantic Ocean. Besides the vile weather, the *Rex* had not updated its position from the day before, causing the thirty-two-year-old LeMay to want "to go somewhere and hide." General Andrews had emphasized the mission's importance to his crews before they boarded their aircraft, telling them that the Navy had buried the results of the *Utah* bombing last year, and that the American public needed to understand bomber capabilities. As the crews departed the operations building, Andrews looked directly at LeMay and said, "Good luck."[2]

Fortunately for LeMay, an update of the *Rex*'s position arrived just before takeoff, allowing him to revise his calculations as he bounced along through turbulence so severe that the aircraft's altitude often shifted by more than five thousand feet in a matter of seconds. He found that his original estimate placed the ship much closer to shore than was actually the case; now the intercept would occur more than 750 miles out to sea. Moreover, an intense headwind slowed the projected ground speed of the B-17s. Before takeoff LeMay estimated sighting the *Rex* at 12:25 p.m., and NBC decided to begin its live radio broadcast based on that prediction. But like any good navigator—and LeMay was deemed the best in the Air Corps—his original estimate contained a time cushion. At 12:21 the aircraft entered a squall. Two minutes later the clouds began giving way to patches of sunlight. Dead ahead was the *Rex*. "It was all a movie. It was happening to someone else, it wasn't real, wasn't happening to us," LeMay recalled.[3]

The impact of the intercept was immediate. Goddard's photograph of two B-17s flying past the liner at mast level appeared on page 1 in newspapers around the nation. Hanson Baldwin's feature in the *New York Times* noted that the B-17s "roared through line squalls, hail, rain and sunshine today in a 1,300-mile overwater flight unprecedented in the history of the Army Air Corps." The mission was "a striking example of the mobility and range of modern aviation."[4] Andrews was elated, yet realized that most officers on the Army's General Staff—who saw bombers only as vehicles for providing close air support to ground troops—would probably view the episode differently. "I notice from some press reports that there is a tendency to indicate that the Army GHQ Air Force is planning to fight a war by itself. I would like to correct that impression," he diplomatically remarked to journalists after the flight. "We must realize that in common with the mobilization of the Air Force in this area, the ground arms of the Army would also be assembling, prepared to take the major role in repelling the actual landing forces. . . . I want to ask that you do not accuse us of trying to win a war alone."[5]

Technological Developments

By the mid-1930s many air power advocates believed that aerial technology had finally begun to catch up to air power theory. The outdated Keystone B-4, a two-engine, fabric-covered biplane that served as the Army's primary bomber when the decade began, gave way to all-metal monoplanes, the Boeing B-9 and Martin B-10. The open-cockpit B-9 could fly at 186 miles per hour at six thousand feet, which made it 60 miles per hour faster than any current Air Corps bomber when it first flew in April 1931. At above twenty thousand feet—the estimated maximum range of antiaircraft artillery—it was faster than the Air Corps' primary *fighter* aircraft, the P-26! The B-10 was faster still, recording a speed of 207 miles per hour at twenty-one thousand feet in 1932, plus it sported internally carried bombs, enclosed crew compartments, and a retractable landing gear.[6] Both aircraft had only two engines, however, which precluded them from carrying heavy bomb loads for long distances.

To overcome this deficiency, Air Corps Chief Major General Benjamin Foulois submitted a request to aircraft manufacturers for a design capable of flying 2,000 miles with a ton of bombs at a speed of 250 miles per hour. Three companies responded to the request, and one, Boeing, built a four-engine model designed for an eight-man crew. That prototype, the XB-17, could reach 250 miles per hour at fourteen thousand feet, could operate as high as thirty thousand feet, and could carry 2,500 pounds of bombs 2,260 miles or 5,000 pounds for 1,700 miles.[7] For airmen it was the manifestation of nirvana. Hap Arnold recalled that the B-17 was "the first real American air power. . . . Not just brilliant prophecies, good coastal defense airplanes, or promising techniques; but, for the first time in history, Air Power that you could put your hands on."[8] The Air Corps wanted to purchase sixty-five B-17s, but the prototype's crash in October 1935, stemming from locked flight controls—and the War Department's desire for a bomber better suited for supporting ground troops—limited the order to thirteen. They began arriving at Langley's Second Bombardment Group in March 1937.

Complementing the B-17 was a device that significantly improved bombing accuracy—the Norden bombsight. In October 1931 Air Corps observers witnessed use of the Navy's new bombsight, the Mark XV. Carl L. Norden, a civilian consultant, and Navy Captain Frederick I. Entwistle had developed the device, and in 1932 Foulois requested twenty-five of them for the Air Corps. The main feature of the black metal bombsight was a gyro-stabilized, motor-driven telescope. The bombardier looked through it during the bomb run, after having inserted the wind speed, altitude, and bomb ballistics information into the bombsight. Its primitive computer updated the aircraft's speed over the ground, which enabled the bombardier to control lateral aircraft movements via an autopilot. Meanwhile, he synchronized the telescope's vertical and horizontal crosshairs on the target. If he had inserted the proper data and aligned the crosshairs over the proper spot, the bombsight would identify the correct point to release bombs and drop them automatically. Under *ideal* conditions at twenty-one thousand feet, he might place *one* bomb out of all those that he dropped into a hundred-foot-diameter circle surrounding the center of the target, although conditions in combat would rarely be ideal. Still, the Norden bombsight dramatically increased the possibility that an air offensive could sever the strands of an industrial web. In 1933 the Air Corps ordered seventy-eight more of the devices, and by the late 1930s the Tactical School had its students estimating the number of Norden-equipped bombers needed to destroy particular targets. The bomber type used in those exercises was the B-17.[9]

Army Opposition

The Air Corps' emphasis on the bomber's independent mission continued despite the Army's growing opposition to it. In the early 1930s, the Air Corps received some promising signals that the Army might support long range bomber operations. In 1931 Chief of Staff General Douglas MacArthur obtained from his naval counterpart, Admiral William V. Pratt, an agreement that the Air Corps would conduct the air defense of the United States and its possessions. Two years later, following Lieutenant Colonel Hap Arnold's nonstop flight of five B-10s from Alaska to Seattle, the War Department endorsed an Air Corps request for a bomber with a five-thousand-mile range, two-hundred-mile-per-hour speed, and two-thousand-pound bomb load that could take off from American soil to defend Hawaii, Alaska, and Panama.[10] In 1936 the War Department also approved a request for a bomber with an eight-thousand-mile range.[11]

The War Department's failure to sanction the B-17, however, indicated that the Army's fundamental view of air power had changed little from the Mitchell era. The Air Corps received a harbinger of Army sentiments in late December 1934, when Brigadier General Charles Kilbourne, chief of the General Staff's War Plans Division, sent a proposed Air Corps doctrinal manual to General

Foulois. Drafted by General Staff officers, the manual stated that success on the battlefield was the decisive factor in war and challenged the notion that air power could win an independent victory. "The effectiveness of aviation to break the will of a well-organized nation is claimed by some," the manual observed, "but this has never been demonstrated and is not accepted by members of the armed services of our nation. So far, well-organized nations have surrendered only when occupied by the enemy's army or when such occupation could no longer be opposed."[12]

Foulois sent the document to Maxwell for comment by the Tactical School. Its faculty responded that the proposed doctrine was neither "reasonable" nor "progressive," and returned aphorisms of industrial web theory to the War Department.[13] Most General Staff officers dismissed such maxims, but when word reached them in 1936 that the school advocated strategic bombing free from ground commanders' control, an Army team came to Maxwell to investigate. Led by Brigadier General Lesley J. McNair, the officers received detailed briefings from Harold George, Larry Kuter, and other instructors on the Tactical School approach to proper bomber employment. McNair concluded that the presentations went far beyond the scope of instruction at other Army schools but refused to revamp Maxwell's curriculum.[14]

Rather than trying to curb the airmen's desire for independent operations, War Department officers restricted the airmen's capability to conduct missions other than Army support. Between October 1935 and June 1939, the Air Corps requested 206 B-17s. Only 14—one more than the original number approved by the War Department in 1935—were in service when Hitler's Germany attacked Poland on 1 September 1939.[15] Major General Hugh Drum, the Army's Deputy Chief of Staff in 1934, reflected the views of many Army senior officers by stating that he saw no reason why an airplane's range should exceed "three days' march by the Infantry."[16] Drum's successor, Major General Stanley D. Embick, was even more vocal in his opposition to heavy bombers such as the b-17. Together with his like-minded Assistant Chief of Staff, Brigadier General George R. Spaulding, Embick in October 1937 persuaded Secretary of War Harry H. Woodring to prohibit further procurement of four-engine bombers. Spaulding decreed that the Army would purchase only equipment that supported a current Army mission, and the b-17—which could be used defensively against a naval force, or offensively against an enemy's vital centers—did not fit that criterion. He dubbed the proposed eight-thousand-mile-range bomber "a weapon of aggression."[17]

Andrews's Advocacy with GHQ Air Force

Brigadier General Frank Andrews, the newly minted commander of the GHQ Air Force, had no intention of allowing the attitude of Embick and Spaulding to prevail. Handsome, athletic, and articulate, Andrews graduated from West Point in 1906, served in the cavalry for eleven years before transferring to the Air Service, and directed the Air Service's postwar European contingent for his father-in-law, General Henry Allen, who commanded American occupation troops in Germany. The Allen connection gave Andrews an inside track into Washington DC social circles, and he used it to further his advocacy of an independent air force. After completing the Air Corps Tactical School in 1928, he served in Washington DC as Air Corps Chief of Training and Operations, where he befriended Florida Congressman Mark Wilcox, a fellow supporter of air force autonomy. Andrews then attended the Army War College and commanded the First Pursuit Group at Selfridge Field, Michigan. While at Selfridge he was a ghostwriter for Wilcox, producing a pro-air power op-ed for the congressman that appeared in the *Washington Star*.[18] In 1934 Andrews returned to Washington DC to help draft plans for the GHQ Air Force. Douglas MacArthur liked his work and selected him to command the new force that would contain all of the Air Corps' combat aircraft—with a jump in grade from lieutenant colonel to brigadier general. General Drum concurred with the appointment. Ironically, he described Andrews as an efficient flyer who "has been in harmony with all the War Department has been trying to do."[19]

In many respects, Andrews's fight for air force autonomy paralleled Billy Mitchell's. Andrews had not been in Mitchell's inner circle, but after Mitchell left the service Andrews became one of his closest confidants.[20] Both men believed that the bomber was the key to obtaining service independence, and both jumped the chain of command and appealed directly to the public to secure a bomber-oriented air force. Andrews was perhaps the more restrained of the two. Initially, he refused to proclaim his ideas too loudly, and he also developed contacts who helped him convey his message. In December 1936 he told General Embick that the heavy bombers under development were for defensive purposes only and that it was "utterly absurd to consider them as anything else."[21] One month later he provided Army Chief of Staff General Malin Craig with a poker-faced endorsement of Representative Wilcox's bill advocating an autonomous air force—when in fact Andrews had drafted the proposal himself.[22]

The GHQ Air Force Commander possessed ties to the government's executive branch as well as its legislative. In late 1937 Andrews sent copies of confidential Navy reports complimenting B-17 bombing accuracy to Colonel Edwin M. "Pa" Watson, military aide to President Franklin Roosevelt. Andrews pleaded to Watson for additional B-17s, noting that the two engine B-18s lacked sufficient range for coast defense.[23] Ultimately, Andrews's zeal for the B-17 resulted in a Mitchell-like banishment to an obscure Texas assignment. But unlike Mitchell, Andrews found support for his beliefs from among the Army hierarchy, and that backing rekindled his air power crusade.

Shortly after taking charge of the GHQ Air Force at Langley

Field, Virginia, Andrews told his staff that unified Air Corps action was essential to convince the public that his new organization was viable; he desired "publicity that can't be beat."[24] The creation of the GHQ Air Force severed the Air Corps into two distinctive units, with reduced authority for each air commander. The Chief of the Air Corps was now responsible only for supply and procurement, and developing doctrine. Meanwhile, Andrews reported directly to the Army Chief of Staff (or the theater commander in time of war), commanded all Air Corps combat aircraft in the United States, and assumed responsibility for training his forces. Those forces consisted of three wings: the First, commanded by Brigadier General Hap Arnold at March Field, California; the Second, commanded by Brigadier General Conger Pratt at Langley; and the Third, commanded by Colonel Gerald Bryant at Barksdale Field, Louisiana. Each wing contained a mixture of bomber, fighter, and ground attack aircraft; observation units remained assigned to ground commanders.

Yet establishing a new command did not mean that it possessed its full complement of airplanes. The authorized strength of GHQ Air Force was 980 aircraft, but Andrews complained to newsman Lowell Thomas in a 1936 national radio broadcast that his command had only 350 combat airplanes, of which 190 were obsolete. The aircraft that Andrews desperately wanted were B-17s. After the crash of the XB-17 prototype in October 1935, he persuaded Brigadier General Augustine W. Robins, Chief of the Army's Material Division, and Major General Oscar Westover, Chief of the Air Corps, to secure War Department approval to buy thirteen B-17s on an experimental basis. Andrews viewed the B-17 as the epitome of American air power, and on radio he voiced views on bomber invincibility that parroted those of the Tactical School. "I do not believe that air attacks can be stopped by any means known," he told an NBC audience in May 1937. "The best defense is a strong offense. We must have an air force capable of going out and meeting an enemy before he can get under way."[25]

Like Mitchell, Andrews stressed the bomber's ability to defend America against a seaborne invasion, and he also revealed a progressive mindset regarding the bomber's capacity to transform war. "The four-engined bombardment airplane, as a coast defense weapon, is one of the greatest steps forward in our airplane development in recent years," he told Air Corps Tactical School students in September 1937.[26] One month later at the Army War College, he elaborated on how air power could best accomplish coast defense—by attacking the enemy "as far from our shores as we can reach him." Only bombers such as the B-17 could accomplish that goal. "Bombardment aviation is, and will always be, the principal force employed in independent air operations," he remarked. "The measure of air power of a nation is really that of its bombardment. It is the striking arm—the arm with punch." Andrews then noted that the application of air power "was a new and entirely different mode of warfare" that sought the same objective as land or sea power—"the destruction of the enemy's will to fight." Given his audience, he avoided saying that bombers could independently achieve victory by destroying enemy morale. Instead, Andrews observed that they could attack enemy will directly, without having to tackle austere terrain or enemy surface forces.[27]

Andrews repeated this mantra to Secretary of War Woodring soon after the start of the new year. He further told Woodring that the Army and Navy "have an important requirement for auxiliary aviation to complete their combat teams, but . . . it must be remembered that the airplane is more than just another supporting weapon." Andrews called for the development of additional bombers as well as auxiliary aircraft for the Army and Navy. "Bombardment is the basic element of air power," he insisted.

"Air power is as vital a requirement to the military efficiency of a great nation as land power and sea power, and there is no hope for victory in a war for a nation in which it is lacking." He concluded by observing: "I cannot escape the conviction that the program I have proposed as a compromise to expediency, instead of being too progressive, is really not progressive enough."[28]

Besides preaching the Tactical School's gospel of air power, Andrews displayed his faith through flying demonstrations. He sent part of his fledgling B-17 force to the West Coast to participate in an August 1937 Army-Navy exercise simulating a seaborne invasion of the United States. In it, seven of his bombers successfully attacked the battleship *Utah* by flying underneath a thick fog. When Navy umpires complained that the overcast prevented sailors from seeing the B-17s and taking evasive action, the bombers attacked in clear weather at altitudes between eight and eighteen thousand feet. They scored hits with 12 percent of the bombs dropped—a higher percentage than Navy aircraft had scored in tests from lower altitudes.[29]

Andrews also used his bombers to convey political messages. In February 1938 Lieutenant Colonel Robert Olds led six B-17s to Buenos Aires for the inauguration of Argentine President Robert Ortiz. The flight demonstrated America's resolve to uphold the Monroe Doctrine in light of fascist encroachment in the area. Despite strong General Staff opposition, Andrews secured the mission by having a journalist friend recommend it to Assistant Secretary of War Louis Johnson, a B-17 proponent. Afterward, the General Staff reiterated its opposition to further long-distance B-17 flights, and General Craig vetoed a request from the Army commander on Hawaii to fly bombers there from the West Coast.[30]

Such resistance did not keep Andrews from striking a blow for air power if the opportunity arose, and the *Rex* intercept in May 1938 was a notable opportunity. The morning after the flight, he received a telephone call from Craig, who told him that future flights over water by the GHQ Air Force would not exceed a distance of one hundred miles from land. The spark for Craig's action perhaps emanated from Navy Secretary Claude Swanson. The Navy had downplayed the success of Andrews's bombers in attacking the *Utah*, and the final report of those maneuvers drafted by Swanson and Secretary of War Woodring discounted the B-17's ability to navigate in clouds or accurately bomb a target.[31] The *Rex* intercept portrayed—for the whole world to see—a surface fleet at the mercy of long-range bombers despite dastardly weather. That vision might cause the American public to question—as had Mitchell seventeen years earlier—the Navy's viability as a first line of defense. If such logic produced an independent air force, the sea service could expect to lose not only its foremost mission, but also a large chunk of its budget.

Such rationale might also cause the Army to lose its air support for ground troops. An autonomous air force founded on strategic bombing as a war-winning instrument would provide little incentive to devote money to ground support. Soon after the *Rex* incident, Secretary Woodring directed that no B-17s in production would be procured during fiscal year 1940. Instead, the Air Corps would confine its 1940 projections to light, medium, and attack bombers. General Embick barked that "our national policy contemplates preparation for defense, not aggression. . . . The military superiority of . . . a B-17 over the two or three smaller planes that could be procured with the same funds remains to be established."[32] Embick asked for a joint Army-Navy board to study the whole issue of heavy bombers and to recommend limits "beyond which Army planes should not be developed."[33] In the spring of 1938, with the Great Depression continuing to ravage America, neither the Navy nor the Army could be complacent about any issue that might affect service budgets. Thus, the im-

79

petus for Craig's directive to Andrews may have stemmed solely from within the General Staff.

Progressive Proponents: Marshall, Arnold, and Roosevelt

The War Department's efforts to curb Andrews's emphasis on heavy bombers intensified during 1938, until the combination of three events abruptly halted the trend: the appointment of Brigadier General George C. Marshall as Chief of the General Staff's War Plans Division, Hap Arnold's appointment as Chief of the Air Corps, and President Roosevelt's growing fear of German aggression.

Unlike many members of the Army's hierarchy, George Marshall was not an opponent of strategic bombing. Andrews would make him an advocate. After assuming his new duties in August, Marshall visited Langley for an update on the GHQ Air Force. Although they had never met, Andrews (now a temporary major general) was not unknown to Marshall, who had once served as chief of staff for Andrews's father-in-law. In addition, the two shared southern backgrounds—Andrews hailed from Nashville; Marshall had attended Virginia Military Institute—and both men possessed an "old-world" sense of courtesy.[34] Andrews told his guest that the B-17 was the essence of his organization, but added that he could not obtain additional bombers. To demonstrate the B-17's fundamental importance, he offered to take Marshall on a nine-day inspection of the GHQ Air Force and aircraft production facilities. Marshall agreed, and afterward wrote his host: "I want to thank you again more formally and definitely for the splendid trip you gave me, and especially for your personal efforts to make it a pleasant one and highly instructive. I enjoyed every moment of the trip and my association with you, and I really think I acquired a fair picture of military-air activities in general."[35]

In October, Marshall replaced Embick as Deputy Chief of Staff and immediately began working to erase his predecessor's hostility to airmen. Kuter, assigned to the General Staff's War Plans Division, recalled that Marshall wanted officers assigned to the staff who "were young, aviators, and not molded into standard conformity by any preceeding [*sic*] series of Army schools."[36] He arrived at his new job from the Tactical School on 1 July 1939, the day that Marshall became Acting Chief of Staff of the Army. Two months later Marshall became the official Chief of Staff. The Air Corps—and its emphasis on independent air power—finally had a friend in a high place.

Marshall's march through the Army hierarchy complemented the appointment of Hap Arnold to replace Major General Oscar Westover as Chief of the Air Corps. After Westover died in an airplane crash on 21 September 1938, Craig originally offered Westover's position to Andrews—provided that he quit promoting the B-17. When Andrews refused, the job went to Arnold.[37] Attempting to assuage the growing split between the Air Corps and the GHQ Air Force, Westover had taken Arnold from command of the GHQ Air Force's First Wing as a temporary brigadier general in January 1936 and made him his Assistant Chief of the Air Corps as a permanent brigadier. Arnold, forty-nine, would serve the final ten and a half years of his career in Washington DC and direct what ultimately became—in terms of men and aircraft—the largest military air organization in history. Leading that force would eventually cost him his health. The cherubic face and frequent smile that earned Arnold his nickname belied a relentless, often chaotic, energy that made him difficult to work for on the best of days. He commanded by relying on instinct and experience, and possessed a diverse military background on which to base his decisions.

Arnold's career did not, however, include combat experience. After graduating from West Point, he learned to fly from the Wright brothers. He twice won the prestigious MacKay Trophy for outstanding feats of airmanship—despite having suffered a severe case of fear of flying that grounded him for four years. During World War I he gained invaluable expertise about the intricacies of American aircraft production—and Washington DC politics—that would serve him well in the next war. His avid backing of Billy Mitchell led to temporary "banishment" at Fort Riley, Kansas, where he commanded a squadron and perfected ground support techniques. He then gained experience in supply and maintenance at Wright Field in Dayton, Ohio. From Dayton he went to March Field.

Arnold did not attend the Air Corps Tactical School, but as a close friend of Mitchell he absorbed the notion that bombing could win wars by destroying the enemy's capacity and will to resist.[38] Arnold, though, was more judicious than Mitchell—or Andrews—in parading the merits of independent air power.[39] He was also more pragmatic. While firmly committed to the goal of air force autonomy, Arnold did not want to press forward until all the pieces were in place. He fully appreciated that the Air Corps consisted of more than simply men and airplanes. "The GHQ Air Force is as much of a revolutionary step as should be tried at this time," he told a congressional committee in July 1936. "We can't at this stage stand on our own two feet."[40] Two years later he still thought that the time for autonomy was not ripe. To avoid antagonizing President Roosevelt and the War Department, he supported Secretary Woodring's limitations on B-17 production. Once rearmament began in 1939, he then shunned "any drastic organizational change" that might hinder the process.[41]

Andrews meanwhile continued his crusade for the B-17, which Army opponents had dubbed "Andrews's folly." His inability to increase the bomber force made him despondent. "I have only a few months in this job of mine and I will be glad to get out of it, for as it works out, I carry the responsibility and very little author-ity," he lamented to Marshall in October 1938. "There is no fu-ture in it, and it is like sitting all of the time on a powder keg."[42] In January 1939, after Secretary Woodring boasted of American air strength, Andrews publicly declared that the United States was a sixth-rate air power. When Andrews's tenure as GHQ Air Force commander expired one month later, Woodring personally ap-proved his assignment to Fort Sam Houston as district air offi-cer.[43] Andrews reverted to his permanent rank of colonel and was given an office that included an open latrine—the same office that Mitchell occupied when banished to Fort Sam Houston in 1925.[44] Yet the penance proved short-lived. In July, one of Marshall's first moves as Acting Chief of Staff was to promote Andrews to brig-adier general and make him Assistant Chief of Staff for Training and Operations—the first time that an airman became one of the four assistant chiefs on the Army's General Staff.

Although Marshall's air power advocacy and Arnold's air power discretion helped curb the Army's resistance to a heavy bomber force, the third—and most important—factor that made Andrews's vision a reality was Roosevelt. The president watched with grow-ing apprehension as Adolf Hitler began rearming Germany and then marched into the Rhineland and Austria; Spain appeared des-tined to fall to fascism; the Japanese had invaded China proper. Despite the isolationist sentiment that still gripped the American public (and Congress) in 1938, Roosevelt saw Nazi Germany and Imperial Japan as direct threats to the United States. The former Assistant Secretary of the Navy was no longer certain that the sea service could protect American shores if war occurred. He realized that air power facilitated much of ongoing fascist aggression, and Andrews's long-range exhibitions with B-17s had caught his eye as well.[45] On 12 September 1938, as the Czechoslovakian crisis intensified, Roosevelt listened to a radio broadcast of Hitler ranting at a Nuremberg party rally. The president was fluent in German and concluded that war was imminent. He dispatched Works Progress Administration (WPA) director Harry Hopkins on a secret tour of American aircraft factories, telling him that he was "sure then that we were going to get into war and he believed that air power would win it."[46] As the British and French cowered before Hitler at Munich, Hopkins reported that the rate of American aircraft production was almost 2,600 airplanes a year.[47] Roosevelt determined that it was not enough.

On 14 November 1938 the president assembled key military and civilian leaders and their assistants, including Secretary of the Treasury Henry Morgenthau Jr., Assistant Secretary of War Louis Johnson, Army Chief of Staff Craig, Army Deputy Chief of Staff Marshall, Arnold, and Hopkins in his office for what Arnold called "a bolt from the blue": he wanted an Army Air Corps of 24,000 airplanes, with 10,000 more a year rolling off the assembly line and an "all-out" capacity to produce 20,000 a year. Roosevelt stated that a new regiment of field artillery or a new barracks in Wyoming or new machine tools in an ordnance arsenal would not scare Hitler one goddamned bit; he wanted airplanes—now—and lots of them! He wanted a large force of Army strike aircraft to protect the Western hemisphere; the Navy should also receive additional airplanes. The president confessed that the isolationist Congress would probably approve only 10,000 aircraft, of which 7,500 should be combat airplanes (with half of those being reserves), and the remaining 2,500 serving as trainers. He then outlined a construction scheme that he likely based on information from Hopkins's travels. Government factories would build one-fifth of the aircraft while commercial factories built the rest. The WPA would construct seven factories, with five of those remaining idle until needed for more expansion. Arnold left the White House believing that the Air Corps had finally "achieved its Magna Carta."[48]

In his January 1939 address to Congress, Roosevelt asked for $500 million for defense spending, with $180 million of it to purchase three thousand airplanes. Several congressmen had accused the president of creating a "pump-priming" spending program when Assistant Secretary Johnson publicly called for increasing the Air Corps after the 14 November meeting, causing Roosevelt to trim his estimate of an acceptable air expansion. The president maintained that government-owned factories, which would also produce aircraft along with commercial aircraft companies, would provide a yardstick for measuring prices charged by the commercial aircraft industry.[49]

Gradually, though, the stark reality of an impotent American military matched by the darkening situation in Europe eclipsed New Deal limits on military spending. Boeing was geared to produce only thirty-eight b-17s a year to add to the thirteen already in operation, and its production rate typified that of other American aircraft manufacturers.[50] Roosevelt, however, now privately indicated that he wanted airplanes available to send to Britain and France as well as to boost Air Corps totals. Envisioning an extensive growth in aircraft production, Arnold asked companies to prepare for it without giving them firm commitments, and many developed machine tools and prepared contracts. Meanwhile, Europe's slide toward war continued as German troops gobbled up the remainder of Czechoslovakia in March. One month later Congress passed Roosevelt's appropriations bill. It raised the authorized strength of the Air Corps to 5,500 aircraft, 3,203 officers, and 45,000 enlisted men. Although not the increases the president had envisioned in November, they were nevertheless dramatic—the allocated money equaled half as much as the Air Corps received in the proceeding *fourteen* fiscal years, while officer strength doubled and enlisted strength increased by 150 percent.[51]

The outbreak of war in Europe heightened the prospects that a global struggle might engulf America and caused Air Corps' planning to shift away from the Japanese threat in the Pacific. On 1 September 1939—the day that the German attack on Poland commenced—Lieutenant Colonel Carl "Tooey" Spaatz, chief of the Air Corps' Planning Division, presented Arnold with an outline for a prospective air campaign against Japan.[52] Spaatz maintained that an invasion of the Japanese home islands would be impractical and unnecessary, while a sea blockade would achieve results too slowly. Independent air power, in the form of heavy bombers from the Philippines, would wreck Japan's vulnerable industry and achieve victory *alone*. Moreover, the presence of American bombers in the Philippines might restrain further Japanese aggression.[53] Ten days later, in an assertion that recalled the *Rex* intercept, Spaatz insisted that two groups of B-17s (eighty-four aircraft) on Hawaii would wreck any carrier force that Japan sent against the islands long before the carrier aircraft launched an attack.[54]

Although he deemed Spaatz's observations valuable, Arnold focused his attention on Europe and sent handpicked observers to Britain and France. Spaatz joined the group on the eve of Dunkirk, and the Battle of Britain provided him with a firsthand appreciation for the difficulties of applying independent air power against a nation's capability and will to resist. He concluded that the Luftwaffe would not win daylight air superiority—or wreck British will—by waging a poorly coordinated offensive against the city of London. In addition, because the Luftwaffe was designed to support ground troops, it lacked a four-engine heavy bomber and an accurate bombsight, and its bombers had meager defensive armament and failed to maintain tight formations. They were no match for the Royal Air Force's combination of a sophisticated command and control system based on radar; maneuverable, high-speed fighters flown by skilled, dedicated pilots; and astute leadership.[55]

From across the Atlantic, Roosevelt watched warily as the Luftwaffe spearheaded Hitler's assaults on Poland, Denmark, and Norway. On 16 May 1940, after the blitzkrieg began to knife its way through France and the low countries, the president asked Congress to raise Army and Navy air arms to a total of fifty thousand airplanes with the capacity to produce fifty thousand more a year. Three days earlier, Arnold had asked the president for $80 million to purchase two hundred B-17s and $106 million for pilot training—a brave request, given that two months before, Roosevelt threatened Arnold with an assignment on Guam if he did not support the planned dispatch of aircraft to Britain and France.[56] Arnold dragged his feet because he believed that the Air Corps' needs outweighed those of the potential allies. He realized that aircraft production took time, and he knew that bombers were necessary to defend the United States and its possessions if war came.

For Roosevelt, an appreciation for the intricacies of bomber production would not occur until late 1940. At a 27 September White House meeting without Arnold—he remained "in the doghouse" for his stand against sending aircraft overseas—the president demanded that B-17s be sent to Britain. Marshall responded that, aside from a few squadrons stationed on the Philippines and Hawaii, the United States possessed a grand total of forty-nine of the heavy bombers for its own defense. "The President's head went back as if someone had hit him in the chest," recalled new Secretary of War Henry Stimson, who believed that Roosevelt "finally saw the situation we were in."[57] On 4 May 1941, the president ordered the production of five hundred heavy bombers per month. He told Stimson that the active defense of the United States required a fleet of heavy bombers, and added: "I know of no single item of our defense today that is more important than a larger four-engine bomber capacity."[58]

Roosevelt's emphasis on the bomber complemented Air Corps

organizational changes that made air power's independent application possible once America entered the war. After Andrews's transfer to Fort Sam Houston, control of the GHQ Air Force returned to the Chief of the Air Corps. The change thrilled Arnold, but it proved transitory. The buildup of Army ground forces that occurred concurrently with Air Corps expansion caused Marshall difficulty in getting his decisions through the General Staff. To decentralize the War Department, he established the GHQ U.S. Army in July 1940. Brigadier General Lesley McNair—who had critiqued the Tactical School's curriculum four years earlier—directed the new organization, which was slated to control the GHQ Air Force. But Arnold believed "it would be suicidal," as he told Marshall on 6 July, "to separate the G.H.Q. from the Air Corps right in the middle of an expansion program."[59]

Arnold instead proposed establishing three Army deputy chiefs of staff—one each for ground, air, and service forces. General Staff officers rejected the idea, and their rationale revealed that many still harbored a hostile view of the Army's air component. "The Air Corps believes that its primary purpose is to defeat the enemy air force and execute independent missions against ground targets," they wrote. "Actually, its primary purpose is to assist the ground forces in reaching their objective."[60] On 19 November GHQ U.S. Army consumed the GHQ Air Force. Marshall, however, had not discounted Arnold's proposal. He made Arnold his deputy chief of staff for air on 30 October, and by March 1941 he gave Arnold authority to direct all air matters not pertaining to war plans or intelligence. Secretary Stimson believed that smooth air operations demanded even greater authority. As a result, on 20 June 1941, Arnold became Chief of the Army Air Forces (AAF), which comprised the Army Air Corps, the GHQ Air Force (redesignated as Air Force Combat Command), and all other Army air units. He also remained Marshall's deputy chief of staff for air.

The holy grail of autonomy now rested tantalizingly close to Arnold's fingertips. The key to embracing it, Arnold believed, was independent air power.

Sanctioning Progressive Air Power: AWPD-1

Providence soon handed Arnold the opportunity to map out a wartime strategy based on strategic bombing. The new Chief of the AAF quickly formed an "air staff" that resembled the Army's General Staff. He asked forty-eight-year-old Lieutenant Colonel Harold Lee George, who commanded the Second Bombardment Group and its B-17s, to leave Langley in early July 1941 and come to Washington DC to establish an Air War Plans Division (AWPD). George agreed and notified Arnold that his division was open for business on 10 July—with a grand total of four people.[61] The previous day, the president had sent a letter to the Secretaries of War and the Navy requesting their estimate of production requirements if the United States fought the Axis. To George, the president's request was a godsend. He asked Arnold to obtain permission for the Air War Plans Division to draft the air portion of the plan.

Arnold agreed that the time was ripe to make a concerted bid for the independent application of air power. He convinced Brigadier General L. T. Gerow, chief of the Army War Plans Division, that George's office was the best suited to determine Army Air Forces requirements. The significance of Arnold's action was not lost on those around him. "We realized instinctively that a major milestone had been reached," recalled then Major Haywood Hansell, who joined George's group from the office of Strategic Air Intelligence. "Suddenly, without anywhere near the opposition we expected, we found ourselves able to plan our own future. How well we would plan and what success we would have in getting that plan past the Army General Staff remained a matter of uncertainty, but for the moment one of our fondest dreams

had been realized."[62] On Monday, 4 August, Lieutenant Colonel
George informed his officers that they would develop a plan for
a prospective air war against Germany and Japan—and that they
would complete the plan in nine days.

To guide the effort George assembled an extraordinary group
of talented men. Lieutenant Colonels Orvil Anderson, Max F.
Schneider, and Arthur W. Vanaman, and Majors Hoyt S. Vandenberg and Samuel E. Anderson were among those who worked on
developing the plan's eighteen separate tabs.[63] Yet the responsibility for the most important of those tabs, analyzing such topics as "Bombardment Operations against Germany" and "Bombardment Aviation Required for Hemispheric Defense," went to
George himself and the three men whom he handpicked to guide
the plan's development: Lieutenant Colonel Kenneth N. Walker,
Major Haywood Hansell, and Major Laurence Kuter. George,
Walker, Hansell, and Kuter knew each other well. All had taught
at the Air Corps Tactical School, and all were stalwart disciples of
the school's strategic bombing theory. "We had one valuable asset
going for us," Hansell recalled. "We embraced a common concept
of air warfare and we spoke a common language."[64]

The red-haired Hansell, who bore the nickname "Possum" because of a scoop-shaped nose and a pointed chin, had already begun analyzing Germany's industrial web. As an officer in Arnold's
Strategic Air Intelligence office since 1940, his job had been to
gather information about the economic structure and air forces
of Germany and Japan. After receiving minimal help—and even
active resistance—from individuals in the War Department's Intelligence office, he turned to specialists from the civilian community who had recently entered the military in the wake of Hitler's
aggression.[65] Hansell relied on "the services of a PhD in industrial
economics and an expert in oil" to pinpoint the vital links connecting the German war machine.[66] He also benefited from the

suggestion of Major Malcolm Moss, a former international businessman who knew that American banks had provided the Germans with most of the capital to construct their electric power system, and thought that those banks might possess drawings and specifications of the German facilities. The hunch proved correct, and also yielded diagrams of oil refineries. Using those materials, as well as information from scientific journals, the advice of his experts, and his own detailed knowledge of production requirements, Hansell prepared target folders for the German electric power and petroleum systems.

The "ABC" discussions between British and American military staffs in early 1941 triggered a summer visit to Royal Air Force (RAF) intelligence offices in Great Britain. While there, Hansell exchanged information on German targets. He found that his studies on oil and electric power were superior to the RAF's but that the British information on transportation, aircraft production, and Luftwaffe organization eclipsed his own findings. The British allowed him to take copies of their reports, and Hansell eagerly did so. He departed in mid-July with a collection of target folders weighing almost a ton, which he crammed into an American bomber. Upon returning to the United States, he joined George's Air War Plans Division.

Ken Walker's operational expertise, and Laurence Kuter's staff work, complemented Hansell's bent for technical data. A quick-tempered chain smoker from Cerrillos, New Mexico, Walker barely missed combat in World War I, earning his wings nine days before the war ended. His work in developing formation tactics at Langley convinced him that defenses could not deter a well-orchestrated bomber attack, and he instilled this belief in his classes at Maxwell. After leaving the Tactical School faculty, he flew bombers in California and Hawaii. George considered him "one of the most brilliant and far-sighted officers in the United States Army."[67]

The restrained Larry Kuter provided a stark contrast to Walker's nervous intensity. Kuter also possessed considerable experience in bombers and had followed Walker as operations officer for Langley's Second Bombardment Group. After his assignment to the General Staff in the summer of 1939—as the sole Air Corps officer in the Operations and Training section—he worked on tripling the size of the Air Corps into a 5,500-plane force adequate to defend the Western hemisphere. Walker deemed his expertise essential to designing a viable plan for a potential air war, and persuaded Spaatz—now Arnold's chief of staff and a brigadier general—to obtain Kuter's temporary relief from the General Staff.[68] Kuter arrived for duty in the War Plans Division on 4 August—the date that George notified his staff of their nine-day deadline.

George's group accomplished their marathon planning session in the recently constructed penthouse on top of the eighth wing of the old Munitions Building, located on Constitution Avenue between the Washington Monument and Lincoln Memorial. Hastily constructed during World War I as a temporary facility, the three-story, steel-and-concrete structure contained cramped offices separated by numerous partitions and concrete pillars. The daytime temperature in Washington DC that August hovered near ninety, and the penthouse absorbed the heat.[69] Oscillating fans did little to relieve the oppressive conditions. Hansell later described the penthouse as "intolerably hot," and recalled that "literally, when you put your hand down on your desk, your papers would stick to it."[70] Despite the heat, the short deadline kept George and his staff working in the penthouse until nearly midnight every night, and on two evenings they did not go home.[71] The heat and the long hours frayed nerves and led to angry confrontations. On one occasion Walker railed at George that he could no longer work with Hansell, precipitating a similar outburst from Hansell.[72] George smoothed the ruffled feathers, and throughout the nine-day ordeal he worked to promote harmony through a mixture of humor, aplomb, and dogged determination.

According to President Roosevelt's directive, George and his staff were to determine Army Air Forces requirements that would guide American industry if war occurred between the United States and the Axis powers. The only restriction given George was that his proposal had to conform to RAINBOW 5, the overall war plan agreed to by the British and American staffs in May 1941. RAINBOW 5 designated Germany as the major Axis threat and stated that Anglo-American efforts would focus on defeating Germany first while maintaining a strategic defensive against Japan. Like Nap Gorrell in 1917, George realized that he could not estimate the number of aircraft needed without first determining *how* air power would be used. In that regard, he faced a dilemma. Although he and his staff were convinced that strategic bombing could independently defeat Germany, they also had to submit a plan that was palatable to the Army hierarchy.

Just as Pershing had expressed concern over the airmen's emphasis on independent air operations in World War I, Marshall, while favorably disposed toward strategic bombing, was likely to reject a plan making no reference to air support for the ground forces. The Chief of Staff had recently called for twelve groups of "Stuka-type" dive bombers in a proposed air expansion to eighty-four groups.[73] Accordingly, George listed the American air mission as: "To wage a sustained air offensive against German military power, supplemented by air offensives against other regions under enemy control which contribute toward that power; to support a final offensive, *if it becomes necessary* to invade the continent; in addition, to conduct effective air operations in connection with Hemisphere Defense and a strategic defensive in the Far East."[74]

By stating that an invasion of continental Europe might not be required, George acknowledged the planners' faith that strategic bombing would eliminate the need for it. Yet George also acknowledged that air power would be available to guarantee an invasion's success if the need arose. Six years earlier, as an Air Corps Tactical School instructor, he had asked his students whether air power could achieve a solo victory in war. He now aimed to construct an air campaign that answered that question with a resounding yes. The progressive notions of Tactical School theory formed the plan's underpinnings; the challenge was to translate accepted beliefs, based on hypothetical applications against generic enemies, into a specific design against an enemy that was very real. Germany—a "modern" nation waging "modern" war—appeared to be an especially apt choice for testing Tactical School principles. If the test proved successful, the bomber offensive would yield victory—and serve as a vindication for air force autonomy.

Having determined that strategic bombing would be the essence of America's air effort, George and his planners worked to identify those parts of Germany's industrial web that contributed the most to Hitler's war effort. Hansell's studies while assigned to the Strategic Air Intelligence office were invaluable in this endeavor. Using them, planners concluded that the electric power, transportation, and oil production systems were the key components of the German economy. They decided that those systems could be wrecked by destroying 124 vital targets—fifty electric power plants, fifteen marshalling yards, fifteen bridges, seventeen inland waterway facilities, and twenty-seven petroleum and synthetic oil plants. This bombing would not only destroy German war-making capability, but also the "means of livelihood of the German people." George's group noted that civilians might also be attacked directly once their morale had weakened due to sustained suffering and a lack of faith in Germany's ability to win the war. "However, if these conditions do not exist," the planners cautioned, "then area bombing of cities may actually stiffen the resistance of the population, especially if the attacks are weak and sporadic." If the industrial web theory was correct, German morale would crack without targeting residential districts.[75]

George and his planners realized that the destruction of Germany's industrial apparatus would be no easy task. German air defenses—which now included radar—were formidable, causing the group to list "neutralization of the German Air Force" as an "intermediate objective, whose accomplishment may be essential to the accomplishment of the principal objectives."[76] Without achieving control of the air, the ability to wreck German warmaking capacity remained problematic; moreover, an invasion of France could not occur unless the Allies first obtained air superiority. George's planners determined that air control through attrition was unlikely. Many industrial targets lay beyond the range of escort fighters, requiring bomber squadrons to rely on Walker's formation tactics as they fought their way across Germany. "We knew that defensive firepower in the air would not suffice to defeat the Luftwaffe," Hansell recalled.[77] Neither would attacking German air bases, which were well dispersed and heavily defended. As a result, planners decided to attack the Luftwaffe before it left the assembly line. They designated eighteen aircraft factories, six aluminum plants, and six magnesium plants as essential to aircraft production, and added them to the list of vital centers earmarked for destruction.

Until negated, German air defenses would likely hamper bombing accuracy, and accurate bombing was essential to wreck Germany's industrial web. Marginal weather also threatened to disrupt the precision bombing effort. Based on studies that Hansell obtained from the British, George's group estimated that an average of only five days a month would be suitable for daylight operations over the Reich.[78] The best weather occurred between

April and September. The prospect of stiff defenses and poor flying conditions, combined with George's own experience from Aberdeen Proving Ground, caused planners to predict that raids on
Germany would be 2.25 times more *in*accurate than peacetime
practice bombing.[79] George demanded that bombers had to attack
each target in sufficient force to achieve a 90 percent probability
of destroying it—the same percentage deemed acceptable in similar problems at the Air Corps Tactical School.[80] In addition—as
Gorrell had pointed out in 1917—bombers would have to attack
many targets more than once to prevent the Germans from repair-
ing the damage. The planners anticipated that the Germans could
repair most targets other than electric power facilities within two
to four weeks; power plants would take longer to restore.[81]

George's group next calculated the number of bombers required
to guarantee a 90 percent level of destruction to the 154 key targets selected, given the expected accuracy and the need for repeated attacks. They determined that 1,100 bombers were necessary to ensure a 90 percent probability of destroying a single
hundred-foot-by-hundred-foot target under combat conditions.[82]
A like number of aircraft would have to return to that target in
two weeks to keep it out of action. Planners quickly realized that
the AAF needed an enormous number of bombers to destroy the
German war effort through constant pounding. George thought
that dismantling German industry required at least six months of
non-stop bombing, and planners anticipated an April–September offensive to coincide with the most favorable flying weather.
Given weather, maintenance, and crew rest limitations, they estimated that a bomb group containing seventy aircraft could send
thirty-six of its bombers against Germany eight times a month.[83]
Thus, to wreck the 154 key targets in a six-month span would require ninety-eight bomb groups—or 6,860 bombers—at the *start*
of the offensive.

Those bombers would consist of ten groups of B-25s and B-26s, twenty groups of B-17s and B-24s, twenty-four groups of B-29s, and forty-four groups of B-36s. Planners noted that the ideal type of bomber for the offensive was the B-29, a recently designed four-engine marvel; two-engine B-25 and B-26 "medium bombers" would suffice "only because they were available."[84] The vast numbers would swamp airfields in Great Britain, which would serve as home base for the B-17s, B-24s, B-25s, and B-26s. B-29s would operate against Germany from Northern Ireland and the Middle East. The B-36, a proposed behemoth with a four-thousand-mile range, could fly from Newfoundland, Greenland, Africa, India, or the northeastern United States. George's staff anticipated that each group engaged in combat would lose 20 percent of its aircraft (and 15 percent of its flying personnel) per month, creating a requirement for an additional 1,272 bombers.[85]

Although the estimate of bombers needed to assault Germany dwarfed previous aircraft projections for the entire Army Air Forces,[86] those bombers were by no means the only airplanes George and his planners envisioned. The massive air offensive against the Third Reich required fighters to defend air bases and support aircraft. Moreover, substantial numbers of fighters and bombers were needed to defend the Western Hemisphere, and the teeth of the strategic defensive in the Pacific would consist of B-29s and B-32s operating from bases in Alaska, Siberia, and the Philippines. All told, George's group calculated that 239 groups and 108 observation squadrons were necessary to defeat the Axis—a grand total of 63,467 airplanes. If the United States began fighting, as anticipated, in the spring of 1942, planners thought that the nation would be hard pressed to produce such an armada before the end of 1943.[87] Still, they believed that a land invasion of Germany in less than three years was unlikely, thus giving air power a chance to achieve an independent victory.[88] A limited air offensive would start as soon as America entered the war, and the six month aerial pounding of the Reich would occur from April to September 1944. Charged with estimating manpower requirements, Kuter determined that by the start of the offensive the Army Air Forces would have expanded from its authorized limit of 152,000 men in August 1941 to 2,164,916, which was a half million more men than were in the entire Army at the end of 1941.[89]

On the afternoon of 12 August 1941, an exhausted Hal George delivered a copy of "AWPD-1: Munitions Requirements of the Army Air Forces" to the Army War Plans office. The plan's appearance reflected the rushed nature of the project. "It was not an impressive looking document," Hansell remembered. "The pages were typed and mimeographed. Corrections were made in ink. The charts were black and white, hastily prepared and crudely pasted together."[90] Nevertheless, despite sweltering conditions and flaring tempers, George's group completed their task on schedule.

Next came the job of persuading civilian and military leaders that the proposal was sound. George submitted the plan to the Army War Plans office without having it approved by Arnold, who was attending the Argentia Conference in Placentia Bay, but he knew that Arnold would have no qualms in endorsing it. Sterner challenges were on the horizon. In the following month, the planners briefed AWPD-1 to Robert Lovett (the new Assistant Secretary of War for Air), Army Chief of Staff Marshall, and Secretary of War Stimson. Lovett received the briefing on 13 August, accompanied by General Gerow from the Army War Plans Division and General Spaatz. A World War I Navy pilot and an outspoken air power advocate, Lovett avidly supported the proposal. Arnold heard the briefing with General Marshall on 30 August. The Army Chief of Staff said nothing until after the presentation was over and discussion had ceased. Then he commented that the plan had merit, and the next day scrawled "Okay, G. C. M." on the cover of his copy.[91] Andrews could claim a measure of credit for that signature. Like most Army generals, Marshall believed that air support for ground troops was essential, but Andrews had opened his eyes to the potential of independent air power. This impetus, coupled with Marshall's practical nature, helped him endorse AWPD-1. He realized that the invasion of Europe could not occur immediately if war came in early 1942, and Germany could not go unscathed during the buildup for the ground offensive. If strategic bombing could topple Hitler and eliminate the need for a risky amphibious assault, Marshall was willing to give it a try.

George's staff culminated their "selling" of AWPD-1 on the afternoon of 11 September and the morning of the next day, when George, Walker, and Kuter briefed Secretary of War Stimson in his office in the Munitions Building. Stimson accepted the plan as "a matter-of-fact statement of the air forces required to defeat the Axis." He cautioned, however, that the enormous number of men and planes necessary to implement the scheme "depended entirely upon the nation being in a war spirit or at war."[92]

With the Japanese attack on Pearl Harbor in December, America obtained the martial spirit that Stimson thought necessary to spur the large-scale production of combat aircraft. The turmoil created by Pearl Harbor canceled a scheduled briefing on AWPD-1 to the president, and Hansell later termed the lost opportunity "a cruel disappointment" because he believed that it prevented bombing advocate Roosevelt from fully understanding the value of a *concentrated* air offensive.[93] Yet the seemingly inevitable march toward war in the late summer of 1941, with the Japanese defying Roosevelt's oil embargo as they advanced across China, and the Germans threatening Atlantic sea lanes while they plowed toward Moscow, was likely a key reason that both Marshall and Stimson endorsed AWPD-1 without complaint. As historian Michael Sherry has observed, "Strategy, then, along with Roosevelt's wishes about how to fight the war, made the War Department amenable to a vision of air war that would have seemed repugnant and fanciful a few years earlier."[94]

Although advocating strategic bombing, air planners understood that their proposal could not neglect the air needs of Army commanders, most of whom were skeptical of air power's ability to achieve victory alone. Just as Gorrell had worked to convince Pershing that his plan for bombing Germany would not deny air support to ground forces, AWPD-1 specifically noted that air power would support an invasion of Europe if such an invasion proved necessary. Some airmen viewed the obligation to demonstrate that they would support their parent service as genuflection.[95] Yet air planners could not ignore the concerns of the theater commander or Chief of Staff, who had to consider the possibility that independently applied air power might not prove decisive. That airmen received the green light to conduct strategic bombing was a tribute to the Andrews-inspired vision of George Marshall.

Marshall's approval of AWPD-1 on the eve of Pearl Harbor guaranteed that the Army Air Forces would use it as a blueprint once war began, but the blueprint was not balanced. Air planners paid a great deal of attention to Germany—the designated primary enemy—and scant attention to Japan. In keeping with the tenor of the industrial web theory, they brushed aside such characteristics of the German state as its totalitarian government and Nazi ideology to focus almost exclusively on a mechanistic economic analysis. They also provided meager allowances for the unexpected— what Prussian military philosopher Carl von Clausewitz called "friction"—and the impact that such elements as chance, uncertainty, danger, and stress might have on an air offensive.[96] The Germany that they depicted had mobilized completely, with its industry running at full bore in the wake of the assault on the Soviet Union. George and his group believed that the taut nature of the

German economy would increase its vulnerability to a precisely aimed air offensive, because no reserve capacity would be available to make up for the damage caused by bombing. The planners, especially Kuter, were painfully aware of America's failure to flex its economic muscle in World War I. They believed that American industry would not allow them to wage total war for two years, and they knew that the Germans were already waging war on a global scale. The logical conclusion, it seemed, was that German factories must be producing at peak capacity.

AWPD-1's analysis of Japan's war machine paled in comparison to the mountain of data accumulated on German industry. "The allowances for defensive measures in the Far East were skimpy, to say the least," Hansell later observed. "It was presumed that the U.S. Navy would be the primary agency for this requirement."[97] While working in the Strategic Air Intelligence section, Hansell had tried to identify Japanese vital centers, but the attempt proved fruitless. "The Japanese had established and maintained a curtain of secrecy that we found absolutely impenetrable. There were not even any recent maps available," he recalled.[98] The lack of information on Japanese production capabilities plagued air leaders throughout the war, and Hansell would learn that frustration firsthand as commander of XXI Bomber Command in late 1944.

Though far from perfect, AWPD-1 marked the culmination of American air power thought from Billy Mitchell through the Air Corps Tactical School. Much of the plan—like much of the Tactical School theory that spawned it—was based on faith. "Opportunities for reality testing were few"; most airmen dismissed the air power applied in Spain and China as too primitive,[99] while the one concrete example of a modern air force attacking a modern nation—the Luftwaffe in the Battle of Britain—did not conform to American bomber technology, tactics, or strategy. Thus, the faith instilled by Mitchell, refined and dispensed by his Tactical School disciples, and blessed by air leaders sharing his vision provided the fundamental underpinning of American air power convictions.

Several articles of faith stood out above the others: the concept of a generic industrial web theory, with its presumed ties between a nation's war-fighting capability and will to resist; the presumed vulnerability of those ties to bombing, and the presumption that severing them would result in surrender; the belief that a properly executed bomber offensive could not be stopped; and, finally, the progressive notion that a victory through air power would be quicker, and cheaper, than one gained through any other medium. At the same time, most airmen thought that an air power victory would vindicate an independent air force. The airmen subscribing to those beliefs were both sincere and pragmatic. They earnestly believed in air power's ability to win a war single-handedly, and in its ability to do so efficiently, yet they realized that without proof for their claims they were unlikely to obtain an autonomous air force. Their faith in an independent air victory melded to their desire for an independent air service until the two became inseparable, as demonstrated by AWPD-1.

In the end, individuals, as well as ideas, were the key elements producing a uniquely American bombing philosophy before Pearl Harbor. The distinctive backgrounds of Gorrell, Mitchell, George, Walker, Kuter, Hansell, Andrews, Spaatz, and Arnold—and countless others—contributed directly to an American approach to air war that manifested itself against Nazi Germany and Imperial Japan. Two years and eight days after the completion of AWPD-1, the man who had found the *Rex* would lead more than one hundred B-17s in a dramatic raid against one of the major industrial targets of Hitler's Third Reich. Curtis LeMay would play a key role in the effort to validate AWPD-1's progressive notions in both the European and Asian skies.

1. British Gen. Sir David Henderson pins the "Companion of the Distinguished Service Order" on twenty-eight-year-old Army Air Service Col. Edgar S. Gorrell in France, April 1919. Relying extensively on British bombing proposals, Gorrell had authored America's first plan for strategic bombing in 1917. (U.S. Air Force)

2. William "Billy" Mitchell spurred the development of progressive air power notions that guided a generation of American airmen. (U.S. Air Force)

3. Mitchell poses beside
his command aircraft, the
Osprey, a DeHavilland DH-4
from which he directed the
bombing of the *Ostfriesland*
in July 1921. (U.S. Air Force)

4. Billy Mitchell's bombers attack the *Ostfriesland* off the Virginia Capes, 21 July 1921. (U.S. Air Force)

5. Air Corps Tactical School students tackle mapping exercises during the 1930s at Maxwell Field, Alabama. (U.S. Air Force)

6. Maj. Gen. Frank Andrews, commander of the GHQ Air Force, sits in the cockpit of the first B-17 to arrive at Langley Field, Virginia, 1 March 1937. (U.S. Air Force)

7. GHQ Air Force B-17s intercept the Italian liner *Rex* seven hundred miles from New York City, 12 May 1938. (U.S. Air Force)

8. Generals George Marshall, Frank Andrews, "Hap" Arnold, and Oliver Echols pose beside a glider at Wright Field, Dayton, Ohio, early in World War II. Marshall provided key support to Andrews and Arnold and their plans for a heavy bomber force. (U.S. Air Force)

9. (*Opposite top*) Hap Arnold and members of his air staff in 1941. Left to right: Lt. Col. Edgar P. Sorenson, Lt. Col. Harold L. George, Brig. Gen. Carl Spaatz (chief of staff), Maj. Gen. Henry H. Arnold, Maj. Haywood S. Hansell Jr., Brig. Gen. Martin F. Scanlon, and Lt. Col. Arthur W. Vanaman. George and Hansell played key roles in designing AWPD-1, the Army Air Forces plan for bombing Germany, while Spaatz would attempt to bring that plan to fruition as Eighth Air Force commander in 1942 and the commander of U.S. Strategic Air Forces in 1944–45. (U.S. Air Force)

10. (*Opposite bottom*) Ira Eaker directed VIII Bomber Command in 1942. During 1943, he led Eighth Air Force in the desperate battles for air superiority over Europe. (U.S. Air Force)

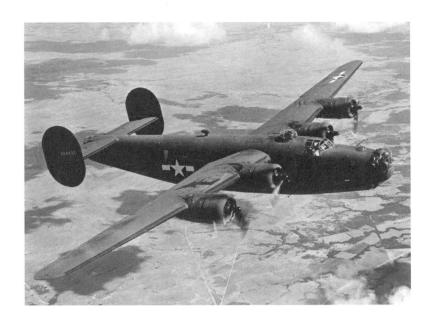

11. (*Opposite top*) Brig. Gen. "Possum" Hansell, First
Wing commander, Eighth Air Force, and Col. Curtis
LeMay, 305th Group commander, stand beside a B-17
at an airfield in Britain in spring 1943. Two years later
LeMay, a major general, replaced Hansell in the Pacific
as the commander of XXI Bomber Command. (U.S. Air
Force)

12. (*Opposite bottom*) The Boeing B-17 "Flying Fortress"
was the workhorse of Eighth Air Force. This "G" model
sported a chin turret to ward off frontal attacks from
Luftwaffe fighters. (U.S. Air Force)

13. (*Above*) The Consolidated B-24 "Liberator" was
one of the two main heavy bombers for the Eighth and
Fifteenth Air Forces in Europe. It could carry a larger
bomb load than its counterpart, the B-17. (U.S. Air Force)

14. The crew of the B-17 *Memphis Belle* at an air base in Britain on 7 June 1943 after completing twenty-five missions over enemy territory. For many bomber crews in 1943–44 the outcome was not as fortunate. (U.S. National Archives)

15. (*Opposite top*) Luftwaffe defenses claim a B-17. The heavy bomber crews of Eighth and Fifteenth Air Forces paid a steep price to win the daylight air superiority needed to launch the Normandy invasion. (U.S. Air Force)

16. (*Opposite bottom*) Bomb release in an Eighth Air Force raid on a ball-bearing plant and an aircraft engine repair facility in Paris, 31 December 1943. Following the costly raid against Schweinfurt on 14 October 1943, Eighth Air Force primarily attacked targets within range of escort fighters. Improvements in the P-47 "Thunderbolt" and P-51 "Mustang," plus the addition of external fuel "drop tanks," enabled bombers to have escort fighters to targets deep in Germany in early 1944. (U.S. National Archives)

17. A fighter pilot in World War I
who shot down three German aircraft,
"Tooey" Spaatz commanded Eighth
Air Force in 1942 and then transferred
to North Africa. He returned to
Britain in 1944 as a lieutenant general
and commander of the new U.S.
Strategic Air Forces, with a mission
to secure daylight air superiority over
Europe to facilitate the Normandy
invasion. (U.S. Air Force)

18. Gen. Dwight D. Eisenhower,
Tooey Spaatz, and Maj. Gen.
Lewis H. Brereton, the Ninth Air
Force commander, at an airfield
in Britain, May 1944. A month
earlier Spaatz had turned over
control of his heavy bombers
to Eisenhower, and Eisenhower
kept control of them until
September to assure invasion
support. (U.S. Air Force)

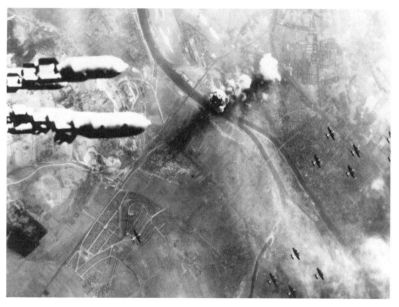

19. (*Opposite top*) Fifteenth Air Force B-24s pound Ploesti oil refineries in summer 1944. Despite the emphasis on supporting the Normandy invasion, Spaatz convinced Eisenhower to let him begin a concentrated attack on oil installations. (U.S. Air Force)

20. (*Opposite bottom*) The Messerschmitt factories at Regensburg, Germany, remained targets long after Curtis Lemay's B-17s first attacked them on 17 August 1943. Here, B-17s attack the complex on 18 December 1944. (U.S. Air Force)

21. (*Above*) Eighth Air Force B-17s unload incendiaries and high explosive bombs over Dresden on 14 February 1945 following a massive area attack by the RAF on the city the night before. Cloud cover obscured the American crews' target, a rail junction near the city's center, and most of their bombs fell on Dresden's main residential district. (U.S. Air Force)

22. B-17s from the 398th Bomb Group proceed to
Neumunster, Germany, on 13 April 1945. By this point in
the war the American portion of the Combined Bomber
Offensive had devastated much of Germany's industrial
capacity and transportation network, but the cost
had been high for the attackers as well as the German
populace. (U.S. National Archives)

23. (*Opposite top*) Frankfurt-am-Main in the aftermath
of the Combined Bomber Offensive. Bombing wrecked
most of Germany's cities. (U.S. Air Force)

24. (*Opposite bottom*) Henry H. "Hap" Arnold
became Commanding General of the Army Air Forces
in June 1941 and soon led the mightiest air armada yet
assembled. A driven, demanding leader, Arnold suffered
four heart attacks during World War II. His first combat
command came when he took charge of Twentieth Air
Force in early 1944, and he directed the B-29 assault on
Japan from his office in the Pentagon. (U.S. Air Force)

25. (*Opposite top*) The Boeing B-29 "Superfortress" was the epitome in bomber technology, sporting pressurized crew compartments plus four gun turrets remotely controlled via General Electric analog computers. The aircraft was World War II's most expensive weapon system, with a three-billion-dollar price tag. (U.S. Air Force)

26. (*Opposite bottom*) Brig. Gen. Haywood S. "Possum" Hansell, XXI Bomber Command commander, briefs B-29 air crews before a mission to Tokyo in late 1944. His steadfast commitment to prewar progressive notions about bombing contributed to Arnold's decision to replace him with LeMay. (U.S. Air Force)

27. (*Above*) Maj. Gen. Curtis LeMay, far left, replaced Brig. Gen. Possum Hansell, center, as XXI Bomber Command commander in January 1945. LeMay, who had previously commanded XX Bomber Command in China, was replaced in that job by Brig. Gen. Roger M. Ramey, far right. (U.S. Air Force)

28. Brig. Gen. Lauris "Larry" Norstad, who served on Hap Arnold's advisory council as a colonel in 1943 before becoming a staff officer in North Africa and Italy, replaced Possum Hansell as Twentieth Air Force Chief of Staff in summer 1944. Norstad wielded considerable power in that position, especially after Arnold suffered his fourth heart attack of the war in January 1945. (U.S. Air Force)

29. The *Enola Gay* dropped the atomic bomb "Little Boy" on Hiroshima on 6 August 1945. (U.S. Air Force)

30. By June 1945 most of Kobe, one of prewar Japan's four most populous cities, was in ruins. (U.S. Air Force)

31. (*Opposite top*) Twentieth Air Force
devastated Tokyo. (U.S. Air Force)

32. (*Opposite bottom*) Col. Paul
Tibbets's *Enola Gay* is prepared
to upload the atomic bomb for
Hiroshima. (U.S. Air Force)

33. (*Above*) Nagasaki following the
atomic strike on 9 August 1945.
(U.S. Air Force)

34. In the post-Vietnam era Col. John A. Warden III emerged as heir to the progressive notions that had sparked Billy Mitchell and Air Corps Tactical School instructors. Many of Warden's ideas underpin current Air Force bombing doctrine. (U.S. Air Force)

4 • Breaching Fortress Europe, 1942–43

War, no matter how it may be glorified, is unspeakably horrible in every form. The bomber simply adds to the extent of the horror, especially if not used with discretion; but when used with the proper degree of understanding, it becomes the most humane of all weapons.
• GEN. HENRY H. ARNOLD, JUNE 1943

I am concerned that you will not appreciate the tremendous damage that is being done to the German morale by these attacks through the overcast, since we cannot show you appreciable damage by photographs. . . . Just imagine for yourself bombs hitting Washington and the Pentagon Building through a thick snowstorm. What will it do? The German people cannot take that kind of terror much longer."
• LT. GEN. IRA C. EAKER TO ARNOLD, NOVEMBER 1943

---

17 August 1943

Thirteen minutes after the last of 139 B-17s from Eighth Air Force's Fourth Bomb Wing had crossed the Dutch coast, the first German fighters appeared. Instantly, the bomber crews knew that their misgivings about the mission against the sprawling Messerschmitt factory at Regensburg were justified. The daylight raid would mark the deepest penetration into Germany yet for an American bomber force, and would occur in tandem with an assault by 222 B-17s of the First Bomb Wing against the ball bearing plants at Schweinfurt, responsible for almost 50 percent of Germany's output. Both the Regensburg and Schweinfurt formations would proceed to their targets largely unescorted despite sixteen squadrons of Spitfires and eighteen squadrons of P-47s that accompanied them across the English Channel, because no Allied fighter possessed the range to fly beyond the German frontier.

Eighth Air Force planners, though, had devised a scheme to get the bombers to their targets and back relatively unscathed. The Fourth Bomb Wing would depart for Regensburg fifteen minutes before the First Wing followed it for Schweinfurt, which would prevent German fighters from attacking both formations on the way to their targets. The Regensburg mission would initially draw the Germans' attention, and by the time the First Wing's bombers approached Schweinfurt, the German fighters would have landed to refuel and rearm, which would allow the Schweinfurt force to proceed to its target unhindered. In the meantime, after the Fourth Wing bombed the Messerschmitt complex at Regensburg, it would avoid further combat by flying south across the Mediterranean to land in North Africa. The Schweinfurt bombers would then battle the rearmed German fighters on the trip home to British bases. If everything worked as planned, the Germans would suffer major damage to two of their most important war-making facilities, and the American bombers would inflict that pain at minimal cost to the attacking force.[1]

Yet the plan that appeared so appealing on paper turned out to be lacking in practice. To succeed, it required near-perfect weather, crisp coordination between multiple layers of command, and zero mishaps as two large formations of heavy bombers took shape in the skies over East Anglia. Those demands were a lot to ask for from a bombing force that had never flown so far across hostile territory. Pre-mission briefers told crews to expect "negligible" opposition, but the airmen had routinely flown missions that summer that produced loss rates approaching 10 percent, and expected the worst. Their fears increased when dense fog shrouded their British bases that morning. "The mission itself started under a cloud of doubt and we didn't know until the last minute whether it would be scrubbed or not," Colonel Curtis LeMay, the Fourth Bomb Wing Commander, said afterward. "Finally, 26 minutes before the take off, we received word from Bomber Command that the mission would go on."[2]

The delayed notification plus the thick fog produced a corresponding delay in getting the bombers airborne. LeMay had trained his crews extensively in instrument take-offs, but even he called the assembly of his seven groups of B-17s "miraculous" given that they had to climb through two dense layers of overcast.[3] The formation finally departed for Regensburg ninety minutes behind the time originally scheduled. Meanwhile, LeMay's counterpart commanding the First Bomb Wing, Brigadier General Robert Williams, did not receive the take-off order until almost an hour and a half after LeMay got the word—which resulted in a departure for Schweinfurt five hours later than the originally scheduled time and almost four hours after LeMay's Fourth Wing had left. Rather than cancel the Schweinfurt part of the mission, the Commander of VIII Bomber Command, Brigadier General Frederick Anderson, determined that the importance of the targets justified the risks involved in dispatching the two bomb wings individually.[4] As a result, almost three hundred Luftwaffe fighters were available to attack both formations for the duration of their time over the Reich.

Unlike the dismal weather in Britain, German skies were crystal clear, making them ideal for bombing—and for fighter assaults against the bombers. LeMay's B-17s formed a stream fifteen miles long at staggered intervals from sixteen thousand to twenty thousand feet. A Messerschmitt Me-110 quickly positioned itself alongside the formation, out of range, and relayed information to waiting German fighters. Colonel Beirne Lay Jr., who flew as a copilot in the bomber stream's last squadron, later wrote: "I had the lonesome foreboding that might come to the last man about to run a gauntlet lined with spiked clubs."[5] An enormous aerial melee soon engulfed the bombers. Lay described what transpired:

Swinging their yellow noses around in a wide U-turn, the 12-ship squadron of Me-109's came in from 12 to 2 o'clock in pairs and in fours and the main event was on.

A shining silver object sailed past over our right wing. I recognized it as a main exit door. Seconds later, a dark object came hurtling through the formation, barely missing several props. It was a man, clasping his knees to his head, revolving like a diver in a triple somersault. I didn't see his 'chute open.

A B-17 turned gradually out of the formation to the right, maintaining altitude. In a split second, the B-17 completely disappeared in a brilliant explosion, from which the only remains were four small balls of fire, the fuel tanks, which were quickly consumed as they fell earthward. . . .

I watched a B-17 turn slowly out to the right with its cockpit a mass of flames. The copilot crawled out of his window, held on with one hand, reached back for his 'chute, buckled it on, let go and was whisked back into the horizontal stabilizer. I believe the impact killed him. His 'chute didn't open.[6]

The hellish fury continued incessantly for an hour and a half, and abated only after the German flak intensified as the bombers approached the target. Lay estimated that the formation had suffered more than two hundred individual fighter attacks, and took grim satisfaction in seeing a column of smoke rising from the Messerschmitt factory once the B-17s headed for the Alps.

The costs of the double strike on Regensburg and Schweinfurt were staggering. LeMay's Fourth Wing lost 24 B-17s—each carrying ten men—and abandoned almost 60 of the aircraft that made it to North Africa because of heavy damage. Williams's First Wing, which suffered through a barrage of fighters that met them on both the inbound and outbound legs to Schweinfurt, lost 36 bombers, with another 27 of those that made it back written off. All told, in terms of aircraft shot down, written off, and abandoned, the missions to Regensburg and Schweinfurt cost Eighth Air Force 147 bombers—40 percent of the attacking force.

For their efforts the American airmen shot down forty-eight German fighters (they claimed in excess of one hundred), with another twelve too damaged to fly again.[7] The Messerschmitt complex at Regensburg, responsible for half of Germany's fighter production, lost three weeks of output, or roughly one thousand Me-109s. The attack on Schweinfurt achieved meager results. While damaging three of the five ball bearing factories, Williams's bombers had little impact on the machine tools that produced the bearings. The Germans negated the destruction that had occurred by turning to reserve stocks and buying additional bearings from Sweden.[8]

Despite his heavy losses and the limited damage inflicted, Major General Ira Eaker, the Eighth Air Force Commander, still considered the industries in Regensburg and Schweinfurt worthy objectives for his bombers. The balding, forty-seven-year-old Eaker was fond of late-night poker games with his staff, but to him Regensburg and Schweinfurt were not gambles—they were exactly the types of targets that would hurt Germany's war-making capability the most. Though a fighter pilot for most of his career, he was well-versed in the principles of high altitude, daylight, precision bombing and had graduated from the Air Corps Tactical School in 1936. Hap Arnold had chosen him as coauthor for two books promoting air power during the late 1930s, plus Arnold had also made him Chief of Air Corps Information. With a degree in journalism from Southern Cal, a charming smile, and a tremendous ability to convey his ideas (his promotion of the *Rex* intercept was just one example), Eaker had been an apt choice to help carve the American public's image of air power. Arnold believed him well suited to lead Eighth Air Force after its initial commander, Tooey Spaatz, departed England in late 1942 to take a command in North Africa.

Eaker had previously led VIII Bomber Command, the bomber component of Eighth Air Force, and had no illusions about the challenges of serving as the Eighth's overall commander in 1943. Bombers, as well as air crews, arrived slowly in Britain, but Eighth Air Force was, at the time, the only American combat unit capable of attacking Germany. Dismayed by the losses from Regensburg and Schweinfurt—German defenses had shot down 15 percent of his attacking force—and disappointed that he could not accompany his crews in the air (his knowledge of the Normandy invasion and the cracking of the German "enigma" codes prevented him from leading the Schweinfurt raid),[9] he had no intention of slowing his air campaign's momentum. He was convinced that the destruction of Germany's vital centers would hasten the war's end, and ultimately yield a victory less costly in Allied manpower than a war without strategic bombing. In the meantime he would continue his appeals for more bombers and crewmen while he continued his effort to deal a mortal blow to the Nazi war machine.

Preparing to Bomb Hitler's Reich, January 1942–January 1943

In the immediate aftermath of Pearl Harbor, most American airmen could not foresee the savage war of attrition that would soon transpire in the skies above Germany. Instead, as they prepared to mount an air campaign against Adolf Hitler's "Fortress Europe," most embraced the progressive views espoused by the Air Corps Tactical School and reflected on paper in AWPD-1. Air leaders like Eaker and Spaatz intended to demonstrate that high altitude, daylight, precision bombing was not only the correct way to apply air power against an enemy nation, but also that its decisive effects justified an autonomous American air force.

In June 1942, Spaatz arrived in Britain as the commander of Eighth Air Force, and he quickly shunned the night "area bombing" campaign against German cities started by Air Marshal Arthur Harris and RAF Bomber Command earlier that year. Spaatz had observed firsthand the German attempt to break British morale with bombs during the Battle of Britain. He disdained the British approach because he thought it much less efficient than the Americans' precision efforts in daylight. "It wasn't for religious or moral reasons that I didn't go along with urban area bombing," he later confided, but instead because precision attacks "could win the war more quickly."[10]

Brigadier General Haywood "Possum" Hansell, a key architect of AWPD-1 who twice commanded an Eighth Air Force Bomb Wing, agreed. "We preferred to avoid mass killings of civilians and we thought there was a better way to 'fatally weaken' an industrialized modern state," he reflected.[11] Hansell noted that "selective strategic air attack served to keep the losses of land war in Western Europe in World War II far below the levels they would have reached if decision had rested entirely upon victory on the battlefield." American air commanders preferred "selective targeting" rather than area bombing to cripple "the entire war-supporting activity of the enemy nation, not simply making the Army's task feasible and easier."[12]

Hansell's observation blended the notions of efficiency and effectiveness with the other great goal of American airmen—to achieve an independent air force. Hansell was not afraid to state that desire openly, and others did as well. Billy Mitchell's former confidant, Frank Andrews, had worked hard for service autonomy as commander of General Headquarters (GHQ) Air Force before the war, and he continued his campaign once the war began. As the Commanding General of Caribbean Command in July 1942, he implored Army Chief of Staff George Marshall's deputy, Lieutenant General Joseph T. McNarney: "We must go further and place air power on an entirely equal footing with the

Army and Navy—and do it soon; a united Air Force entirely and completely coequal with the other two services, with one commander for all three."

Andrews knew that his line of reasoning found a sympathetic audience. While GHQ Air Force Commander, he had befriended Marshall and given him a favorable impression of air power, especially air power in the form of heavy bombers. In addition, McNarney, Marshall's deputy, was an Army Air Forces pilot who had directed much of the St. Mihiel air offensive for Billy Mitchell in World War I. "I am firmly convinced that we must fight this Air Force question out now," Andrews continued. "We are obliged to put our own house in order before we can win this war and you know as well as I do that our leadership in the Air Force is uncertain and worried and continually upset, and will remain so until this problem is solved."[13]

Hap Arnold—the man at the pinnacle of the Army Air Forces pyramid—was indeed concerned about the status of the organization that he led. Receiving his third star a week after Pearl Harbor, he intended for the Army Air Forces to make the *decisive* contribution to victory over the Axis.[14] To Arnold, the best way to achieve a telling impact was a bomber offensive against the Axis homelands. He wrote Robert Lovett, the Assistant Secretary of War for Air, in October 1942 that the mission of the Air Forces was "to destroy the capacity and will of the enemy for waging war," adding that "*no other offensive effort open to us can bring us this success.*"[15] Arnold emphasized air power's ability to achieve "independent" results through strategic bombing, rather than its role in supporting ground or sea forces, not only because he believed that strategic bombing could yield victory, but also because he thought that the success of the independent mission could lead to service autonomy. He told his commanders in June 1943: "Air power is still but an infant among the arms, and its useful growth

110

is dependent upon proper handling now. This is particularly true of heavy, long-range bombardment aviation which comprises the main striking power of air forces and which, *alone*, lifts an Air Force from the status of an auxiliary arm to that of an equal with arms which serve in other mediums."[16]

Arnold worked relentlessly to assure that the strategic bombing mission spurred air force independence. No detail was too small to avoid his attention, and his intensity often rattled those who worked with him—one materiel officer fell dead from a heart attack after Arnold berated his performance early in the war.[17] The non-stop parade of seven-to-seven days ultimately took its toll, and Arnold would have four heart attacks of his own in a twenty-three-month span from February 1943 to January 1945. As a result, Lovett and others close by, including relatively junior officers like Lauris Norstad, Jacob Smart, and Hoyt Vandenberg, who served on Arnold's handpicked Advisory Council, would sometimes speak on Arnold's behalf.[18] All of them understood—and accepted—the Commanding General's unwavering commitment to wrecking the Axis with air power—and to accomplishing that goal in such a way that air power's contribution to victory would provide an unmistakable impetus for an independent air force.

Marshall did little to curb Arnold's zeal. After becoming Chief of Staff, Marshall had added the study of air power to the Army's Command and General Staff College curriculum.[19] Following Pearl Harbor he emphasized his "desire to impress upon higher commanders especially their responsibility for taking all measures which will contribute to our control of the air."[20] Andrews's prewar overtures influenced Marshall's favorable view of the Army Air Forces, but so too did a shared strategic vision with the AAF Commanding General. The Army Chief of Staff seldom overruled Arnold during the war, and in many respects the Army Air Forces had already obtained the autonomy that so many of its leaders sought.[21] Arnold was free, for the most part, to direct his air commanders as he thought best, and he kept especially close tabs on those like Spaatz and Eaker who controlled heavy bombers. Marshall commented after the war that he had intended to make Arnold "as nearly as I could Chief of Staff of the Air without any restraint," but added that Arnold was "very subordinate" and complemented Marshall's strategic inclinations.[22] Indeed, Arnold once confided to Eaker, "If George Marshall ever took a position contrary to mine, I would know I was wrong."[23]

Marshall's support proved insufficient, though, to give Arnold and his cohorts a true appreciation for the magnitude of the task they faced at the start of their air offensive against Hitler's Europe; moreover, they could not envision how the momentum generated by a war against an equally committed foe would transform their progressive notions about bombing. The men who had crafted AWPD-1's requirements had done so based on their faith in a uniquely American approach to applying air power, but had no empirical evidence to back their claims. They largely dismissed previous examples of bombing because those episodes did not correspond to the theory, equipment, and techniques that they deemed essential for a successful air campaign.[24] Instead, as they began to assemble a bombing force in England, they did so with the belief that their precision air offensive would quickly and efficiently wreck German war-making capability—and hence its will to resist—in contrast to the RAF's bludgeon aimed directly at German morale. They were reluctant to heed their British counterparts who sported more than two years of bombing experience, including a disastrous daylight effort against Germany in 1939–40.[25]

In July 1942, Eighth Air Force finally received its first complement of 180 aircraft, which included 40 B-17 "Flying Fortresses."[26] Those B-17s were "E" models and differed significantly from the "C" models that the British had acquired in 1941. Unlike its predecessor, the "E" model boasted increased fuel capacity that extended its combat radius to four hundred miles with a five-thousand-pound bomb load, plus it had an armament of eleven .50 caliber machine guns, many in electric-powered turrets, that offered far more protection than the "C" model possessed.[27] The protection was vital for a bomber force that would rely on self-preservation rather than fighter escort to survive its most grueling missions during its first year and a half of existence.

The fighters that initially arrived as part of Eighth Air Force did so to protect friendly bomber airfields from German attack; AWPD-1's designers had intended them for that purpose, not to protect bombers in flight.[28] Although Hansell and a few others argued before the war that pursuit aircraft (fighters) would prove useful as bomber escorts, their pleas fell on mostly deaf ears, and those who listened did not believe that a suitable single-seat fighter could be built with sufficient range to accompany bombers to target.[29] The B-17 and the B-24 (the other four-engine bomber that comprised Eighth Air Force's "heavy" bomber force) would have to fight through the toughest German defenses alone, as would two-engine "medium" bombers such as the B-25 and B-26 that also were a part of the Eighth.

Spaatz, for one, expressed little concern about the challenges ahead. One week after the Eighth Air Force's first bombing raid of the war, a 17 August 1942 attack by 12 B-17s against a marshalling yard near Rouen, France, he wrote Arnold that with 1,500 heavy and medium bombers, plus 800 fighters to defend his airfields, he would have "complete aerial supremacy over Germany within a year, with the resultant insurance of her rapid defeat." He added: "The force listed above is considerably less than that proposed in AWPD-1. However, the experience so far in this theatre and our experience in the Far Eastern theatre indicates that contrary to the assumption in AWPD-1, bombing accuracy does not diminish under fire, but rather increases. As a result the force set up above, plus what the RAF may have, will in my mind accomplish the objectives set forth in AWPD-1."[30]

The Rouen attack belied Spaatz's optimism. He and Eaker, then Commander of VIII Bomber Command, had carefully selected the relatively friendly confines of French airspace for Eighth Air Force to make its first strike, and they had also picked their top crews to fly the mission. The pilot of the lead aircraft was one of the best in the Army Air Forces, Major Paul Tibbets Jr., and the gifted commander of the Ninety-seventh Bomb Group, Colonel Frank Armstrong Jr.—who would serve as the model for "Frank Savage" in the novel and movie *Twelve O'Clock High!*—flew as copilot. Eaker was also aboard one of the aircraft, despite having been stung by twenty-seven hornets while hunting the previous day.[31] The target chosen was one that endangered few French civilians, the weather was superb, and 108 Spitfires escorted the 12 "Flying Fortresses" to and from Rouen, which was well within their range. Yet, despite the fanfare resulting from America's first bombing raid in Europe, few bombs hit the target, and the overall results were marginal, though no bombers were lost.

Four similar missions against French targets followed, again with no bombers lost. When Arnold received Spaatz's glowing assessment of the Eighth's first week of activity—which claimed that fifty-eight of seventy-two B-17s had hit their targets, dropping 107 tons of bombs at twenty-two thousand feet—the AAF Commanding General proudly announced to a gathering of the Combined Chiefs of Staff in early September: "I realize that these operations were too limited to permit the drawing of definite conclusions but the following statements are of interest: (1) Precision bombing can be conducted against the continent with B-17's from high altitudes. (2) These operations lend encouragement to a belief that daylight operations may be extended into the heart of Germany, with or without fighter protection—if the proper size force is used."[32] Arnold aimed his ebullient declaration to mollify British colleagues skeptical about the prospects for daylight bombing and eager for Americans to join the RAF's night campaign against Germany proper. Still, he wanted to see more such updates, which he considered tangible revelations of progress.

As the first week of Eighth Air Force operations drew to a close, President Franklin Roosevelt asked for an estimate of the number of combat aircraft that the United States and its Allies should produce in 1943 to have "complete air ascendancy over the enemy."[33] Arnold turned to Possum Hansell to provide the answer. Hansell, who served in England as air planner for Lieutenant General Dwight Eisenhower, relied on his expertise in crafting AWPD-1 after he returned to Washington DC along with Eaker. Ten days later, Hansell and a small staff produced AWPD-42.

Much like AWPD-1, AWPD-42 estimated America's air needs in broad terms that went beyond the scope of the original request, and it also hearkened to the progressive notions that had guided the earlier plan. Hansell concluded that the United States would need to produce 139,000 aircraft in 1943, of which the Army Air Forces would require 63,000 combat aircraft, organized into 281 groups. In the Pacific, defensive operations would dominate, but in Europe Hansell envisioned that 78 groups would fly from Great Britain, and many of those would begin a bomber offensive against Germany. That campaign would destroy German warmaking capability in six months of constant bombing once the attacking force reached maturity.

AWPD-42 "contemplated a degree of destruction of internal Germany which would make invasion feasible and relatively inexpensive in terms of U.S. lives," Hansell reflected.[34] The destruction of the Luftwaffe again received emphasis as "an intermediate objective with overriding priority," followed by submarine yards, transportation systems, electric power facilities, oil installations, and aluminum and rubber plants. The U-Boat scourge during the Battle of the Atlantic dictated second billing for the submarine yards, but the remainder of the list differed little from AWPD-1's priorities. Hansell estimated that forty-two groups of heavy bombers, composed of 48 aircraft each and totaling 2,016 aircraft, would arrive in the United Kingdom by 1 January 1944, along with 960 medium bombers. The plan estimated 2,500 fighters as well, but did not consider them as bomber escorts. "Our heavy bombers are far superior in fire power and capacity to absorb punishment to the bombers used by the Germans," AWPD-42 observed. "Our daylight penetration of German defenses has up to this time indicated a relatively low attrition rate to our bombers and a relatively high attrition rate to German fighters."[35]

Despite AWPD-42's optimistic appraisal, prospects for bombing Germany were dim, and the Rouen raid set the pattern for the next five months of Eighth Air Force operations. Spaatz never came close to receiving the 1,500 bombers he had mentioned in his prediction to Arnold and was unwilling to risk his meager force against targets in Germany. President Roosevelt had spurred bomber production with his May 1941 order to build 500 "heavies" a month, but it took time for assembly lines to gear up for that total. By March 1942 American industry topped the 4,000 mark in monthly aircraft production, yet 40 percent were trainers, and transport aircraft and fighters consumed a sizable chunk of the rest.[36] In October, just as the Eighth Air Force had gained four more groups of heavy bombers, each containing 35 aircraft, Spaatz received word that he had to surrender 1,250 airplanes and their crews to help create Twelfth Air Force for the invasion of North Africa.[37] Eighth Air Force would have only seven "heavy" groups remaining, and of those, only two were fully operational at the end of October.[38]

Moreover, many crews arriving in Britain had minimal training in the types of missions they would have to fly. Most bombardiers trained at "high" altitudes of twelve thousand feet, rather than at the twenty-thousand-foot level they would frequently use for combat.[39] Gunners arrived without having fired at tow targets. Pilots arrived with no experience in formation flying, essential not only for mutual protection, but also to assure concentrated bombing patterns. Not until LeMay appeared with his 305th Bomb Group in November 1942 did Eighth Air Force truly begin to solve the problems of formation flying. After several days of directing training missions from the top turret of his B-17, he devised the "combat box" formation that massed three squadrons of six aircraft each to form a combat group of eighteen aircraft.[40] Two or more combat groups formed a combat wing.

LeMay further took his best pilots, navigators, and bombardiers, and made them "lead" crews who dictated by radio when the entire group formation dropped its bombs. Most B-17s had their bombsights removed and replaced by a machine gun in the aircraft's Plexiglas nose. The resulting "pattern bombing" technique ultimately became standard operating procedure for Eighth Air Force. "At one stroke you raised the accuracy of the whole Group from the common denominator to the level of your best man, and navigation improved accordingly," he later remarked.[41] LeMay also mandated that his crews fly "straight and level" two minutes prior to target to allow the gyro in the Norden bombsight to stabilize while the lead bombardier fed in ground speed and cross-wind information. Though initially apprehensive about the inability to take evasive action on the bomb run, crews found that their loss rate to German flak actually declined with a steady approach to target. LeMay had already reached that conclusion by using the artillery manual from his Ohio State ROTC course to calculate that each piece of German antiaircraft artillery would have to fire 273 rounds to score one hit on a B-17.[42]

Yet LeMay's innovations could not instantly—or entirely—erase the difficulties of bombing factories or rail yards from four miles up while under fire, and after five months of attacking targets in occupied Europe, Eighth Air Force's loss rate inched upward, with little to show for the effort other than increasing claims of German fighters shot down.[43] British concerns for merchant shipping losses mandated that many missions went against German submarine pens in French ports, but the sub pens were relatively small structures with thick concrete ceilings that were difficult to hit and more difficult to damage.[44] In December, Spaatz left England to take command of Twelfth Air Force in North Africa, and Eaker took charge of the Eighth, with Brigadier General Newton Longfellow taking Eaker's former job as Commander of VIII Bomber Command. Eaker soon found himself on the defensive from the British, led by Prime Minister Winston Churchill, who contended that the Americans should abandon daylight bombing and join the RAF's night campaign against German cities.

On the evening of 13 January 1943—while hosting his first dinner guests after becoming Eighth Air Force Commander—Eaker received a telephone call from General Eisenhower, ordering him to report at once to Casablanca, where Churchill would meet Roosevelt in top-level strategy discussions. Arnold and the rest of the Combined Chiefs of Staff would attend as well, and Arnold wanted Eaker to dissuade the prime minister from recommending American night bombing to Roosevelt. Eaker needed little persuasion. Three months earlier, after comparing British and American bombing methods, he had written Spaatz: "I believe it is clearly demonstrated that the efficiency of day bombardment over night bombardment is in the order of ten to one."[45] Churchill had spoken favorably of Eaker in the past, and Arnold believed that he had the best chance to change Churchill's mind. Eaker would return to the notion of efficiency to do so, but his version of efficient was one that maximized the experience of each force. When the prime minister appeared before the Eighth Air Force Commander in the uniform of an RAF air commodore, Eaker was ready with a one-page memo stressing the persistent nature of a "round-the-clock" offensive that would give the Germans no respite from air attack. Churchill found the notion appealing and relented, though his change of mind also came at a price—Eaker promised the prime minister that the Eighth Air Force would begin bombing Germany before the end of the month.[46]

Yet at Casablanca it was a statement made by Roosevelt, not Churchill, that had the greatest impact on future American bombing. The president and the prime minister had both determined well before the conference that they would pursue a policy of complete surrender for the Axis powers; Roosevelt believed that the failure to crush the German regime in World War I had spawned the stab-in-the-back theory that facilitated Hitler's rise, and after Pearl Harbor he contended that total victory was necessary to erase the threat of future militarism from Germany, Italy, and Japan.[47] At Casablanca, following the November 1942 North African landings, Roosevelt and Churchill aimed to assure their domestic publics—and their Soviet ally—that the Anglo-American forces would not make deals with German collaborators, nor would they make a separate peace with the Germans.[48] As a result, on 24 January 1943, the president announced to a group of reporters that the war aim sought by the Allied powers was the "unconditional surrender" of the Axis nations, which called for "the destruction of the philosophies in those countries which are based on conquest and subjugation of other people."[49] He repeatedly emphasized that objective for the war's duration.[50]

The ramifications of Roosevelt's declaration were profound for

a bomber force that had yet to bomb the homeland of its strongest foe. On one hand, if American political and military leaders
adhered to the guidelines of AWPD-1 and AWPD-42, and those estimates proved correct, then the American air offensive against
Germany should result in an efficient air campaign that eviscer-
ated the Third Reich six months after intensive bombing began.
On the other hand, if political and military leaders deviated from
those guidelines—and Eaker's promise to Churchill and the high
demand for bombers in North Africa and elsewhere guaranteed
that the Eighth Air Force would begin its portion of the "Combined Bomber Offensive" (CBO) with less than the desired number of aircraft—then the time required would take far more than
half a year. Moreover, the six-month estimate assumed (1) a high
degree of bombing accuracy on a consistent basis, (2) the bombing force would prevail against German defenses in a reasonable
amount of time, and (3) the Germans would yield as a result of
destruction rendered. Those premises were thin reeds at best, and
"unconditional surrender" made the final notion especially problematic. Roosevelt's declaration now defined German defeat not
only as military loss, but also as the eradication of the Nazi regime. Using bombs to sever the delicate strands of Germany's industrial web might not suffice to cause the Germans to throw in
the towel.[51]

Target Germany, January–June 1943

On 27 January 1943, Eighth Air Force finally launched its first
raid against Germany when heavy bombers attacked naval facilities at Wilhelmshaven. Only 91 bombers flew on the raid, and
of those, only 53 located the cloud-obscured target. Still, only 2
B-24s and 1 B-17 were lost, and crews claimed 50 German fighters shot down.[52] After dismal weather grounded the bombers for
much of February, the Eighth attacked the submarine construction

yard at Vegesack on 18 March with 91 B-17s and B-24s, recording many hits on the target while losing only 3 aircraft.[53] When 107 B-17s raided the Focke-Wulf factory at Bremen a month later, fierce German defenses claimed 16 bombers, with another 46 damaged.[54] Eaker tried to husband his strength in early 1943 by interspersing his attacks on Germany with raids on targets in France and the Low Countries, where he could count on fighter escorts. The Bremen mission indicated that stern tests awaited Eighth Air Force over the Reich.

Eaker faced the challenge of trying to achieve positive results with a bombing force lacking in potency, and to assist him in target selection, Arnold created the Committee of Operations Analysts (COA) in December 1942. The group was a mix of civilian professors, lawyers, industry executives, and Army Air Forces officers based in Washington DC who received intelligence information on German war-making facilities and tried to determine which ones to attack to achieve maximum impact. Major General Muir S. "Santy" Fairchild, an Army Air Forces officer on the Joint Staff who had taught bombing theory at the Air Corps Tactical School, prodded Arnold to create the committee to deflect criticism from Army and Navy intelligence officers who questioned the utility of Eighth Air Force bombing. Arnold directed Colonel Byron E. Gates, who oversaw the COA, to prepare a report analyzing how bombing could systematically wreck the German war effort and to determine "the date when the deterioration will have progressed to a point to permit a successful invasion of Western Europe."[55]

In Arnold's mind—as Hansell had likewise reflected in AWPD-42—the proper application of air power would dictate the timing of the invasion, and that meant wrecking German capability and will to such a degree that the invasion would occur against minimal resistance—if any. Substantial ground forces might be needed to fight German defenders, but, if bombing did its job, they would become more important as an occupying force. "Even if we believe that Germany can be defeated by air power alone," the COA's Colonel Ed Sorenson wrote to Brigadier General Lawrence Kuter, the Eighth Air Force's First Bomb Wing Commander in early January 1943, "we must concede the practical necessity of the presence of the strong ground forces of our own to take control, if not to fight, [then] to obviate the undesirable necessity of occupation being taken over by our allies from the farther East."[56] Kuter sent the letter to Hansell, who had just replaced him as First Wing Commander, and noted that Hansell should relay its contents to Eaker.[57]

In the meantime, the COA members divided themselves into groups examining the individual components of what they deemed Germany's "Priority A" targets—those offering the most promise in terms of wrecking German military power in 1943. Their conclusions paralleled Hansell's earlier findings in AWPD-42. The COA initially placed aircraft, electric power, oil, rubber, transportation, chemicals, and electric equipment at the top of their Priority A list.[58] Arnold placed enormous weight on their priorities, and directed that his commanders follow the committee's recommendations in selecting targets.[59] Initially skeptical of the group and prospects that it might "try to run the air war from Washington," Eaker relented after meeting many committee members, and for the remainder of his tenure as Eighth Air Force commander he frequently consulted the COA on targeting possibilities.[60]

Besides considering COA suggestions, Eaker also had to address Allied concerns. His success at Casablanca in preserving a daylight offensive had resulted in an official acknowledgment of daylight bombing in the "Casablanca Directive." Issued at the conference by the Combined Chiefs of Staff, the directive merged the American and British air efforts in a "Combined Bomber Offensive" that had as its objective "the progressive destruction and dislocation of the German military, industrial and economic system and the undermining of the morale of the German people to a point where their capacity for armed resistance is fatally weakened."[61] The directive came with its own set of target priorities, similar to those outlined in AWPD-42 and by the COA, but not exact. The directive's priorities were, in order of importance: submarine construction yards, the aircraft industry, transportation facilities, oil plants, and other components of war industry. The directive further noted that its priorities would likely shift as the war progressed and "other objectives of great importance either from the political or military point of view must be attacked." Examples included submarine bases on the Bay of Biscay and "Berlin, which should be attacked when conditions are suitable for the attainment of especially valuable results unfavorable to the morale of the enemy or favorable to that of Russia."[62] Also at Casablanca, General Marshall agreed that, until Army Air Forces aircraft outnumbered British airplanes—and Americans had proven the efficacy of daylight bombing—American bombers in Britain would remain under the operational direction of the British, who would dictate targets and times of attack, while operational procedures and bombing techniques would remain the prerogative of American commanders.[63]

In reality, Air Chief Marshal Sir Charles "Peter" Portal, Eaker's nominal commander in the aftermath of Casablanca, did little to interfere with Eaker's target choices, but the vagaries of weather, increasing strength of German defenses, and continued diversion of bombers to other theaters made Eaker's successful orchestration of an air campaign a thorny prospect. Dense banks of winter clouds frequently obscured targets in Germany. Meanwhile, the Germans increased their homeland fighter strength by transferring units from the Mediterranean and Russian fronts to defend the Reich. Eaker had told Arnold at Casablanca that with three hundred heavy bombers per mission he could attack any target with a low rate of loss.[64] He believed that a strong bombing force guaranteed an efficient air campaign and informed Arnold's deputy, Brigadier General Barney Giles, that his bombers had a six-to-one kill ratio against German fighters.[65] Not only were such claims excessive, but at the time of Casablanca, Eighth Air Force had still not bombed Germany, and the experience that bomber crews had thus far received did not compare to what awaited them over the German heartland without escorts. Indeed, statistics in early December 1942 revealed that Eighth Air Force bombers had a 2 percent loss rate when escorted, compared to a 7 percent loss rate without the "little friends."[66]

Eaker appreciated the value of escorts to a degree, writing that "it is most important to have some fighter protection" on raids with fewer than three hundred bombers.[67] His preference, though, was to increase the size of the bomber force until its own defensive firepower would suffice to protect it. On the eve of Casablanca he learned that Spaatz's Twelfth Air Force would receive twenty-eight B-17 replacements originally slated for the Eighth. Eaker notified Arnold's air staff that his average bomber group strength had shrunk from thirty-five to eighteen aircraft—the total needed to put in the air on combat missions—which meant that he now had zero bombers available for spares or as a reserve force.[68] For the next four months he refused to commit more bombers and crews than he could replace with the meager numbers of aircraft and men heading his way.[69]

Eaker's struggle to obtain more bombers merged with efforts to determine how best to use the force that he had. In early February he met with COA representatives to exchange views on targets that Eighth Air Force might attack with precision bombing. Eaker offered that "no judgment could be made as to the results obtainable through precision bombing at this time inasmuch as the force requisite to put it into effect had not been available."[70] He asserted that more bombers would saturate German defenses and reduce the percent of bombers lost on a raid; with one hundred bombers on a mission he would likely lose 5 percent of his attacking force, while with three hundred only 3 percent would be lost, and one thousand would produce a negligible loss rate.[71] Eaker's calculations presumed that more bombers attacking would produce a corresponding increase in bombs on target and hence reduce the need to return to it; otherwise, his decreasing loss rates actually produced an *increase* in the number of bombers lost. The Eighth Air Force Commander initially persuaded the COA members to include a call for additional bombers in the March report that they submitted to Arnold, but that paragraph disappeared in the final draft that listed sixty key targets for attack.[72] Eaker responded with an angry memorandum to Arnold that proclaimed, "The current position of the Eighth Air Force is not a credit to the American Army. After 16 months in the war we are not yet able to dispatch more than 123 bombers toward an enemy target."[73]

While he did not dismiss Eaker's outcry, Arnold chose instead to focus on the prospects of an efficient air campaign portended in the COA report. Unknown to Eaker, the Army Air Forces Commanding General had suffered his first heart attack at the end of February. Roosevelt waived the regulation that would have required Arnold to leave the service, provided that the Commanding General provided monthly updates on his health to the president. Accordingly, Arnold aimed to accent not only his fitness for command, but also the distinctive contributions of air power to the war effort. After receiving the COA report, he wrote Roosevelt's trusted assistant, Harry Hopkins, that bombing could paralyze Germany's war-making capability "by the destruction of not more than five or six industries, comprising not more than fifty or sixty targets." As an example, he noted that "a stoppage, or a marked curtailment, of the production of ball bearings would probably wreck all German industry."[74]

Arnold also wrote Eaker: "We know that the strength of our striking force will always be relatively limited. We must, therefore, apply it to those specially selected and vital targets that will give us the greatest return." Arnold added that the president, as well as the American public, was very aware of Eighth Air Force's bombing and wanted to know its specific accomplishments. Thus, he told Eaker to provide him with bi-monthly bombing summaries that "will help us a great deal in defending your operations and in building up a correct picture of the results being accomplished."[75]

With his public relations background, Eaker appreciated the need to "sell" the air campaign, but his first priority was to assure that the effort had a reasonable chance for success, and that meant securing more bombers for it. His quest for additional aircraft ultimately reached the highest level. Lieutenant General Frank Andrews—who had moved from commanding Caribbean defenses to Commanding General, U.S. Forces in the Middle East in November 1942, and had also appealed for daylight bombing to Churchill at Casablanca—replaced Eisenhower as Commander of U.S. European Theater of Operations in February when Eisenhower became Supreme Commander of Allied Forces in the Mediterranean. The change thrilled Eaker because it placed an avid air power proponent in a high command position. He wrote Arnold that Andrews's appointment "will be a big boon for us. We have been about bled to death by the African operation."[76]

After arriving in Britain Andrews wasted no time in notifying his friend Marshall of how bomber diversions had depleted Eighth Air Force.[77] The Army Chief of Staff, in turn, took that message to the president. "Up to the present time the Army Air

Forces have never been able to even approximate the technique on which they have built up the proposition of daylight precision bombing," Marshall informed Roosevelt in March. "I might further say, without greatly exaggerating, that Army Air elsewhere in the world, except in the Australian theater, has been somewhat misused by the employment of Army planes and crews in a manner for which the planes were not designed nor the crews trained, all of which has been a constant embarrassment to the Air Corps."[78] Marshall's blunt notice, Eaker's continued clamor, and the realization among Allied leaders that an invasion of Europe could not occur without control of the air finally produced noticeable increases in Eighth Air Force bomber strength.

Bolstered by the rising numbers, Eaker came to Washington DC in late April to brief his plan for a Combined Bomber Offensive to the Joint Chiefs of Staff. His proposal reflected extensive collaboration with members of the COA, as well as assistance from RAF analysts and commanders. He gave top emphasis to the destruction of German fighter strength—"an intermediate objective second to none in priority"[79]—and then outlined a series of phased attacks on industrial centers and war-making facilities that would wreck the essential components of Germany's ability to fight. A steady increase in bomber strength was vital to success. Eaker argued that he would need a total force of at least 800 bombers to dispatch 300 on a regular basis, and ultimately he would require a force of 2,700 "heavies." After limited debate, the Joint Chiefs concurred. They approved Eaker's plan in early May and recommended "implementing it to the maximum extent practicable, consistent with aircraft production, available shipping, and current strategic commitments."[80]

At the Trident Conference later that month, the Combined Chiefs of Staff endorsed Eaker's plan as well. Moreover, they tied a cross-channel invasion—tentatively set for May 1944—to the successful conduct of the Combined Bomber Offensive.[81] For American airmen, the approval of the Combined Bomber Offensive plan was a bittersweet success, because two of their leaders were not present to witness it—Frank Andrews had died in a B-24 crash in Iceland on 3 May, and Arnold had suffered his second heart attack seven days later.[82] Still, Eaker's plan portended a significant increase in bomber strength for Eighth Air Force and the chance for it to have a decisive impact on the war. By the end of May 1943 Eaker wrote his British counterpart, Air Marshal Arthur Harris, that bombers and crews had begun to arrive "according to schedule" and expressed optimism that Eighth Air Force would receive 2,700 heavy bombers by April 1944.[83]

The plan that spurred Eighth Air Force's bomber total was a masterpiece of mechanistic logic solidly anchored to progressive roots. It noted that the COA had identified sixty targets, the destruction of which "would gravely impair and might paralyze the Western Axis war effort."[84] Eaker added sixteen targets to the mix and divided them all into six "systems," comprising seventy-six precision targets that, once destroyed, would critically damage the German war machine. Those systems included: submarine construction yards and bases, the aircraft industry, ball bearings, oil, synthetic rubber and tires, and military transport vehicles. The plan linked Germany's aircraft industry to the overriding intermediate objective of eliminating fighter strength in Western Europe. Wrecking the associated targets would destroy 43 percent of Germany's fighter capacity and 65 percent of its bomber capacity and "produce the effect desired."[85]

The plan also highlighted ball bearings, which the COA had emphasized since early February. "The critical condition of the ball bearing industry is startling," the plan observed. "The concentration of that industry renders it outstandingly vulnerable to air attack." Eaker noted that the destruction of the plants at Schweinfurt would eliminate almost half of Germany's ball-bearing production and instantly stymie the production of tanks, airplanes, artillery, and "all the special weapons of modern war." Because of Schweinfurt's importance, he recommended attacking it as one of two "deep penetration" raids in the first phase of combined operations. Yet he cautioned: "It would be most unwise to attempt it until we are perfectly sure we have enough force to destroy the objective in a single operation. Any attempt to repeat such an attack will meet with very bitter opposition."[86]

While acknowledging the strength of German air defenses, Eaker insisted that they would not prevent effective bombing, provided that he received adequate bombers and crews. Once more he turned to statistical analysis to make his case. Eaker contended that the twenty daylight bombing missions that the Eighth Air Force had flown from 3 January to 6 April 1943 "definitely establish the fact that it is possible to conduct precision pattern bombing operations against selected precision targets from altitudes of 20,000 feet to 30,000 feet in the face of anti-aircraft artillery and fighter defenses." He rated twelve of those missions as "highly effective," and added that the destruction produced by an average of eighty-six bombers was "highly satisfactory." Thus, he surmised, "From this experience it may be definitely accepted that 100 bombers dispatched on each successful mission will provide entirely satisfactory destructive effect of that part of the target area within 1000 feet of the aiming point; and that two thirds of the missions dispatched each month will be successful."[87]

Eaker likely knew that he had overstated his case. His First Bomb Wing Commander, Hansell, had written Arnold's intelligence chief in February regarding the difficulty of discerning the number of bombs that fell in the target area and noted, "To date we have been unable to account for approximately fifty percent of the bombs which we take out." He added that future bombing analysis should "not harp too much on small precision targets. We find they are hard to hit, particularly in the face of heavy AA [anti-aircraft] fire and determined fighter opposition."[88] Besides enemy defenses, Hansell remarked that the wind and sun also played a role in bombing accuracy. The Norden bombsight could not compensate for cross-wind bombing approaches when the winds exceeded 80 mph, and on crystal clear days a haze developed that was "frequently literally impenetrable toward the sun."[89] The "precision pattern bombing" that Eaker had mentioned in his April briefing to the Joint Chiefs was fantasy; LeMay's technique significantly increased the odds that a group formation bombed in unison, but even ideal conditions could not guarantee "precision."[90] Too many variables affected bombing accuracy, and Eighth Air Force bomber crews had no control over most of them.[91]

Eaker privately acknowledged that limitation as Allied leaders prepared to endorse his plan for the Combined Bomber Offensive. But he downplayed the significance of his admission by focusing instead on the growing strength of Eighth Air Force, writing Arnold in May 1943:

> As a result of the additional force we have just received and the increased rate of supply of replacement aircraft and crews, *we are changing our operating policy*. In the past as I told you, we have matched our rate of operation to our receipt of replacements, so that our Air Force would not waste away and go downhill. We have, therefore, in the past, waited for good days when we could be reasonably sure of seeing our targets from high altitude. *We are going now on a new basis when we will go out in force on days when we may not be able to bomb our exact small point targets due to more than 5/10ths cloud cover, but we will at any rate be able to hit our second or last resort targets, the built-up industrial area*, and what is even more important, we will be able to work on the German Air Force in combat.[92]

Eaker refused to allow paltry numbers, German defenses, and poor weather to halt the American experiment in daylight bombing that he had fought so hard to preserve, but he could do little to improve the accuracy of his bomber force. Now, with the strength of that force increasing, he faced new challenges—to gain control of the skies over Western Europe by spring 1944 to facilitate an invasion—and to demonstrate, in a year's time, that air power could wreck an enemy's war-making capability and will to resist. He still lacked the numbers that he felt were essential to accomplish those objectives efficiently; the buildup envisioned in AWPD-42 had suffered substantial delays. British bombing would help to offset that deficiency to some extent, but the RAF would contribute little to achieving daylight air superiority. Still, adopting British area bombing methods during daylight might damage some vital industries on days when clouds obscured precision targets.

Eaker knew that area bombing was a bludgeon, not a scalpel, but he lacked the time and equipment to create an aerial razor. The longer he waited, the stronger his enemy grew. Intelligence reports revealed that increased production now bolstered Germany's homeland fighter force by more than one hundred airplanes each month.[93] Trident, meanwhile, had started the clock ticking for air power to achieve decisive results. If the Combined Bomber Offensive defeated the Luftwaffe, air power could wreck Germany's vital centers with impunity, perhaps scoring a knockout blow that ended the war. Hansell believed that bombing could achieve an independent victory;[94] so too did Brigadier General Frederick Anderson, Eaker's new Commander of VIII Bomber Command. Anderson contended in late July: "The VIII Bomber Command is destroying and will continue to destroy the economic resources of Germany to such an extent that I personally believe no invasion of the Continent or Germany proper will ever have to take place with the consequent loss of thousands and possibly millions of lives."[95] Provided the buildup of Eighth Air Force continued, Eaker believed that his bombers might fulfill that progressive goal. Regardless, he had little choice in the matter—indeed, he had put himself in his current predicament with his successful arguments to Churchill and the Joint Chiefs. It was his turn to transform faith into fact.

The Realities of Air War, July–October 1943

The objectives that Eaker now sought did not exactly match those touted by airmen before the war. The limitations of his force and the unforgiving environment in which it operated altered the prospects for "efficient" results within the time constraints set by the Trident Conference. Anderson acknowledged Eaker's problem: "There are unavoidable conditions, not immediately correctable, which preclude present attainment of the desired results and which necessitate acceptance of less than maximum efficiency."[96] The premium was on *fast* results, and fast did not necessarily guarantee efficient. Moreover, the overall war aim did not lend itself to rapier thrusts of air power; bludgeoning with bombs better suited Roosevelt's goal of "unconditional surrender." That objective called for speed, but only from the standpoint of ending the war quickly to save *Allied* lives. It also demanded *enough* destruction to erase the future desire for war from the collective psyche of the Axis populations. Roosevelt and Churchill—as well as Joseph Stalin—intended not only to wreck Germany's war-making capability and will to fight, but also to destroy the Nazi philosophy that fostered the German war effort—and to assure that a similar world view never again materialized. "Practically all Germans deny the fact that they surrendered in the last war, but this time they are going to know it," the president would tell journalists in summer 1944. "And so are the Japs."[97]

To the Commander of RAF Bomber Command, the April 1943

Combined Bomber Offensive plan ably reflected the ideals that he believed should guide an air campaign. Air Marshal Arthur Harris had directed the RAF's bombing of Germany for more than a year, and had staged his first "thousand plane raid" in May 1942 against Cologne. He thought that the opportunity to employ two "highly specialised and well equipped" bomber forces in tandem simply made sense, plus it offered the chance to achieve maximum efficiency. "There is no difficulty in achieving our object at minimum cost in life, material and effort," Harris remarked to Eaker in April 1943. "There is difficulty only in convincing those in whose hands lies the power to grasp the opportunity." Having received the blessing of Combined Chiefs in May, Harris set out to achieve aerial effects in concert with his American ally that he believed would "decide all."[98]

In actuality the Combined Bomber Offensive, officially designated "Operation Pointblank," provided few instances of genuine cooperation between the two bomber forces. Their distinctive targeting philosophies, exemplified by the RAF's night bombing aimed at morale and the Army Air Forces' daylight effort aimed at industrial production—along with the intense American desire to demonstrate independent success to bolster the bid for service autonomy—led to largely separate air campaigns.[99] A notable exception occurred at the end of July when Harris turned his attention to Hamburg. For more than a week, the RAF and Eighth Air Force pummeled the city, with the American raids occurring on 25 and 26 July against naval installations and an aircraft factory. Army Air Forces crews had difficulty seeing their targets because of the thick smoke created by RAF attacks after midnight on 25 July, when 733 bombers had unleashed 2,290 tons of bombs, almost half of which were incendiaries. One-third of the 147 B-17s dropped incendiaries as well.[100] The series of raids ultimately produced a massive firestorm; 42,600 German civilians perished, and 755,000 more lost their homes.[101] Harris deemed "Operation Gomorrah" a success, and colored away the city's burned out sections in the "Blue Books" he kept that displayed aerial photographs of Germany's major urban areas.

Hamburg also made a distinct impression on American political and military leaders. Roosevelt saw the raids as "an impressive demonstration" of what American air power might accomplish against Japan.[102] Fred Anderson, who flew aboard an RAF Lancaster bomber over Hamburg on the night of 27 July, offered that the raids showed the German populace "that we can hit any place in Germany anytime we propose to do so."[103] Hamburg portended that bombs might break German morale, much like the 19 July attack by Spaatz's bombers on marshalling yards in Rome that Arnold believed "had a deep psychological effect on the Italian people" and led to the overthrow of Benito Mussolini.[104] Arnold's perspective downplayed the impact of Allied landings in Sicily the previous week and conformed to his belief that bombing could achieve independent success. Indeed, the Army Air Forces Commanding General had asked the COA in March to determine what targets air power could destroy "to knock Italy out of the war," and requested a similar study on Japan.[105]

Arnold further envisioned three uses for incendiary bombs by Eighth Air Force: "burning down suitable precise industrial objectives; starting fires by day in the densely built up portions of cities and towns to serve as beacons for the R.A.F. to exploit at night; [and] burning down the densely built-up portions of cities and towns by day attack alone when the occasion warrants."[106] Although he emphasized to his commanders in June that the bomber, "when used with the proper degree of understanding, becomes, in effect, the most humane of all weapons," Arnold had relayed a very different message to his air staff two months earlier: "The way to stop the killing of civilians is to cause so much damage and destruction and death that the civilians will demand their government cease fighting. This does not mean that we are making civilians or civilian institutions a war objective, but we cannot 'pull our punches' because some of them may get killed."[107]

Arnold condoned ruthlessness only as long as it did not tarnish the image of the Army Air Forces. He returned to progressive ideals in specifying the message that he wanted Eaker and the Eighth Air Force to convey to the American people: "It is very important, for whole-hearted public and official support of our Air Forces in their operations, that the people understand thoroughly our Air Force's precepts, principles, and purposes," he wrote. "Still more, it is important for the people to understand that our prime purpose is destruction of the enemy's ability to wage war, by our planned persistent bombing and sapping of his vital industries, his transportation, and his whole supply system. And finally, it is important for them to realize that this takes time, as well as money and planes and planning and work—but that it will win the war and save perhaps millions of lives which otherwise would be sacrificed in bloody ground combat."[108] As the Eighth Air Force prepared to attack Hamburg, he told Eaker to guarantee that postraid press releases stressed "the mission aiming point rather than the city or town in which the aiming point is located."[109]

Eaker appreciated Arnold's concerns, but the Eighth Air Force Commander placed his emphasis on assuring that his crews could actually drop their bombs in the vicinity of the aiming point. The weather in summer 1943 had turned especially nasty, with clouds covering Germany during the months that should have provided ideal daylight bombing conditions. The British had developed various methods of radar bombing that allowed them to bomb at night, and Eaker wanted to use those devices to enhance the Eighth Air Force's daylight efforts during periods of poor weather. "We are looking for a considerable degree of accuracy, sufficient

at least that we can dump our bombs in the heavily built-up industrial areas," he informed Arnold—a far cry from the notion
of precision bombing that he had espoused less than a year before.[110] The best of the British instruments was H2S, a ground mapping radar that the RAF employed with great effect against Hamburg. The British were reluctant to provide their allies with it for
the same reason that American airmen refused to share the Norden bombsight with the RAF—they feared that a downed bomber
might reveal its secrets to the Germans. At the end of July, Air
Chief Marshal Portal relented, and Eaker reported that he would
soon have a squadron "ready to go with one of these gadgets" in
the lead aircraft.[111]

In the meantime, whenever the weather cooperated, Eaker remained true to the principles that had guided the development of
an American bombing force. In August Eighth Air Force participated in two dramatic raids against perceived linchpins of the Nazi
industrial web. The first occurred on 1 August against the complex of petroleum refineries at Ploesti, Romania, which refined
60 percent of Germany's crude oil needs. Eaker had mentioned
Ploesti in his brief to the Joint Chiefs in April, and the COA had
long had it on its list of targets. Eighth Air Force contributed two
groups of B-24s for the raid, plus another slated for the Eighth,
and the remaining two groups came from Spaatz's Northwest Africa Air Force. They took off from the Libyan base at Benghazi
and flew across the Mediterranean at only one hundred feet to
avoid radar detection.

Chance disrupted the plan from the start. The aircraft carrying the lead navigator mysteriously crashed in the sea on the way
to Ploesti, and the bomber with the deputy mission navigator developed mechanical problems and had to return to base. Mission
navigation devolved to a new second lieutenant; two of the bomb
groups refused to trust his skills and mistakenly flew to Bucharest

when the lieutenant had correctly called for a turn to Ploesti. By the time the B-24s arrived in staggered disarray over the target, German defenses were primed and downed 41 of the 177 bombers dispatched. Other factors claimed an additional 13, and 55 more suffered major damage. Although the raid wrecked 42 percent of the refineries' total capacity, the Germans had operated them at only 60 percent, which meant that Ploesti suffered a long-term loss of only 2 percent in production capability. Within weeks it refined oil at a higher rate than it had before the raid.[112]

Eaker's own dual attack on 17 August against the Messerschmitt factory at Regensburg and the ball bearing complex at Schweinfurt met a similar dismal fate and produced similar meager results.

Ploesti, Regensburg, and Schweinfurt exemplified the carnage that Luftwaffe defenses inflicted on Eighth Air Force throughout the summer and early autumn of 1943. Eaker tried to offset the losses by increasing his total of bombers and crews. He possessed almost 700 bombers by July, allowing him to launch some raids with as many as 300 aircraft, but he still lacked the numbers to do so on a consistent basis, plus his crew totals remained insufficient.[113] Production problems in the United States left him short 240 bombers, and the diversions that had plagued him during the spring continued.[114] At his April briefing to the Joint Chiefs, he stated that he would likely need to replace a third of his force *each month* because of attrition,[115] but loss rates often neared 10 percent on the missions flown against Germany in August. Losses among new crews were higher still—four new groups that arrived in April averaged a loss of 21 aircraft in eighteen missions, while four experienced groups on the same missions averaged 9.[116] Eaker told Arnold that new crews needed at least two weeks of training to make them mission ready and that several losses occurred because "the formations are not always flown as instructed." Yet he also acknowledged that part of the losses stemmed from "the unusual ferocity of the defense put up by the German fighter over his homeland as contrasted with the defense put up by him over occupied territory."[117]

In the summer of 1943, Eighth Air Force had no real answer for the German fighter force, which was responsible for the vast majority of bomber losses.[118] The P-47 "Thunderbolt" and the P-51 "Mustang," two single-seat fighters with promising capabilities as escorts, lacked the range to venture far beyond the German border, and German fighter pilots waited until the escorts turned back to pounce. Engineers thus far had limited success developing "drop tanks" to extend the American fighters' range. Attempts to protect bombers with the YB-40, a B-17 that carried no bombs and sported extra turrets and machine guns, failed miserably—the aircraft's performance characteristics differed too much from standard bombers to keep place in formation. Eaker believed that with more bombers he could ultimately overcome the Luftwaffe, and that his bomber crews had already inflicted substantial losses on the German fighter force. He surmised that more bombers and larger formations offered greater firepower to shoot down German fighters. Eaker also pressed for fighter escorts, but he did not completely dismiss the YB-40, which he thought was "a good idea but we have not quite gotten the correct aircraft for carrying it out."[119]

To the pilots, navigators, bombardiers, and gunners who battled the Luftwaffe, the prospects for success appeared grim indeed. Most bomber crewmen did not focus on whether their actions contributed to Germany's demise. Instead, their definition of success was simple—survival. In January 1943, Eaker and Arnold gave heavy bomber crews a requirement of twenty-five combat missions, after which they would transfer to assignments free of combat duty. The crew of the *Memphis Belle* was the first to complete the requirement and departed England in May 1943 to fanfare that included immortalization in a classic documentary by Hollywood director William Wyler. Other crews were not so fortunate. By August 1943 the life expectancy of a typical bomber crewman had dipped to fifteen missions—and would stay at that number for the remainder of the year.[120] Eaker wrote Arnold in October, "I think it is perfectly marvelous the morale we have been able to maintain,"[121] but the truth was better revealed in the first stanza of a poem written by one of LeMay's crewmen:

They call him the "Aerial Gunner."
His hopes, they say, are dim
And his life is said to hang by a thread
That is long and weak and slim.[122]

The progressive tenets of the Air Corps Tactical School had forecast a bomber offensive that achieved success by minimizing crew losses instead of through attrition. Yet the longer the daylight campaign persisted, the more it resembled an aerial slugfest that would continue until only one side demonstrated that it could still respond after absorbing massive punishment. Eaker could not allow that fight to persist indefinitely, but he could see no way to avoid the slaughter in the sky given the time constraints that he faced. Indeed, based on his receipt of intercepted German message traffic, he believed that the Luftwaffe fighter force had suffered severe losses that threatened its ability to control the air.[123] If he could break that force through continued assaults on vital centers, then he might yet achieve daylight air superiority within the allotted time. The time available, though, continued to slip away. In mid-August, the Combined Chiefs of Staff solidified the 1 May 1944 date for the invasion of France and reaffirmed that the successful prosecution of the Combined Bomber Offensive was a prerequisite for it.

Still, Eaker did not abandon his faith that bombing could wreck Germany's war-making capability. He continued to attack Point-blank targets that the COA had recommended despite suffering losses that again neared 10 percent for raids over the Reich in September and the first half of October. On 14 October—a date that bomber crews would dub "Black Thursday"—Eighth Air Force returned to Schweinfurt. Of the 319 B-17s that attacked the ball bearing complex, 60 fell to German defenses.[124] The magnitude of the loss caused even Roosevelt to remark that the United States could not afford to have 60 bombers shot down on a regular basis.[125] Arnold called a press conference proclaiming, "Now we have got Schweinfurt!" and added that losses as high as 25 percent on some missions could be expected—and accepted.[126]

In truth the damage inflicted on ball bearing production once again had little impact on German war production, and Eaker had to send a notice to his crews that Arnold had been misquoted about condoning such a high loss rate.[127] The grim assessment of the Army Air Forces Commanding General also did not go unnoticed by *Time* magazine writers, who summarized Eaker's new measure of efficiency in their 25 October issue: "Suddenly the cost of victory loomed large. . . . The price was not exorbitant: without bearings the mechanized German war machine would be helpless. But the cost was high enough to elicit a spate of explanation."[128]

Arnold wanted an explanation as well. Eaker sent him a cable in the immediate aftermath of the raid confirming the loss of sixty B-17s in combat and another five when their crews elected to bail out over England rather than attempt landing with heavily damaged aircraft. Eaker further noted that his crews had shot down ninety-nine German fighters, with another thirty probably destroyed and fourteen damaged.[129] "This does not represent a disaster," he asserted. "It does indicate that the air battle has reached its climax." Eaker then asked Arnold to expedite the arrival of additional bombers and crews, provide auxiliary fuel tanks for escort fighters, and "send every possible fighter here as soon as possible. We must show the enemy we can replace our losses; he knows he cannot replace his. We must continue the battle with unrelenting fury."[130] Arnold agreed that the Luftwaffe had also suffered much but wanted proof that its end was near. "It appears from my viewpoint that the German Air Force is on the verge of collapsing," he cabled Eaker. "We must not (repeat) must not miss any symptoms of impending German collapse. . . . Can you send me any substantial evidence of collapse?"[131]

The Intensifying Demand for Results, October–December 1943

Arnold's request crystallized the great dilemma for Eaker as the clock continued ticking toward Operation Overlord, the codename given for the invasion of France. Intelligence assessments indicated that his bombing—and the air battles that accompanied it—had a detrimental impact on the German war effort, yet the question remained—*how much* of an impact? Eaker could not say with certainty. He could express success in numerical terms—the amount of bombs dropped, the percentage that hit the target, the numbers of enemy fighters shot down—but even with photographic reconnaissance and Ultra intercepts he could not know for sure whether the destruction that he claimed had actually occurred, or, more importantly, if the actual destruction had produced the desired effect on Germany's capability and will to keep fighting.

Eaker's inability to divine his enemy's response to bombing was a problem that did not lend itself to easy solutions. Besides scrutinizing intelligence reports, he examined German newspaper accounts of raids to determine if the tone of articles revealed the German public's willingness to keep supporting the war.[132] Many COA members relied on their knowledge of American industry to determine the likely impact of destroying similar features of German war production. Planning for the first Schweinfurt raid typified the mirror-image approach. "Industrialists think in terms of what destruction of American ball bearing plants would mean to them, and they are completely unable to suggest a method by which they could long continue in operation if this [destruction] should occur," wrote the COA's Colonel Guido Perera. "There is every reason to believe that the German situation is identical, for in both countries the industry has the same essential characteristics."[133]

Such logic ignored actions that the Germans might have already taken to forestall production losses or that they would take afterward to replace their capability; it also presumed that German industry operated at peak capacity (it did not, and would not until 1944). Thus, determining *when* aerial destruction would produce tangible results remained a tall order. Regarding future attacks on Ploesti and the German oil system, COA members concluded, "It is impossible to state the precise time when the effects of such destruction would become apparent. German military leaders would at some point realize that the future was hopeless."[134]

Until they did so, Eaker would keep bombing. With the onset of winter, the dismal weather that had plagued Eighth Air Force over northern Europe deteriorated even further. Eaker had no intention of giving the Germans a respite from his daylight campaign, but the losses that he had suffered limited his ability to attack deep inside the Reich. In addition, Arnold stripped away replacement aircraft and crews to help create the Fifteenth Air Force that would attack Germany from Italian bases.[135] The creation of the Fifteenth cut deeply into an already depleted Eighth.[136] To preserve his bomber force, Eaker confined most raids to targets within range of his escort fighters. Dense clouds compelled his crews to use radar bombing for the majority of those missions.

The need to protect bombers and use radar methods limited Eaker to attacking coastal targets in Germany, where the contrast between land areas and water produced the strongest radar images and the distances were short enough to provide escorts most of the way. Bomber losses declined as a result, but bombing accuracy declined as well. Eighth Air Force analysts estimated that for the twenty-seven radar bombing missions flown between the end of September 1943 and the end of January 1944, only 5 percent of the bombs fell within *one mile* of the aiming point.[137]

Yet Eaker refused to believe that he had lost his chance for success. The emphasis remained on achieving rapid results, and he believed that radar bombing could help achieve that objective. On 16 November he wrote Arnold: "I am concerned that you will not appreciate the tremendous damage that is being done to the German morale by these attacks through overcast, since we cannot show you appreciable damage by photographs. . . . The German people cannot take that kind of terror much longer."[138] If the destruction rendered to Germany's industrial web and its homeland fighter force failed to wreck its *capability* to fight in the allotted time, the radar attacks appeared to offer the prospect for quickly breaking Germany's *will* to keep fighting.

Eaker understood that his radar raids resembled the RAF's night area bombing in terms of destruction, but to him they were unique—and hence more terrorizing—because they demonstrated the ability to bomb a city enshrouded in a dense cloud cover.[139] He knew such raids killed large numbers of civilians but was untroubled by that result. "I have always believed that civilians supporting [the] national leadership were equally responsible with the military," he reflected after the war. "I thought, and still believe, that the man who builds the weapon is as responsible as the man who carries it into battle."[140]

Although many air leaders likely felt the same way, Eaker's decision to stress radar bombing revealed how the war's momentum had altered the progressive ideals that initially guided American airmen in World War II. Eaker had not abandoned those beliefs, but he had helped transform them into notions that stressed speed over all else, including the goal of minimizing casualties on both sides. The desire for an efficient air campaign that limited losses gave way to an air offensive that produced high American casualties and now condoned a direct attack on urban areas that was certain to produce widespread civilian deaths. The failure to achieve air superiority, combined with the vagaries of weather, was largely responsible for the loss of lives that occurred both in the air and on the ground from the American portion of the Combined Bomber Offensive, and the emphasis on controlling the air as quickly as possible led to further losses in both domains. *Fast* results became the sine qua non of a victory through air power, but fast did not necessarily equate to efficient, especially in terms of lives spared. The emphasis on achieving rapid success endured for the remainder of the war.

Eaker's shift to radar bombing did not impress Arnold, who downplayed the impact of the weather on Eighth Air Force. The AAF Commanding General wanted fast results as well, but thought that the best way to get them was by attacking aircraft factories. Air Chief Marshal Portal confirmed airframe and engine plants as the top targets in Germany at the end of October, stressing that "the success of 'Overlord' hangs on the extent to which, by the date of the operation, we have been able to achieve a reasonable reduction of the enemy fighter forces."[141] The COA echoed Portal's message, noting that Overlord placed "increasing emphasis on the need for short-term results."[142] Accordingly, Arnold directed Eaker on 1 November to conduct radar bombing, when cloud cover prohibited precision attacks, against area targets that would adversely affect the Luftwaffe fighter force.[143]

Germany's aircraft factories, though, were all small, "precision" targets scattered deep inside the Reich. Eighth Air Force could not hit them using radar techniques; furthermore, Eaker lacked the strength to send bomber formations across Germany unescorted.[144] At the end of November, after contemplating a mission against Berlin as a part of Harris's offensive against the city, Eaker decided against it.[145] He continued to highlight the destruction that his radar bombing had rendered to German cities, and hence to German morale.[146] He further confided to Air Secretary Lovett, "I think those who discount and discredit the effect that our overcast bombing on German cities is having on the enemy are unrealistic and unwise."[147] Yet he also acknowledged to Major General Barney Giles, who directed Arnold's air staff, on 13 December:

> There seems to be a feeling there of great irritation that we have not attacked the fighter factories recently. The plain truth of the matter is that there has been no day since November 1 when we could see these factories well enough to bomb them visually. We have not reached a state of either technical or tactical development where we can attack fighter factories with overcast devices. These factories, as you know, are scattered and isolated and they also require deep penetration. We are not justified in striking at them unless the conditions augur for success. These deep penetrations and the impossibility of fighter escort will cost us 80–120 bombers. We will suffer this loss any time we penetrate in force to these targets. We must, therefore, be reasonably certain of their destruction before we launch any expedition entailing such cost.[148]

The Army Air Forces Commanding General—who had never commanded any force in combat—failed to empathize with Eaker's plight. Arnold could also hear the clock ticking to produce air power results, and he did not like his chances. Even though his diversions of bombers to the Mediterranean and Pacific had helped emasculate Eaker's force, Arnold felt that the situation demanded a new commander for America's bomber offensive against Germany. Eisenhower would soon arrive in Britain to command the forthcoming invasion and had asked that Spaatz, who had served as his air commander in the Mediterranean, accompany him. The overall Allied air commander in the Mediterranean, Air Marshal Arthur Tedder, would join Eisenhower as well, creating a vacancy that needed to be filled by an experienced airman. In addition, Arnold had long desired a single air commander for "strategic" air operations, and with the creation of the Fifteenth Air Force, he now had two bomber forces engaged in the bombing of Germany. His solution was to make Spaatz the Commander of the "U.S. Strategic Air Forces," which would encompass the bomber commands in the Eighth and the Fifteenth, and shift Eaker to command the Mediterranean Allied Air Forces.

Eaker, who had received a promotion to lieutenant general in September, was bitter over the transfer. He learned of it on 18 December, just as Eighth Air Force had finally begun to receive many of the bombers and crews originally promised in the CBO plan, and fighters with long-range drop tanks had begun to arrive that would enable them to accompany bombers deep into Germany. Four days later, he wrote his friend Major General James Fechet, a former commander of the Army Air Corps: "I feel like a pitcher who has been sent to the showers during a world series game."[149]

Eaker, though, had done much to shape how the remainder of the "game" would be played. Spaatz and his subordinate commanders, Lieutenant General James "Jimmy" Doolittle, the new Commander of the Eighth Air Force, and Lieutenant General Nathan Twining, Commander of Fifteenth Air Force, would adhere to the methods that Eaker had established for bombing the Third

Reich. The Air Corps Tactical School's progressive proposition that bombing could precisely sever the strands of an enemy's industrial web to produce quick, inexpensive results had morphed into an air campaign that placed a higher priority on rapid success than it did on producing inexpensive gains. The emphasis on speed would guarantee—for the both the attacker and the attacked—that the American air offensive against Germany was anything but "cheap."

5 • Bludgeoning with Bombs

Germany, 1944–45

It has been an unhappy fact for the rest of the world that these gullible and warlike people [the Germans] should have developed a powerful industrial and technical organization to support a huge military machine. This machine depends on some 90-odd industrial centers of which perhaps 50 are of major importance. If these centers can be destroyed or seriously damaged it must be obvious that her *means* to make war will be reduced. And in the process of destroying them the people can be given their first searing lesson, in the heart of their hitherto untouched homeland that crime doesn't pay. This should reduce their *will* to fight. If, therefore, we can reduce the *means* to fight and the *will* to fight, the tasking of overpowering her is made easier or the time shortened. That, very simply, is the contention of the Air Forces.

• ASSISTANT SECRETARY OF WAR FOR AIR, ROBERT A. LOVETT, 9 DECEMBER 1943

Hit oil if visual assured; otherwise, Berlin—center of city.

• GEN. CARL A. SPAATZ TO LT. GEN. JAMES DOOLITTLE, 1 FEBRUARY 1945

---

14 February 1945

As the crews of 311 B-17s approached their target, a smoky black haze arose from the city surrounding it and mingled with dense clouds. Dresden, the medieval capital of Saxony, was in ruins. More than 750 RAF Lancasters had dropped 1,471 tons of high explosive bombs and 1,175 tons of incendiaries on the refugee-filled city the night before, and now the Eighth Air Force would add to that total.[1] The thick blanket of clouds across northern Europe had caused the target to change as the B-17s crossed the English Channel. Originally, it had been the vast marshalling yard on the southern bank of the Elbe. By the time crews could see the smoke rising from the city, the target had become a rail intersection in Dresden's center, west of the main residential area.

Clouds obscured the rail junction, though, and when the lead bombardier signaled "Bombs away!" he was actually over Dresden's most densely populated district—the same area that the RAF had pummeled just hours before. Using radar bombing techniques, the B-17s dropped more than seven hundred tons of bombs, almost half of which were incendiaries. The next day, 211 B-17s attacked Dresden's marshalling yard, and cloud cover once again prevented accurate bombing. Almost five hundred tons of high explosive bombs fell on the city's center.[2] The series of raids created a firestorm similar in intensity to the one almost two years earlier at Hamburg; between twenty-five thousand and thirty-five thousand German civilians died, and an estimated five hundred thousand lost their homes.[3]

On the afternoon of 15 February, RAF Air Commodore C. M. Grierson conducted a press conference in Paris in which he highlighted the Dresden raids. Grierson stated that bombing population centers caused the Germans difficulty because it forced them to send in trains carrying relief supplies and send out trains carrying homeless civilians, thereby disrupting transportation and contributing "greatly to the break up of the German economic system." Concerning Dresden, Grierson noted that the city was a communications center that the Germans used to relay men and equipment to the Russian front, and that refugees fleeing the Russians clogged the city. He maintained that the principal reason for the raids was to stop communications rather than to kill refugees.[4]

Grierson's comments had an immediate effect on the journalists in attendance. One of them, the AP's Howard Cowan, wrote on page 1 in the 18 February edition of the *Washington Star*: "The Allied Air Commanders have made the long awaited decision to adopt the deliberate terror bombing of great German population centers as a ruthless expedient to hasten Hitler's doom." Cowan added that "more raids such as the British and American heavy bombers carried out recently on the residential sections of Berlin, Dresden, Chemnitz, and Cottbus are in store for the Reich, and their avowed purpose will be creating more confusion in the German traffic triangle and sapping German morale."[5] The article created an uproar at Army Air Forces headquarters in Washington DC, and at Coral Gables, Florida, where recently promoted five-star General Hap Arnold was recovering from his fourth heart attack of the war. Arnold demanded an explanation. He cabled General Carl Spaatz, the Commander of the U.S. Strategic Air Forces (USSTAF), and told him to "transmit as a matter of urgency the specific text of your present directive to USSTAF, together with any further comments in order to clarify in my mind completely the entire present situation as to directives and priorities for strategic bombing."[6]

Spaatz was away from his headquarters near London visiting units in the Mediterranean, and his deputy commander, Major General Frederick Anderson, received the Cowan article as well as Arnold's request from a Colonel Rex Smith, who lamented, "This is certain to have nationwide serious effect on the Air Forces as we have steadfastly preached the gospel of precision bombing against military and industrial targets."[7] Anderson replied to Arnold on 19 February, contending that Cowan's article was an exaggeration that had slipped past the censors. "We have not, or do not," he asserted, "intend to change the basic policy which has governed the direction of effort of the United States Strategic Air Forces in Europe from the time they first started operations in this Theater. Our attacks have been in all cases against Military objectives."[8] Colonel Alfred R. Maxwell, USSTAF's Director of Operations, followed with another message written on Spaatz's behalf: "It has always been my [Spaatz's] policy that civilian populations are not suitable military objectives."[9] An Army Air Forces spokesman in Washington DC mirrored those replies in a 21 February press conference, remarking that Americans stressed precision bombing over "wasteful and ineffective" indiscriminate attacks and adding, "We have never done deliberate terror bombing . . . we are not doing it now . . . we will not do it."[10]

Such statements were half-truths at best. Since May 1943 when Ira Eaker, then the Commander of Eighth Air Force, acknowledged that cloud cover prevented precision bombing, the American bomber force had often resembled RAF Bomber Command on days that weather obscured the target area. The distinction between the two bomber forces became especially thin once the Eighth Air Force received radar bombing equipment in autumn 1943 and Eaker informed Arnold of his intention to break the morale of the German public. Spaatz had refused to state such an objective since taking charge of USSTAF in January 1944. Yet he consistently bombed Germany using radar whenever the weather was disagreeable, and he possessed many more bombers than had Eaker.

Moreover, the longer the war progressed, the louder the clamor grew to end it, and the closer Spaatz's targets crept to residential districts in German cities. Both Dresden's marshalling yard and the rail junction selected for the 14 February attack were less than a mile from the heart of the city's residential area. Even with the Norden bombsight in excellent weather, bomber crews were certain to hit more than just their aiming point; using radar against a "precision" target in the midst of a city guaranteed many civilian deaths. Indeed, the "last resort" target for the 14 February Dresden mission was: "Any military objective definitely identified as being in Germany and east of the current bomb line."[11] By February 1945 the impetus to end the war quickly provided few limits to the definition of "military objective."

Spaatz and the Battle for Air Superiority

When Arnold tapped Spaatz in late 1943 to lead USSTAF, the new command comprising the heavy bombers of Eighth and Fifteenth Air Forces, both men understood that the paramount need for rapid results might forestall the conduct of an efficient air campaign. Spaatz had to gain daylight air superiority, and do so quickly— Overlord could not occur without it. He possessed a wealth of experience for the task at hand. A fighter pilot in World War I, Spaatz arrived at the front three weeks before the armistice and shot down three German aircraft, earning him the Distinguished Service Cross. During the interwar years, he commanded both a bomb group and a bomb wing, plus he helped set a flight endurance record of 150 hours (along with Ira Eaker and three other crewmen) aboard the *Question Mark* in 1929. He had been Arnold's choice to command Eighth Air Force when it began the daylight assault on Hitler's Europe, and competently led the Northwest African Air Force as it supported the American ground advance from North Africa to Italy.

Moreover, Tooey Spaatz was a man Arnold could trust, and trust implicitly, to get him the desired results. The two had established an enduring friendship through many assignments together, and a 1920 incident in San Francisco typified the depth of that connection—after Colonel Arnold, who served as air officer for the Army's Ninth Corps Area, reverted to his prewar rank of captain, Major Spaatz, who had been Arnold's executive officer, requested a transfer rather than take command of a unit that he thought rightfully belonged to Arnold.[12] Modest in appearance with a graying mustache, loyal and selfless, Spaatz commanded respect from all who knew him. Dwight Eisenhower rated him, along with Omar Bradley, as the two American generals who contributed the most in the war against Germany, and Bradley ranked Spaatz second, after Eisenhower's chief of staff, Bedell Smith.[13]

Eaker, asked to rank Army Air Forces officers in November 1944 in terms of their merit for postwar leadership, listed Spaatz second behind Arnold.[14]

Arnold presented Spaatz with USSTAF in January 1944 to achieve daylight air superiority over Europe and facilitate the Normandy invasion—and, if all went well, to score a knockout blow against German industry. Arnold had long believed that a single air commander was essential for the maximum efficiency of a heavy bomber force and to prevent ground commanders from taking air elements piecemeal to pursue their own objectives.[15] With Spaatz he had the desired unity of command and the prospect that air power could make the decisive contribution to ending the European war.

Much like Eaker before him, Spaatz heard the steady ticking of a clock as he set out to snatch control of the European sky from the Luftwaffe. He would have preferred to have set his own timetable for destroying Germany's capability and will to fight, and viewed the invasion "as a necessary temporary diversion of the strategic air forces, not a primary objective of strategic air war."[16] Indeed, when he heard that the Combined Chiefs of Staff had selected a date for Overlord, he reportedly said, "This means the death of the strategic air war."[17] Spaatz would support the invasion with all the force that he possessed, but to him, the primary reason for achieving air superiority was to enhance the bomber offensive's prospects for independent success.

Compared to Eaker, Spaatz had a vast array of force at his command; American production had finally begun to catch up to wartime requirements. New crews began to arrive in theater as well. By the end of December 1943 Eighth Air Force possessed twenty-six heavy bomber groups compared to eleven the previous May—so many aircraft and crews that Lieutenant General James "Jimmy" Doolittle, the new Eighth Air Force Commander, could regularly send out missions with a mix of seven hundred

B-17s and B-24s. Many of Doolittle's B-17s were new "G" models, which had a combat radius of seven hundred miles—nearly three hundred miles more than most of Eaker's B-17s—plus they could carry two thousand more pounds of bombs. The "G" model also possessed a chin turret under its Plexiglas nose to ward off head-on fighter attacks, a favorite tactic of the Luftwaffe pilots. The B-24 had received a nose-turret as well, though it was manned instead of remotely operated as in the B-17 and made the bomber a bit wobbly in flight, yet the "Liberator" could still carry the same seven-thousand-pound bomb load as the "G" model "Flying Fortress."[18] B-24s comprised two-thirds of the heavy bombers in Fifteenth Air Force, headquartered in Foggia, Italy, and capable of attacking targets in southern Germany, Austria, and the Balkans. By February 1944, the Fifteenth possessed twelve groups of "heavies."[19]

An increase in fighter strength for Eighth and Fifteenth Air Forces matched the sizable gains in heavy bombers—and Army Air Forces engineers finally began to perfect 75- and 108-gallon drop tanks that allowed fighter escort for a distance of six hundred miles, enough to reach Berlin. The P-47 "Thunderbolt" and P-51 "Mustang" were the key escort fighters; both could fly in excess of 430 mph above 25,000 feet, and the P-47 could approach 550 in a dive. At the beginning of 1944 Eighth Air Force possessed eleven fighter groups containing between seventy-five and ninety-six aircraft each, and by February Fifteenth Air Force would have four fighter groups of its own. In addition, Spaatz and Doolittle decided that Eighth Air Force fighter pilots, who had thus far flown escort by staying close to the bombers that they defended, could now roam freely to seek out Luftwaffe fighters. Eighth Air Force fighter pilots also received the same amount of credit for destroying enemy aircraft on the ground as they did in aerial combat to encourage the strafing of airfields. Bomber crews were initially dismayed by these policies, but the new directives soon paid dividends over Germany.[20]

Spaatz realized that "cutting loose" his fighters would produce increased combat—and hence increased losses—for his fighter force. Given the situation that he faced, he felt that he had little choice. He had three months to wrestle control of the air from the Luftwaffe; in April, General Eisenhower would take charge of USSTAF (and RAF Bomber Command) for invasion support. Yet Spaatz also knew that he had an abundance of numbers and a steady stream of replacements, while Ultra intelligence intercepts told him that the German fighter force had suffered severely during Eaker's fall offensive—so much that Luftwaffe commanders had reduced recuperation times for wounded pilots, and even ordered test and transport pilots to fly against American bombers.[21]

In late January, Spaatz wrote Arnold that he could not simply wait for decent weather to bomb German aircraft factories—destroying them would not suffice to gain daylight air superiority in the time allotted. Thus, Spaatz would also bomb German airfields, and he would further attack "objectives which force German fighters into combat action within range of our fighters." In short, he would wage attrition warfare, and use his bombers as bait. "Losses will be heavy," he stated, "but we must be prepared to accept them."[22] He was confident not just that he could sustain the losses, but also that the magnitude of destruction inflicted on the Luftwaffe would produce air superiority in the shortest amount of time. Spaatz even acknowledged a willingness to risk bombers without fighter escort if such attacks yielded corresponding damage to the Luftwaffe. "Under peculiar weather conditions when all of Germany is fog-bound," he told Arnold, "raids might be made well beyond fighter cover on area targets, such as Berlin, to force the German fighters into the air under conditions which will result in heavy operational losses to their fighters."[23]

Until the weather cleared, Spaatz would continue radar bombing, much like Eaker in late 1943. American engineers at MIT had perfected their own version of the British H2S device, and the American model, dubbed H2X, employed a shorter microwave length that resulted in a sharper radar picture of the ground. But H2X did not appreciably increase bombing accuracy, and the Army Air Forces official historians glumly noted that with radar "the aiming point became a highly theoretical term."[24]

Arnold knew that radar bombing was far from precise, but he did not want his air commanders to convey that impression publicly. He directed Spaatz to avoid the phrase "blind bombing" when referring to raids with H2X, and Spaatz agreed to label such attacks "overcast bombing technique," "bombing through the overcast," or "bombing with navigational devices over clouds extending up to 20,000 feet."[25] Regardless of the terminology used, Eighth Air Force bombers mounted six weeks of radar raids, including a mission by more than eight hundred B-17s and B-24s against Frankfurt on 29 January, which mirrored RAF Bomber Command's area attacks in terms of methods used and damage inflicted. Remarked the AAF historians: "It seemed better to bomb low-priority targets frequently, even with less than precision accuracy, than not to bomb at all."[26]

While Spaatz likely agreed with that assessment, he could not wait indefinitely to achieve significant results. On 8 February he directed that "Operation Argument," the anticipated assault against the German aircraft industry by the Eighth and Fifteenth Air Forces, would conclude by 1 March 1944. Primary targets would consist of airframe and final assembly plants for single- and dual-engine fighters as well as ball bearing production facilities, which members of the Committee of Operations Analysts (COA) and USSTAF planners alike deemed essential to aircraft construction.[27] Those targets all demanded "precision" bombing, and to attack them successfully Spaatz needed a week-long stretch of decent weather. Thick clouds had canceled Argument on numerous occasions, but Spaatz could no longer wait for ideal conditions and accepted that poor weather might lead to losses exceeding two hundred bombers for a single mission.[28]

On 19 February USSTAF's weather officers predicted a period of clear skies across Europe, in contrast to the forecast made by weather officers at Eighth Air Force. Major General Frederick Anderson, Spaatz's deputy commander who had led VIII Bomber Command for Eaker, urged Spaatz to begin Argument. Spaatz gave the order and risked that clouds and icing might ground many of his escort fighters. His fears proved illusory. The next day, sixteen combat wings of heavy bombers—more than 1,000 aircraft—supported by seventeen groups of escort fighters took off for targets in southern Germany. USSTAF's forecasters proved correct, and 941 heavy bombers attacked fighter assembly plants in the vicinity of Leipzig and Brunswick. German defenses claimed 21 bombers, but the bombing results were good.[29]

The 20 February mission marked the beginning of a six-day series of attacks dubbed "Big Week." Not only did Eighth and Fifteenth Air Forces jointly participate in many of the attacks, but the RAF contributed as well by pounding many of the target cities the night before American bombers attacked specific installations in them. The Luftwaffe fought back fiercely and losses were heavy. On 22 February the Eighth lost forty-one bombers and the Fifteenth lost nineteen; on 24 February the Eighth lost forty-nine bombers and the Fifteenth lost seventeen; and on 25 February, when both Air Forces jointly attacked the Messerschmitt plants at Regensburg, the Eighth lost thirty-one bombers and the Fifteenth lost thirty-two, which was 19 percent of the Fifteenth's attacking force. All told, Big Week cost the Eighth Air Force alone three hundred aircraft, most of which were bombers, and 2,500 airmen killed, wounded, or taken prisoner.[30] Yet on Spaatz's balance sheet, the advantage was decisively his—in February the Germans lost 33 percent of their single-engine fighters and 18 percent of their fighter pilots, many of whom had shot down more than one hundred aircraft.[31] Improved P-47s with water-injection engines were responsible for most of the damage done to the Luftwaffe; only two groups of Mustangs participated in the air battles.[32] The Thunderbolts tipped the balance for control of the skies in favor of the Americans.

Besides inflicting substantial damage in the air, Big Week also hurt the German aircraft industry. Radar bombing occurred on few missions; crews conducted most attacks with the Norden bombsight.[33] B-17s and B-24s dropped more than ten thousand tons of bombs during the six-day span—more tonnage than the Eighth Air Force had dropped on all targets for all of 1943.[34] The attacks completely wrecked the Regensburg complex and damaged other facilities as well, but analysts' claims that the attacks had reduced production to 650 aircraft a month were wishful thinking. In actuality, the large amount of slack in the German aircraft industry enabled the monthly production rate to increase despite the raids; many factories with only one shift of workers changed to twenty-four-hour operations.[35] Still, Big Week stymied German production plans. Nazi economic leaders had calculated that they could produce 80,000 aircraft a year by 1945, yet they reached only 36,000 in 1944.[36] Big Week was a key reason that they could not produce more.

Buoyed by Big Week's success, Spaatz turned his attention to the target that American airmen had most wanted to bomb since their first raid over Hitler's Europe—Berlin. The first raid against the German capital was a feeble one, when 29 B-17s failed to get a weather recall message on 4 March and pressed on to their target; they survived because three groups of P-51s stayed with them.

Two days later, Spaatz unleashed 730 heavy bombers and 800 escorting fighters in an aerial stream sixty miles long. The Luftwaffe defended tenaciously, and 75 bombers were shot down, crashed, or written off. Yet the statistic that mattered most to Spaatz was enemy losses, and his fighter pilots claimed 82 German aircraft downed for a cost of 14 American fighters.[37]

On 8 March the onslaught continued. Spaatz sent 600 bombers and 900 fighters against Berlin, losing 13 bombers and 17 fighters. Three hundred bombers returned the next day, bombing through the clouds with H2X. Nine heavies fell to flak—but none were lost to Luftwaffe fighters, which did not oppose the attack. On 22 March 650 bombers returned to Berlin, and flak claimed all 12 that fell.[38] For the month, Luftwaffe fighter units wrote off 56 percent of their single-engine fighters, while crew losses reached almost 22 percent of the pilots present for duty at the beginning of March.[39] American bomber crews suffered as well; Spaatz lost 345 heavy bombers in March alone.[40] Yet, in blunt terms, he felt he could afford the losses; he knew the Germans could not. At the end of the month, with the Luftwaffe reeling, Arnold raised the tour length for bomber crews from 25 to 30 missions. Spaatz had given him daylight air superiority.

Spaatz had achieved what Eaker could not because Spaatz possessed an abundance of resources that allowed him to conduct an air campaign based on attrition.[41] Eaker had counted on the Luftwaffe's aerial losses to spur his quest for air superiority as well, but anxiety about the survival of his bomber force prevented persistent attacks deep into Germany. Neither Eaker nor Spaatz completely abandoned their progressive belief that the destruction of key targets like aircraft factories and ball bearing plants would produce rapid results; their concern was whether the results would occur rapidly enough. As the countdown toward Overlord continued, a negative answer appeared likely. Spaatz chose to forego the progressive goal of "cheapness" to obtain the higher priority objective of speed, and, in the end, was successful. Yet the cost was enormous. Eaker's painstaking commitment of a weak bomber force that lacked escort fighters, and Spaatz's ruthless use of the strength that he possessed, combined to make a staggering 77 percent of all American airmen who flew against the Third Reich before D-Day casualties.[42]

Eaker and Spaatz had accurately surmised the importance of the German aircraft industry to Hitler's war machine. The Luftwaffe was not going to risk losing its production centers without a fight—which was exactly what Spaatz hoped in early 1944. Between January and the end of April, the Germans had 1,684 pilots killed, and Ultra intercepts made Spaatz aware of the loss.[43] Eaker, who now "owned" Fifteenth Air Force as a part of his Mediterranean Allied Air Forces (Spaatz, as USSTAF Commander, directed the heavy bombers of the Fifteenth and coordinated with Eaker on all missions for that force), gained bittersweet satisfaction in knowing that the plan he had set in motion finally bore fruit. Without the damage that Eaker's Eighth Air Force had inflicted on the Luftwaffe, Spaatz could never have gained air superiority in the time allotted.

In one sense, the achievement of air superiority that enabled Overlord fulfilled the progressive goal of inexpensive results by guaranteeing that fewer Allied soldiers would die in the invasion than if the Germans had retained control of the air. Whether the Allies would have attempted a cross-Channel assault lacking control of the air remains doubtful, though, especially in light of the disastrous Dieppe raid in August 1942.[44] American air leaders hoped that the bomber offensive might eliminate the need for an invasion by wrecking German capability and will to fight once the air campaign gained control of the sky. Army Air Forces planners designed both AWPD-1 and AWPD-42 with that goal in mind, and that objective still resonated at the Casablanca Conference in January 1943, when the Combined Chiefs of Staff defined the purpose of the Combined Bomber Offensive as destroying German military, industrial, and economic capability, and the morale of the German people "to a point where their capacity for armed resistance is fatally weakened."[45]

By the time of the Trident Conference four months later, the Combined Chiefs defined "fatally weakened" as "so weakened as to permit initiation of the final combined operations on the Continent."[46] Arnold, Eaker, and Spaatz would have defined it differently if given the choice. Instead, they had to temper their expectations for independent success and hope that air power could still play a decisive role in Overlord's aftermath. Arnold in particular would view the failure of the bomber offensive to forestall the invasion of France as impetus to make sure that a similar air campaign in the Pacific did not lead to similar results.

Ground Support versus Independent Operations

On 1 April 1944, with daylight air superiority secured, Operation Pointblank officially ended, and two weeks later Eisenhower assumed operational control of USSTAF and RAF Bomber Command. He retained the authority for the next five months. During that span he used the heavy bombers to disrupt transportation routes in northern France that the Germans could use to thwart the invasion, as well as to spur the drive of Allied armies across France after the landings. Winston Churchill initially balked over the prospect of substantial French casualties from the bombing, but relented when President Franklin Roosevelt stated an unwillingness to restrict any military action that "might militate against the success of 'Overlord' or cause additional loss of life to our Allied forces of invasion."[47] Approximately 4,750 French civilians died from the bombing of transportation lines before D-Day.[48] To

Roosevelt and Churchill, those deaths were a small price to pay for a successful invasion that would shorten the war, especially since both leaders placed a higher premium on the lives of their own combatants than they did on the lives of civilians in occupied countries. Eisenhower sympathized with those views. On 6 June, he used B-17s to demolish twelve French towns and block roads in them that the Germans could use to move reinforcements to the invasion beachhead.[49]

American air commanders shared the progressive desire for rapid victory, but continued to maintain that independent bombing operations, rather than those devoted to ground support, offered the most inexpensive way to end the war quickly. Before departing England for his Mediterranean command, Eaker reviewed the Overlord plan and deemed the proposed use of B-17s and B-24s to support ground forces a mistake. "Heavy bombers are inefficient artillery," he observed. "They have a more important assignment in the war effort which, incidentally, is more important to winning the battle on the beaches as well."[50] Arnold concurred in his response for "Eaker's Eyes Only," which Eaker received in the midst of his effort to prevent widespread use of Fifteenth Air Force bombers as "flying artillery" in the Italian campaign. "I have reason to fear that we will be dragged down to the level and outlook of the Ground Forces," Arnold fumed. "Our airmen thoroughly know the capabilities of their Arm. They, and they alone, must control the operations of their Air Forces. It is, in my opinion, impossible for Ground Force officers to fully utilize vision and imagination in air action, since they are not well acquainted with air capabilities and limitations."[51]

Spaatz despaired as well over the extensive use of his bomber force to support Overlord. In June, he scoffed at Eisenhower's suggestion to have B-17s drop supplies to partisans in southern France, and also complained that British ground commanders "visualize the best use of our tremendous air potential as plowing up several square miles of terrain in front of the ground forces to obtain a few miles of advance!"[52] Yet without a massive infusion of air power, Eisenhower's invasion may well have stagnated in the Normandy hedgerows. For almost two months after D-Day, German troops and tanks prevented Allied armies from moving more than twenty miles inland from the invasion beaches. Operation "Cobra" made the difference. On 25 July, 1,495 American heavy bombers, 380 medium bombers, and 559 fighters blasted German positions near Saint-Lô.[53] A follow-up attack by 200 medium bombers and five fighter groups the next morning broke the spirit of the German defenders, enabling American troops to pour into the gap and begin their drive to the German frontier.

Although he realized that air power had played a useful role in supporting Allied armies, Spaatz wanted to use his bombers independently, not as an auxiliary force, and in a way that would have a more decisive impact on Germany's capability to fight—as well as highlight the distinctive contribution of strategic bombing to the Allied war effort.[54] He was of course familiar with AWPD-1, AWPD-42, and Eaker's proposal for the Combined Bomber Offensive, and all stressed oil as a vital component of Germany's war-making capacity. In January 1944, COA members had examined prospects for attacking oil production and refining centers. They rejected such raids because they estimated that the Germans would not feel effects from them for at least six months, too long a time to influence the battle for air superiority that Spaatz had to win by April.[55] Once he had gained daylight control of the air, the desire to attack those targets resurfaced.

In late March, Spaatz argued that destroying Germany's oil supply would provide the greatest support to the invasion by restricting enemy troop movements, but Eisenhower thought that attacks on transportation lines in northern France and Belgium would pay more immediate benefits.[56] Still, in his initial bombing directive on 17 April, Eisenhower called for continued pressure on the Luftwaffe, and Spaatz reasoned that raids on oil facilities would compel the Luftwaffe to fight—and suffer attrition—much like the Big Week attacks on the aircraft industry. Spaatz pressed Eisenhower for limited attacks on oil—and even threatened resignation over the issue.[57] Eisenhower relented, and gave him permission to use two good-weather days to attack synthetic oil facilities.

Spaatz knew that the plans for bombing Germany called for six months of concentrated attacks on key industries to produce telling results, yet he thought that he could inflict significant damage to the Nazi oil system with intermittent raids while the focus remained on supporting Overlord. He now possessed a vast force of more than three thousand heavy bombers, and Fifteenth Air Force provided the capability to attack key Balkan targets like Ploesti on a regular basis.[58] In fact, Spaatz had already begun the assault on Ploesti under the guise of attacking the city's rail yards to support the Russian advance in Romania—most of the bombing in three April raids caused "incidental" damage to Ploesti's oil refineries.[59] Despite the scattered nature of the oil system, comprising more than eighty facilities in Nazi-controlled Europe, the COA determined that certain targets were system linchpins—for instance, four Bergius synthetic oil plants produced half of Germany's aviation fuel supply.[60]

Spaatz began the oil offensive with Eisenhower's blessing on 12 May against the synthetic oil plants at Merseburg-Leuna, Zwickau, Bohlen, and other cities. More than eight hundred B-17s and B-24s attacked, with heavy fighter escort, and three hundred German fighters rose to intercept them. Eighth Air Force lost forty-six bombers and seven escorts, while the Luftwaffe lost sixty-five fighters.[61] The enemy response following the raid showed that Spaatz's bombers had indeed hit a vital part of the industrial web.

On 16 May, Spaatz received an Ultra intercept that the Germans had canceled the movement of nine flak batteries to France and sent them instead to synthetic oil plants, along with ten other flak batteries—some of which had defended aircraft factories.[62] The Nazi Minister of Armaments, Albert Speer, recalled: "I shall never forget the date May 12. . . . On that day, the technological war was decided. . . . It meant the end of German armaments production." A week after the attack Speer told Field Marshal Wilhelm Keitel, "The enemy has struck us at one of our weakest points. If they persist at it this time, we will no longer have any fuel production worth mentioning."[63]

The results of the raids pleased Eisenhower, and he not only approved additional attacks on German oil targets for 28 and 29 May, but also permitted Spaatz to make oil USSTAF's top priority target on 8 June. Heavy bombers knocked out nine-tenths of aviation fuel production before Spaatz had to return his focus to invasion support on 22 June.[64] For the next month, attacks on oil facilities fluctuated according to the needs of the ground offensive in France.

COA members spent much of June examining Germany's oil system and revised their earlier estimate. This time they determined that oil was particularly vulnerable to bombing. Analysts concluded that the Germans could not easily hide or disperse their sprawling refineries and synthetic production facilities. In addition, the Germans possessed no excess refining capability. Ploesti was essential to the Nazi war effort, but other refineries in Germany, France, Belgium, and Hungary were also important. The COA identified twelve key refineries and five synthetic oil plants that, if destroyed in a single month, two months later would produce "a very serious curtailment in German military operations." One analyst estimated that after three months, if other refineries remained at current production levels, "you will have immobilized the German economy. They will not be able to either fight or manufacture."[65]

Such assessments intensified Spaatz's desire to wreck German oil. As the air power demands in the Italian ground war began to subside, he dispatched Fifteenth Air Force heavies to wreck the oil target at the top of the list once and for all. He had begun a direct assault on Ploesti's refineries with attacks on 18 and 31 May, with almost 500 bombers participating in the latter raid. The last week of June he ordered three more strikes, and then five more in July. The July raids cost Fifteenth Air Force nearly 100 bombers—by the end of the month it had lost 30 percent of its bomber strength. Spaatz, though, could count on a steady stream of aircraft and crews to replace the losses, and waged an attrition campaign against Ploesti similar to his Big Week battles against the aircraft industry. Four more attacks followed in August, with the RAF joining in the assault with night raids. The Luftwaffe did not oppose the final mission against the refineries on 19 July; intelligence officers estimated that Ploesti's oil production was now a mere 10 percent of its peak output. The Soviet army overran the smoldering complex at the end of the month. Fifteenth Air Force dropped almost fourteen thousand tons of bombs in the five-month campaign that eliminated nearly half of Germany's ability to refine oil. In the process it lost 350 bombers, 200 fighters, and more than one thousand men.[66]

Spaatz wanted to continue hammering oil installations, but other requirements diverted him from that effort. Soon after D-Day, the Germans began launching v-1 "buzz" bombs against England from northern France and Belgium. While the attacks caused little damage compared to the Luftwaffe's blitz in the Battle of Britain, they killed almost six thousand civilians in two and a half months and produced widespread anxiety.[67] Churchill persuaded Eisenhower to make the launch sites the top target for USSTAF and RAF Bomber Command. Spaatz began attacking them in mid-June, though he thought the effort yielded minimal results against well-camouflaged targets that had a minimal impact on the war. At the end of the month he met with Eisenhower and persuaded the Supreme Allied Commander to allow attacks against targets in Germany when the weather cooperated, the ground forces did not face an emergency, and the V-weapons did not demand the complete attention of the strategic air forces.[68]

Nonetheless, the demand for air support from Allied armies continued. Fifteenth Air Force heavies devoted substantial assistance to the "Anvil" landings in southern France in August. Operation "Market Garden," the airborne assault in Holland, consumed much of Eighth Air Force's heavy bomber fleet in September. Spaatz reported to Arnold that using heavy bombers to resupply ground and airborne troops for ten days in Market Garden cost Eighth Air Force the equivalent of a B-24 wing for six weeks. During the ten-day span, Spaatz bemoaned, his bombers lost the chance to conduct precision raids against German targets on two days, and radar attacks on another six.[69] Spaatz's deputy commander, Fred Anderson, also voiced his displeasure over the need to provide air support to ground forces. "The Armies cannot move forward without help from the Air," Anderson confided to Major General Curtis LeMay in early October. "They stay until we blast the way, and once the way is blasted they move the extent that their supplies allow; then they stop. And when they stop the German digs in, and the way must be blasted again before they move."[70]

Prospects for Peace through a Thunderclap

As Allied armies pushed toward the German frontier, the question of how best to use the heavy bomber force to speed the end of the war surfaced yet again. In early July, the Combined Chiefs

167

of Staff determined that a time might come when a massive assault against German morale might prove decisive. A month later, Air Chief Marshal Sir Charles "Peter" Portal, Chief of the British Air Staff and the ranking officer in the RAF, produced a proposal for such a catastrophic blow from the air. Portal argued that a massive attack on the German civilian populace was unlikely to produce an overthrow of German leadership; at best it might spur rioting, but the rioting would probably occur among foreign workers only. Direct attacks on the morale of political and military leaders themselves, though, might lead to significant results. "Our object must be to influence the minds of German high political and military authorities in the desired direction to the point where the High Command must either accept the necessity of surrender or be replaced by an alternative Command which does so," Portal maintained. He believed that heavy attacks on government and military control centers in Berlin (five thousand tons of high explosive ordnance on a 2 ½-square-mile area), backed by "well judged propaganda," could lead to German capitulation.[71]

Codenamed "Thunderclap," the proposed operation received intense scrutiny from Spaatz's USSTAF staff in the United Kingdom, as well as from Arnold's air staff in the Pentagon. Spaatz's officers examined the British proposal from a progressive mindset that presumed a faster end of the war meant a better end of the war—at least as far as Allied combatants were concerned. "If the operation should succeed in curtailing the duration of the war by even a few weeks it would save many thousands of Allied casualties and would justify itself many times over," their critique stated. They further noted that a large portion of the German government had evacuated Berlin, making the operation's ability to cause a sudden administrative breakdown problematic. Still, the daylight population of the targeted area was roughly 375,000, of whom 275,000 would likely die or be seriously injured, and "it may well be that an attack on the proposed area of Berlin would have a greater effect upon national administration than is at present appreciated."[72]

Spaatz disagreed. In March, he had shunned a British plan to attack "political targets" in the Balkans to reduce Nazi support there,[73] and felt that Portal's current proposal was unsound as well. He informed Eisenhower that American bombing policy condoned attacks on military objectives, not morale. "I am opposed to this operation as now planned," he declared. "We are prepared to participate in an operation against Berlin, but in so doing will select targets for attack of military importance."[74]

Eisenhower had initially been receptive to Thunderclap. After reviewing the proposal on 7 August, he penciled: "Since conditions stated are 'that military defeat is certain and obvious'—I agree the project would be a good one. (We would no longer require bombing strictly military targets.)"[75] Once he received Spaatz's critique, Eisenhower hedged—but only slightly. The Supreme Allied Commander acknowledged that he had always insisted on bombing precision targets, yet he was "always prepared to take part in anything that gives real promise to ending the war quickly." Given the losses suffered during the invasion and breakout from the Normandy beachhead—with the likelihood of tougher fighting as his troops neared Germany—Eisenhower found air power's prospects for achieving a rapid victory enticing. He told Spaatz: "The policies under which you are now operating will be unchanged unless in my opinion an opportunity arises where a sudden and devastating blow may have an incalculable result."[76] On 9 September, he directed Spaatz to make certain that Eighth Air Force would be ready to bomb Berlin at a moment's notice. Spaatz then had Jimmy Doolittle, the Eighth Air Force Commander, scrub plans to attack military objectives in Berlin and prepare for bombing "indiscriminately on the town" when Eisenhower gave the order.[77]

169

Major General Laurence Kuter, one of AWPD-1's designers who now served as Arnold's assistant chief for plans and combat operations, critiqued Thunderclap as well. AWPD-1 had included the possibility of attacking German civilians directly if their morale weakened during the war, but cautioned that a miscalculation of their resolve could cause bombing to stiffen their desire to resist. Kuter was therefore reluctant to endorse Thunderclap. He surmised that the impetus for the British proposal stemmed from their desire to retaliate for the recent buzz bomb attacks against England. Although he realized that Thunderclap's intent was to break the will of the German leaders, he noted that civilians would bear the brunt of the attacks. "The bombing of civilian targets in Germany cannot be expected to have similar effects to those which might be expected in a democratic country where the people are still able to influence the national will," he asserted. Kuter reiterated that it was "contrary to our national ideals to wage war against civilians." Yet—consistent with AWPD-1's caveat three years before—he conceded that a time might arrive when attacks "against other than objectives immediately related to the battle" might tip the balance and end the war. Thus, while opposed to the British proposal, he recommended planning for it—just in case.[78]

After examining the arguments, General Arnold directed USSTAF to develop a plan for including British and American air forces in an "all-out, widespread attack" against Germany that would last roughly a week. Its purpose would not be to obliterate cities or towns, nor would Berlin be the sole target. Rather, the assault would strike "military objectives of numerous types . . . to give every citizen an opportunity to see positive proof of Allied air power." Arnold stated that such an operation could be "decisive" if conducted at the proper moment.[79] In mid-September, Spaatz's headquarters began working on a plan for attacking morale that did "not harbor the cold-blooded slaughter of civilians."

Planners selected targets "designed to destroy such necessities of life as are normally required from day to day [to] produce a morale effect over a longer period of time than would an indiscriminate direct attack on a town."[80]

Focus on Oil, September–December 1944

In September Eisenhower returned operational control of the USSTAF to Spaatz, and the USSTAF commander intensified his assault on the target that he thought would end the war most rapidly—oil. Eighth Air Force launched "thousand bomber raids" on synthetic oil plants, refineries, and related industries on 27 and 28 September and again on 3, 6, and 7 October, with the last day's effort totaling more than 1,300 heavies, of which 52 were lost, and most of those to flak.[81] The weather, though, refused to cooperate. In October American bombers launched only three entirely "precision" raids on oil targets, and Germany's synthetic oil production tripled from its output the previous month. Radar attacks produced dismal results—of 81,654 tons of bombs dropped by Eighth Air Force using H2X between 1 September and 31 December 1944, only 674 tons—*0.8 percent*—fell within one thousand feet of the aiming point.[82] Clear skies did not guarantee good bombing, however. Despite the large size of the oil facilities, only small parts of them contained equipment truly vital to production. Those components were hard to hit, even with the Norden bombsight, and flak bursts made the task especially difficult.

The Combined Chiefs of Staff kept oil as the top target for both USSTAF and RAF Bomber Command when they met in late October. Germany remained overcast for most of November, and Allied ground forces continued to demand air support. In addition, the Luftwaffe revealed a new threat—the Me-262 jet fighter—that could fly 100 mph faster than the Mustang and could also fly on cheap, plentiful kerosene. Despite those concerns, Eighth Air

Force flew four raids a week throughout November that averaged more than one thousand heavy bombers against oil and transportation targets, which occupied the second spot on the Combined Chiefs' target list.[83] Eighth Air Force heavies dropped 39 percent of their bombs that month on oil targets, and the Fifteenth's heavy bombers did the same with 32 percent of their ordnance, but radar bombing occurred on most attacks. RAF Bomber Command also contributed 24 percent of its November ordnance to the oil campaign, again by radar techniques. The German oil system that had suffered so severely in the summer continued to rebound.[84]

Still, Spaatz thought that the weight of ordnance dropped on oil and transportation targets might prove decisive. On 13 December he informed Arnold: "There is increasing evidence that the attacks on rail communications and industrial areas in Germany are having a cumulative effect. There is [a] possibility that the breaking point may be closer at hand than some of us are willing to admit."[85] Three days later Spaatz realized that the desired breaking point remained elusive.

The Ardennes and Its Aftermath

On 16 December 1944, the Germans demonstrated in convincing fashion that they still possessed both the capability and will to continue the war. The Ardennes offensive stunned Allied leaders, most of whom had assumed that Germany was on the brink of collapse. Spaatz shifted USSTAF's focus from oil to transportation centers west of the Rhine, and Eighth Air Force flew only one mission against oil targets between 16 December and 8 January.[86] By 28 January the "Battle of the Bulge" claimed eighty-one thousand American casualties—making it the bloodiest engagement in American military history.[87] Soon after it began Eisenhower considered asking for ten additional divisions. Although he decided against the extra manpower, he ordered the first American execution of a deserter in eighty years to stiffen the resolve of his troops against the German onslaught.[88] Intelligence appraisals now estimated that the war might last until 1946, while the Selective Service upped draft quotas for January and February 1945 from sixty thousand to eighty thousand.[89] In early January, Army Chief of Staff General George Marshall stated: "We now face a situation requiring major decisions to prevent this war from dragging on for some time." He asked for Eisenhower's "broad personal estimate of the resources required and the steps to be taken to bring this war in Europe to a quick conclusion."[90]

As Allied losses mounted the progressive rationale originally presented for Thunderclap became more and more appealing: an aerial Armageddon might actually wreck Germany's will to fight, end the war, and save Allied lives. Arnold had expressed similar sentiments in waxing about how America would approach future conflicts to scientist Theodore von Karman a month before the Bulge attack. "It is a fundamental principle of democracy that personnel casualties are distasteful," Arnold opined. "We will continue to fight mechanical rather than manpower wars."[91] The European struggle now threatened to become an extended battle of attrition on the ground, and the bomber seemingly offered the mechanical means to stop the slaughter in one fell swoop. Moreover, the goal of unconditional surrender dictated the destruction of the Nazi government and its administrative apparatus, and that government appeared more than capable of continuing the conflict. The planned air assault would wreck key Nazi offices in Berlin. Their location near the city's main residential area guaranteed that the civilians supporting that government would feel the full fury of a raid that illustrated the bankrupt nature of the Nazi regime. Marshall agreed, and also recommended that a similar attack on Munich "would probably be of great benefit because it would show the people that are being evacuated to Munich that there is no hope."[92]

In the meantime, the Red Army's advance in the East had reached the point where it would benefit directly from the destruction of transportation hubs like Berlin—and Arnold wanted to demonstrate the impact of American air power to the Soviets.[93] He was dismayed over bombing's failure to defeat Germany on its own, writing to Spaatz that despite a five-to-one superiority in the air, and "in spite of all our hopes, anticipations, dreams and plans, we have as yet not been able to capitalize to the extent which we should. We may not be able to force capitulation of the Germans by air attacks, but on the other hand, with this tremendous striking power, it would seem to me that we should get much better and decisive results than we are getting now."[94] Arnold further despaired over the paltry results achieved thus far by the B-29 offensive against Japan—stress that would help trigger his fourth heart attack on 17 January. The proposed attack on Berlin promised independent success that could overshadow the meager performance in the Pacific. A bombing-induced German collapse would not only save a multitude of Allied lives, it would cause political and military leaders around the world to acknowledge air power as the source of salvation. Thunderclap thus offered the chance to satisfy numerous concerns. A 31 January 1945 directive made selected cities in eastern Germany, "where heavy attack will cause great confusion in civilian evacuation from the east and hamper reinforcements," the Combined Bomber Offensive's highest priority targets after oil.[95]

Those factors, together with the abundance of bombers available, led Spaatz to attack Berlin, Leipzig, and Dresden in February 1945. Yet the magnitude of the 3 February Berlin assault did not approach Thunderclap proportions.[96] The expectation of clouds over the city precluded precision attacks on oil targets and made transportation facilities and an array of government buildings—both of which had larger "footprints" than individual synthetic oil plants—the primary objectives for radar attacks. Once over Berlin, however, crews found the skies predominantly clear, and most bombed visually. Almost one thousand b-17s dropped 2,279 tons of bombs on the city, causing heavy damage to the Reichschancellery, Air Ministry, Foreign Office, Ministry of Propaganda, and Gestapo headquarters, as well as to many railroad marshalling yards.[97] The raid may have killed as many as twenty-five thousand people.[98] Against Leipzig and Dresden, the Eighth Air Force again attacked rail yards. In the 14–15 February raids on Dresden, clouds obscured the target, and crews mistakenly dumped their bombs on Dresden's main residential district, which had been heavily bombed the night before by the RAF. Refugees fleeing the Russians clogged the city, and between twenty-five thousand and thirty-five thousand civilians perished in the multiple assaults.[99]

Technically, the attacks on Berlin and Dresden were aimed at military objectives. Two days after the Berlin mission, Spaatz revealed that he had little faith in the notion that a single, massive bombing raid could compel German surrender, telling Arnold: "Your comment on the decisiveness of results achieved by air power leads me to believe that you might be following the chimera of the one air operation which will end the war. I have concluded that it does not exist. I also feel that in many cases the success of our efforts is unmeasurable, due to our inability to exploit the decisive results achieved."[100] Nevertheless, Spaatz showed that he had viewed the Berlin assault as more than simply an attempt to destroy German war-making capacity. When asked by Doolittle before the raid if he wanted "definitely military targets" on the outskirts of Berlin hit if clouds obscured oil installations, Spaatz replied: "Hit oil if visual assured; otherwise, Berlin—center of City."[101] Dresden's marshalling yard bordered the city's major residential district, virtually guaranteeing that bomb misses would kill civilians.

Moral qualms and the conviction that attacks aimed at war-making capability were more productive than those aimed at the enemy populace combined to prevent American air leaders from launching a wholesale campaign to kill German civilians. Air commanders maintained that the essence of German morale was public support for the war, and that such support was fragile, but they agonized over how best to attack it. While Eaker, with radar bombing in late 1943, and Spaatz, with the 3 February raid on Berlin, attacked civilian morale directly, it was not their preference to do so. They, as well as their counterparts, believed that attacking civilians *indirectly*—by terrorizing people rather than killing them, or by depriving them of needed goods and services—was the answer to breaking their will.

Yet the difference between attacks intended to terrorize and those intended to kill was a fine one, and the distinction blurred as the war progressed. The impetus to end the war quickly led to the selection of targets—like Dresden's rail yards—that would also have a maximum impact on civilian morale. When Secretary of War Henry Stimson learned of Dresden's devastation, he requested information on the attacks and asked that "the City be thoroughly photographed to establish that our objectives were, as usual, military in character." Arnold received the request while recuperating in Coral Gables and scribbled across it: "We must not get soft—War must be destructive and to a certain extent inhuman and ruthless."[102] By 1945, German civilians had no argument with Arnold's assessment. For them, no distinction existed between the RAF Bomber Command's area attacks and American raids against specific targets in or near cities.

For Eighth Air Force, the 3 February raid on Berlin was the tenth against the German capital. More than 600 bombers had attacked it on several occasions; on 21 June 1944 935 heavies had pummeled the city; and on 26 February 1,100 more would strike it.[103] Spaatz understood that whether his crews bombed urban targets using the Norden bombsight or radar, they would kill many civilians, and "dehouse" many more. To him, though, intent mattered. *Why* counted more than *how* in evaluating success, and the purpose of the raid provided criteria by which to judge results. With photographic reconnaissance and Ultra intercepts, he could calculate the damage rendered to Germany's oil producing capability caused by bombing a specific synthetic oil plant. What he could not do, however, was translate those figures into an accurate estimate of *when* Germany's oil supply would cause it to quit fighting—and the time factor was the ultimate judge of success. He had faced a similar dilemma the previous spring in trying to determine when his bombers and fighters might gain daylight air superiority, and resorted to aerial attrition to achieve his goal in the time allotted. Now, in the aftermath of Hitler's Ardennes offensive, the impetus for quick success—in this case, quick victory—helped to mold the intent of his actions.

The desire for a rapid end to the war courtesy of American air power was nothing new to Spaatz—or Arnold—or any Army Air Forces commander. They entered the war with that goal in mind, but *they* also sought to dictate when the war ended, and the demands of the ground war had upset their calculations. Ideally, they had wanted to build an enormous bomber force and then pound the key nodes of German industry with it for six months, after which they thought Germany would surrender. The diversion of bombers to support ground advances in the Mediterranean, followed by requirements to support the Normandy invasion, not only prevented air commanders from testing their theory, but also from estimating when bombing would end the war. While rapid victory remained the airmen's goal, they wanted an air power-induced success, and the opportunities for that result diminished the closer Allied troops came to Berlin.

In early 1945, with the Anglo-American armies poised to advance into Germany, Spaatz was uncertain that his oil campaign could stymie Germany's capability to fight before those forces advanced deep into the Reich. His 3 February Berlin raid may have mirrored his other attacks against the city in terms of conduct, but his intent paralleled Eaker's desire in late 1943 to win the war by shattering German morale through radar bombing.[104] As for the attacks on Dresden ten days later that achieved much more notoriety, statements made afterward by Spaatz and other American air leaders were closer to the mark—those raids were little different in either conduct or intent from American bombing missions that began more than a year before.

Gradually, though, the mindsets of American air commanders morphed into a mentality that viewed radar bombing in the same vein as precision raids. Regardless of the equipment used, the emphasis remained on the targets attacked rather than on the methods used to attack them. American air leaders retained their convictions regarding the importance of Germany's industrial web and devoted considerable attention to pinpointing the key connections in it—even though they knew that they lacked the capacity to attack those strands with true precision bombing. What they did not lack were numbers. By fall 1944 Spaatz could regularly send one thousand bombers against a particular target, and did so.

The demand for rapid results—part of which stemmed from the airmen's own desires to demonstrate that they could achieve "independent" success—pushed them relentlessly onward, and the overriding war aim of unconditional surrender condoned the massive destruction that followed.[105] Arnold had told his commanders in June 1943, "We are not in a position to ignore the costs and win by brute force."[106] A little more than a year later, Spaatz and

USSTAF could try to do exactly that. Throughout their portion of the Combined Bomber Offensive, American airmen failed to note that the emphasis on rapid results distorted the progressive ideals of efficiency and economy at the heart of their beliefs about the virtues of bombing. American bomber crews paid a heavy price for achieving dominance in the European skies, and radar bombing wreaked a terrible toll on the German civilian populace. Still, the public statements of air leaders, as well as much of their private correspondence, often sounded as if their efforts were beyond reproach.

In private, though, they also frequently agonized over the prospects of using brute force to secure victory—especially in terms of the legacy that it might foster. Eaker, who contributed the heavy bombers of Fifteenth Air Force to Spaatz's campaign against Germany, commented at length on the dilemma. Spaatz had requested his views on "Clarion," a plan designed not only to disrupt transportation links in small towns, but also to showcase the might of Allied air power to German citizens unfamiliar with its fury. Eaker did not mince his words on the proposal:

> It [Clarion] will absolutely convince the Germans that we are the barbarians they say we are, for it would be perfectly obvious to them that this is primarily a large-scale attack on civilians as, in fact, it of course will be. Of all the people killed in this attack over 95% of them can be expected to be civilians.
>
> It is absolutely contrary to the conversations you and [Air Secretary] Bob Lovett had with respect to the necessity of sticking to military targets. . . .
>
> If the time ever comes when we want to attack the civilian populace with a view to breaking civil morale, such a plan as the one suggested is probably the way to do it. I personally, however, have become completely convinced that you and Bob Lovett are right and we

should never allow the history of this war to convict us of throwing the strategic bomber at the man in the street. I think there is a better way we can do our share toward the defeat of the enemy, but if we are to attack the civil population I am certain we should wait until its morale is much nearer [the] breaking point and until the weather favors the operation more than it will at any time in the winter or early spring.[107]

Eaker—who had himself attempted to subdue German morale with bombs—did not completely dismiss the possibility that air power might break civilian will, but he thought that the current odds were low. Despite his concerns, Operation Clarion transpired in early 1945. On 22 February more than two thousand USSTAF bombers, with heavy fighter escort, roamed over Germany bombing and strafing railroad stations, marshalling yards, and bridges. The RAF supported the effort with intense attacks on lines of communication in the Ruhr. The pattern was repeated the next day and produced a temporary halt to rail traffic throughout much of the Reich. Yet it did not significantly affect the morale of the populace. The bland statement appearing in the Army Air Forces' official history, "Nothing in particular happened after the German people beheld Allied warplanes striking towns which usually escaped bombings," made a fitting epitaph for the operation.[108]

The remainder of America's contribution to the Combined Bomber Offensive continued with the same intensity that Spaatz had displayed since taking command of USSTAF a year before. Oil and transportation remained the two top targets. Winter weather made attacks on both difficult, but the magnitude of the air offensive ultimately made a difference. Every day between 19 February and 4 March Eighth Air Force attacked targets in Germany with more than one thousand bombers; Fifteenth Air Force heavies raided Germany on twenty days in February. Germany's synthetic oil production fell from thirty-seven thousand tons a month in January to thirteen thousand in February, less than 4 percent of the production total for January 1944.[109]

USSTAF actually dropped more bombs on transportation targets than it did on oil, with 54,000 tons out of the 74,400 dropped in February going to roads, bridges, rail lines, and marshalling yards.[110] Marshalling yards in particular received an abundance of ordnance, most of which fell via radar bombing during periods of poor weather.[111] Those attacks produced telling results because the sheer amount of bombs dropped disrupted rail traffic to such a degree that trains could not deliver loads of coal to German factories—and most industries, including synthetic oil production—operated by burning coal.

Coal delivery emerged as the truly vital strand of Germany's industrial web, and the attacks against transportation lines and marshalling yards eliminated what remained of Germany's industrial capability more by happenstance than design.[112]

Assessment

On 26 April 1945, with Anglo-American armies across the Rhine and Berlin ringed by Soviet legions, American heavy bombers flew their last mission in the Combined Bomber Offensive. More than 70 percent of almost 2,700,000 tons of bombs that the Army Air Forces and RAF dropped on Axis Europe fell during the war's last nine months.[113] Most of the destruction to German industry occurred during that span, aided by factories finally producing at peak capacity and without slack to compensate for the damage. The nine months of intense bombing after achieving daylight air superiority paralleled the six-month requirement forecasted by AWPD-1, AWPD-42, and Eaker's April 1943 CBO plan, though none of those plans anticipated the substantial diversion of the heavy bomber effort to battlefield support. RAF Bomber Command made sizable contributions to the air campaign, dropping 67,000 tons of bombs alone in March 1945.[114] The destruction of Germany's ability to fight accelerated after Eisenhower released control of Bomber Command and USSTAF in September 1944. By December, bombing had destroyed half of Germany's supply of all petroleum products. The attack on German transportation lines, which began in earnest in September 1944 and generally received second billing to oil targets, reduced the volume of railroad car loadings by 75 percent in February 1945.[115]

The clamor for fast results removed the emphasis on efficiency that was a hallmark of American air power's prewar progressive notions. When combined with the overarching objective of unconditional surrender, the impetus for speed had dismal consequences for the attacker as well as the attacked. The requirement for total victory "with minimum suffering and loss for the victors . . . could justify almost any action that accelerated triumph," remarked historian Michael Sherry.[116] The Combined Bomber Offensive killed 305,000 German civilians, wounded at least 780,000, destroyed the homes of 1,865,000, forced 4,885,000 to evacuate, and deprived 20 million of public utilities. By the third quarter of 1944 the air offensive had tied down an estimated 4.5 million workers, almost 20 percent of the non-agricultural labor force, in air raid-related activities.[117] The goal of rapid success, though, impelled Spaatz and, to a lesser extent, Eaker to wage a campaign of aerial attrition that produced enormous losses for American airmen in the skies over Hitler's Europe. By the end of the war Eighth Air Force had suffered 26,000 fatal casualties—more than the entire United States Marine Corps.[118] All told, the Army Air Forces in the European and Mediterranean theaters lost almost 36,000 men killed.[119] Eighth and Fifteenth Air Forces combined lost 8,759 heavy bombers.[120] RAF Bomber Command, which fought for almost three years more than the Americans, had 55,888 men killed, a majority of whom lost their lives to the Luftwaffe's formidable night fighter force.[121]

The United States Strategic Bombing Survey, produced after the conflict by a team of primarily civilian analysts, concluded that "Allied air power was decisive in the war in western Europe."[122] It further surmised that had Allied armies not overrun Germany, bombing would have halted its armament production by May 1945, resulting in the collapse of resistance a few months later.[123] Yet air power did not produce an independent victory in the European war, and the vast efforts of Allied armies and navies were essential to destroying the Third Reich's capability and will to fight. The Survey acknowledged that strategic bombing complemented those efforts by achieving air superiority and reducing the quantity, and quality, of materiel that the Germans could bring to the battlefield.

Though the dream of a distinctive "victory through air power" remained unfulfilled in Europe, American airmen would have one more chance to make it a reality. As Spaatz signed Germany's unconditional surrender to the Soviet Union in the smoldering Berlin suburbs just before midnight on 8 May, half a world away, the crews of 302 B-29s of Hap Arnold's Twentieth Air Force prepared for missions against Tokuyama, Otake, and Amami-O-Shima. They had been burning Japan's cities for two months. Another massive effort to achieve a rapid, independent victory with air power was underway.

6 • Fire from the Sky

Japan, 1944–45

Results of incendiary attacks have been tremendous. The first areas assigned were selected on the basis of a compromise between industrial importance and susceptibility to fire. With a greater respect we now have for our fire-making ability and the greater weight that we are able to lay down, these new areas which have just been sent to you represent more nearly the top industrial areas. They also appear to be most susceptible to fire attack, but they do not represent any compromise.

● BRIG. GEN. LAURIS NORSTAD TO MAJ. GEN. CURTIS LEMAY, 3 APRIL 1945

I am influenced by the conviction that the present stage of development of the air war against Japan presents the AAF for the first time with the opportunity of proving the power of the strategic air arm.

● MAJ. GEN. CURTIS LEMAY TO BRIG. GEN. LAURIS NORSTAD, 25 APRIL 1945

Night of 9–10 March 1945

As midnight on 9 March passed into the wee hours of the next day, Major General Curtis LeMay could not sleep. Instead, he paced back and forth through the Quonset hut that served as the operations control room of Headquarters XXI Bomber Command on Guam, nervously smoking his trademark cigars. The thirty-eight-year-old LeMay had reason to be anxious. That afternoon he had watched 54 B-29 "Superfortresses" take off from Guam for Tokyo, to be joined by 110 B-29s from Tinian, and another 161 from Saipan.[1] As the Commander of XXI Bomber Command in Twentieth Air Force, LeMay had ordered the raid, and every aspect of it contradicted the fundamental tenets guiding the American approach to strategic bombing: the heavy bombers would attack at night, without any defensive armament, at extremely low altitudes between 4,900 and 9,200 feet, and they would target the most densely populated part of the world's most populous city with an enormous amount of incendiary bombs.

About an hour before the first bombing results were to arrive, Lieutenant Colonel St. Clair McKelway, the public relations officer of XXI Bomber Command, wandered into the Quonset hut. LeMay had given McKelway notice of the raid only a few days before and, in fact, had not notified General "Hap" Arnold, the Commander of Twentieth Air Force as well as Commanding General of the Army Air Forces, until less than thirty-six hours before the attack.[2] LeMay grimaced at McKelway through cigar-clenched teeth, which was actually his way of smiling—an attack of Bell's palsy years earlier had frozen the corners of his mouth so that he could not raise them. After rhetorically asking McKelway why he was still awake, the man who had found the *Rex* in the Atlantic, designed the Eighth Air Force's formation tactics, and led the grueling August 1943 mission against Regensburg, admitted: "I'm sweating this one out myself. A lot could go wrong." Yet LeMay also believed that his new approach would pay dividends that made the risks worthwhile. "If this raid works out the way I think it will," he told McKelway, "we can shorten this war. . . . I think we've figured out a punch he's not expecting this time. I don't think he's got the right flak to combat this kind of raid and I don't think he can keep his cities from being burned down— being wiped right off the map. . . . I never think anything is going to work until I've seen the pictures after the raid, but if this one works we will shorten this damned war out here."[3]

LeMay's progressive desire to end the Pacific War quickly and decisively with air power mirrored that displayed in Europe by Tooey Spaatz. Like Spaatz's 3 February attack on Berlin, LeMay's raid a month later against Tokyo was an attempt to speed the end of the war by obliterating the center of the enemy's capital city.

The progressive notion that bombing would limit enemy civilian casualties had faded after more than three years of war; "progressive" now meant hastening the war's end and saving *American* lives in the process. LeMay still believed that the *precise* destruction of the key elements of enemy industrial power would end the war more quickly—and inexpensively in terms of American lives lost—than any other approach. "If you don't destroy the Japanese industry, you're going to have to invade Japan," he reflected. "And how many Americans will be killed in an invasion of Japan?"[4] Unlike Germany, though, targeting Japan's industry posed a much different problem. Japanese cities contained few factories set apart from residential districts. Instead, a multitude of "cottage industries," each employing fewer than 250 workers, spread throughout most urban areas. Despite this blending, Army Air Forces planners divided Japan's largest cities into separate zones that they thought contained the most factories, the most residences, and the most commercial enterprises.

In Tokyo, the city's most densely populated residential district, not its primary industrial area, was the target for the B-29s on the night of 9 March. That guidance came from Brigadier General Lauris Norstad, who served from the Pentagon as the Twentieth Air Force's Chief of Staff.[5] Arnold had vetoed Norstad's plan to firebomb Tokyo's Imperial Palace on 8 December 1944 as retribution for Pearl Harbor, though he disagreed more with the choice of target and its political ramifications than with the desire to bomb Japanese urban areas intensively. Since Arnold's heart attack on 17 January, and his subsequent recuperation in Florida, much of the real power driving Twentieth Air Force operations now came from Norstad. When Arnold's impatience with poor bombing results had led him to relieve LeMay's predecessor, Brigadier General "Possum" Hansell, from command in early January, he had sent Norstad to Guam to convey the news. On the night of 9 March Norstad was on Guam once again, asleep in LeMay's quarters after having arrived from Washington DC that morning. LeMay viewed the visit as a threat since his own bombing had thus far produced results mirroring Hansell's.[6] "There are plenty of wolves around who were looking for the job—Norstad one of them," LeMay recalled.[7] In the meantime, Norstad and Arnold had called for a "maximum effort" against Japan, and LeMay planned to provide it. He would attack the target that he had received with as much strength as he could muster, although, as he informed Norstad, he would continue "working on several very radical methods of employment of the force."[8]

Many of LeMay's crews—who had regularly flown high altitude, daylight missions—were dumbfounded upon learning of his "radical" tactics at their pre-mission briefing on 9 March, but as they began arriving over Tokyo shortly after midnight, Japanese time, they gained an appreciation for his approach.[9] For the next three hours the 279 B-29s reaching their target dropped 1,665 tons of incendiaries on a city constructed largely out of wood.[10] The crews at the end of the two-hundred-mile-long bomber stream beheld an awesome sight—from more than *one hundred miles* away, the horizon glowed a bright yellow. The B-29s razed sixteen square miles of Tokyo, including the area of the greatest population density, and, with the help of 30 mph winds, created a firestorm so intense that glass melted and water boiled from temperatures in excess of five hundred degrees.[11] At least eighty-three thousand people died and more than one million survivors lost their homes.[12] Several crewmen reported the smell of charred flesh in the cabin; the assault remains the world's most devastating air attack.

Yet the comparative cost of rendering such massive destruction was much less than many airmen had feared. While LeMay had dismissed the negligible Japanese night fighter force, his antiaircraft experts and several squadron commanders had estimated that low altitudes might result in the loss of 70 percent of his bombers to flak.[13] LeMay disagreed, contending that the heaviest amount of Japanese antiaircraft artillery was the high altitude variety, and that the remainder was ill-suited for aircraft flying between five thousand and ten thousand feet. His instincts proved correct, and flak claimed only two B-29s, with another twelve lost to reasons other than enemy defenses.[14]

LeMay and McKelway received initial word of the attack's progress via radio from Brigadier General Thomas Power, the 314th Wing Commander, who orbited Tokyo at twenty thousand feet and colored in areas of a city map as fire consumed them. LeMay, his staff, and Norstad met Power at his aircraft and complimented him upon his return to Guam, but LeMay waited for more definitive results from B-29 photoreconnaissance aircraft dispatched to Tokyo on 10 March before proclaiming success. When the post-strike photographs arrived, LeMay and Norstad reviewed them and confirmed the enormity of the destruction that the B-29s had inflicted.

LeMay then issued a press release exemplifying his conviction that air power was the key to a rapid defeat of Japan: "I believe that all those under my command on these island bases have by their participation in this single operation shortened this war. . . . They are fighting for a quicker end to this war and will continue to fight for a quicker end to it with all the brains and strength they have."[15] Norstad added his praises as well. "After study of post attack photographs, it is very apparent that this last operation was most successful," he wired Arnold. "The results far exceed my optimistic expectations."[16] Arnold notified LeMay: "I am exceptionally well pleased with the March Ninth attack upon Tokyo. This mission, flown under the most difficult operating conditions, proves again the courage and efficiency of your command."[17]

The great raid against Tokyo set the pattern for the next week of bombing, with the emphasis on incinerating the main residential areas of Japan's four largest cities. Coming on the heels of the Eighth Air Force's pounding of Berlin and Dresden, LeMay's attacks resembled Spaatz's in terms of fury and destructiveness. They also demonstrated a willingness to target civilians directly rather than relying on the complementary pain caused by targeting nearby government offices (Berlin) or rail yards (Dresden). Norstad noted that in the Japanese case, the target "areas assigned were selected on the basis of a compromise between industrial importance and susceptibility to fire."[18] He would later provide LeMay with targets that stressed industrial production, yet for now, Norstad thought that destroying urban areas would wreck Japan's will to fight and produce victory in the shortest amount of time.

While the revenge motive missing from the European war might have contributed to the targeting shift, the main reason for it was the same one that had led Spaatz to demolish the center of Berlin—the desire for a rapid end to the war.[19] Despite their "precision bombing" rhetoric, air commanders did not aim the Tokyo raid and those that followed in its immediate aftermath at Japanese industry. Their intent was to kill people and destroy homes, which would *indirectly* affect industrial production—an argument that stood one of the chief bombing tenets of Maxwell Field's Air Corps Tactical School on its head. Air commanders believed that the attacks would demonstrate to Japanese leaders that they could not stop the urban annihilation and cause them to end a futile conflict. If they failed to yield, the devastation would continue unabated until bombing wrecked any remaining capacity to resist. Either way, air commanders surmised, air power promised to save American lives.

To guarantee that promise, though, air chiefs had to produce *rapid* success—and produce it quickly enough to prevent the invasion of Japan. "The factor of time was taking on a new insistence," Hansell reflected. "The invasion of the Japanese home islands—whose necessity had become an obsession with the Army planners—had been agreed upon. If air power was to end the war without a massive bloodletting on the ground, its application could not be delayed."[20] Victory via bombing would not only save American lives, it would also go a long way toward vindicating the quest of Army Air Forces leaders to make their organization an independent service. The emphasis on speed, when combined with the overarching goal of unconditional surrender, would again produce enormous suffering for those on the receiving end of American air power.

Still, the prewar progressive belief endured that destroying key elements of production would collapse the dominos connecting the enemy's war effort. While targeting Japan's densely populated districts, air leaders never abandoned their conviction that the precise destruction of industry would yield the quickest, most inexpensive path to success. McKelway referred to the Tokyo raid as "pin-point incendiary bombing from a low level, designed not simply to start fires or destroy a single factory but to start one great conflagration whose fury would double and redouble the destructive force of the bombs."[21] LeMay continued to stress the damage to industry even though Tokyo and the four raids that followed primarily targeted residential districts. Indeed, the target description given to crews on 9 March referred to the "Tokyo Urban Industrial Area" and highlighted that the average population density of 103,000 people per square mile was "an average probably not exceeded in any other modern industrial city in the world."[22]

Preparations for an Air Campaign

Much like the European air war, the shift away from precision bombing against Japan resulted more from happenstance than design. Despite Army Chief of Staff General George Marshall's November 1941 warning that Americans would "fight mercilessly" in the event of war, and that B-17s from the Philippines would "be dispatched immediately to set the paper cities of Japan on fire," Marshall intended his admonition to deter Japanese military activity rather than to provide a blueprint for American actions.[23] The United States had only thirty-five B-17s on the Philippines when Japan attacked on 8 December, and by March 1942 had fewer than thirty "Flying Fortresses" in Australia.[24] The dramatic raid by Lieutenant Colonel "Jimmy" Doolittle's sixteen B-25s, launched from the aircraft carrier *Hornet* on 18 April 1942, was an effort to bomb specific industrial and military targets in Tokyo even though most of the bombs fell on residential areas. Hap Arnold and his Army Air Forces commanders intended to conduct a sustained, high altitude, daylight, precision bombing campaign against Japanese industries once they could place a substantial bomber force within range of Japan's home islands. The guiding strategy for a bomber offensive, Arnold insisted, would be the "destruction of Japanese factories in order to cripple production of munitions and essential articles for maintenance of economic structure in Japan."[25] Yet Arnold and his cohorts had little information on the nature of the Japanese industrial complex and its key components.

To fill that void, in March 1943 Arnold asked the Committee of Operations Analysts (COA) to identify the appropriate targets for an air campaign against Japan that "would knock [it] out of the war."[26] The COA, composed of civilian "experts" that included bankers and economists, as well as Army Air Forces officers, had directed their previous efforts to dissecting the key war-making components of Adolf Hitler's Third Reich. The committee members began their examination of Japan in similar fashion by listing industrial linchpins that, if destroyed, would negate Japan's capability to fight. By November, they determined that steel was a key strategic target, and noted that the destruction of six coke plants, essential to the production of steel, would "cause a reduction of 30 percent of total Japanese steel capacity for several months until new sources of fuel could be found." Moreover, "the immediate effects upon the industrial process would be substantial. . . . It is believed that Japan's power to wage war effectively would be gravely impaired probably within six months and certainly within one year after the destruction had occurred."[27]

Steel was one of the six most important strategic targets identified by the COA; others included merchant shipping, aircraft factories, ball bearing plants, radar and radio facilities, and urban industrial areas. The COA did not stress one set of targets over the other, and the inclusion of "urban industrial areas" recognized the important contribution made by cottage industries to Japan's war production—as well as the susceptibility of those areas to fire. "Japanese war production (aside from heavy industry) is peculiarly vulnerable to incendiary attack of urban areas because of the widespread practice of subcontracting to small handicraft and domestic establishments," the COA report stated. "Many small houses in Japan are not merely places of residence, but workshops contributing to the production of war materials."[28] The COA recommended attacks against urban industrial targets between December and May to take advantage of probable weather conditions such as high winds that would maximize the damage from firebombs. The analysts also noted that striking many urban areas simultaneously might "overwhelm the relief and repair facilities of the country as a whole."[29]

At first glance, the COA recommendation of "urban industrial areas" as targets appeared inconsistent with the notions of strategic bombing that had guided America's initial planning for World War II air campaigns. Both AWPD-1, developed before the United States entered the war, and AWPD-42, designed soon after the Eighth Air Force had begun bombing Hitler's Europe, stressed precision attacks against key centers of production to wreck Axis war-making capability. Army Air Forces planners intended those raids to achieve rapid, efficient results once the bomber force received the desired number of aircraft, crews, and logistical support. Japan's industrial pattern, though, did not match Germany's, and both AWPD-1 and AWPD-42 focused on the European war. The COA determined that Japan's cottage factories were an important part of its industrial complex, and the only way to attack that component successfully would be through area bombing. AWPD-1 had not completely dismissed area attacks, and in fact had stated that such raids might occur late in the European war when German morale reached the breaking point.

By the time of the COA report on Japan, Ira Eaker's Eighth Air Force—with Hap Arnold's blessing—had begun using radar to area bomb German cities in attacks ostensibly aimed at industrial targets but actually designed to break German morale. In the case of Japan, the primary purpose of the COA-recommended attacks would be to wreck industry, although the raids would also kill large numbers of civilians. If the bombing worked as intended, it would provide the most efficient means possible to eliminate a key element of Japan's production capability.

While the COA tried to identify Japanese targets, Brigadier General Orvil Anderson, the chief of the planning section of Arnold's air staff, asked the intelligence branch to investigate how the Army Air Forces might best attack them with incendiary bombs. The subsequent October 1943 report compared German cities to those in Japan, observing that Japanese cities were more congested than their German counterparts and that Japanese residences were much more flammable. Combustible material in residential construction could serve as "kindling" for attacks that would also destroy factories and other necessities of war. The report created three categories of vulnerability that applied to Japan's twenty major cities:

Zone I—Most Vulnerable Zone, the commercial center of the inner city containing the most residential congestion, greatest mix of residences and cottage industries, and an average population density of ninety thousand people per square mile; *Zone II—Less Vulnerable Zone,* less congested residential areas containing port facilities, rail yards, warehouses and some completely industrial areas with a population density of fifty-four thousand people per square mile; and *Zone III—Non-Incendiary Zone,* the suburban residential, park, and completely industrial areas, containing factories vulnerable to incendiaries but with fire-resistant business districts and low population density.[30]

AAF intelligence officers also estimated how many tons of bombs were required to destroy the two incendiary zones. They calculated that six tons of incendiaries per square mile would suffice to destroy Zone I completely, while the total destruction of Zone II would require ten tons per square mile. They did not consider Zone I more important than Zone II, because Zone II contained more factories that would affect war production. Zone I, though, contained more people, and its destruction would produce a significant indirect effect on Japan's war effort by killing and dislocating its work force.[31] The recommended instrument of destruction was the M-69 incendiary bomb, a 6.2-pound gasoline gel device tested against simulated German and Japanese residences at Dugway Proving Ground, Utah, between May and September 1943.[32]

Despite the attention given Japan's "Urban Industrial Areas" as potential targets in late 1943, they were only one of many possible target categories, and the emphasis remained on precision bombing with that marvel of air power technology created by American engineering prowess, the B-29 "Superfortress." The B-29 was the war's most expensive weapon system at $3 billion, compared to the next costliest arms project, the $2.2 billion atomic bomb.

The Superfortress traced its roots to a 1939 Army Air Corps production board that had included Charles Lindbergh. Board members called for a heavy bomber with twice the range of a B-17, while Arnold demanded an aircraft that could attack targets two thousand miles away from its home base. Boeing won the contract and took two years to build a prototype, which first flew in September 1942.

The B-29 suffered from production delays and design problems, including four Wright R-350 engines prone to overheating, but contained unique features that made it a truly revolutionary design. The bomber sported the world's first pressurized cabins (it had three—the cockpit, gunners' compartment, and tail gunner's compartment), enabling its eleven-man crew to fly at altitudes in excess of twenty-five thousand feet without having to wear the cold weather gear required by crews on B-17s or B-24s. The high operating altitude made the B-29 difficult for slow-climbing Japanese fighters to intercept. It had a top speed of 350 miles per hour, and a combat radius of 1,600 miles with twenty thousand pounds of bombs (roughly three times the bomb load of a B-17), which allowed it to attack targets in Japan from bases in the Marianas. It further possessed four gun turrets, remotely controlled via four General Electric analog computers, containing a total of twelve .50-caliber machine guns, plus a high-velocity 20 mm long-range cannon in the tail.[33] AWPD-1 and AWPD-42 had both envisaged the B-29 for the European war, flying against Germany from bases in the United Kingdom and Egypt. The need for a heavy bomber that could fly the vast distances required to bomb Japan, combined with lagging B-29 production and the build-up of B-17s and B-24s in Europe, relegated the Superfortress to the Pacific theater.

There, the B-29 formed the mainstay of the Twentieth Air Force, created in April 1944 and directed from Washington DC, by Hap

Arnold. Arnold later claimed that the genesis for an independent bombing force in the Pacific under his command stemmed from his visit to bases in the region in autumn 1942. "There was nothing else I could do, with no unity of command in the Pacific," he contended. "It was something that I did not want to do."[34] That admission rang hollow, however. Arnold had no intention of allowing Army generals and Navy admirals to direct his high-priced bombers as auxiliary support for surface forces and divert them from their primary mission of destroying Japan's vital centers.

The prospects for the B-29s to accomplish that independent goal received a substantial boost in late 1943 at the Sextant Conference of the Combined Chiefs of Staff. At this Cairo gathering, the Combined Chiefs approved the "Overall Plan for the Defeat of Japan," which outlined grand strategy for the conclusion of the Pacific War. The document noted "the possibility that the invasion of the principal Japanese Islands may not be necessary and the defeat of Japan may be accomplished by sea and air blockade and intensive air bombardment from progressively advanced bases." Planning for a possible invasion would continue "if this should prove necessary."[35] Arnold was determined that it would not be. After several discussions with his Joint Chief counterparts—including a session with the Chief of Naval Operations, Admiral Ernest J. King, in which Possum Hansell argued for an independent B-29 force[36]—the Joint Chiefs sanctioned the Twentieth Air Force. The new air force would operate directly under the Joint Chiefs with Arnold serving as "executive agent" to implement their directives. In actuality, the Army Air Forces Commanding General had secured control over his prized B-29s with minimum oversight, and had gained for himself his first ever combat command.

While he received limited interference from the Joint Chiefs in directing Twentieth Air Force, Arnold did have to contend with one higher authority—Franklin Roosevelt. In February 1943, the president proclaimed his progressive hope that air power might provide a relatively inexpensive victory in the Pacific. He called for the bombing of Japan to begin soon to prevent an American advance "inch by inch, island by island" that "would take about fifty years before we got to Japan."[37] Arnold promised that B-29s would begin bombing from China no later than March 1944, but that deadline did not satisfy Roosevelt. On 15 October 1943 the president wrote Marshall that he was "pretty thoroughly disgusted with the India-China matters. The last straw was the report from Arnold that he could not get the B-29s operating out of China until March or April next year."[38] Roosevelt continued to press for an air campaign against Japan from China that he thought would bolster the Chinese war effort. At the Sextant Conference in late November, the president formally committed American support to Chiang Kai-shek and his Chinese army, and the impetus for a B-29 campaign from Chinese bases increased. However, production delays and logistical difficulties shifted the new proposed start date for bombing to 1 May 1944.

Arnold was desperate to fulfill Roosevelt's wishes, not just because they came from the president but also because he believed that the B-29 could make the decisive contribution to ending the Pacific War. His preference was to begin bombing from the Marianas once the Navy and Marines secured those islands. Roosevelt, though, had promised Chiang that American bombers would soon head his way. Until the capture of the Marianas, China offered the only friendly location from which B-29s could attack Japan—and even then, they had the range to strike only Kyushu, the southernmost main island.

When Arnold briefed Roosevelt in February 1944 on "Operation Matterhorn," the projected B-29 assault on Japan from China, as well as on his plans to bomb from the Marianas, he noted that Japanese cities were especially vulnerable to fire. Yet he also re-

197

marked that he aimed to do more than simply create "uncontrol-lable conflagrations in each of them." "Urban areas are profitable targets," he observed, "not only because they are congested, but because they contain numerous war industries."[39] Roosevelt approved Arnold's plan, as well as the provision that would make the Army Air Forces leader the Twentieth Air Force Commander.[40] The president's action heightened the increasing momentum to get the Superfortress into combat—and to obtain rapid results with it once it finally began operations. But as with the European war, the desire for fast results would ultimately overcome the progressive desire to minimize casualties among enemy civilians. From the perspective of those on the ground, a quick victory did not necessarily equate to fewer lives lost.

Despite Arnold's zeal to begin bombing, numerous difficulties delayed the start of "Matterhorn." Mass production of B-29s had finally begun in autumn 1943, yet deliveries occurred slowly, and many of the new bombers suffered from problems because of constant design changes. Only sixteen of the ninety-seven B-29s produced in January 1944 were flyable.[41] To remedy the situation, Arnold created an array of "production modification centers" in central Kansas where design updates occurred en masse to the newly produced bombers; Boeing provided six hundred mechanics to assist. Once the B-29s received the necessary modifications to make them operational, their combat crews arrived and flew them to India—where they faced a new set of challenges to prepare them for their missions against Japan.

Bombing from China

The first B-29s began arriving at Indian bases near Kharagpur in April 1944, and from there they would fly east for one thousand miles to their advanced airfields at Chengtu, China, the site of four 8,500-foot runways that more than three hundred thousand Chinese peasants had constructed by hand. Major General Kenneth "K. B." Wolfe commanded the force of roughly one hundred Superfortresses, their crews, and support personnel that comprised the XX Bomber Command of Arnold's Twentieth Air Force. Wolfe, a pilot from Denver and one of the Army Air Forces' top engineers, had supervised B-29 flight tests and had organized, trained, and led XX Bomber Command from its inception. Still, he never anticipated the logistical nightmare that he would face to get his bombers positioned to raid Japan. To provide the necessary fuel and munitions, C-46 cargo aircraft typically carried one thousand pounds of gasoline and three thousand pounds of bombs on resupply missions across the "Hump" of the Himalayas. B-29s had to shuttle fuel as well, and required *seven* flights from India to China just to build up the needed gasoline for *one* flight from Chengtu against Japan.[42] As Twentieth Air Force Commander, Arnold tried to provide as much assistance as he could from his office half a world away. The stress took its toll, however, and helped trigger his third heart of attack of the war on 10 May. For the next month Possum Hansell, who served from the Pentagon as Twentieth Air Force Chief of Staff, provided Wolfe with guidance while Arnold recuperated.

On 15 June 1944, after a preliminary raid from Indian bases against a Bangkok rail junction, XX Bomber Command finally launched the aptly named "Operation Matterhorn." The attack against the Yawata Iron and Steel Works on Kyushu revealed that the beginning of the bomber offensive did not mean the end of adversity for the B-29 force. To conserve fuel the Superfortresses attacked at night in a bomber stream flying one behind the other; formation flying in daylight would have burned more gasoline. Ninety-two B-29s departed India for Chengtu; seventy-five made it to China; sixty-eight managed to get airborne for the 1,600-mile flight to attack the Yawata factory; of those, only forty-seven dropped their bombs against it—and most of the bombs missed. Darkness, smoke, and haze combined with inexperienced B-29 radar operators to produce the inaccuracies. Only one bomber fell to enemy defenses, though various malfunctions claimed another seven.[43]

Matterhorn continued, but persistent logistical difficulties and dismal weather caused it to occur in fits and starts. Most attacks occurred against steel production facilities, the only significant targets in range from the Chinese bases. Not until 7 July did XX Bomber Command again bomb Japan, and only fourteen bombers completed the mission. The next major raid did not transpire until 29 July, an attack on coke ovens at the Showa steelworks in Anshan, Manchuria, responsible for a third of Japan's steel supply.

Arnold was grateful for the positive response that the B-29s raids elicited from the American press and public, especially in the aftermath of the acclaim received by the Army and Navy for the Normandy invasion, but he could not tolerate a feeble effort that produced minimal bombing results.[44] He decided to replace Wolfe with an innovative bomber commander from the European theater who had a sterling reputation but whom Arnold had never met—the Army Air Forces' youngest major general, Curtis LeMay. Wolfe possessed an excellent engineering background, yet he lacked combat experience. Arnold wanted a combat leader—an "operator"—and LeMay ably fit the bill. He took control of XX Bomber Command on 29 August. A week later, he participated in a renewed attack against the Showa steelworks at Anshan by ninety-five B-29s that produced significant damage.

LeMay was not impressed by the success and instituted a rigorous training program for his crews. It included daylight formation tactics similar to those he had devised for Eighth Air Force, with an emphasis on "lead crews" to guide the formations and signal the remaining crews when to drop their ordnance. To assure that such "pattern bombing" could occur in all weather conditions, both the bombardier and radar operator in the lead aircraft monitored the bomb run so that either could take control of the aircraft depending on the amount of visibility present over the target. By carefully managing his supplies, LeMay increased the frequency and intensity of XX Bomber Command raids. He also increased bombing accuracy. "We are now ten times more efficient than we were in August," he boasted to Arnold at the end of November.[45]

Pleased by the results, Arnold wrote Tooey Spaatz in Europe: "With all due respect to Wolfe he did his best, and he did a grand job, but LeMay's operations make Wolfe's very amateurish."[46] Arnold's letters to LeMay transitioned from a salutation of "Dear LeMay" on 22 September to "Dear Curt" on 17 November.[47] A month later, Arnold complimented LeMay for a recent attack on Singapore that placed 41 percent of the bombs within one thousand feet of the aiming point. "I follow the work of the XX Bomber Command in far greater detail than you probably think," Arnold remarked. "The B-29 project is important to me because I am convinced that it is vital to the future of the Army Air Forces." In a handwritten note at the end of the letter, he added: "Tell all concerned how much the good work being done is appreciated."[48]

By December 1944, questions of "where" and "how" to accomplish good work against Japan loomed large. Ten months earlier the COA had examined target possibilities for Chengtu-based B-29s, and listed shipping concentrations, coke and steel production, aircraft factories, radar and radio installations, petroleum facilities, and urban areas. The COA cited seven urban areas in Kyushu, with a total population of 1,182,000, and noted that in raids against them, the "essential public utilities and thousands of small plants, as well as a number of large plants, would be destroyed."[49]

In August 1944, though, COA members changed their minds. Based on their examination of attacks against German "urban industrial areas," they concluded that "the economic consequences of attack upon such areas [in Japan] are not likely to be large." Acknowledging an inability to estimate the psychological effects of area raids, they pointed to "the successful results achieved in Europe by concentration upon precision target systems," and recommended that the B-29 force do the same. "Attacks upon urban industrial areas should be postponed until ample forces are available *after* completing the attack on precision targets," the COA advised. "The attack should then be concentrated upon the most important industrial areas which are Tokyo, Kobe-Osaka and Nagasaki."[50]

The Offensive Begins from the Marianas

The August COA study went not only to Arnold, but also to Hansell, the Twentieth Air Force's Chief of Staff. As an early disciple of high altitude, daylight, precision bombing, Possum Hansell took its progressive message to heart. He had taught strategic bombing theory at the Air Corps Tactical School during the 1930s; he was a principal architect of AWPD-1 and the primary architect of AWPD-42, both of which called for precision bombing offensives to forestall an invasion of Europe and knock Germany out of the war; and he had put theory into practice as commander of Eighth Air Force's First Bomb Wing from 1 January to 30 June 1943. He had also served as de facto commander of Twentieth Air Force when Arnold had been incapacitated with his third heart attack. Arnold's selection of Hansell to lead XXI Bomber Command from the Marianas came as no surprise. When he landed on Saipan at the controls of *Joltin' Josie, the Pacific Pioneer* on 12 October, Hansell prepared to initiate the main B-29 offensive against Japan that Arnold had long counted on to produce decisive results.

From the Marianas, XXI Bomber Command could attack most of Japan's major cities, but Hansell faced an array of problems before a raid against them could occur. Tokyo was the obvious choice for the first attack, and the COA had designated the Nakajima aircraft engine plant at Musashino, in the northwest part of the capital, as the initial target in a series of raids designed to destroy the aircraft industry. Hansell, though, possessed only one partially finished runway on Saipan while Army engineers struggled to complete complementary airfields on Tinian and Guam. The prospect of constant long-range, high altitude attacks in formation also presented challenges. In stateside practice missions, flown from Kansas to Batista Field in Cuba (the same 1,400-mile distance as from Saipan to Tokyo), engines had caught fire after exhaust valves burned out, and the gunners' plastic viewing bubbles had frosted over above twenty-five thousand feet. Hansell had asked to fly his bombers from the United States to Saipan in formation to gain additional experience. Air Transport Command denied his request, he later observed, "on the grounds that the airplane lacked the range to fly from Sacramento to Hawaii in formation, even without a bomb load and in good weather. The distance was 2,400 miles. We would have to fly 3,200 miles, with a bomb load, in the face of enemy fighters, without weather reporting or navigation aids."[51]

Besides the difficulties encountered in long-range formation flying, Hansell faced a dearth of target information, plus he also had to deal with crews and aircraft unprepared for the missions ahead. His initial orders were to destroy Japan's aircraft industry, but he had no target folders to guide his mission planning. "Our strategic air intelligence was simply non-existent in regards to Japan," he recalled.[52] Not until the 1 November arrival of two B-29s specially modified for photographic reconnaissance did Hansell obtain the needed targeting clues; the aircraft took seven thousand photographs from thirty-two thousand feet, beyond the range of

Japanese flak.[53] More reconnaissance missions followed. Hansell and his staff then had to review the photographs and prepare for the first raid, which Arnold wanted by the middle of November.[54] Hansell scheduled it for the seventeenth. In the meantime, the Seventy-third Wing, originally slated for General Wolfe's XX Bomber Command in China and trained in radar bombing at night, had begun arriving at Saipan at the rate of two or three aircraft per day. Japan's aircraft factories were precision targets that demanded visual bombing with the Norden bombsight. The Seventy-third's B-29s had APQ-13 bombsights designed for radar attacks and ill-suited for precision bombing.[55] Limited time was available for training, and with the first mission looming, several crews would fly against Tokyo without any practice flights in the combat theater at all.

Arnold's impatience for a rapid start to the Marianas offensive stemmed in part from high-level developments in the orchestration of Allied strategy. At Quebec's Octagon Conference in September 1944, the Combined Chiefs of Staff foreshadowed an invasion of Japan's home islands by stating that the Allied mission in the Pacific included seizure of "objectives in the industrial heart of Japan."[56] Once the invasion began, Arnold would lose his chance to score "decisive" results with air power in the Pacific. He knew that the clock had begun ticking for the B-29s to achieve independent success—much as it had for Eighth Air Force in May 1943 after the Combined Chiefs of Staff selected a projected date for Overlord. Three weeks before Hansell took XXI Bomber Command from its training location in Colorado Springs to the Marianas, Arnold wrote him:

> As you well know the original conception of the B-29 was an airplane that would carry tremendous loads for tremendous distances. We have not to date fulfilled this promise. We have flown great distances but we have not carried any sizeable bomb loads. In fact we

have not carried any more bombs and in most cases considerably less than the B-24s and B-17s carry. One of the greatest factors in the defeat of Japan will be the air effort. Consequently every bomb that is added to each airplane that takes off for Japan will directly affect the length of the war. . . .

I know that you, in your position as commander of one of our great striking forces, will do your utmost to help accomplish the earliest possible defeat of Japan. This can only be done by making the best possible use of the weapon at your disposal.[57]

In November, the Joint Chiefs of Staff approved a tentative plan for invading Kyushu in September 1945. Hansell's race against the clock had officially begun.

On 24 November 111 B-29s took off to attack Tokyo's Nakajima aircraft engine factory, responsible for an estimated 30 to 40 percent of all Japanese combat aircraft engines.[58] Brigadier General Emmett "Rosy" O'Donnell, the Commander of the Seventy-third Wing, led the mission, with Major Robert K. Morgan, who had commanded the famed *Memphis Belle* in the European theater, flying as his co-pilot. Vile weather had compelled Hansell to cancel the mission five times. Shortly before it finally occurred, he received a portent that it might not go well. O'Donnell, a Brooklyn native who had commanded a B-17 squadron in the Philippines after Pearl Harbor, and who had also served as a favored colonel on Arnold's Advisory Council, came to Hansell with a handwritten letter. It concerned the forthcoming mission and warned that "the hazards and the lack of training produced risks which exceeded the limits of prudent military judgment." O'Donnell thought that the raid could produce a "disaster," and urged Hansell to forego a daylight attack and instead bomb at night "until the command had a chance to build up its competence."[59] Hansell thanked Rosy for his views, and then burned the letter in his presence to prevent misinterpretation if the raid succeeded.

The attack was far from successful, though not for the reasons that O'Donnell had suspected. Only twenty-four B-29s bombed the engine factory, while another sixty-four dropped their bombs on the city and its docks. An additional seventeen aborted en route to the target, and mechanical difficulties prevented the remainder from bombing at all.[60] The chief problem encountered was unforeseen—jet stream winds of more than 150 mph that whipped through the high altitudes above Tokyo and tossed the bombs randomly across the city. Out of more than one thousand bombs dropped, only forty-eight landed within the Nakajima plant's boundaries.[61] Two bombers were lost, one to a Japanese fighter that rammed it, and the other ditched after running out of fuel on the trip back.

On 27 November eighty-one bombers again took off for the Nakajima factory, but clouds obscured the target and none hit it; on 3 December seventy B-29s attacked it, again with dismal results. Hansell's crews had few answers for the jet stream, which pushed the Superfortresses along at a staggering 445 mph over the ground—much too fast for the Norden bombsight to compensate for its effects.[62] If the crews flew perpendicular to the winds, they still could not correct for the wind velocity. If they flew into the winds, they risked flying so slowly that they would become easy prey for antiaircraft batteries. Hansell tried flying upwind during a 13 December raid against the Mitsubishi aircraft engine factory at Nagoya and had thirty-one bombers damaged by flak, although bombing accuracy showed marked improvements.[63]

Frustration and Debate

Meanwhile, the invasion clock continued ticking, and Arnold grew increasingly frustrated. The Japanese had responded to the attacks on their homeland by launching two night raids from Iwo Jima against Saipan that wrecked four B-29s, left three more unserviceable, and damaged six more.[64] Hansell remained committed to the high altitude, daylight, precision attacks. "I considered that the whole concept of strategic air warfare as a war-winning strategy, carried out by unified air command, was hanging in the balance," he later wrote.[65] At the suggestion of his chief of staff, he had attacked Tokyo with twenty-four bombers in a night raid at lower altitudes on 29 November with incendiaries—his B-29s had dropped high explosive bombs on the other raids—though the results remained disappointing. "I still feel that our primary effort should be by visual bombing, when possible, because it is always inherently more accurate," Hansell wrote Arnold on 16 December, "but with the improvement in radar bombing, I feel that our efforts can be directed against our primary target every time and that it will not be necessary to waste our bombs on large city areas as a secondary effort."[66]

Arnold likely never saw this bit of reasoning. Across the top of Hansell's letter, he scrawled: "Gen. Norstad summarize for me— HHA." Brigadier General Lauris Norstad had replaced Hansell as Twentieth Air Force Chief of Staff when Hansell took over XXI Bomber Command. Norstad had been one of Arnold's "fair haired boys" as an Advisory Council colonel in early 1943, and had served in staff positions in North Africa and Italy before returning to Washington DC in summer 1944. He observed Arnold's impatience when Hansell delayed the initial B-29 raid against Tokyo, and watched the frustration mount as the poor bombing results from XXI Bomber Command arrived at the Pentagon. Norstad encouraged Hansell to send his problems to him, rather than Arnold. "If there are really serious major problems which you feel absolutely must be brought to his attention, don't hesitate to do so," he wrote Hansell on 7 December, "but I think the normal run of difficulties will only be an annoyance to him and can be better handled by me anyway."[67]

Larry Norstad had developed his own ideas about how to address Hansell's difficulties, and many of those notions stemmed from observing targeting deliberations that continued among COA members. In September 1944, soon after he became Twentieth Air Force Chief of Staff, Norstad attended COA meetings regarding target priorities for Japan. Once more, the analysts considered the utility of attacking "urban industrial areas" and focused on the prospects of area bombing Zones I and II in Japan's six most populous cities. Colonel John F. Turner remarked, "We have been intrigued with the possibilities . . . of complete chaos in six cities killing 584,000 people."[68] Turner noted that "successful" raids might produce even more casualties and that Japan's industrial production would drop roughly 15 percent. Later calculations indicated that a drop of only 11 percent would occur, mostly from the output of machine tools, because Zones I and II contained fewer industries than originally thought.[69]

The analysts also considered the psychological impact that such raids might have. While their expert on Japanese culture thought that the panic and fear of fire might cause civilians to demand political reorganization, he did not believe that the Japanese would accept unconditional surrender until the arrival of American troops.[70] The COA members suggested that an "experimental" incendiary raid from Saipan or China against a densely populated area of a city would provide data from which they could make more accurate estimates. In the meantime, they agreed that aircraft factories, especially those producing engines, were priority targets and that the Saipan force should attack them, while XX Bomber Command in China should continue to attack steel production.

The COA's September conclusions underpinned the 10 October 1944 report that they submitted to Arnold—their last formal product of the war. In it, the analysts culled the target systems that they believed would have the most telling impact on Japan's war effort to three: the aircraft industry, urban industrial areas, and shipping. The analysts deemed that the U.S. Navy's sea-control campaign had "checked the expansion of the Japanese economy and rendered the attack on steel through coke much less important," and the same logic applied to other materiel resources.[71]

Most of the report focused on the forthcoming operations of the Marianas-based XXI Bomber Command. The committee members recommended that attacks begin against Japan's five major aircraft engine plants, followed by "an attack upon the industrial areas of Tokyo, Yokohama, Kawasaki, Nagoya, Kobe and Osaka." Such raids would "burn out all housing in Zones I and II" and likely "increase and prolong losses effected by precision attacks on war industries."[72] Still, the analysts noted that area bombing would minimally impact Japan's "front-line strength" because of "the apparent existence of considerable stocks of aircraft components and of excess manufacturing capacity in tanks and trucks."[73] They recommended that area attacks "should be postponed until they can be delivered in force and completed within a brief period."[74] B-29s could also assist in isolating Japan by mining sea lanes.

The committee members further stressed flexibility in adopting their proposed program. They noted that once bombing began from the Marianas, it might reveal "that Japanese fighter defense is so ineffective that attack upon the aircraft industry should not be given precedence over a mining campaign or attacks on urban industrial areas." The analysts further called for a "trial attack against an industrial area on Kyushu or Honshu" during the initial phase of XXI Bomber Command operations before the force had built up to full strength.[75] The target priorities listed in the report became the priorities sent to Hansell in November.[76]

Norstad in particular was impressed by the COA report and thought that its recommendations offered the best chance for air power to make a rapid—and decisive—contribution to victory. On 17 November he wrote Major General Lawrence Kuter, Arnold's assistant chief for plans who frequently oversaw COA activities: "The work of this Committee as represented by its report, was superior. Conclusions reached have been the subject of serious study by this Headquarters and have lead [*sic*] directly to the directive covering the operations of this command for the next three months."[77] That same day Hansell was to begin bombing Japan's aircraft industry from the Marianas, in accordance with the COA outline for operations. While those raids produced meager results, they also showed that Japanese fighters offered feeble resistance to the B-29 force. Arnold remained impatient for bombing success, and Norstad deemed that the time had come to test the prospects of urban area attacks. On 18 December he sent Hansell a message to attack the main residential district of Nagoya with one hundred B-29s dropping the new M-69 gasoline gel incendiary bombs.

Hansell responded to Norstad's directive within hours. "I have with great difficulty implanted the principle that our mission is the destruction of selected primary targets by sustained and determined attacks using precision bombing methods both visual and radar," he answered. "The temptation to abandon our primary targets for secondary area targets is great and I have been under considerable pressure to do so, but I have resisted so far. I am concerned that a change to area bombing of the cities will undermine the progress we have made. However, I am accepting your No. S-18-2 [message number] as an order from you and a change in my directive and I will launch this operation next."[78] Norstad replied that XXI Bomber Command's primary mission remained the destruction of Japanese air power, but the requested strike was a "special requirement resulting from the necessity of future planning."[79]

Hansell did indeed attack Nagoya next. Yet he did so with forty-eight B-29s, not one hundred; his crews aimed at the Mitsubishi aircraft factory, not the city's residential area; and they dropped M-76 incendiaries, not the M-69s that Norstad had requested—the five-hundred-pound M-76 could penetrate brick and concrete structures (like the roof and walls of the Mitsubishi factory), while the lightweight M-69 could not.[80] On 27 December the bombers returned to Tokyo once more to attack the Nakajima factory with high explosive bombs, and once more the results were meager. That same day an exasperated Arnold, mindful of the impression that B-29 operations made on an American public eager for success against Japan—and retribution for the Bataan Death March and Kamikaze attacks—admonished Hansell:

> To oversimplify our basic operating policy, it is our purpose to destroy our targets. For this reason we have avoided announcing in advance what we propose to do and we have carefully screened our news releases to avoid the public's becoming overoptimistic. We want to let the results speak for themselves. However, we must accept the fact that we have a big obligation to meet. To fulfill this we must in fact destroy our targets and then we must show the results so the public can judge for itself as to the effectiveness of our operations. . . .
>
> To me the best evidence of how you are getting along is the pictures of the destruction that you have accomplished against your primary targets.[81]

On 28 December, Hansell's press statement assessing his first raids against Japan appeared in several American newspapers. Despite praising the excellence of the B-29 and its crews, he also noted that "we have much to learn and many operational and other technical problems to solve."[82] Arnold decided that he had heard enough. He told Norstad to head to the Marianas and notify Hansell that he had been relieved from command.

Lemay to the Marianas

LeMay was Arnold's choice for a successor. With the establishment of bases in the Marianas, the offensive from China had lost its urgency, and Arnold directed his staff in late September to study the implications of withdrawing the B-29s from Chengtu.[83] A month and a half later he told LeMay to prepare to take XX Bomber Command to a new location. Arnold added, "I cannot at this time tell you where you will go or when your bases will be ready" and thus LeMay would likely have to stay put "for a matter of months."[84] Hansell's dismissal changed the equation. Moreover, Hansell was a brigadier general, LeMay wore two stars, and LeMay was a B-29 commander who was in-theater and available.[85] Arnold ordered LeMay to proceed to Guam, the new site of XXI Bomber Command, and to arrive there immediately after Norstad. Once Norstad conveyed the news to Hansell, Arnold wanted LeMay available to discuss operations with the man that he would replace.

Hansell accepted his relief with a minimum of complaint, though his ten-page, typed letter to Arnold on the eve of his departure from Guam—a highly detailed discussion of problems that he had faced leading XXI Bomber Command—typified his communications with his boss. At the end of his report, Hansell stated: "I feel, on reflection, that I have erred in not passing on to you my problems in more detail. I have felt that my first consideration should be to solve my problems as best I could, rather than to send complaints to you. Perhaps I have overdone this conception."[86] Ironically, such lengthy explanations of why he had failed to achieve success probably contributed to Hansell's relief. In contrast, LeMay had provided short, pithy summaries of his results directing XX Bomber Command. Those synopses usually contained bomb tonnages along with the amount of damage inflicted to the target—"hard" data that Arnold could show his Joint Chief counterparts to justify his control of Twentieth Air Force and its expensive bombers—and that Arnold could himself use as solace that his B-29s were on their way to achieving decisive results. "Statistics of tons of bombs dropped and of sorties flown are easily compiled, seem factual and specific, and are impressive. Photographs of burned-out cities also speak for themselves," Hansell later remarked.[87]

LeMay fully appreciated the desire for tangible results in Washington DC, but his selection to lead XXI Bomber Command stemmed as much from his flexible attitude, especially his willingness to try new bombing methods, as it did from the numbers that he actually produced. The initial bombing by XX Bomber Command, including several raids after LeMay had taken charge, was particularly poor. A December 1944 study of the command's first ten missions revealed that only 269 bombs out of 5,554 fell within one thousand feet of the aiming point, followed by the comment: "A look at planes lost on these missions brings the realization that it cost us one B-29 to place twelve 500 G.P. [General Purpose] bombs within 1,000 feet of the target." Arnold underlined that sentence and wrote in the margin beside it, "Oh, Lord!"[88] The numbers improved as a result of LeMay's rigorous training policies, yet LeMay—like Hansell in the Marianas—stressed precision attacks against specific industrial targets.

Not until an 18 December mission against the *Chinese* city of Hankow did LeMay conduct an area attack. He initially opposed the raid, but ordered it in response to requests from Lieutenant General Albert C. Wedemeyer, commander of American forces in China, and Major General Claire Chennault, Commander of Fourteenth Air Force, to attack the city that was a key staging area for a Japanese offensive. Eighty-four B-29s dropped 511 tons of incendiaries that burned down half of Hankow and produced a smoke cloud that billowed three miles high.[89] Even though Arnold had not ordered the raid, he wrote Secretary of War Henry Stimson that it provided a valid test of the "efficacy" of firebombing and was significant "from a long range as well as an immediate viewpoint."[90]

Arnold was always looking ahead, because he knew that he had limited time to affect the outcome of the Pacific War. Hansell later reflected upon the overriding importance of achieving rapid results: "'Time' had become an obsessive compulsion—the time for the invasion of Japan. Washington placed great stress upon the end of the war, emphasizing that this carnage must not go on a single week longer than necessary to achieve victory."[91] The progressive vision had indeed become an obsession for Arnold, who realized that the B-29 offensive from the Marianas was the Army Air Forces' last, and best, chance to secure the ideals espoused by his friend and mentor Billy Mitchell—which included service independence. "I am still worried," he wrote Norstad on 14 January. "We have built up ideas in the Army, the Navy, and among civilians of what we can do with our B-29s . . . and yet . . . our average delivery rate against Japan is very, very small. . . . Unless something drastic is done to change this condition soon, it will not be long before the B-29 is just another tactical airplane."[92] Three days later he collapsed with his fourth heart attack of the war. The pursuit of decisive results with air power would continue, but, during its key phase in the Pacific War, the newly minted five-star Commanding General of the Army Air Forces would no longer appear at the forefront of the B-29 campaign. Instead, the standard bearer of the Twentieth Air Force's effort to score a knockout blow now became its Chief of Staff, Larry Norstad.

LeMay and Norstad had communicated frequently during LeMay's tenure with XX Bomber Command, and both shared Arnold's views about the B-29's importance to the war effort as well as to future force structures. "I think we all agree that the composition and size of our post war Air Force depends a great deal on the B-29 performance in the Pacific," LeMay wrote Norstad on 16 November 1944.[93] Norstad concurred, telling LeMay after his assumption of command in Guam: "I am convinced that the XXI Bomber Command, more than any other service or weapon, is in a position to do something decisive."[94] Those perspectives mirrored Arnold's, and his guiding hand never truly left Twentieth Air Force as he read mission reports and message traffic from his recuperation bed in Coral Gables, Florida. Still, Arnold could not actively lead the force that mattered most to him, and he would have to count on Norstad and LeMay to make his vision of rapid success a reality. "General Arnold was absolutely determined to get results out of this weapons system," LeMay recalled.[95] The new commander of XXI Bomber Command did not intend to disappoint his ailing boss.

LeMay soon realized that satisfying Arnold—and Norstad—would not be easy. LeMay was especially upset with the staff that Hansell had left him, which he described to Norstad as "practically worthless." He further told Norstad that Rosy O'Donnell's Seventy-third Wing was "in bad shape" and that "you better start warming up a sub for Rosy in case we have to put him in. . . . I get the impression from Rosy on down they think the obstacles too many and the opposition too heavy to crash through and get the bombs on target."[96] Much as he had with XX Bomber Command, LeMay started an intensive training program for his crews in the Marianas. Yet he discovered that training alone would not cure the problems that had plagued Hansell.

Like his predecessor, LeMay believed in the merits of high altitude, daylight, precision bombing against specific targets essential to enemy war production. That faith could not overcome the obstacles of wind, clouds, and distance. Jet stream winds continued to scatter bombs, clouds frequently obscured targets, and 1,600-mile flights to and from cities like Tokyo and Nagoya tested the limits of the B-29's range, often leading to ditchings on the way back to the Marianas. From his 20 January assumption of command through the first week of March, LeMay conducted six precision raids, and all produced miserable results. A 27 January attack by seventy-six B-29s on Hansell's nemesis, the Tokyo Nakajima aircraft plant, placed *no* bombs on the target at a cost of nine Superfortresses.[97]

From Precision to Obliteration

The bleak production dismayed LeMay, Arnold, and Norstad, who all searched for alternatives to achieve success. Three days before he had taken charge of XXI Bomber Command, LeMay asked his friend Major General Fred Anderson, the Deputy Commander of Eighth Air Force Operations, for information on night photography that could assist in night bombing missions. "This weapon [the B-29] has tremendous possibilities, and I do not believe that we have more than scratched the surface of new developments, modifications, and methods," LeMay stated. "Certainly, I will never permit the operations of a Command to which I am assigned to become routine and if there is a means of getting more bombs on to the target I propose to find it."[98] Arnold revealed similar thinking in his scribbles on a 30 January memorandum brought to him by his deputy, Lieutenant General Barney Giles. Giles noted that Japanese fighter opposition had increased in intensity over Tokyo and Nagoya, and wrote: "To offset this apparent concentration of fighter strength, we are instructing LeMay to direct his efforts at more widely dispersed targets and to engage in night fighter operations until our long-range fighters are available for employment, which should be in the latter part of February." Arnold marked out the second use of the word "fighter" and put parentheses around the word "night," and then wrote "OK" across the sentence.[99]

Norstad's answer to overcoming the lack of precision was the same that he had provided Hansell—area attacks on the densely populated centers of Japanese cities. He had failed to get Arnold's endorsement for his plan to commemorate Pearl Harbor's anniversary with a fire raid on the emperor's Tokyo palace, though Arnold's response indicated that he opposed the target, not the concept of incendiary attack. "Not at this time," Arnold wrote on the proposal. "Our position—bombing factories, docks, etc., is sound. Later destroy the whole city."[100] He had not demurred earlier when Norstad directed Hansell to attack the center of Nagoya with incendiaries, which Arnold could convey to the press and the public as an attack on Japan's cottage industry.

That rationale still applied, Norstad surmised, after the change at the top of XXI Bomber Command. Norstad suggested firebombing the most densely populated part of Kobe, and LeMay complied. On 4 February—one day after almost one thousand B-17s targeted government buildings in Berlin's main residential district with 2,279 tons of bombs—sixty-nine B-29s attacked the center of Kobe with 159 tons of incendiaries.[101] Norstad deemed results of the raid "inconclusive" after reconnaissance photographs showed fire damage covering 0.15 square miles of the city and three of twelve industrial targets damaged.[102] Eight days later he told LeMay to prepare to create a "conflagration that is beyond the capacity of fire-fighting control" in Nagoya.[103] The following week LeMay received a directive stating that aircraft engine plants remained his primary objective, but "selected urban areas for test incendiary attack" were now second in priority.[104]

On 20 February Norstad requested a maximum effort, telling LeMay to choose between Nagoya and Tokyo and send as many aircraft as possible from the 73rd, 313th, and newly arrived 314th

Bomb Wings. LeMay countered that he needed additional time for training. Norstad responded that "circumstances beyond our control" dictated the mission, which historian Michael Sherry suspects was the savage fight for Iwo Jima then underway. Similar logic had helped persuade LeMay to firebomb Hankow, and now the effort would support his own force—the capture of Iwo Jima would eliminate Japan's ability to attack the Marianas and would provide an emergency landing field for battered B-29s that could not make it to the Marianas after a raid.

Yet another reason likely caused Norstad to demand an attack. On 16–17 February, Navy fighters and fighter bombers of Admiral Marc A. Mitscher's Task Force Fifty-eight flew almost one thousand sorties over Tokyo, despite taking off in rain and snow squalls for many of their missions. They claimed more than five hundred Japanese aircraft destroyed, plus they also attacked the Nakajima aircraft engine factory and damaged it severely.[105] The carrier raids garnered headlines in the United States, including from the *New York Times*, which described them as "the most daring operation of the Pacific war to date."[106] Recuperating in Florida, Arnold noted the attention that the Navy attack received, as well as another headline announcing the one-thousandth B-29 produced by Boeing's Wichita plant. He commented to Giles that if only sixty or eighty B-29s could attack Japan at a time, "a change in management is certainly in order."[107]

LeMay needed little prompting in the aftermath of the Navy's attack on Tokyo. On 19 February he sent 150 B-29s against the same Nakajima factory that he and Hansell had bombed so many times—and that the Navy had now bombed successfully—and once again scored no hits on it, this time at a cost of six bombers.[108] On 25 February, in response to Norstad's prodding, XXI Bomber Command mounted its largest mission to date with 172 Superfortresses using radar to bomb Tokyo's Zone I with 411 tons of M-69 incendiaries.[109] The B-29s attacked at altitudes of twenty-three thousand to thirty thousand feet, though most crews bombed individually because heavy cloud cover prevented attacks in formation. LeMay had originally wanted them to return to the onerous Nakajima factory, but the prediction of dense clouds over the target—along with the lack of success against it thus far—persuaded him to condone the area attack. Despite the B-29s' dispersal, the raid was brutally effective, and the bombs—which fell in the midst of a heavy snowstorm—burned out one square mile of the city. No B-29s were lost to Japanese defenses.

In his report to LeMay following the mission, Brigadier General Thomas Power, commander of 314th Wing that had recently arrived at Guam, posed a question: If the crews had attacked at a lower altitude with a larger bomb load, would more destruction have resulted? The vile weather forced Power to fly his B-29 at a low altitude to Japan before climbing to twenty-five thousand feet to release his bombs, and the lower altitude reduced fuel consumption by producing less stress on the engines—which could have permitted his aircraft to carry more bombs.[110] In the meantime, LeMay dispatched 192 Superfortresses on yet another precision strike against Tokyo's Nakajima factory, and once more the results were dire; cloud cover obscured the target and most bombs fell in the city's urban areas.[111]

LeMay began to accept the reality that the high altitude, precision bombing of Japanese targets was impossible. In early March he ordered twelve of Rosy O'Donnell's crews to bomb a tiny island near Saipan at an altitude of fifty feet with delayed-fuse bombs to determine the feasibility of a low-level attack.[112] He also wrote Norstad:

We have been having a hell of a time with the weather lately. . . . If we put our formations on top of it going in, the bomb load drops to

219

practically nothing. To try and beat these weather conditions, I am going to try to assemble a formation over Japan itself. I think we can get away with it a few times anyway.

Another out is to try some night bombing. I don't believe it is an efficient method of operation but this is another case of a few bombs on the target being better than no bombs at all.[113]

LeMay knew that this letter would likely not reach Norstad before he saw Norstad in person; perhaps he wanted to provide a written rationale to justify the radical approach that he planned to take. On 2 March Giles had notified Arnold, "I am sending Norstad out to the Pacific to discuss questions with LeMay that can be ironed out only through personal contact," and LeMay received word of the impending visit.[114] He had little doubt what it meant, or that its impetus came from Arnold. "General Arnold needed results," LeMay recalled. "Larry Norstad had made that very plain. In effect, he had said: 'You go ahead and get results with the B-29. If you don't get results, you'll be fired.'"[115]

Norstad's directive to attack Zone I in both Tokyo and Nagoya had not changed, and area bombing—with incendiaries—offered the best means to inflict some damage to Japan's war effort as well as provide photographic proof of the damage rendered. LeMay knew that the night, low-level area attacks that he envisioned were certain to kill thousands of Japanese civilians, yet, based upon his calculations of Japanese defenses, they also provided the best chance for his crews to survive. His goal now matched the cold-blooded thinking that rationalized the obliteration of German cities—an air power–induced early end of the war that would save American lives. LeMay aimed to achieve it by losing the minimum number of his own men in the process,[116] and he viewed his action as ethical as well as laudatory. "Actually, I think it's more immoral to use *less* force than necessary, than it is to use *more*," he later wrote. "If you use less force, you kill off more of humanity in the long run, because you are merely protracting the struggle."[117]

Like his counterparts in Europe, LeMay's logic presumed that increased brutality would hasten victory, and that fewer people would die from his incendiary campaign than would perish if he failed to initiate it. That projected outcome, though, remained uncertain, and many Japanese would reach a different conclusion.

Aerial Deluge

While much of the credit for the 9 March raid against Tokyo went to LeMay, in reality he simply implemented a strategic design set in motion by the Committee of Operations Analysts, approved by Arnold, and pushed forward by Norstad. Arnold endorsed area attacks because they offered the best prospect for rapid, tangible results—results that he also believed would prove decisive in ending the war. LeMay's low-level tactics and stripping armament and gunners from his B-29s conserved fuel and doubled the bombs that his aircraft could carry. Yet the key decisions—the choice of targets and the type of ordnance to drop on them—came from Arnold and Norstad. As Michael Sherry notes, LeMay "had the illusion of making his own choices . . . because the details were left to him. LeMay would also sincerely believe that he made the command decision."[118] Arnold and Norstad were content to have him believe it. LeMay demonstrated that he could achieve the destruction that they demanded and continued to display that capability in the raids that followed. After returning to Washington DC in mid-March, Arnold addressed his letters to LeMay as "My dear Curt."[119]

LeMay's low-level, night campaign continued against Japan's major urban areas. More than three hundred B-29s attacked Zone I in Nagoya on 11 March and burned down two square miles of

221

the city. Two nights later 274 Superfortresses torched the heart of Osaka and wiped out eight square miles. On 16 March 307 bombers attacked Kobe, destroying three square miles. Finally, on 18 March, 290 B-29s again bombed Nagoya, wrecking another three square miles and completing the series of incendiary attacks on Japan's four most populous cities. Combined, the five raids incinerated nearly thirty-two square miles of urban real estate—which equated to 41 percent of the destruction inflicted on German cities by the Army Air Forces *during the entire war*. The devastation required less than 1 percent of the total bomb tonnage dropped on Germany, and it cost twenty-two B-29s and their crews.[120] From the progressive perspective—as it had evolved among American airmen by 1945—LeMay's series of five incendiary attacks marked the epitome of efficient destruction.

Arnold and Norstad now focused on how others would perceive that destruction—and how rapidly it would translate into decisive results. Banner headlines in many newspapers announced the devastation of Japanese cities. While grateful for the attention, Arnold cautioned LeMay and Norstad that "editorial comment [is] beginning to wonder about blanket incendiary attacks upon cities therefore urge you to continue hard hitting your present line that this destruction is necessary to eliminate Jap home industries and that it is strategic precision bombing."[121] Norstad continued that mantra in a 23 March press conference after he returned to Washington DC. Resorting to statistical analysis, he noted that the Tokyo raid alone resulted in "1,200,000 factory workers made homeless [and] 369,000 square feet of highly industrialized land . . . leveled to ashes." Incendiary bombing was just "the economical method of destroying the small industries in these areas . . . of bringing about their liquidation." When asked if any change had occurred "in the basic policy of the Air Forces in pin-point bombing [and] precision?" Norstad replied, "None."[122]

Many American newspapers accepted that explanation and stressed the "precise" nature of attacks "to cripple the enemy's war potential."[123] Yet Norstad and fellow Army Air Forces leaders knew the all too obvious truth—that LeMay's bombers killed tens of thousands of Japanese civilians in some of the most horrible ways imaginable. Moreover, intelligence reports stated that most Japanese factories lacked the necessary resources to operate them, and that cottage industries now made a meager contribution to the limited amount of front-line war production that remained.[124]

Still, the message that Army Air Forces commanders presented—both to themselves as well as to the rest of the world—was one highlighting their progressive faith in efficient precision bombing to wreck Japan's industrial web. For the 11 March raid against Nagoya, Twentieth Air Force headquarters described the city as "home of the world's largest aircraft plant . . . with the Mitsubishi aircraft engine works exceeding in size our own Willow Run plant," even though the Mitsubishi factory was not in the target area and received only "minor damage" during the attack.[125] Likewise, the XXI Bomber Command report summarizing the raids on Tokyo, Nagoya, Osaka, and Kobe observed: "It is noteworthy that the object of these attacks was *not* to bomb indiscriminately civilian populations. The object was to destroy the *industrial and strategic targets* concentrated in the urban areas of these four cities."[126]

Such internal statements demonstrated the depth of the conviction among Army Air Forces leaders to their progressive ideals. Indeed, for some, the vision had become reality—they saw no distinction between the theory of precision bombing against specific industrial targets to achieve rapid, efficient results, and the reality of area attacks on residential districts to achieve the same goal. Colonel Cecil E. Combs, a member of the XXI Bomber Command staff with both Hansell and LeMay, wrote his former boss: "Without abandoning the concept of precision destruction of priority targets the Twenty-first [wings] have been experimenting with incendiary missions and the results . . . indicate the high degree of vulnerability of Japanese industry as a whole."[127] After the war LeMay added: "Japanese targets being largely inflammable, we hit vulnerable areas with firebombs. Let me emphasize that this was not a deliberate deviation from precision to area bombing. We hit only areas when enemy war-making capacity was spread over large areas, as in the 'cottage industries' surrounding factories or when weather forced us into radar bombing, visual precision being impossible."[128]

LeMay's postwar comment was disingenuous, for at the time he knew that his four-city series of attacks had targeted Zone I in each—the densest area of population that also contained the least amount of industry. Norstad wrote him on 3 April with a new list of targets, noting that those assigned in March "were selected on the basis of a compromise between industrial importance and susceptibility to fire," but that new areas "represent more nearly the top industrial areas. They also appear to be most susceptible to fire attack, but they do not represent any compromise."[129] Like Tooey Spaatz, his counterpart in Europe who had unleashed savage area attacks against German cities, LeMay hoped that his raids' intensity would pay dividends with a quick end to the war. "The destruction of Japan's industry by air blows alone is possible," he declared on 15 April in a comment that drew a reprimand from Norstad for openly predicting victory through air power.[130]

While Spaatz did not announce that prospect, he harbored the same hope, and both he and LeMay could claim that their bombing had a tangential connection to industrial capability. Yet Spaatz knew that his radar-directed area attacks missed most of the factories that he targeted, and LeMay knew that his low-level area raids hit the parts of Japanese cities contributing the least to the war effort in terms of industrial production. For both, achieving rapid results had become the overriding concern, and brute force became the methodology to assure speed.

The enormous bomb tonnages, aimed at urban areas, ably supported the overarching political objective of unconditional surrender, while against the Japanese, the desire for retribution further condoned area attacks. As long as the Japanese (and the Germans) refused to yield, they would pay an indelible price. Roosevelt believed that memories of such destruction would help dissuade the Axis populations from pursuing future war.[131] Against the Japanese, American airmen generally reflected the sentiments of most Americans and felt little compassion for an enemy that they increasingly viewed as treacherous.[132] By early 1945, the American public had learned of atrocities that the Japanese had committed against captured American troops in the Philippines, which heightened the hunger for revenge that had emanated from Pearl Harbor.

Kamikaze attacks that began at Leyte Gulf in October 1944 also intensified the call for retribution. Arnold, who visited the Philippines in June 1945, noted in his diary: "There is no feeling of sparing any Japs here, men, women or children: gas, fire, anything to exterminate the entire race exemplifies the feeling."[133] Rosy O'Donnell wrote LeMay a week after the war ended that his service in XXI Bomber Command "gave me an opportunity, not only to repay the humiliating experience which I suffered at the hands of the Japs in the early days of hostilities, but also to put in a lick for the many fine men who were not so fortunate in getting out of their clutches."[134] The priority on quickly ending the war to save *Allied* lives meshed well with the desire for revenge. Yet even without the yearning for retribution, the emphasis on achieving rapid results with air power, when combined with the goal of unconditional surrender, virtually guaranteed the devastation of an urbanized, militaristic society that viewed the war as a righteous endeavor.

Momentum Builds

The Japanese refused to succumb to the massive March bombings, and LeMay lacked the capability to continue constant incendiary attacks. Despite the terrible toll of civilians killed and the enormous destruction rendered to their cities, the Japanese kept fighting with the same intensity they had demonstrated before raids. American Army and Marine forces invaded Okinawa on 1 April and did not control the islands until 21 June—at a cost of almost fifty thousand American casualties, of whom more than twelve thousand were killed or missing.[135]

The mounting losses in the fight for Okinawa intensified the demand for an air power–generated victory that would forestall an invasion of the home islands. LeMay's March attacks had expended most of his supply of incendiaries, and, with the exception of two mid-April raids against Tokyo and another against Kawasaki, no more firebombing occurred until mid-May after the Navy had replenished his incendiary stocks. In the meantime, he returned to precision methods with high explosive bombs to strike new targets that he received from Norstad. Those targets consisted of aircraft engine plants, oil, chemical production facilities, and, after 16 April, airfields to support the Okinawa invasion.[136] The B-29s also conducted extensive aerial mining operations in the Sea of Japan that severely restricted movement among the home islands and ultimately sank or disabled eighty-three ships.[137]

Arnold was eager to reignite the incendiary campaign, which, unlike mining, produced immediate empirical evidence of the damage inflicted. He urged LeMay to "put the maximum weight of effective bombs on Japanese targets" and noted that the Army Air

Forces "alone are able to make the Japanese homeland constantly aware of the price she will pay in this futile struggle." Observing that LeMay would control almost a thousand B-29s by July (he had received XX Bomber Command's Superfortresses when Japanese troops threatened Chengtu early in 1945, and newly manufactured aircraft continued to arrive in the Marianas), Arnold asserted: "Under reasonably favorable conditions you should then have the ability to destroy whole industrial cities should that be required." Arnold left no doubt that it would be. Yet he persisted in emphasizing attacks on industry, remarking that "it is apparent that attacks similar in nature to that against Tokyo have a most significant effect on industrial production."[138]

LeMay returned to his incendiary campaign on 14 May with a daylight assault on Nagoya. A follow-on night attack against the city on 16 May was so successful that it no longer appeared on the Twentieth Air Force target list.[139] Fire raids against Tokyo, Osaka, Kobe, and Kawasaki followed, and by mid-June a total of 105.6 square miles in Japan's six largest cities were smoldering ruins with an estimated 112,000 civilians in them dead.[140] The devastation came at a price—in May alone eighty B-29s were lost, though many more made it to the emergency landing field on Iwo Jima.[141] Meanwhile, the Japanese kept fighting.

New president Harry S. Truman called a meeting with the Joint Chiefs on 18 June to determine, "Can we win the war by bombing?"[142] Marshall answered that the United States could not, based on the example of the European war, and outlined the plan for an invasion.[143] At the gathering—which Arnold missed because of touring Pacific bases—Truman expressed his intention "of economizing to the maximum extent possible in loss of American lives" and that "economies in time and money [were] relatively unimportant."[144] Time, however, was vital to Arnold. He sent LeMay to Washington DC in his stead to brief Marshall and the Joint

Chiefs on the progress of the B-29 campaign and its prospects for eliminating an amphibious assault on Japan.[145] LeMay told the Chiefs, as he had told Arnold on Guam, that by 1 October B-29s would have destroyed all Japanese industrial facilities and Japan could not continue fighting with its reserve supplies wrecked.[146] Marshall fell asleep during his briefing.[147] Preparations for Operation Olympic, the invasion of Kyushu scheduled for 1 November, continued.

When LeMay returned to Guam he intensified his campaign against Japan's urban areas. He began incinerating twenty-five of Japan's smaller cities, often with as many as five hundred B-29s on a single raid. Arnold fully backed the effort, telling LeMay, "We have the Nip where we want him."[148] On 16 July Superfortresses attacked Oita, a town of sixty thousand that contained *no* industry and only "a vital naval air depot" that was not a target.[149] LeMay complemented his offensive in late July by having his B-29s drop leaflets that warned of attacks on potential target cities and urged surrender. The ability to announce future attacks and then conduct them made a powerful impression on the Japanese, and actually contributed to achieving the prewar progressive aim to avoid civilian casualties—many people who read the notices survived LeMay's onslaught by evacuating the cities listed.[150]

While the B-29s mauled Japan, a debate over the viability of the incendiary effort raged in Washington DC between members of the United States Strategic Bombing Survey (USSBS), a largely civilian research team analyzing the impact of American air campaigns, and the Joint Target Group (JTG), an intelligence organization created by the Joint Chiefs in September 1944 to identify and evaluate Japanese air targets.[151] Based on their examination of European bombing, the USSBS members argued that attacks on Japan's transportation network, especially rail and watercraft traffic, would produce the most benefit, followed by raids on oil, chemical production, and electric power. They discounted the effectiveness of the incendiary attacks, which they compared to the RAF's effort against German morale, and recommended that Twentieth Air Force return to precision bombing.[152]

Culminating Devastation

Tooey Spaatz, now wearing four stars and in Washington DC en route to the Pacific to command the United States Strategic Air Forces there, agreed with the USSBS representatives when he met with them in late July. Arnold had yielded control of Twentieth Air Force to Lieutenant General Nate Twining, and Eighth Air Force would reconstitute on Okinawa, commanded by its former European commander, Lieutenant General "Jimmy" Doolittle, while Spaatz oversaw both organizations as USSTAF Commander, with LeMay serving as his chief of staff. Yet when Spaatz arrived on Guam at the end of the month, he continued the incendiary campaign in addition to attacking precision targets. Indeed, on the night of 1 August, B-29s burned Hachioji, another town of roughly sixty thousand people.

Spaatz also arrived on Guam with written orders to drop the atomic bomb. He was uncertain that such a device was necessary to induce Japanese capitulation. After examining the post-strike photographs from LeMay's raids, he sent a message to Arnold that "unless the Japanese were intent to commit national suicide they would surrender under the present strategic bombing."[153] *When* they might surrender, though, remained the great unknown. LeMay believed that the bomb offered the chance to end the war but was skeptical that it would work as advertised. "I knew we had a big bang coming," he later recalled, "but it really was a little beyond my comprehension how big a bang it was going to be."[154] In planning the Hiroshima raid, LeMay determined that the mission would attract less notice from the Japanese if it appeared as a typical attempt to gather weather information. Accordingly, only three B-29s participated on 6 August, with the bomb-laden *Enola Gay* flown by Colonel Paul Tibbets Jr.—the same officer who had piloted the lead aircraft in the Eighth Air Force's first heavy bomber mission against Hitler's Europe. Once over Hiroshima, the careful Tibbets polled his crew to verify that he was indeed above the target city, and then began the bomb run.[155]

Between seventy thousand and eighty thousand people, mostly civilians, died from the bomb dubbed "Little Boy," though many others would later perish from burns and radiation sickness.[156] Norstad's thoughts on the attack revealed just how far his commitment to air power's progressive ideals had taken him. In a private message to Spaatz on 8 August, he noted that he wanted pictures of Hiroshima released showing the aiming point in the city's center so that "the accuracy with which this bomb was placed may counter a thought that the Centerboard [atomic bomb delivery] project involves wanton, indiscriminate bombing."[157] Spaatz displayed a different mindset and tried to prevent a second atomic attack on an urban area. After Hiroshima, he called for dropping the second atomic bomb outside a city as a show of force.[158] His plea went unheeded, and on 9 August at least thirty-five thousand people died instantly in the atomic raid against Nagasaki.[159] On 14 August, with peace negotiations ongoing, 449 B-29s attacked Japan that day and 372 that night.[160] Arnold "wanted as big a finale as possible" and aimed to guarantee in no uncertain terms that air power played *the* decisive role in ending the war.[161]

Following Hiroshima, Spaatz informed reporters that the atomic bomb probably precluded an invasion of Japan and that a similar bomb against Germany could have shortened the European war by at least six months—remarks that drew the ire of George Marshall.[162] After Nagasaki, had the Japanese failed to surrender, Spaatz now wanted to drop a third atomic bomb on Tokyo to

compel a rapid end to the war.[163] Most American air commanders agreed that the atomic attacks broke Japan's will to fight and
saved an enormous number of Allied lives.[164]

Allied political leaders reflected those sentiments as well. Truman claimed after the war that Marshall had estimated an invasion might cost five hundred thousand American lives,[165] though
in the 18 June 1945 meeting with the Joint Chiefs (that Arnold
had missed), the president had received conflicting projections.
Marshall's calculation of thirty-one thousand casualties in the first
thirty days of fighting on Kyushu was among the lowest totals,
but that estimate omitted potential Navy losses and did not project when the fighting would end; Admiral William Leahy anticipated Kyushu losses exceeding two hundred thousand.[166] Ultra intelligence intercepts in the month after the meeting indicated that
triple the number of estimated Japanese troops actually defended
the selected Olympic invasion beaches, and Marshall likely notified Truman of the update in late July.[167] The impetus to obtain a
rapid, inexpensive victory—from the American perspective—led
Truman to approve the atomic attacks even if his numbers were
indefinite. Yet he framed the first atomic raid from a progressive
perspective resembling Norstad's and noted on 9 August that Hiroshima was "a military base . . . because we wished in this first
attack to avoid, insofar as possible, the killing of civilians."[168] British Prime Minister Winston Churchill provided a similar progressive view of the atomic bomb's utility—with questionable numbers as a rationale—in his typically vivid prose:

> To quell the Japanese resistance man by man and conquer the coun-
> try yard by yard might well require the loss of a million American
> lives and half that number of British. . . . Now all this nightmare pic-
> ture had vanished. In its place was the vision—fair and bright in-
> deed it seemed—of the end of the whole war in one or two violent

shocks. . . . To avert a vast, indefinite butchery, to bring the war to an end, to give peace to the world, to lay healing hands upon its tortured peoples by a manifestation of overwhelming power at the cost of a few explosions, seemed, after all our toils and perils, a miracle of deliverance.[169]

Assessment

LeMay would have argued that Churchill's remarks appropriately described the rationale for the incendiary attacks, and that those raids alone would have ultimately compelled surrender without an invasion—an assertion supported by the U.S. Strategic Bombing Survey.[170] That contention downplayed the Soviet Union's 8 August entry into the Pacific War and the condition of Japanese troops in Manchuria opposing the Soviet advance, factors that—along with the lack of resources, relentless thrust of America's island-hopping campaign, devastation of cities, and shock of the atomic bombs—likely combined to produce Japanese capitulation.[171] Indeed, for all the emphasis AAF leaders placed on destroying Japan's industry through incendiary attack, the Survey observed that strategic bombing had less impact on Japan's production capability than did shortages imposed by sea blockade and merchant shipping losses.[172] Production hours lost because of bombing rose from 20 percent in 1944 to more than 40 percent in July 1945, by which time industrial production had declined to 35 percent of its wartime peak.[173]

The Survey also claimed that the LeMay's fire raids undercut Japanese public support for the war. Data collected after the conflict showed that only 19 percent of the populace believed that Japan could not win before LeMay's incendiary assault began; the number had increased to 68 percent on the eve of surrender, of which more than half credited air attacks *other* than the atomic raids as the reason for their beliefs.[174] Still, the people's morale never cracked, and faith, stoicism, and apathy enabled them to endure the horrors suffered at the hands of the Army Air Forces. In fire raids against sixty-six urban areas, 8.5 million Japanese civilians lost their homes—roughly one-third of all Japanese living in cities. The Survey estimated total civilian deaths from "conventional" bombing and the atomic raids at 330,000, though they may well have exceeded 900,000.[175] More Japanese civilians likely died from American weaponry than did Japanese combatants, and the vast majority of civilians died from American bombs.[176]

For most American airmen, air power finally fulfilled the progressive promise of a rapid, efficient victory—the b-29 campaign lost 1.38 percent of all combat sorties and cost the lives of 2,148 men in fourteen months of bombing, compared to 26,000 men killed in Eighth Air Force alone after thirty-one months of attacks in Europe.[177] Most air commanders viewed the offensive against Japan as proof that a powerful, concentrated bombing effort, unhindered by diversions, could produce dramatic results. "Our campaign against Japan was a more clear-cut case of the proper use of air power than Europe," LeMay contended after the war. "The true buildup of air power in Europe came after the invasion."[178]

The Japanese example further provided significant impetus to fulfill the dream of service independence. With the war over, the campaign for an autonomous Air Force loomed, and many airmen were eager for it to start. Eleven days after Japan's surrender, LeMay wrote his friend Fred Anderson, who now served in the Pentagon on Arnold's air staff:

Do you know what General Arnold's thought is on my returning to Washington now that the war is over? My interest in this theater has more or less folded with the Japs and I am anxious to get into the fight for a separate Air Force. Most of us believe out here that we must get it quick or not at all. My own personal views are that we must get the ball rolling in the next 30 days or fail again. None of us of course have any desire to finish out our service under the same conditions that we have had for the last fifteen years.[179]

In LeMay's eyes—and those of many of his contemporaries—the air campaign in the Pacific had now achieved the progressive ideals proclaimed by Nap Gorrell, Billy Mitchell, and the Air Corps Tactical School. Service independence was a natural consequence of that victory. The principles of progressive American air power, LeMay and his cohorts believed, would work well to justify that autonomy in the future.

7 · Progressive Legacies

It is a fundamental principle of democracy that personnel casualties are distasteful. We will continue to fight mechanical rather than manpower wars.

• GEN. HENRY H. ARNOLD, 1944

Only air power can frequently circumvent enemy forces and attack strategic centers of gravity directly. Other components, on the other hand, need to fight their way in—normally with large casualties. Air operations—especially with modern weapons and accuracy as used in the Gulf war—are very much likely to result in fewer casualties to either side. Air power then becomes quintessentially an American form of war; it uses our advantages of mobility and high technology to overwhelm the enemy without spilling too much blood, especially American blood.

• COL. JOHN A. WARDEN III, 1992

---

2 September 1945

Tooey Spaatz stood on the deck of the USS *Missouri* and watched a seemingly endless stream of B-29s pass low overhead. The spectacle, which also included vast formations of Army Air Forces and Navy fighters, was an awesome display of American air power following the formal Japanese surrender in Tokyo Bay. Spaatz was the only American representative present at each of the war's major surrender ceremonies—at Rheims and Berlin in May 1945, as well as at Tokyo—and he could take grim satisfaction in knowing that much of the devastation that he observed in the two enemy capitals resulted from men and aircraft that he had led. As he watched on the *Missouri* with the other Allied representatives, he was the acknowledged commander of the world's mightiest aerial strike force.

Postwar Perceptions

The American public and its political leaders also acknowledged the Army Air Forces' contribution to concluding the Pacific War, and they viewed that contribution from a progressive perspective. Yet their definition of "progressive air power"—had they used such a term—would have now mirrored the definition that air commanders would have given it since at least the summer of 1943 in Europe and March 1945 in the Pacific: air power designed to end the war as rapidly as possible with the fewest American lives lost in the process. Most Americans believed that the atomic attacks on Hiroshima and Nagasaki had accomplished exactly that. That conviction—along with the belief that the nation would rely on strategic bombers and atomic bombs to decide a future conflict—enabled airmen to embrace the grail of service autonomy in September 1947. As Billy Mitchell had predicted, the new U.S. Air Force became the nation's first line of defense, and the key to defending the country now rested on the ability to attack and destroy any potential aggressor with air power.

For American airmen, World War II did not perfectly fit the progressive ideals that many of them had held on the eve of the conflict. They had entered the war believing that they possessed the necessary technology and a blueprint for using it that would enable them to wage war in pristine fashion. Relying on high altitude, daylight precision bombing, they would sever the key strands of an enemy's industrial web, bring its war-making capability to a halt, and compel surrender—while at the same time they would validate the need for a separate air force. The entire process would be quick, inexpensive, and efficient—the precise destruction of a small number of vital targets would risk few airmen and would kill a small number of civilians, thus averting the carnage from a clash of armies like that generated by World War I's Western Front.

Although the character of World War II matched that envisioned by Mitchell and Air Corps Tactical School instructors—a global struggle against enemies viewed as direct threats to America's security—the conflict soon developed its own momentum that proved difficult to restrain. "Unconditional surrender" was an outgrowth of the war's evolution, and unconditional surrender and rapid victory were not complementary objectives against fanatical foes like Nazi Germany and Imperial Japan. The former goal demanded the destruction not only of war-making capability, but also of hostile governments and the way of life that they fostered, and those objectives could not be obtained quickly. In addition, the aim of unconditional surrender may have inadvertently lengthened the war by causing German and Japanese leaders to fight harder than they might otherwise have done since early capitulation provided them with no benefit.[1] When combined with the goal of rapid victory, unconditional surrender produced such brutal applications of force as the area bombing seen in both theaters. In the meantime, unexpected "frictional" developments further shaped the air campaigns and undercut the progressive predictions of prewar planners.[2] Diversions and production problems delayed the buildup of heavy bomber forces; key industrial targets proved difficult to identify and destroy under wartime conditions; weather, wind, and climate produced constant challenges to effective bombing; and bombers, especially in the European theater, were much more vulnerable than anticipated.

Given the aim of rapidly destroying the fascist regimes, the aerial technology available, and the impact of friction on the technology's employment, air power was not the antiseptic instrument of finite destruction that Mitchell and Tactical School instructors had forecasted, nor was it necessarily "cheap" in terms of men or money. American bomber crews in Europe paid a heavy price for their attempts to gain daylight air superiority over the continent in time to permit an invasion of France in spring 1944. The B-29 was the war's costliest weapon, which contributed to Hap Arnold's zeal to gain a return on the investment in it. The desire to achieve quick success, and hence limit American losses, consistently trumped the desire to limit enemy civilian casualties—and also produced losses among civilian populations in occupied countries.

Still, many airmen during the war continued to think in prewar progressive terms. They sincerely *believed* that their bombing benefited all concerned because they were certain that it guaranteed a quicker end of the war than a reliance on surface forces alone—and the sooner the killing stopped, the better for the world as a whole. Their assertion presumed a strategic equation: a quicker end of the war = fewer deaths. But that logic was uncertain, even regarding the likelihood of saving American lives, because other outcomes were possible. For instance, reducing the incendiary effort against Japan, eliminating the atomic bombs, and increasing aerial mining might, in concert with a vigorous Soviet advance in Asia, have produced Japanese surrender later than mid-August but before the 1 November date scheduled for Operation "Olympic." Such an outcome would have likely saved more American lives by exposing B-29 crews to less danger than they endured from overflying Japanese cities, and probably would have produced fewer civilian casualties. Similarly, a less intense bombing of German urban areas, and greater emphasis on close air support, might have yielded victory in more time but with fewer losses—for all concerned—than actually occurred. The faith of air leaders in the perceived progressive merits of strategic bombing—which they viewed as the surest path to service autonomy—led them to dismiss alternatives for using heavy bombers in an auxiliary role to surface forces.

For most air commanders, the great dilemma was *how* strategic bombing would hasten the war's end. Assuming that they correctly identified the targets that would fatally damage the enemy's war effort and destroyed them, what assurances did they have that the destruction would induce rapid surrender? Curtis LeMay told Arnold in June 1945 that the war would end by 1 October because by then B-29s would have destroyed all Japanese industry.[3] Likewise, the Committee of Operations Analysts often estimated how the loss of certain industries in the United States would impact America's war-making capability, and then applied those projections to Germany and Japan. Such mirror-imaging presumed "rational" behavior and downplayed the enemy's will to keep fighting (it downplayed American will as well). Most air commanders understood that will was an essential part of the enemy's war effort and that breaking it *would* produce collapse. Indeed, AWPD-1 noted that an attack against German morale late in the war might prove decisive, and both Eaker and Spaatz launched area attacks designed to break Germany's will to fight. LeMay's initial incendiary raids—as well as the atomic bombs—targeted Japan's will. Yet airmen could only guess at the impact such bombing might have on speeding the end of the war, especially against the fanatical opposition that they faced.

The time element had a significant impact on the conduct of the air campaigns in both Europe and the Pacific, and Arnold was always conscious of a ticking clock as he pressed his commanders to achieve results independent of land and sea forces—the pursuit of service autonomy added to the impetus for rapid results. At great cost, the Eighth and Fifteenth Air Forces achieved air superiority over the European continent, but they could not forestall the Normandy invasion, nor could they score a knockout blow against Germany before ground forces overran much of the country. Eaker and Spaatz relied on widespread radar bombing—precision methods were useless for much of the weather encountered—

239

against Germany's war-making capability as well as its will, and radar bombing devastated the residential areas of German cities. The goal of rapid victory subsumed all other prewar progressive rationales; it sanctioned heavy losses of aircrews and civilians, and air commanders relentlessly pursued that goal convinced that it assured fewer losses than would the war's continuation.

That logic guided the bombing of Japan as well as Germany. Against Japan, weather conditions foiled high altitude precision bombing, and the nature of Japanese industry would have made the utility of such bombing problematic even in the absence of jet stream winds. Air commanders on the Marianas could point to a nine-month campaign that was remarkably efficient from the American perspective. For the loss of fewer than 2,500 airmen, the B-29 offensive (punctuated by two atomic bombs) incinerated almost all of Japan's most populous cities and helped to compel a surrender prior to an invasion of the home islands. Untold numbers of Americans—and Japanese—were spared from savage ground fighting that might have persisted for more than a year. Precluding that combat cost the lives of at least 330,000 Japanese civilians.

In the war's aftermath, many airmen continued to view air power's contribution to victory in prewar progressive terms. Shortly after he replaced Arnold as Commanding General of the Army Air Forces in 1946, Spaatz wrote an article for *Foreign Affairs* that lauded strategic bombing's ability to minimize the war's total costs:

> Our land and sea forces, supported by air, could be expected to contain the most advanced echelons of our enemies, and gradually drive their main armies into their heavily fortified citadels. But the essential question remained. How was their military power to be crushed behind their ramparts without undertaking an attritional war which

might last years, which would cost wealth that centuries alone could repay and which would take untold millions of lives? . . . The development of a new technique was necessary. Some new instrument had to be found. . . . The outcome of the total war hung in the balance until that new technique had been found and proved decisive in all-out assault. The new instrument was Strategic Air Power.[4]

After the war, LeMay contended that his bombers had efficiently destroyed Japan's war-making capability before Hiroshima, and noted that the atomic bomb "was anticlimactic in that the verdict was already rendered."[5] He also maintained that his bombing, in producing a quicker end to the conflict, had saved Japanese lives as well as American. LeMay further claimed—in his memoirs— that some postwar Japanese understood his motives and had reacted positively to them.[6]

Ira Eaker agreed that civilian death and destruction caused by bombing was regrettable but necessary. He observed after the war that Allied leaders "deeply regretted the necessity of endangering 'defenseless women and children' in the vigorous prosecution of their campaigns, but all realized that such was necessary to prevent a greater loss of human life." Eaker also stressed that the goal of quickly ending the war dictated many of his decisions as an air commander, and he referenced the 1944 bombing of the medieval monastery at Monte Casino to make his point. "Our purpose in bombing Monte Casino was the hope that it would break the stalemate; save future U.S. and Allied casualties; and affect [sic] an earlier end of the campaign against the Germans in Italy," he recalled. "Thus, we did not permit our knowledge that on top of Monte Casino was one of the oldest churches in Christendom, prevent us from accomplishing our primary mission— the earliest end of the war."[7]

Possum Hansell argued that the European war could have ended sooner if American political and military leaders had adhered to AWPD-1, the plan that he had helped craft in August 1941 to guide a bomber offensive against Germany. "If we had followed the plan which was eventually approved the devastation which characterized Germany in March of 1945 might have been imposed by mid-summer of 1944," he maintained. "Invasion, if it were needed under those conditions, might have been an operation of 'occupation' against slight resistance."[8] LeMay agreed that an invasion of France was not essential to produce Allied victory once the Army Air Forces had achieved daylight air superiority over the continent. "I believed that once we had the complete upper hand in the air we could have waited for an inevitable German capitulation," he contended in 1982.[9] Hansell remarked after the war that achieving control of the air sped victory in Europe, making it less costly for the Allies. "The air offensive did achieve the latter part of the objective of AWPD-1," he wrote. "It did make an invasion feasible without excessive losses. It did achieve the defeat of the German Air Force. Without that achievement, there would have been no invasion."[10]

Progressive Doctrine

Following the war the views of air leaders like Spaatz, LeMay, Eaker, and Hansell solidified into doctrine for the new U.S. Air Force. Much of that doctrine reflected the progressive ideals that airmen had possessed before the war, and many airmen believed the war validated those notions. Their convictions, strengthened by the attainment of service autonomy soon after the conflict, made World War II a template for "victory through air power," and that template highlighted the belief that bombing had scored a knockout blow in the Pacific. Major General Fred Anderson typified the perspective of many postwar air leaders in a letter to Spaatz eight days after Nagasaki: "I wish to congratulate you and your staff on your superior handling of the final stages of the strategic war against Japan. I wish to congratulate you upon proving to the world that a nation can be defeated by air power alone."[11]

Most airmen thought that America's vast superiority in strategic bombers and atomic bombs assured that future wars would be quick, cheap, and efficient compared to the savagery that had killed tens of millions from 1939–45. Even in the aftermath of the Korean War—a "limited" conflict that did not conform to airmen's expectations—the progressive notions underpinning Air Force doctrine remained little changed from the ideals espoused at the Air Corps Tactical School. The authors of the 1955 edition of the Air Force's Basic Doctrine Manual anticipated a conflict with the Soviet Union but were mindful of the recent experience in Korea. Regardless of the type of conflict that next emerged, they believed that air power would decide it quickly and efficiently. They noted: "War has been characterized in the past by a general pattern of events in which military forces were engaged in an extended struggle of attrition in surface battles. With air forces and modern weapons systems available, it no longer is necessary to defeat opposing armed forces as a prerequisite to conducting major operations directly against an opponent either in his sovereign territory or in any other locality."[12] The manual further stated: "Of the various types of military forces, those which conduct air operations are most capable of decisive results. . . . They provide the dominant military means of exercising the initiative and gaining decisions in all forms of international relations, including full peace, cold war, limited wars of all types, and total war."[13]

The total war with the Soviets never materialized, but eight years of limited war in Vietnam produced no substantial changes to the Air Force's progressive mindset. The 1984 edition of the Basic Doctrine Manual stressed that "aerospace forces have the power to penetrate to the heart of an enemy's strength without first defeating defending forces in detail."[14] The manual identified the enemy's heart as a "selected series of vital targets," which, if destroyed, would wreck the enemy's capability and will to fight.[15] Of the ten possible targets listed, six were components of a nation's industrial apparatus. The manual also noted that strategic bombing could occur successfully "at all levels of conflict,"[16] an obvious reference to Vietnam and President Richard Nixon's December 1972 bombing of the North that many airmen believed produced the Paris Accords a month later. LeMay expressed that conviction when an interviewer asked him in 1986 if America could have won in Vietnam. "In any two-week period you want to mention," he answered.[17] LeMay believed—as did many other airmen—that the political controls restraining much of the bombing in the North had prevented air power from producing a rapid, inexpensive victory much earlier in the conflict.[18]

For air commanders today, the political restrictions inherent in limited war are givens, yet service doctrine continues to stress a progressive viewpoint. The current edition of the Air Force's Basic Doctrine Manual, written in 2003, lists "strategic attack" first among a list of seventeen "air and space power functions."[19] The manual further emphasizes that strategic attack not only gives the United States a unique capability to defeat an enemy without bloody ground combat, but also provides the means to transform the character of war itself:

> Air and space power is inherently a strategic force and an offensive weapon. Unlike other forms of military power, air and space power may simultaneously hold all of an enemy's instruments of power at risk—military, economic, and diplomatic. Employed properly, it offers the capability of going to the heart of the enemy sources of strength, avoiding prolonged attrition-based surface combat operations as a precursor. . . . Strategic attack, as envisioned today, is more than just

a function—it is also a different approach for thinking about war. It is the manifestation of the Airman's perspective: thinking about defeating the enemy as a system.[20]

Warden and the New Progressives

The concept of "the enemy as a system" originated with Colonel John A. Warden III, the modern Air Force's intellectual heir to the progressive notions developed by Mitchell and the Air Corps Tactical School.[21] Warden had flown as a forward air controller in Vietnam, and his frustrations in that restrained conflict caused him to consider a new approach for applying air power to achieve quick success. During the decades that followed he developed ideas that would form the basis of America's air campaign plan for the 1991 Persian Gulf War—and for much of the Air Force's planning in subsequent conflicts.

Like Mitchell, Warden stressed air power's "revolutionary" characteristics, and he fully shared Mitchell's progressive vision. For both men aerial technology was the key to reforming war. The incredible accuracy possible with an array of precision-guided "smart" munitions was a linchpin of Warden's ideas. He believed that those munitions, which included bombs with significant penetrating power, and the development of stealth aircraft gave the United States a dramatic capability to fight limited wars by relying almost exclusively on air power. He argued that those technological developments enabled American air forces to attack a prospective enemy's "centers of gravity" directly, which they could do by circumventing its surface forces. "Air power then becomes quintessentially an American form of war; it uses our advantages of mobility and high technology to overwhelm the enemy without spilling too much blood, especially American blood," he insisted.[22]

For Warden, the key center of gravity of a nation—or any organized group capable of fighting—was leadership. That element comprised the center ring of his five-ring model that specified the major components, or systems, essential to war-making capability. Surrounding leadership was a ring of key production, which for most states included electricity and oil. Surrounding key production was a ring of infrastructure, comprising transportation and communications, and surrounding it was a ring of population, which included food sources. Finally, a ring of fielded military forces surrounded the population.

Warden contended that leadership was the most critical ring because it was "the only element of the enemy . . . that can make concessions" and that attacking it promised "the quickest and cheapest" path to obtaining victory.[23] If that ring could not be attacked directly, the goal then became to confound the leadership's ability to direct war-making activities, and air power could target the outer rings. Yet the focus of the attacks remained their impact on the center ring. He cautioned against attacking military forces, which he labeled "a means to an end," and urged that they "be bypassed—by strategy or technology."[24] Warden also eschewed direct attacks on civilians, and his rationale for attacking industry mirrored an Air Corps Tactical School text: "If a state's essential industries (or, if it has no industry of its own, its access to external sources) are destroyed, life becomes difficult, and the state becomes incapable of employing modern weapons and must make concessions."[25]

Warden's beliefs reinforced the Air Force's progressive vision, and that vision has meshed well with the war aims of American presidents during the last two decades. Beginning with the 1991 Persian Gulf War, American presidents have consistently embraced air power's progressive notions in their pursuit of victory. At the time of Saddam Hussein's invasion of Kuwait in August 1990, Warden was the Air Staff's deputy director of "Checkmate," its plans and war-fighting division. A combination of factors led to his ideas forming the basis for the Desert Storm air campaign against Iraq, and chief among them was that his notions complemented President George H. W. Bush's objectives. Bush viewed Saddam's aggression as a grave threat to the energy needs of the United States and its allies, but he would not condone devastating Iraq to remove the threat. Bush also viewed America's need to respond as a moral crusade, part of "the burden of leadership and the strength that has made America the beacon of freedom in a searching world."[26] He outlined his war aims as the removal of Iraqi troops from Kuwait, restoration of the Kuwaiti regime, protection of American lives, and conditions that would provide "security and stability" in the region.[27] An air campaign that targeted Saddam—whom Bush equated to Hitler—or his power base would help fulfill those goals.

Bush intended to remove Iraqi troops from Kuwait in the most effective, inexpensive way possible. Thirty-seven days of bombing by a vast coalition air armada against targets in Iraq and Kuwait facilitated a four-day ground offensive that liberated Kuwait for a cost of only 148 American combat deaths.[28] Although an estimated 2,300 Iraqi civilians died in the forty-one-day air campaign,[29] the image that much of the world—and, in particular, the U.S. Air Force—took from the war was one of a remarkably efficient, high technology air offensive that rapidly produced maximum results for minimum costs.

That image resonated with Bush's successor. Beginning in 1993 in Bosnia, President William Clinton committed American air power to UN and NATO efforts to preserve a multiethnic state in Bosnia and halt Bosnian Serb ethnic cleansing against Muslim and Croat populations. He eschewed sending ground forces, convinced that such an option might prove too costly in terms of lives risked and damage inflicted. Air power's sensational precision capability promised to minimize both concerns. In Operation "Deliberate Force" against the Bosnian Serbs—twelve days of bombing in August and September 1995 in which 708 of 1,026 bombs dropped were precision-guided munitions—NATO aircraft struck forty-eight Bosnian Serb targets.[30] Bosnian Serb leaders halted their attacks against Bosnia's Croat and Muslim populations, and Clinton declared that "the NATO air campaign in Bosnia was successful."[31]

His announcement omitted the likely impact of a fast-moving hundred-thousand-man offensive from the Croatian army against the northern areas of Serb-held Bosnia, as well as an invasion from the south mounted by the Muslim-Croat forces of the Bosnian Federation. Those ground assaults reclaimed significant chunks of Bosnian territory that the Serbs had controlled and threatened to take more.[32] To the president, though, air power rapidly achieved success and eliminated the need for American ground forces. The air attacks risked few American lives—only one aircraft was shot down and its pilot rescued—plus enemy civilians emerged relatively unscathed—the Bosnian Serbs claimed that bombing had killed just twenty-five noncombatants.[33]

Clinton's perception that air power had coerced the Bosnian Serbs caused him to return to that formula in response to Serb ethnic cleansing in Kosovo, and his motivations for bombing in 1999 paralleled his 1995 objectives. "Why are we in Kosovo?" he asked rhetorically during the midst of the air campaign designated Allied Force. "Because we have a moral responsibility to oppose crimes against humanity and mass ethnic and religious killing where we can. Because we have a security responsibility to prevent a wider war in Europe, which we know from our two World Wars would eventually draw America in at far greater cost in lives, time, and treasure."[34]

Although the 1999 Kosovo conflict was a periodically waged

guerrilla struggle unlike the conventional war that Bosnia had become by 1995, Clinton believed that air power offered the best chance to accomplish his Kosovo goals at a minimum cost. He further thought that bombing was a more acceptable solution than a ground invasion not only to the American public but also to the nineteen states comprising NATO, and he placed a high premium on preserving the alliance. Yet he understood that maintaining NATO support—as well as an endorsement from the global community at large—would be difficult "at a time when footage of airstrikes is beamed to homes across the world even before our pilots have returned to their bases, a time when every accidental civilian casualty is highlighted."[35]

The seventy-eight-day Allied Force air campaign produced mixed results, but the impression of a rapid, efficient application of air power persisted with many observers. Much of the bombing targeted Serb installations in the vicinity of Belgrade. American aircraft flew the bulk of the sorties and dropped most of the twenty-eight thousand munitions expended, 38 percent of which were precision-guided.[36] The war did not end, however, until the Serbs had expelled eight hundred thousand Kosovar Albanians from Kosovo, and Serbia's loss of Russian backing and the threat of a NATO invasion may have contributed to Serbian President Slobodan Milosevic's decision to stop fighting.[37] Precision bombing also did not guarantee infallibility, as B-2 pilots mistakenly bombed the Chinese embassy on the evening of 7 May, and several instances occurred in which bombs injured civilians. Still, the bombing killed just five hundred Serb noncombatants, and only one American aircraft—and no pilots—were lost.[38] Given that air power was the sole instrument of military force used, some onlookers, like the distinguished British military historian John Keegan and Dartmouth professor Andrew Stigler, claimed that bombing had achieved a dramatic solo victory.[39] "There are certain dates

in the history of warfare that mark real turning points," declared
Keegan. "Now there is a new turning point to fix on the calendar: June 3, 1999, when the capitulation of President Milosevic
proved that a war can be won by airpower alone."[40]

Such seemingly antiseptic displays of air power led President
George W. Bush to rely on bombing as a significant component
of his military ventures in Afghanistan and Iraq. Bush's father
had relied heavily on bombing to liberate Kuwait, and the elder
Bush's use of air power likely heightened his son's perception that
bombing could achieve dramatic results. Against Taliban and al
Qaeda forces in Afghanistan, U.S. Air Force and Navy aircraft in
Operation "Enduring Freedom" were by far the dominant components of American military force marshaled in the aftermath of
the 11 September terrorist attacks. Bush relied on twenty thousand troops of the Afghan Northern Alliance for support on the
ground, supplemented by small numbers of American and NATO
Special Forces.[41] The collapse of the Taliban regime in December
2001 after two months of bombing, and with only twelve fatalities suffered by American ground forces, further vindicated Bush's
belief that air power could achieve a quick, inexpensive victory.[42]
He commented in December 2001 that precision-guided munitions offered "great promise" and "have been the majority of the
munitions we have used. We're striking with greater effectiveness,
at greater range, with fewer civilian casualties." Thus, he insisted,
America was "redefining war on our terms."[43]

The president concluded from the destruction of the Taliban regime that air power could help in deposing a recalcitrant Saddam
Hussein thought to possess weapons of mass destruction. Bombing provided the initial thrust of Operation "Iraqi Freedom" in
March 2003. When intelligence reports indicated the Iraqi dictator was in a farm near Baghdad, Bush ordered an air strike on
the facility. The attack by two F-117 stealth fighters with laser-

guided bombs failed, but precision bombing remained the centerpiece of the "shock and awe" air campaign that began on 21 March. More than 1,500 bombs and cruise missiles struck Iraqi governmental and military installations that night in a fantastic display of American military prowess. Although the raids caused few civilian casualties, they garnered widespread media attention, and much of the coverage from around the globe was highly critical.[44] Bush was upset that many observers failed to appreciate the American ability to apply lethal doses of air power precisely. He later remarked that "it was not understood that the United States had found a way to wage war that as much as possible spared civilians, avoided collateral damage and targeted the leaders and their means to fight and maintain power. Wars of annihilation, carpet-bombing, and fire-bombing of cities should be a thing of the past."[45]

Twenty-First-Century Dilemmas of Progressive American Air Power

Progressive sentiments have continued to guide America's application of air power in both Iraq and Afghanistan, but the results have not matched the rhetoric. Both conflicts have evolved into struggles against irregular units in which ground combat has dominated. Enemy fighting techniques have varied from guerrilla warfare, replete with suicide terrorism, booby traps, and roadside bombs, to occasional massed uprisings. Generally, when the enemy chooses to fight, civilians are likely to be close at hand, which increases the chances of bombing mistakes even with the sophisticated technology now available in the likes of Predator drones and satellite-guided bombs. In Iraq, an estimated 1,560 civilian deaths resulted from air strikes between 2006 and 2008.[46] In Afghanistan, according to UN assessments, air raids killed 116 civilians in 2006, 321 in 2007, and 522 in 2008.[47]

The trend is especially discouraging in Afghanistan, where efforts to compensate for the lack of ground troops with air power have given way to increased restrictions on bombing near civilians, and in Pakistan, where American drones have attacked Taliban and al Qaeda forces in the tribal areas on Afghanistan's border.[48] America's success in stabilizing Afghanistan depends in large measure on how public opinion—both locally and throughout the Muslim world—perceives America's use of force. Afghan President Hamid Karzai has condemned American air strikes on several occasions, noting that civilian casualties continue to undermine the support of the Afghan populace for the American war effort.[49] Episodes of collateral damage in Pakistan, where air strikes that killed fourteen terrorist leaders have also killed an estimated seven hundred civilians, have produced intense anti-American protests in an already fragile nation that possesses nuclear weapons.[50] Aware of the negative impact of civilian losses, Taliban and al Qaeda insurgents have tailored their tactics accordingly, and work hard to guarantee that the news media broadcast bombing mistakes to the world at large.

Besides dealing with collateral damage, American political leaders and air commanders today still face the same great problem that confronted Roosevelt and his air chiefs—determining *how* bombing that destroys the desired targets will speed the end of a conflict. The odds that current precision-guided munitions will hit their desired target are exponentially higher than they were for the high explosive and incendiary bombs carried by B-17s and B-29s. Yet determining the ultimate impact of such bombing that does strike home—whether the target is a supply of roadside explosives, a suspected nuclear facility, or a notorious terrorist leader—remains incredibly difficult. The task is especially arduous when confronting enemies, reminiscent of the Germans and Japanese in World War II, who are utterly committed to the cause that they support. Historian Robert F. Futrell, in his analysis of the Air Force in the Korean War, commented on this problem that remains a great dilemma for those who tout air power's ability to achieve rapid, inexpensive success: "Air intelligence could target physical objectives for attack and could calculate the physical damage done to the air targets by air strikes, but it was not able to determine what significance a particular physical objective might have to the Communist regime nor could it project the effect of a given amount of destruction upon the hostile regime's primarily political decision to end the fighting."[51]

The progressive vision that has shaped American air power during the past eight decades has created enormous challenges for it in the years ahead. That vision portrays bombing as a rational, just military instrument that helps achieve victory more quickly, with less destruction and fewer lives lost—on both sides—than surface combat. This notion of efficiency has had an enduring appeal to American air commanders and presidents alike. In many respects those political chiefs have found air power's siren song even more enticing than have the airmen, for it seemingly offers political leaders a way to eliminate a perceived evil cheaply, and without having to inflict undesired pain. In the classic phrasing of Johns Hopkins professor Eliot Cohen, "Air power is an unusually seductive form of military strength, in part because, like modern courtship, it appears to offer gratification without commitment."[52]

Much like President Roosevelt, Presidents George H. W. Bush, Clinton, and George W. Bush all turned to bombing to help fight wars that each viewed as a just crusade, and each believed that air power's progressive ideals blended well with the war's righteous cause. President Barack Obama has also relied on bombing to thwart America's enemies.[53] The presidents have all tried to achieve success by risking the fewest American lives, and relying on air power has risked fewer Americans than turning to armies or navies. Yet the war aims sought and the type of war encountered have profoundly affected *how* air power could be applied. Roosevelt pursued unconditional surrender in a total war. That political objective condoned such methods as area bombing to produce victory as rapidly as possible. His successors have all pursued goals far more circumscribed in conflicts far more constrained. Despite having vastly more sophisticated technology available, presidents can no longer apply it in unlimited fashion—limited goals demand limited applications of violence. In the age of CNN and al Jazeera, collateral damage is an American enemy's best friend, and perceptions of damage inflicted often count more than reality. The limited goals sought in the wars that America is most likely to fight will demand not only extreme precision from air power, but also, in many cases, infallibility, and that is a very tall order for any type of military force.

Ultimately, tying air power's progressive ideals to a wartime crusade leads to a strategy based more on faith than sound reasoning. Episodes of collateral damage will continue to offset positive pronouncements of air power accomplishments made by American leaders. Although proponents may proclaim that air power can end wars quickly and cheaply, skeptics—in particular, non-American skeptics—can argue that such progressive views apply only to proponents who are also U.S. citizens. The emphasis on the speedy conclusion of hostilities and a small loss of life appears ideally suited to Americans, who have the world's greatest air power and have displayed a willingness to use it, in the last two decades, as their first choice of military options.

To some observers, the espoused progressive notions are morally bankrupt, and really equate to assuring the smallest possible loss of life for American combatants, rather than guaranteeing no civilian casualties—as was indeed the case during the last years of World War II. Author David Halberstam summarized Operation "Allied Force" against Serbia as follows: "The war may have started with Milosevic's brutality against the Albanians, but what much of the world was soon watching was a big, rich, technologically advanced nation bombing a poor, little country, and doing it in a way that showed its unwillingness to accept casualties itself."[54] Air Force Lieutenant General Michael Short, the air commander responsible for conducting Allied Force, seemingly confirmed that assessment by listing one of his primary objectives as "zero losses. . . . I wanted to destroy the target set and bring this guy [Milosevic] to the negotiating table without losing our kids."[55] Many of the world's onlookers likely nodded at Short's admission, and believe that such emphasis will continue to guide applications of American air power.

Many around the globe also discount American assurances that precision bombing will not threaten noncombatants. Although American political and military leaders continue to make such promises, bombing mistakes consistently prove them wrong. The more limited the conflict, the greater the progressive rhetoric seemingly becomes, and the greater the probability that "collateral damage" will undermine the political goals sought.

The key problem in stressing progressive air power as an aspect of American military prowess is that it does not suit war's basic nature, much less the types of war that America now faces. As Prussian military philosopher Carl von Clausewitz observed, the fundamental nature of war is constant, a swirling mix of violence, hatred, and enmity; calculated reason; and probability and chance.[56] No amount of technological wizardry can remove those components, no matter how sophisticated the technology, or how sound the intentions of those who apply it.

Clausewitz added: "Kind-hearted people might of course think there was some ingenious way to disarm or defeat an enemy without too much bloodshed, and might imagine this is the true goal of the art of war. Pleasant as it sounds, it is a fallacy that must be exposed: war is such a dangerous business that the mistakes which come from kindness are the very worst."[57] More than half a century after Spaatz stood on the deck of the *Missouri* in Tokyo Bay, American air commanders and their political leaders still control the world's mightiest air force. As long as they continue to rely on it to help achieve their objectives in war, they must emphasize Clausewitz's realism, not the progressive notions of Mitchell and his successors. In the end, progressive air power is an enticing idea waiting to be victimized by conflicting goals, uncooperative enemies, and the imposing momentum that every war generates.

NOTES

Introduction

1. Even after serving as president, Roosevelt was frequently addressed as "Colonel," an acknowledgment of his service as a colonel with the Army's First Volunteer Cavalry Regiment (the Rough Riders) during the Spanish-American War.

2. "Roosevelt Up in Aeroplane," *New York Times*, 12 October 1910; Missouri Writers Project, *Missouri: A Guide to the "Show Me" State* (New York: Duell, Sloan, and Pearce, 1941), 104; "TR's flight was risky, flier says," *Cleveland Press*, 12 October 1910, reprinted at upi.com and accessed at http://about.upi.com/?q=AboutUs/index.php%3FContentID%3D20051018121141-32491.

1. Genesis in the Great War

Lt. Col. E. S. Gorrell to Chief of Air Service, memorandum, 2 January 1918, in Maurer Maurer, ed., *The U.S. Air Service in World War I* (Washington DC: U.S. Government Printing Office, 1979), 2:154.

1. "Curtiss Flies, Albany to New York, at the Speed of 54 Miles an Hour," *New York Times*, 30 May 1910.

2. "Col. Gorrell Dead; Chief of Airlines," *New York Times*, 6 March 1945; *The Howitzer: The Yearbook of the United States Corps of Cadets—1912* (New York: Charles L. Willard, 1912), 83; Juliette A. Hennessy, *The United States Army Air Arm: April 1861 to April 1917* (Washington DC: Office of Air Force History, 1958, 1985), 167–70.

3. Thomas H. Greer, *The Development of Air Doctrine in the Army Air Arm, 1917–1941* (Washington DC: Office of Air Force History, 1955, 1985), 1–2.

4. Quoted in Alfred H. Hurley, *Billy Mitchell: Crusader for Air Power* (New York: Franklin Watts, 1964; new ed., Bloomington: Indiana University Press, 1975), 17.

5. Greer, *Development of Air Doctrine*, 2. Baker did replace Brig. Gen.

George P. Scriven, the chief signal officer, with Brig. Gen. George O. Squier. Scriven had labeled aviators "unbalanced as to grades, young in years and service, and deficient in discipline and the proper knowledge of the customs of the service and the duties of an officer."

6. Joint Army and Navy Airship Board to Secretary of War through Secretary of Navy, "Organization of Technical Staff and Estimate of Funds Needed to Obtain One Rigid Airship," 26 March 1917, file General Correspondence, 1907–1917, box 6, William Mitchell Papers, Library of Congress.

7. John H. Morrow Jr., *The Great War in the Air: Military Aviation from 1909 to 1921* (Washington DC: Smithsonian Institution Press, 1993), 185, 265; Hennessy, *U.S. Army Air Arm*, 196–97; Edgar S. Gorrell, *The Measure of America's World War Aeronautical Effort* (Northfield: Norwich University, 1940), 2; Hurley, *Billy Mitchell*, 20; Edward M. Coffman, *The War to End All Wars: The American Military Experience in World War I* (Madison: University of Wisconsin Press, 1986), 190.

8. I. B. Holley, *Ideas and Weapons* (New Haven: Yale University Press, 1953; repr., Washington DC: Office of Air Force History, 1983), 45.

9. Holley, *Ideas and Weapons*, 54.

10. Hurley, *Billy Mitchell*, 31.

11. Raymond H. Fredette, *The Sky on Fire: The First Battle of Britain 1917–1918 and the Birth of the Royal Air Force* (New York: Holt, Rinehart, and Winston, 1966), 53–67; David Nevin, *Architects of Air Power* (Alexandria VA: Time-Life Books, 1981), 27; Lee Kennett, *A History of Strategic Bombing* (New York: Charles Scribner's Sons, 1982), 24–26.

12. Holley, *Ideas and Weapons*, 54.

13. Holley, *Ideas and Weapons*, 42–45, 54–55.

14. On 24 May 1917, 140 Italian aircraft, including 29 Caproni bombers, dropped ten tons of bombs on Austrian positions near the Carso River. By August, the Italians would mass 260 aircraft in a single raid. See "Caproni's Warfare" (22–30), an English-language synopsis of Italian bombing missions from August 1915 to February 1918, file 168.661-162, Air Force Historical Research Agency (hereafter AFHRA), Maxwell Air Force Base AL. Not until the end of 1918, however, did the Italians possess a bombing force capable of conducting *sustained* combat operations. See Kennett, *History of Strategic Bombing*, 29–30.

15. J. L. Boone Atkinson, "Italian Influence on the Origins of the American Concept of Strategic Bombardment," *Air Power Historian* 4 (July 1957):

NOTES TO PAGES 13–17

142. At the time of the Bolling mission, Douhet was serving a prison term for his outspoken denunciation of Italian military leadership.

16. Quoted in Holley, *Ideas and Weapons*, 55.

17. "Bolling Report, 15 August 1917," in Maurer, *U.S. Air Service*, 2:131.

18. Maurer, *U.S. Air Service*, 2:133.

19. Maurer, *U.S. Air Service*, 2:132.

20. Holley, *Ideas and Weapons*, 56.

21. Bill to Maj. William Mitchell from the Atlantic Coast Aeronautical Station of the Curtiss Aviation School, Newport News, Virginia, 1 March 1917, file General Correspondence, 1907–1917, box 6, Mitchell Papers. Mitchell tried to bill the government for his training, but the treasury comptroller ruled that individual payments made to civilian flying schools were not refundable.

22. Hurley, *Billy Mitchell*, 21.

23. William Mitchell, *Memoirs of World War I* (New York: Random House, 1960), 59. The book contains a series of articles published in *Liberty* magazine in 1928.

24. Mitchell, *Memoirs*, 103–11; Isaac Don Levine, *Mitchell: Pioneer of Air Power* (New York: Duell, Sloan, and Pearce, 1943, 1958), 94–97; Nevin, *Architects of Air Power*, 51; Hurley, *Billy Mitchell*, 25–27; Morrow, *Great War*, 271.

25. Mitchell to Chief of Staff, AEF, memorandum, 13 June 1917, quoted in Holley, *Ideas and Weapons*, 47.

26. Mitchell to Chief of Staff, AEF, memorandum, 13 June 1917, extract in Maurer, *U.S. Air Service*, 2:108.

27. In the United States, however, the Signal Corps maintained control over its Aviation Section.

28. Hurley, *Billy Mitchell*, 32.

29. Mitchell, *Memoirs*, 153–54, 157. Mitchell used the Chateau to inspire his staff to converse in French, which he encouraged to enhance Allied cooperation.

30. Quoted in Holley, *Ideas and Weapons*, 135.

31. Robert F. Futrell, *Ideas, Concepts, Doctrine: Basic Thinking in the United States Air Force, 1907–1984* (Maxwell Air Force Base AL: Air University Press, 1989), 1:25.

259

32. Gorrell, "History of the Strategical Section, Air Service, American Expeditionary Force," 1 February 1919, 2–3, file 167.4017-1, AFHRA.

33. Atkinson, "Italian Influence," 147.

34. Gorrell to Caproni, 31 October 1917, file 168.661-83, AFHRA.

35. Nino Salveneschi, *Let Us Kill the War; Let Us Aim at the Heart of the Enemy* (Milan: Milesi and Nicola, 1917), 36–37.

36. Salveneschi, *Let Us Kill the War*, 38.

37. Salveneschi, *Let Us Kill the War*, 62.

38. Salveneschi, *Let Us Kill the War*, 47.

39. Salveneschi, *Let Us Kill the War*, 43, 46.

40. George K. Williams, "'The Shank of the Drill': Americans and Strategical Aviation in the Great War," *Journal of Strategic Studies* 19 (September 1996): 390–94. See also Tami Davis Biddle, *Rhetoric and Reality in Air Warfare: The Evolution of British and American Ideas about Strategic Bombing, 1914–1945* (Princeton: Princeton University Press, 2002), 38–39.

41. Williams, "Shank of the Drill," 400–402; Biddle, *Rhetoric and Reality*, 54.

42. Williams, "Shank of the Drill," 400.

43. Gorrell, "Strategical Bombardment Plan," 28 November 1917, in Maurer, *U.S. Air Service*, 2:141.

44. Gorrell, "Strategical Bombardment Plan," in Maurer, *U.S. Air Service*, 2:143.

45. Gorrell, "Strategical Bombardment Plan," in Maurer, *U.S. Air Service*, 2:142–43.

46. Gorrell, "The Future Role of American Bombardment Aviation," ca. February–March 1918, 9, 15, file 248.222-78, AFHRA.

47. Gorrell, "Strategical Bombardment Plan," in Maurer, *U.S. Air Service*, 2:150.

48. Gorrell, "Strategical Bombardment Plan," in Maurer, *U.S. Air Service*, 2:150.

49. Holley, *Ideas and Weapons*, 135.

50. Quoted in Holley, *Ideas and Weapons*, 135.

51. Williams, "Shank of the Drill," 411–22.

52. Gorrell, "Future Role," 1, file 248.222-78, AFHRA.

53. Gorrell, "Future Role," 4–6, file 248.222-78, AFHRA.

54. Gorrell, "Future Role," 14–15, file 248.222-78, AFHRA. Gorrell lifted

this passage almost verbatim from Trenchard's report. See Williams, "Shank of the Drill," 419–20.

55. Gorrell, "Future Role," 1–2, file 248.222-78, AFHRA.

56. Gorrell, "Future Role," 9, file 248.222-78, AFHRA.

57. Greer, *Development of Air Doctrine*, 10.

58. Quoted in Kennett, *History of Strategic Bombing*, 26–27.

59. Gorrell, "Early History of the Strategical Section, Air Service, AEF," January 1919, in Maurer, *U.S. Air Service*, 2:152.

60. Gorrell, "Early History," in Maurer, *U.S. Air Service*, 152; Kennett, *History of Strategic Bombing*, 29.

61. Carman P. Felice, "The Men and the Machines: Air Operations in World War I," *Aerospace Historian* 5 (January 1958): 41; Greer, *Development of Air Doctrine*, 9.

62. Biddle, *Rhetoric and Reality*, 76–81. See also Greer, *Development of Air Doctrine*, 9.

63. James J. Hudson, *Hostile Skies: A Combat History of the American Air Service in World War I* (Syracuse: Syracuse University Press, 1968), 250. The Italians also trained American airmen in bombing techniques beginning in the spring of 1918, and 80 Americans flew combat missions with them. By the end of the war, 131 Americans had completed the Italian bombing program. See Maurer Maurer, "Flying with Fiorello: The U.S. Air Service in Italy," *Aerospace Historian* 11 (October 1964): 115–17.

64. Maj. Gen. J. W. McAndrew to Chief of Air Service, endorsement, 18 June 1918, in Maurer, *U.S. Air Service*, 2:192.

65. Bruce C. Hopper, "American Day Bombardment in World War I," *Aerospace Historian* 4 (April 1957): 88–91; Hudson, *Hostile Skies*, 175–95.

66. Chief of Air Service, First Army Corps to Commanding General, First Army Corps, memorandum, 16 February 1918, file General Correspondence, 1918, box 6, Mitchell Papers.

67. Mitchell, *Memoirs*, 146.

68. Hurley, *Billy Mitchell*, 32; Futrell, *Ideas, Concepts, Doctrine*, 1:22.

69. Major General McAndrew to Chief of Air Service, endorsement, 18 June 1918, in Maurer, *U.S. Air Service*, 2:192.

70. Gorrell, "Strategical Bombardment Plan," in Maurer, *U.S. Air Service*, 2:155.

71. Gorrell, "Strategical Bombardment Plan," in Maurer, *U.S. Air Service*, 2:155–56.

72. Gorrell, "Early History," in Maurer, *U.S. Air Service*, 2:157.

73. Quoted in DeWitt S. Copp, *A Few Great Captains* (Garden City NY: Doubleday, 1980), 24–25.

74. Copp, *A Few Great Captains*, 24.

75. Mitchell to General Foulois, memorandum, "Notes on the letter of Chief of Staff to C.A.S., A.E.F., regarding air units," 23 July 1918, file General Correspondence, 1918, box 6, Mitchell Papers.

76. John J. Pershing, *My Experiences in the World War* (New York: Frederick A. Stokes, 1931), 2:337.

77. Quoted in Holley, *Ideas and Weapons*, 161–62.

78. Henry H. Arnold, *Global Mission* (New York: Harper and Brothers, 1949), 48, 57–59. The Aviation Section's name changed to the Aeronautical Division during the war.

79. Arnold, *Global Mission*, 67–68.

80. Morrow, *Great War*, 270; Holley, *Ideas and Weapons*, 142.

81. Holley, *Ideas and Weapons*, 142–43.

82. Morrow, *Great War*, 268–70. See the autumn 1917 entries in "Translated Extracts from Caproni's Diaries, 1913–1918," file 168.661-27, AFHRA, for Caproni's insights on the difficulty of negotiating a contract for Americans to produce his bombers.

83. Morrow, *Great War*, 271.

84. Holley, *Ideas and Weapons*, 142.

85. Arnold, *Global Mission*, 70.

86. Holley, *Ideas and Weapons*, 145.

87. Gorrell, "Early History," in Maurer, *U.S. Air Service*, 2:157.

88. Quoted in Levine, *Mitchell*, 148.

89. Quoted in Levine, *Mitchell*, 147.

90. Woodrow Wilson, "Address Delivered at a Joint Session of the Two Houses of Congress, April 7, 1917," in *Public Papers of Woodrow Wilson: War and Peace* (New York: Harper and Brothers, 1927), 1:14.

91. Quoted in Hurley, *Billy Mitchell*, 37.

92. Mitchell, "Tactical Application of Military Aeronautics," 5 January 1919, 3, file 167.4-1, AFHRA.

93. Kennett, *History of Strategic Bombing*, 24, 33. In a study made in 1915, the Allies found that against objectives such as railway stations and junctions, only two bombs in a hundred would hit the target.

94. "Area vs. Precision Bombing," in Maurer, *U.S. Air Service*, 2:253.

2. Progressive Prophecy

William Mitchell, *Winged Defense* (New York: G. P. Putnam's Sons, 1925; repr., New York: Dover, 1988), 16.

Maj. Harold Lee George, "An Inquiry into the Subject 'War,'" lecture, ACTS, ca. 1934–36, 2, file 248.11-9, Air Force Historical Research Agency (hereafter AFHRA), Maxwell Air Force Base AL.

1. "2,000-Pound Bombs from Army Planes Sink Ostfriesland," *New York Times*, 22 July 1921; Isaac Don Levine, *Mitchell: Pioneer of Air Power* (New York: Duell, Sloan, and Pearce, 1943, 1958), 230–70; David Nevin, *Architects of Air Power* (Alexandria VA: Time-Life Books, 1981), 58–68; Alfred H. Hurley, *Billy Mitchell: Crusader for Air Power* (New York: Franklin Watts, 1964; new ed., Bloomington: Indiana University Press, 1975), 67–71; Mitchell to Chief of Air Service, memorandum, "Report on the operations of the 1st Provisional Air Brigade, Langley Field, from Apr–Aug 1921," 29 August 1921, file General Correspondence, 1925, box 11, William Mitchell Papers, Library of Congress.

2. On the nature of progressivism and its lingering impact in the 1920s, see Richard Hofstadter, *The Age of Reform: From Bryan to F.D.R.* (New York: Alfred A. Knopf, 1955, 1968), esp. 5, 91–93, 131–72, 270–326; Robert H. Wiebe, *The Search for Order* (New York: Hill and Wang, 1967), 286–302; Arthur M. Schlesinger Jr., *The Age of Roosevelt: The Crisis of the Old Order* (Boston: Houghton Mifflin, 1957), 72–89; Arthur S. Link, "Not So Tired," in *The Progressive Era: Liberal Renaissance or Liberal Failure*, ed. Arthur Mann (New York: Holt, Rinehart, and Winston, 1963), 105–19; and David Traxel, *Crusader Nation: The United States in Peace and the Great War, 1898–1920* (New York: Alfred A. Knopf, 2006), 354–59.

3. William Mitchell, "Aeronautical Era," *Saturday Evening Post*, 20 December 1924, 99. Mitchell repeats this message in *Winged Defense*, 16, and *Skyways* (Philadelphia: J. B. Lippincott, 1930), 262.

4. Mitchell, *Winged Defense*, x.

5. The pacifist inclinations were perhaps best exemplified by the 1928 Kellogg-Briand Pact outlawing war, which was co-authored by U.S. Secretary of State Frank B. Kellogg.

6. Quoted in Hurley, *Billy Mitchell*, 50; Mitchell, diary entry, 24 December 1924, file Diaries, December, 1924, box 3, Mitchell Papers.

7. Quoted in Andrew Boyle, *Trenchard* (London: Collins, 1962), 472.

8. Mitchell had outranked Foulois, an ex-enlisted man, before the war, and when Gen. John J. Pershing elevated him to Chief of the Air Service in November 1917, Mitchell was furious. His dislike of Foulois endured long after the war. Gorrell had become chief of the Air Service's Technical Section because of Mitchell's recommendation, but the friendship between the two disappeared once Gorrell joined Pershing's staff and began no-notice inspections of Mitchell's squadrons. See John F. Shiner, *Foulois and the U.S. Army Air Corps 1931–1935* (Washington DC: Office of Air Force History, 1983), 9–11; Mitchell to Foulois, 19 July 1918, file General Correspondence, 1918, box 6, Mitchell Papers.

9. Levine, *Mitchell*, 272–73.

10. Mitchell, "War Memoirs," draft, 3, file Diaries, May 1917–February 1919, box 1, Mitchell Papers.

11. Mitchell, *War Memoirs*, 2; Mitchell, *Skyways*, 253.

12. Mitchell, "Aeronautical Era," 99–103; see also Mitchell, *Winged Defense*, 16–17.

13. Mitchell, *Winged Defense*, 214.

14. Mitchell, "Aeronautical Era," 3.

15. Mitchell, *Winged Defense*, 126–27; Hurley, *Billy Mitchell*, 87; Mitchell, *Notes on the Multi-Motored Bombardment Group Day and Night*, 1922, 76, 81, 93–94, file 248.222-57, AFHRA.

16. Mitchell, "Aeronautical Era," 3.

17. Mitchell, *Skyways*, 263.

18. Mitchell to Major General Patrick, memorandum, 10 May 1923, file General Correspondence, 1925, box 11, Mitchell Papers; Thomas H. Greer, *The Development of Air Doctrine in the Army Air Arm, 1917–1941* (Washington DC: Office of Air Force History, 1955, 1985), 57. By 1925 Mitchell had substituted Bangor, Maine, for Boston as the apex of his triangle. See Mitchell, *Winged Defense*, 184.

19. Mitchell, *Notes on the Multi-Motored Bombardment Group*, 94, file 248.222-57, AFHRA.

20. Hurley, *Billy Mitchell*, 75. Hurley notes that not until 1932 did Mitchell acknowledge having "frequent conversations" with Douhet, and may have referred to Caproni and Douhet when he stated that he met "more men of exceptional ability in Italy than we did in any other country." Yet "Mitchell never attributed any special influence on his thinking to Douhet" despite receiving a summary of *The Command of the Air*.

21. Douhet observes in *Command of the Air* that "Victory smiles upon those who anticipate the changes in the character of war, not upon those who wait to adapt themselves after the changes occur" (30), while Mitchell notes in *Winged Defense* that "Victory always comes to that country which has made a proper estimate of the equipment and methods that can be used in modern ways" (127). See Douhet, *The Command of the Air* (New York: Coward-McCann, 1942; repr., Washington DC: Office of Air Force History, 1983), 30; Mitchell, *Winged Defense*, 127.

22. Mitchell, *Winged Defense*, xiv, 9; Douhet, *Command*, 25, 54–55.

23. Douhet, *Command*, 34.

24. Mitchell, *Winged Defense*, 9–10.

25. Douhet's concern with defending Italy was a key consideration in his ideas. See Phillip S. Meilinger, "Giulio Douhet and the Origins of Airpower Theory," in *The Paths of Heaven: The Evolution of Airpower Theory*, ed. Phillip S. Meilinger (Maxwell Air Force Base AL: Air University Press, 1997), 13–14.

26. The development of radar during the 1930s would remove a large measure of uncertainty in regards to the intentions of an attacking air force.

27. Douhet, *Command*, 18, 52–55.

28. Col. Townsend F. Dodd, "Recommendations concerning the Establishment of a 'Department of Aeronautics,'" 17 April 1919, 19, file Aeronautics—Separate Department Recommendations (1), box 31, Mitchell Papers.

29. Mitchell, *Winged Defense*, xvii–xix, 6, 11–17.

30. Mitchell, "Why We Need a Department of the Air," 21 December 1919, file Aeronautics—Separate Department Recommendations (3), box 31, Mitchell Papers.

31. Mitchell, *Notes on the Multi-Motored Bombardment Group*, 72, file 248.222-57, AFHRA.

32. Adjutant General to the Chief of Air Service, memorandum, 7 February 1925, with attached memorandum from Mitchell to Chief of Air Service, 2 March 1925, and W. G. Kilner to Mitchell, memorandum, 30 January 1925, with attached memorandum from Mitchell to Chief of Air Service, 5 February 1925, file General Correspondence, 1925, box 11, Mitchell Papers.

33. Weeks did not mince his rationale to President Calvin Coolidge. The Secretary remarked: "General Mitchell's course has been so lawless, so contrary to the building up of an efficient organization, so lacking in reasonable team work, so indicative of a personal desire for publicity at the ex-

pense of everyone with whom he is associated that his actions render him unfit for a high administrative position such as he now occupies." See Weeks to the President, 4 March 1925, file General Correspondence, 1925, box 11, Mitchell Papers.

34. "The personnel of these permanent establishments often tend to become uniformed office holders instead of public servants entirely engaged in furthering the betterment of their nation," Mitchell wrote. See *Winged Defense*, 136.

35. Elizabeth Mitchell to William Mitchell, 2 September 1925, file General Correspondence, 1925, box 11, Mitchell Papers. The letter was sent special delivery.

36. Quoted in Hurley, *Billy Mitchell*, 101.

37. Quoted in Eugene M. Emme, "The American Dimension," in *Air Power and Warfare: Proceedings of the Eighth Military History Symposium, USAF Academy, 1978*, ed. Alfred F. Hurley and Robert C. Ehrhart (Washington DC: U.S. Government Printing Office, 1979), 67.

38. Emme, "American Dimension," in Hurley and Ehrhart, *Air Power and Warfare*, 67.

39. For an excellent brief analysis of the trial, see Rondall R. Rice, *The Politics of Air Power: From Confrontation to Cooperation in Army Aviation Civil-Military Relations* (Lincoln: University of Nebraska Press, 2004), 1–8.

40. Hurley, *Billy Mitchell*, 108.

41. See, for instance, Harvey F. Trumbore to General Mitchell, 27 January 1926, Elverton H. Wicks to Colonel Mitchell, 31 December 1925, and Horace C. Carlisle to Colonel and Mrs. Mitchell, 21 December 1925, file General Correspondence, 1926, box 12, Mitchell Papers.

42. Henry H. Arnold, *Global Mission* (New York: Harper and Brothers, 1949), 158–59.

43. Quoted in Robert F. Futrell, *Ideas, Concepts, Doctrine: Basic Thinking in the United States Air Force, 1907–1984* (Maxwell Air Force Base AL: Air University Press, 1989), 1:48. Emphasis added.

44. Ira C. Eaker, "Maj. Gen. James E. Fechet: Chief of the Air Corps, 1927–1931," *Air Force Magazine*, September 1978, 96; Jeffery S. Underwood, *The Wings of Democracy: The Influence of Air Power on the Roosevelt Administration 1933–1941* (College Station: Texas A&M University Press,

1991), 30–31; Emme, "American Dimension," in Hurley and Ehrhart, *Air Power and Warfare*, 72.

45. Eaker, "Fechet," 96; James Parton, "The Thirty-One Year Gestation of the Independent Air Force," *Aerospace Historian* 34 (September 1987): 153.

46. Futrell, *Ideas, Concepts, Doctrine*, 1:67.

47. Quoted in Futrell, *Ideas, Concepts, Doctrine*, 1:70–71.

48. Arnold, *Global Mission*, 122.

49. Quoted in Shiner, *Foulois*, 51.

50. Underwood maintains in *Wings of Democracy* that the failure of Mitchell's controversial public appeals to produce an independent air force caused his successors—with the notable exception of Air Corps Chief Benjamin Foulois—to work "within the system" to secure their goal. While certainly true of many airmen, Brig. Maj. Gen. Frank Andrews, the commander of GHQ Air Force, and his chief of staff Col. Hugh Knerr sometimes resorted to controversial publicity when they thought it would further the cause of an independent air force. See Rice, *Politics of Air Power*, 135–36, 143–47.

51. Mitchell, *Winged Defense*, 220. See also Ronald Schaffer, *Wings of Judgment: American Bombing in World War II* (New York: Oxford University Press, 1985), 17–18.

52. Quoted in Parton, "Thirty-One Year Gestation," 152.

53. Maj. Gen. Mason Patrick to the War Department Adjutant General, memorandum, "Reorganization of the air forces for national defense," 19 December 1924, file Aeronautics—Separate Department Recommendations (4), box 31, Mitchell Papers.

54. For an examination of how Generals Patrick and Fechet, ably assisted by Assistant Secretary of War for Air F. Trubee Davison, instilled an attitude of compromise in the Air Corps during its dealings with the Army from 1926–32, see Rice, *Politics of Air Power*, 74–95.

55. For a superb analysis of the Air Corps Tactical School (ACTS) and its subsequent impact on American strategic bombing doctrine, see Peter R. Faber, "Interwar U.S. Army Aviation and the Air Corps Tactical School: Incubators of American Airpower," in Meilinger, *Paths of Heaven*, 183–238.

56. Faber, "Interwar," 212. See also Robert T. Finney, *History of the Air Corps Tactical School, 1920–1940* (Maxwell Air Force Base AL: Air University, 1955; repr., Washington DC: Office of Air Force History, 1992), 43. Of the three-star generals in the Army Air Forces at the end of the war, eleven of

thirteen were Tactical School graduates, and three four-star generals—Joseph McNarney, George Kenney, and Carl Spaatz—graduated from the school.

57. Greer, *Development of Air Doctrine*, 29.

58. Faber, "Interwar," 216; Finney, *History*, 64–68.

59. Finney, *History*, 19. The school changed its name from the Air Service Field Officers' School to the Air Service Tactical School in 1922; it became the Air Corps Tactical School on 18 August 1926.

60. Maj. Gen. Clayton Bissell, USAF Oral History Interview by Brig. Gen. George W. Goddard, 22 February 1966, 8–10, file K239.0512-987, AFHRA; Hurley, *Billy Mitchell*, 128. I am grateful to Mr. Joe Carver at the AFHRA for providing me the dates of the bombing manual's use at the ACTS.

61. Gen. Laurence S. Kuter, USAF Oral History Interview by Hugh N. Ahmann and Tom Sturm, Naples, Florida, 30 September–3 October 1974, 118, file K239.0512-810, AFHRA.

62. Eaker, "The Air Corps Tactical School," *Air Corps Newsletter*, 15 April 1936, file Miscellaneous Correspondence, 1936, box 3, Ira C. Eaker Papers, Library of Congress.

63. Finney, *History*, 34–41.

64. Kuter, interview, 107.

65. Futrell, *Ideas, Concepts, Doctrine*, 1:62.

66. One hundred eighteen Army officers who were not in the Air Corps—roughly 11 percent of the total number of graduates—completed the ACTS. See Finney, *History*, 42.

67. Maj. Harold Lee George, "An Inquiry into the Subject 'War,'" lecture, ACTS, ca. 1934–36, 2, file 248.11-9, AFHRA.

68. George, "Inquiry," 2–8, file 248.11-9, AFHRA.

69. George, "Inquiry," 8–9, file 248.11-9, AFHRA.

70. George, "Inquiry," 9, file 248.11-9, AFHRA.

71. Wesley Frank Craven and James Lea Cate, *The Army Air Forces in World War II* (Chicago: University of Chicago Press, 1948–58; repr., Washington DC: Office of Air Force History, 1983), 1:50–52. See also Donald Wilson, "Origin of a Theory for Air Strategy," *Aerospace Historian* 18 (March 1971): 19–25; Michael S. Sherry, *The Rise of American Air Power: The Creation of Armageddon* (New Haven: Yale University Press, 1987), 49–58; and Thomas Fabyanic, *Strategic Air Attack in the United States Air Force: A Case Study* (Manhattan: Kansas State University/Aerospace Historian, 1976). Wilson, who served as Chief of the "Air Force" section from

1931–34 and Director of the Department of Air Tactics and Strategy from 1936–40 at the ACTS, was highly influential in the development of the industrial web theory.

72. *Employment of Combined Air Force*, text, ACTS, 1925–26, 3, file 248.101-7A, AFHRA.

73. "Principles of War Applied to Air Force Action," lecture, Air Force course, ACTS, 1934–35, 5, file 248.101-1, AFHRA. On the overlapping nature of Tactical School bombing objectives, see Sherry, *American Air Power*, 54–55.

74. "Principles of War Applied to Air Force Action," 5; quoted in Greer, *Development of Air Doctrine*, 77.

75. *General Air Force Principles*, text, Air Force course, ACTS, 1934–35, 2, file 248.101-1, AFHRA.

76. "Doctrine of the Army Air Corps," introductory remarks, ACTS Comments on War Plans Division Study, 31 January 1935, folder ACTS Correspondence, May 1932–May 1939, file 145.93-116, AFHRA.

77. Kuter, "Growth of Air Power," 129–30, Papers of Laurence S. Kuter, USAF Academy Library Special Collections, USAF Academy CO.

78. Kuter, "American Air Power—School Theories vs World War Facts," lecture, ACTS, 1937–38, 23–24, file 248.11-2, AFHRA.

79. *Air Force Objectives*, text, Air Force course, ACTS, 1934–35, 4, file 248.101-1, AFHRA.

80. "The Primary Objective of Air Forces," lecture, ACTS, 13 April 1936, 5, file 248.2017A-10, AFHRA.

81. Maj. Muir S. Fairchild, "National Economic Structure," lecture, ACTS, 5 April 1938, 3–5, file 248.2019A-10, AFHRA.

82. "Testimony Presented by Major Donald Wilson, Captain Robert Olds, Captain Harold Lee George, Captain Robert M. Webster, and 1st Lieutenant K. N. Walter before the Federal Aviation Commission, Washington, DC," 1934, 9–10, file 248.121-3, AFHRA.

83. Fairchild, "National Economic Structure," 8, file 248.2019A-10, AFHRA.

84. Fairchild, "National Economic Structure," 24, file 248.2019A-10, AFHRA.

85. Kuter, "Growth," 119, USAF Academy Library Special Collections.

86. Fairchild, "National Economic Structure," 24, file 248.2019A-10, AFHRA.

87. Fairchild, "National Economic Structure," 24, file 248.2019A-10, AFHRA.

88. *Air Force Objectives*, text, Air Force course, ACTS, 1934–35, 5.

89. Kuter, "Growth," 111, 118, USAF Academy Library Special Collections.

90. Quoted in Greer, *Development of Air Doctrine*, 81.

91. On the Tactical School's penchant for quantification, see Barry D. Watts, *The Foundation of U.S. Air Doctrine: The Problem of Friction in War* (Maxwell Air Force Base AL: Air University Press, 1984).

92. "The Air Force," lecture, Air Force course, ACTS, 1934–35, 1, file 248.101-1, AFHRA.

93. ACTS Comments on War Plans Division Study, "Doctrine of the Army Air Corps," 31 January 1935, 3, folder ACTS Correspondence, May 1932–May 1939, file 145.93-116, AFHRA.

94. George, "Inquiry," 7, file 248.11-9, AFHRA.

95. See Raymond Flugel, "United States Air Power Doctrine: A Study of the Influence of William Mitchell and Giulio Douhet at the Air Corps Tactical School, 1921–1935" (PhD diss., University of Oklahoma, 1965).

96. Mitchell, *Winged Defense*, 6.

97. Finney, *History*, 66; Futrell, *Ideas, Concepts, Doctrine*, 1:64.

98. Quoted in Futrell, *Ideas, Concepts, Doctrine*, 1:64.

99. Finney, *History*, 77; Kuter, interview, 111, file K239.0512-810, AFHRA.

100. Haywood S. Hansell Jr., *The Air Plan that Defeated Hitler* (Atlanta: Higgins-McArthur/Longino and Porter, 1972), 19–20.

101. Kuter, interview, 131–32, file K239.0512-810, AFHRA. Original emphasis.

3. From Prophecy to Plan

Frank M. Andrews, "Comments to Army War College," 15 October 1936, folder Data for Speeches, Address, and Talks, 1 March 1935–9 October 1937, file Wilcox Bill 1937, box 11, Frank M. Andrews Papers, Library of Congress. Original emphasis.

Frank M. Andrews, "Text of NBC Radio Broadcast, 'Your Government at Your Service,'" 20 May 1937, folder Data for Speeches, Address, and Talks, 1 March 1935–9 October 1937, file Wilcox Bill 1937, box 11, Andrews Papers.

1. John T. Correll, "Rendezvous With the *Rex*," *Air Force Magazine*, December 2008, 56.

2. Curtis E. LeMay with MacKinlay Kantor, *Mission with LeMay* (Garden City NY: Doubleday, 1965), 189.

3. LeMay with Kantor, *Mission*, 191. See also DeWitt S. Copp, *A Few Great Captains* (Garden City NY: Doubleday, 1980), 418–23; and Jeffery S. Underwood, *The Wings of Democracy: The Influence of Air Power on the Roosevelt Administration 1933–1941* (College Station: Texas A&M University Press, 1991), 114–15.

4. Hanson W. Baldwin, "'Flying Fortresses' Meet Liner at Sea," *New York Times*, 13 May 1938.

5. Quoted in LeMay with Kantor, *Mission*, 193.

6. Thomas H. Greer, *The Development of Air Doctrine in the Army Air Arm, 1917–1941* (Washington DC: Office of Air Force History, 1955, 1985), 45; Laurence S. Kuter, "Growth of Air Power," 82, Laurence S. Kuter Papers, USAF Academy Library Special Collections, USAF Academy CO.

7. Alfred Goldberg, ed., *A History of the United States Air Force, 1907–1957* (Princeton NJ: Van Nostrand, 1957), 41–42; Greer, *Development of Air Doctrine*, 46; Robert F. Futrell, *Ideas, Concepts, Doctrine: Basic Thinking in the United States Air Force, 1907–1984* (Maxwell Air Force Base AL: Air University Press, 1989), 1:81.

8. Henry H. Arnold, *Global Mission* (New York: Harper and Brothers, 1949), 154.

9. Wesley Frank Craven and James Lea Cate, eds., *The Army Air Forces in World War II* (Chicago: University of Chicago Press, 1948–58; repr., Washington DC: Office of Air Force History, 1983), 1:598–99; Robin Cross, *The Bombers* (New York: Macmillan, 1987), 77–78; Michael J. Nisos, "The Bombardier and His Bombsight," *Air Force Magazine*, September 1981, 106–13; Kuter, "Growth," 122–23, USAF Academy Library Special Collections; Gen. Laurence S. Kuter, interview by Hugh N. Ahmann and Tom Sturm, Naples, Florida, 30 September–3 October 1974, 148, file K239.0512-810, Air Force Historical Research Agency (hereafter AFHRA), Maxwell Air Force Base AL.

10. Boeing developed an aircraft, the XB-15, which flew in 1937, but the bomber's engines could not adequately support it and the project was canceled.

11. This bomber, the massive XB-19, was built by Douglas. Like the XB-15, it proved too slow for combat and only the prototype was completed.

12. War Plans Division Study, "Doctrine of the Air Corps," 21 December 1934, folder ACTS Correspondence, May 1932–May 1939, file 145.93-116, AFHRA.

13. ACTS Comments on War Plans Division Study, "Doctrine of the Army Air Corps," introductory remarks, 31 January 1935, folder ACTS Correspondence, May 1932–May 1939, file 145.93-116, AFHRA.

14. Kuter, "Growth," 134–35, USAF Academy Library Special Collections.

15. Greer, *Development of Air Doctrine*, 101.

16. Quoted in Thomas M. Coffey, *Hap* (New York: Viking Press, 1982), 157.

17. Greer, *Development of Air Doctrine*, 94–99.

18. See J. Mark Wilcox, "Adequate Air Force U.S. Need," *Washington Star*, 14 December 1933, in file National Defense, 1933–42, box 11, Andrews Papers.

19. Quoted in DeWitt S. Copp, "Frank M. Andrews: Marshall's Airman," in *Makers of the United States Air Force*, ed. John L. Frisbee (Washington DC: Office of Air Force History, 1987), 52.

20. Copp, "Frank M. Andrews," in Frisbee, *Makers*, 52.

21. Quoted in Greer, *Development of Air Doctrine*, 90.

22. Copp, *A Few Great Captains*, 374–79.

23. Underwood, *Wings of Democracy*, 97; Andrews to Col. Edwin M. Watson, memorandum, Field Artillery, Military Aide to the President, November 1937, file Assistant Secretary of War, 1937–42, box 11, Andrews Papers.

24. "Notes of Propaganda Talk," 12 March 1935, file GHQ Air Force Directives, box 9, Andrews Papers.

25. Texts of Radio Broadcasts on 13 January 1936 and 20 May 1937, folder Data for Speeches, Addresses, and Talks, 1 March 1935–9 October 1937, file Wilcox Bill, 1937, box 11, Andrews Papers.

26. Andrews, "Address at the Opening Exercises of the Air Corps Tactical School," 7 September 1937, 7, folder Data for Speeches, Addresses, and Talks, 1 March 1935–9 October 1937, file Wilcox Bill, 1937, box 11, Andrews Papers.

27. Andrews, "The General Headquarters Air Force—Lecture before the Army War College," 9 October 1937, 10–11, folder Data for Speeches, Ad-

dresses, and Talks, 1 March 1935–9 October 1937, file Speeches, box 19, Andrews Papers.

28. Andrews to the Secretary of War, memorandum, "Air Corps Procurement Program," 24 January 1938, file Secretary of War, 1938–42, box 11, Andrews Papers.

29. LeMay with Kantor, *Mission*, 142–52.

30. Underwood, *Wings of Democracy*, 105–8.

31. Underwood, *Wings of Democracy*, 91–92.

32. Quoted in Goldberg, *History*, 43.

33. Quoted in Greer, *Development of Air Doctrine*, 99.

34. Copp, "Frank M. Andrews," in Frisbee, *Makers*, 45.

35. Marshall to Andrews, 19 August 1938, file Personal Correspondence, "M," 1929–39, box 5, Andrews Papers.

36. Kuter, "Growth," 139, USAF Academy Library Special Collections.

37. Copp, "Frank M. Andrews," in Frisbee, *Makers*, 59.

38. Eric Larrabee, *Commander in Chief: Franklin Delano Roosevelt, His Lieutenants, and Their War* (New York: Simon and Schuster, 1987), 220.

39. For a comparison of the different approaches used by Arnold and Andrews as air power advocates, see Rondall R. Rice, *The Politics of Air Power: From Confrontation to Cooperation in Army Aviation Civil-Military Relations* (Lincoln: University of Nebraska Press, 2004), esp. 139–50.

40. Arnold, *Global Mission*, 161.

41. Quoted in Underwood, *Wings of Democracy*, 142.

42. Andrews to Marshall, 18 October 1938, file Personal Correspondence, "M," 1929–39, box 5, Andrews Papers.

43. Copp, "Frank M. Andrews," in Frisbee, *Makers*, 59.

44. Copp, *A Few Great Captains*, 473; Larrabee, *Commander in Chief*, 213.

45. Underwood, *Wings of Democracy*, 109–12, 144–46.

46. Cited in Robert E. Sherwood, *Roosevelt and Hopkins: An Intimate History* (New York: Harper and Brothers, 1948), 100.

47. Henry H. Adams, *Harry Hopkins* (New York: G. P. Putnam's Sons, 1977), 140.

48. Arnold, *Global Mission*, 177–79; Underwood, *Wings of Democracy*, 133–36; Copp, *A Few Great Captains*, 455–57; Larrabee, *Commander in Chief*, 214. Arnold incorrectly provides the date of this meeting as 28 Sep-

tember 1938, and also states that Secretary of War Woodring attended, when in fact he was not present.

49. Underwood, *Wings of Democracy*, 135–37.

50. Larrabee, *Commander in Chief*, 214.

51. Craven and Cate, *Army Air Forces*, 1:104.

52. Spaatz, who had red hair, received the nickname "Tooey" as a plebe at West Point because of his striking resemblance to a redheaded upperclass cadet, F. J. Toohey. The moniker stuck, although the *h* in the original name was dropped. See David R. Mets, *Master of Airpower: General Carl A. Spaatz* (Novato CA: Presidio Press, 1988), 7.

53. Michael S. Sherry, *The Rise of American Air Power: The Creation of Armageddon* (New Haven: Yale University Press, 1987), 90.

54. Spaatz to Arnold, memorandum, 11 September 1939, folder 381 "B" War Plans, Central Decimal Files, 1939–42, series 2, box 207, Record Group (hereafter RG) 18, National Archives (hereafter NA), Washington DC.

55. Carl Spaatz, "Leaves from My Battle of Britain Diary," *Air Power Historian* 4 (April 1957): 66–75; Mets, *Master of Airpower*, 110–12.

56. Arnold, *Global Mission*, 186–87; Underwood, *Wings of Democracy*, 151. Arnold incorrectly states that his admonishment from Roosevelt came in early 1939.

57. Quoted in Larrabee, *Commander in Chief*, 223.

58. Quoted in Underwood, *Wings of Democracy*, 166.

59. Maj. General Arnold, memorandum for record, 9 July 1940, file Miscellaneous Correspondence, January–July 1940, box 3, Henry H. Arnold Papers, Library of Congress.

60. Quoted in Futrell, *Ideas, Concepts, Doctrine*, 1:103.

61. Besides George, Lieutenant Colonels Howard Craig, Orvil Anderson, and Kenneth Walker comprised the division on its first day.

62. Haywood S. Hansell Jr., *The Air Plan that Defeated Hitler* (Atlanta: Higgins-McArthur/Longino and Porter, 1972), 65–66.

63. Futrell, *Ideas, Concepts, Doctrine*, 1:109.

64. Haywood S. Hansell Jr., "USAAF Plans and Strategic Effects," in *Impact: The Army Air Forces' Confidential Picture History of World War II* (Harrisburg PA: Historical Times, 1982), 4:v.

65. James C. Gaston, *Planning the American Air War: Four Men and Nine Days in 1941* (Washington DC: National Defense University Press, 1983), 30.

66. Hansell, *Air Plan*, 51.

67. Hansell, *Air Plan*, 4.

68. Hansell, *Air Plan*, 67.

69. Gaston, *Planning*, 22.

70. Quoted in Gaston, *Planning*, 21–22.

71. Gaston, *Planning*, 16.

72. Gaston, *Planning*, 58.

73. Futrell, *Ideas, Concepts, Doctrine*, 1:102.

74. "AWPD-1: Munitions Requirements of the Army Air Forces," 12 August 1941, tab no. 1, 1, file 145.82-1, AFHRA. Emphasis added.

75. "AWPD-1," 2–7, AFHRA.

76. "AWPD-1," 2, AFHRA.

77. Hansell, *Air Plan*, 83–84.

78. Hansell, *Air Plan*, 86.

79. Hansell, *Air Plan*, 86.

80. Gaston, *Planning*, 56.

81. Hansell, *Air Plan*, 86.

82. Gaston, *Planning*, 56–57.

83. Gaston, *Planning*, 57.

84. Futrell, *Ideas, Concepts, Doctrine*, 1:111.

85. Gaston, *Planning*, 25.

86. On 14 March 1941 the War Department had approved an Air Corps strength of eighty-four groups, consisting of 7,799 aircraft divided as follows: 1,520 heavy bombers; 1,059 medium bombers; 770 light and dive bombers; 2,500 pursuit interceptors; 525 pursuit fighters; 806 observation, liaison, and photo aircraft; 469 transport airplanes; and 150 amphibian aircraft. See Futrell, *Ideas, Concepts, Doctrine*, 1:102.

87. Futrell, *Ideas, Concepts, Doctrine*, 1:110–11. The B-36 groups were unlikely to be fully operational before 1945.

88. "AWPD-1," 2, AFHRA. The plan stated: "If the air offensive is successful, a land offensive may not be necessary."

89. Gaston, *Planning*, 42.

90. Hansell, "USAAF Plans," viii.

91. Hansell, "USAAF Plans," viii; quoted in Futrell, *Ideas, Concepts, Doctrine*, 1:111

92. Futrell, *Ideas, Concepts, Doctrine*, 1:111.

93. Hansell, "USAAF Plans," ix.

94. Sherry, *American Air Power*, 100. Official Army Air Forces historians Wesley Frank Craven and James Lea Cate offer this explanation: "Perhaps its [AWPD-1's] ready acceptance was partly due to the pressure of time in meeting the President's directive, for irrespective of the intrinsic merits of AWPD-1, the views expressed therein were not wholly consistent with those of the War Department." See Craven and Cate, *Army Air Forces*, 1:146. See also David E. Johnson, *Fast Tanks and Heavy Bombers: Innovation in the U.S. Army, 1917–1945* (Ithaca NY: Cornell University Press, 2003), 169–71.

95. Walker reflected the contempt that many airmen felt toward mainstream Army views on air power. He sarcastically told the Federal Aviation Commission in 1934: "I have been impressed with the refusal of military advisers to consider that the Air Force is of real value, other than to cover the mobilization of the Army." See "Testimony Presented by Major Donald Wilson, Captain Robert Olds, Captain Harold Lee George, Captain Robert M. Webster, and 1st Lieutenant K. N. Walter before the Federal Aviation Commission, Washington, DC," 1934, 3, file 248.121-3, AFHRA.

96. Carl von Clausewitz, *On War*, ed. and trans. Michael Howard and Peter Paret (Princeton: Princeton University Press, 1976), 104, 119, 121. Barry D. Watts provides an extensive analysis of the airmen's failure to plan for friction in *The Foundations of U.S. Air Doctrine: The Problem of Friction in War* (Maxwell Air Force Base AL: Air University Press, 1984).

97. Hansell, "USAAF Plans," viii.

98. Hansell, *Air Plan*, 50.

99. Sherry, *American Air Power*, 56; Underwood, *Wings of Democracy*, 95–96.

4. Breaching Fortress Europe

H. H. Arnold to All Air Force Commanders in Combat Zones, "Evaluation of Bombing Methods and Purposes," 10 June 1943, file 36 (Bombing), box 41, Henry H. Arnold Papers, Library of Congress.

Eaker to Arnold, 16 November 1943, folder Bombing—Overcast Operations, box 82, Carl A. Spaatz Papers, Library of Congress.

1. For a detailed analysis of the 17 August 1943 missions against Regensburg and Schweinfurt, see Edward Jablonski, *Double Strike: The Epic Air Raids on Regensburg/Schweinfurt* (Garden City NY: Doubleday, 1974); Martin Middlebrook, *The Schweinfurt-Regensburg Mission* (New York: Charles

Scribner's Sons, 1983); and Thomas M. Coffey, *Decision over Schweinfurt* (New York: David MacKay, 1977), 1–75.

2. "Minutes of the Group Commanders' Meeting, 28 August 1943," folder Regensburg—Mission Report—17 August 1943, box B5, Curtis E. LeMay Papers, Library of Congress.

3. "Minutes of the Group Commanders' Meeting, 28 August 1943," folder Regensburg—Mission Report—17 August 1943, box B5, LeMay Papers.

4. James Parton, *Air Force Spoken Here: General Ira Eaker and the Command of the Air* (Bethesda MD: Adler and Adler, 1986), 299.

5. Col. Beirne Lay Jr., USAAF, "Personal report on the REGENSBURG mission, 17 August 1943" submitted to Commanding Officer, One Hundredth Bombardment Group (H), 25 August 1943, folder Regensburg—Mission Report—17 August 1943, box B5, LeMay Papers.

6. Lay, "Personal report," 25 August 1943, folder Regensburg—Mission Report—17 August 1943, box B5, LeMay Papers.

7. Geoffrey Perret, *Winged Victory: The Army Air Forces in World War II* (New York: Random House, 1993), 268–69; Parton, *Air Force Spoken Here*, 300; Jablonski, *Double Strike*, 110–11.

8. Perret, *Winged Victory*, 269.

9. Parton, *Air Force Spoken Here*, 300.

10. Gen. Carl Spaatz, USAF, Ret., interview by Brig. Gen. Noel F. Parrish and Dr. Alfred Goldberg, 21 February 1962, file K239.0512-754, U.S. Air Force Historical Research Agency (hereafter AFHRA), Maxwell Air Force Base AL.

11. Maj. Gen. Haywood S. Hansell Jr., Ret., to Mr. Devin B. Herbert, 8 April 1983, Hansell Small Manuscript Collection, MS 6, Special Collections Branch, U.S. Air Force Academy Library CO (hereafter HSMC).

12. Hansell to Lt. Col. David MacIsaac, 24 August 1975, MS 6, HSMC.

13. Andrews to Lieutenant General McNarney, Deputy Chief of Staff, 20 July 1942, file Letters—"M" 20 July–15 October 1942, box 19, Frank Andrews Papers, Library of Congress.

14. Arnold told AAF Maj. Gen. Eugene Eubank in May 1944: "There can be but one justification for our tremendous and expensive Air Forces organization—it must play a decisive role in the decisive defeat of our enemies." Quoted in William W. Ralph, "Improvised Destruction: Arnold, LeMay, and the Firebombing of Japan," *War in History* 13 (Winter 2006): 504.

15. Arnold to Lovett, 19 October 1942, quoted in Eric Larrabee, *Com-*

mander in Chief: Franklin Roosevelt, His Lieutenants, and Their War (New York: Simon and Schuster, 1987), 220. Original emphasis.

16. H. H. Arnold to All Air Force Commanders in Combat Zones, memorandum, "Evaluation of Bombing Methods and Purposes," 10 June 1943, file 36 (Bombing), box 41, Arnold Papers. Emphasis added.

17. Ronald Schaffer, *Wings of Judgment: American Bombing in World War II* (New York: Oxford University Press, 1985), 15.

18. Retired Air Force General C. P. Cabell, who served on the Advisory Council as a colonel in 1942, commented on the council's main function in an April 1969 letter to David MacIsaac: "Their [council members'] principal interest was in the need for a careful assessment of the whole bomber offensive, essentially on the basis of the postwar necessity for an authoritative and unbiased answer to the inevitable question: 'Who won the war?'" See David MacIsaac, *Strategic Bombing in World War Two: The Story of the United States Strategic Bombing Survey* (New York: Garland, 1976), 29, 155.

19. Thomas M. Coffey, *Hap: The Story of the U.S. Air Force and the Man Who Built It* (New York: Viking Press, 1982), 201.

20. Marshall to Gen. Brehon Sommervell, 29 March 1942, Army AG Classified Decimal File 1940–42, folder 381 (26–31 March 1942), box 638, Record Group (hereafter RG) 407, National Archives (hereafter NA), Washington DC.

21. Michael S. Sherry, *The Rise of American Air Power: The Creation of Armageddon* (New Haven: Yale University Press, 1987), 221–25.

22. Quoted in Sherry, *American Air Power*, 221.

23. Gen. Ira C. Eaker, interview by Thomas M. Coffey, 18 April 1975, quoted in Coffey, *Hap*, 337.

24. Tami Davis Biddle contends that British and American airmen dismissed the results of interwar conflicts because "they were not 'first-class' wars between major states." See her *Rhetoric and Reality in Air Warfare: The Evolution of British and American Ideas about Strategic Bombing, 1914–1945* (Princeton: Princeton University Press, 2002), 8.

25. Kenneth P. Werrell, *Death from the Heavens: A History of Strategic Bombing* (Annapolis: Naval Institute Press, 2009), 69–70; John Terraine, *A Time for Courage: The Royal Air Force in the European War, 1939–1945* (New York: Macmillan, 1985), 140–47.

26. Wesley Frank Craven and James Lea Cate, eds., *The Army Air Forces in World War II* (Chicago: University of Chicago Press, 1949; repr., Wash-

ington DC: Office of Air Force History, 1983), 1:644. See also Parton, *Air Force Spoken Here*, 168.

27. Perret, *Winged Victory*, 97–98; "Memorandum of Conference with Major General I. C. Eaker at Wide Wings," 4 February 1943, file 118.01, V.2, AFHRA.

28. "The doctrine of bomber penetration was evolved before the development of radar," Hansell reflected, "when high-performance bombers had enormous advantage in terms of initiative, selection of time and place of penetration, mass, altitude, and superior speed over pursuit, which was operating blind and would have to climb to interception." See Hansell to Col. Kenneth Alnwick, 10 May 1983, MS 6, HSMC.

29. Hansell, "Air War College Lecture," 16 February 1951, MS 6, HSMC.

30. Spaatz to Arnold, 24 August 1942, folder Personal Correspondence, 16–31 August 1942, box 8, Spaatz Papers. Spaatz also stated that "it is of the utmost importance that the maximum amount of the above [listed force] be placed in this theatre at the earliest practicable date." David R. Mets contends that Spaatz intended this letter to persuade Arnold to stop sending bombers originally bound for Britain to other fronts, but the letter also raised Arnold's expectations regarding Eighth Air Force. See Mets, *Master of Airpower: General Carl A. Spaatz* (Novato CA: Presidio Press, 1988), 134.

31. Parton, *Air Force Spoken Here*, 173.

32. "To be read by General Arnold at the C.C.S. Meeting of Sept. 4, 1942," file 39 (Bombing), box 41, Arnold Papers.

33. Quoted in Haywood S. Hansell Jr., *The Air Plan that Defeated Hitler* (Atlanta: Higgins-McArthur/Longino and Porter, 1972), 100.

34. Hansell, *Air Plan*, 107.

35. Quotes from AWPD-42 taken from Hansell, *Air Plan*, 106–7. See Craven and Cate, *Army Air Forces*, 2:277–79.

36. Perret, *Winged Victory*, 140, 167.

37. Perret, *Winged Victory*, 247. Spaatz had to send two of his most experienced "heavy" Bomb Groups, the 97th and 301st, to North Africa.

38. Craven and Cate, *Army Air Forces*, 2:235.

39. "Study of Bombing Accuracy (Bombardment Aviation), Bombing Analysis Report No. 6," 5 May 1943, folder Director, Dr. Theodore von Karman, 1941—August 1947, box 8, Office, Chief of Air Staff Advisory Group, RG 18, NA. The period of the report covered 1 July–31 December 1942.

40. The specifics of the combat box formation were: the six bombers in

each squadron divided into two elements of three aircraft each, with each three-aircraft element forming an inverted "V" and flying one behind the other at staggered 50-foot altitudes. The group formation consisted of a lead, high, and low squadron, with the six bombers in the lead squadron flying in front of the formation, while the low squadron flew 250 feet below and to the right of the lead squadron, and the high squadron flew 250 feet above and to the left of the lead. See Hansell, *Air Plan*, 115–18.

41. Gen. Curtis E. LeMay, USAF, Ret., "The Command Realities," in *Impact: The Army Air Forces' Confidential Picture History of World War II* (Harrisburg PA: Historical Times, 1982), 5:xii.

42. Lemay, "Command Realities," 5:xi. Army Air Forces engineers ultimately developed Automatic Flight-Control Equipment (AFCE), which allowed the lead bombardier to guide his aircraft to target in level flight through a linkage with the bomber's automatic pilot. Its first use occurred in March 1943. See Parton, *Air Force Spoken Here*, 243.

43. During November–December 1942, Eighth Air Force bombers flew eighteen missions with an overall loss rate of 6 percent, but the last two missions had loss rates of 8 and 7 percent respectively. See Parton, *Air Force Spoken Here*, 185.

44. Typical submarine pens had roof slabs of reinforced concrete, 11.5 to 13 feet thick. See "An Appreciation of the Air Effort Against Submarines," January 1943 COA study in file 118.01, v.2, AFHRA.

45. Eaker to Spaatz, "Night Bombing," 8 October 1942, folder September–October Official Correspondence, box 10, Spaatz Papers. Eaker added: "This is true because, targets can be located easier, they can be seen and identified through the bombs sights, and the bombing pattern can, with greater ease and certainty be placed on target. . . . A force of 100 bombers can, by concentration which is possible in daylight, effect the destruction of a material objective, which a force of at least 1,000 bombers would be required to execute, with any degree of certainty, in a night operation."

46. Churchill had already been leaning in the Americans' direction. Air Marshal Sir Charles Portal, RAF Chief of the Air Staff, wrote the prime minister in early November 1942 endorsing the American daylight effort, and in mid-December Air Marshal John Slessor and Secretary of State for Air Sir Archibald Sinclair added their endorsements. In part, the British believed that daylight bombing might work; in part, the British did not want to risk that the American bomber force might transfer to the Pacific theater. See Parton, *Air Force Spoken Here*, 193, 217; Biddle, *Rhetoric and Reality*, 215. For

Eaker's firsthand description of his meeting with Churchill at Casablanca, see Ira C. Eaker, "Some Memories of Winston Churchill," *Aerospace Historian* 19 (Fall 1972): 121–24.

47. Gerhard L. Weinberg, *A World at Arms: A Global History of World War II* (Cambridge: Cambridge University Press, 1994), 438–39; Raymond G. O'Connor, *Diplomacy for Victory: FDR and Unconditional Surrender* (New York: W. W. Norton, 1971), 4–5, 50; Bernard Brodie, *War and Politics* (New York: Macmillan, 1973), 39.

48. An uproar had occurred in both Britain and the United States after Lt. Gen. Dwight Eisenhower, the Allied commander of the North African invasion force, negotiated an agreement with French Admiral Francois Darlan (who had earlier served as Henri Petain's deputy in the Vichy French government) for Vichy French forces in North Africa to surrender. Roosevelt and Churchill both wanted to assure their publics that no more such deals with "collaborators" would occur, plus they wanted to assure the Soviets that they would continue fighting until Germany's ultimate defeat, even though they could not launch an invasion of France in 1943. See Weinberg, *World at Arms*, 432–39; O'Connor, *Diplomacy for Victory*, 49–51.

49. "The Eight Hundred and Seventy-fifth Press Conference, Joint Conference by the President and Prime Minister Churchill at Casablanca, January 24, 1943," in Samuel I. Rosenman, comp., *The Public Papers and Addresses of Franklin D. Roosevelt, 1943* (New York: Harper and Brothers, 1950), 39.

50. See Roosevelt, "The Nine Hundred and Sixty-second Press Conference, Waikiki, Honolulu, July 29, 1944" (209–11), "'International Cooperation on Which Enduring Peace Must Be Based Is Not a One-Way Street'— Annual Message to Congress on the State of the Union, January 6, 1945" (495), "'We Cannot Fail Them Again, and Expect the World Again to Survive'—Address to the Congress Reporting on the Yalta Conference, March 1, 1945" (575), in Rosenman, *Public Papers, 1944–45*.

51. Whether the declaration of unconditional surrender made the Germans fight harder is subject to debate. Anne Armstrong asserts that "had the German generals been able to act to end the war and had the Allies been willing to negotiate, the war might have ended earlier, nine months to two years earlier, depending on the degree of compromise." See *Unconditional Surrender: The Impact of the Casablanca Policy on World War II* (New Brunswick NJ: Rutgers University Press, 1961), 254; O'Connor, *Diplomacy*

for Victory, 53–54; Sherry, *American Air Power*, 236; and Johannes Steinhoff, Peter Pechel, and Dennis Showalter, eds., *Voices from the Third Reich: An Oral History* (Washington DC: Regnery Gateway, 1989), 387. Gerhard Weinberg counters, "A careful examination of National Socialist propaganda has shown that, in spite of post-war assertions to the contrary, the Unconditional Surrender formula had little resonance there" and references the work of Günter Moltmann. See Weinberg, *World at Arms*, 1044n94. Robert A. Pape argues that the combination of unconditional surrender and fear of the Soviets kept the Germans fighting until the bitter end. See *Bombing to Win: Air Power and Coercion in War* (Ithaca: Cornell University Press, 1996), 296–311. Albert Speer, the Nazi minister of armaments, thought that Roosevelt's announcement resonated with the man who led the Third Reich: "Hitler was probably the only German leader who entertained no illusions about the seriousness of this statement [unconditional surrender]. . . . Now, during the situation conferences, he more and more often declared, 'Don't fool yourself. There is no turning back. We can only move forward. We have burned our bridges.' In speaking this way, Hitler was cutting his government off from any negotiation." See *Inside the Third Reich* (New York: Avon Books, 1970), 381.

52. Actual German losses were seven fighters. See Parton, *Air Force Spoken Here*, 230; Perret, *Winged Victory*, 250.

53. Craven and Cate, *Army Air Forces*, 2:326–27.

54. Craven and Cate, *Army Air Forces*, 2:330.

55. Arnold to Assistant Chief of Air Staff, Management Control, "Research and Analysis to Fix Earliest Practicable Date for Invasion of Western Europe," 9 December 1942, file 118.01, v.2, AFHRA.

56. Sorenson to Kuter, 3 January 1943, MS 6, HSMC.

57. Kuter to Hansell, 28 January 1943, MS 6, HSMC.

58. Edward M. Earle to Mr. Winfield W. Riefler, Economics War Division, U.S. Embassy, London, 23 December 1942, file 118.01, v.2, AFHRA.

59. Hansell to Robert F. Futrell, 5 July 1988, MS 6, HSMC.

60. Hansell to Sorenson, 11 February 1943, MS 6, HSMC; Parton, *Air Force Spoken Here*, 251.

61. "Excerpts from CCS 166/1/D, The Bomber Offensive from the United Kingdom," Attachment to Portal's letter to Arnold, 15 April 1943, box 16, Eaker Papers.

62. "Excerpts," Attachment to Portal's letter to Arnold, 15 April 1943, box 16, Eaker Papers.

63. Craven and Cate, *Army Air Forces*, 2:304.

64. Perret, *Winged Victory*, 249.

65. Perret, *Winged Victory*, 249.

66. Perret, *Winged Victory*, 249. During the second half of 1942, the bulk of German fighters were on the Russian or Mediterranean fronts, which helped to keep American losses low during the first six months of Eighth Air Force operations. See Biddle, *Rhetoric and Reality*, 223.

67. Eaker to Brig. Gen. E. L. Eubank, Director of Bombardment, Headquarters AAF, 19 February 1943, folder Eubank File, box 17, Eaker Papers.

68. Eaker to Maj. Gen. George Stratemeyer, 2 January 1943, cited in Parton, *Air Force Spoken Here*, 212–13.

69. Gen. Ira Eaker, interview by James Parton, 30 March 1972, cited in Parton, *Air Force Spoken Here*, 233.

70. "Memorandum of Conference with Major General I. C. Eaker at Wide Wings," 4 February 1943, file 118.01, v.2, AFHRA.

71. "Memorandum," 4 February 1943, file 118.01, v.2, AFHRA.

72. Gates to Arnold, memorandum, "Report of Committee of Operations Analysts," 25 March 1943, file 118.01, v.2, AFHRA.

73. Eaker to Arnold, memorandum, March 1943, quoted in Parton, *Air Force Spoken Here*, 245.

74. Arnold to Harry L. Hopkins, the White House, 25 March 1943, file Strategy and Command, box 39, Arnold Papers.

75. Arnold to Eaker, 10 April 1943, box 16, Eaker Papers.

76. Eaker to Arnold, 30 January 1943, box 16, Eaker Papers.

77. DeWitt S. Copp, "Frank M. Andrews: Marshall's Airman," in *Makers of the United States Air Force*, ed. John L. Frisbee (Washington DC: Office of Air Force History, 1987), 70.

78. Marshall to the President, memorandum, "High Altitude Bombing in the European Theater," 22 March 1943, file Miscellaneous Correspondence, 1943, box 3, Arnold Papers.

79. "Joint Chiefs of Staff Minutes of Special Meeting," 29 April 1943, 5, folder Joint Chiefs of Staff Meetings, 71st–86th, RG 218, NA.

80. Craven and Cate, *Army Air Forces*, 2:372.

81. At Trident, the Combined Chiefs repeated the purpose of the Combined Bomber Offensive as stated in the Casablanca Directive: "the progres-

sive destruction and dislocation of the German military, industrial and economic system and the undermining of the morale of the German people to a point where their capacity for armed resistance is fatally weakened." They then added the following sentence to that statement: "This is construed as meaning so weakened as to permit initiation of final combined operations on the Continent." See Hansell to Lt. Col. David MacIsaac, 24 August 1975, MS 6, HSMC; Parton, *Air Force Spoken Here*, 263.

82. Marshall delivered the eulogy at Andrews's Arlington National Cemetery funeral.

83. Eaker to Harris, 31 May 1943, folder Eighth Air Force Correspondence to RAF Officers, 31 December 1942–1 January 1944, box 19, Eaker Papers.

84. "Joint Chiefs of Staff Minutes of Special Meeting," 29 April 1943, 2, folder Joint Chiefs of Staff Meetings, 71st–86th, RG 218, NA. Eaker's phraseology regarding the sixty targets came directly from the COA report to General Arnold on 8 March. See Memorandum for General Arnold, "Report of Committee of Operations Analysts with Respect to Economic Targets Within the Western Axis," 8 March 1943, 2, file 118.02, v.2, AFHRA.

85. "Joint Chiefs of Staff Minutes of Special Meeting," 29 April 1943, 2–5, folder Joint Chiefs of Staff Meetings, 71st–86th, RG 218, NA.

86. "Joint Chiefs of Staff Minutes of Special Meeting," 29 April 1943, 3–8, folder Joint Chiefs of Staff Meetings, 71st–86th, RG 218, NA.

87. "Joint Chiefs of Staff Minutes of Special Meeting," 29 April 1943, 7, folder Joint Chiefs of Staff Meetings, 71st–86th, RG 218, NA.

88. Hansell to Colonel Sorenson, Air Staff A-2, 11 February 1943, MS 6, HSMC.

89. Hansell to Sorenson, 11 February 1943, MS 6, HSMC.

90. An Eighth Air Force examination of bomb plots for missions occurring from 17 August–31 December 1942 revealed that 5.5 percent of the bombs dropped on any target were within a thousand-foot circle around the aiming point; with the adoption of pattern bombing techniques, the average total within the circle had increased to 14.6 percent by the end of August 1943. See Eaker to Arnold, 30 August 1943, file 312.1-F Operations Letters, June–October 1943, box 194, RG 18, NA.

91. For an excellent analysis of this point, see Barry D. Watts, *The Foundations of U.S. Air Doctrine: The Problem of Friction in War* (Maxwell Air Force Base AL: Air University Press, 1984), 47–54.

92. Eaker to Arnold, 13 May 1943, box 16, Eaker Papers. Emphasis added.

93. "Joint Chiefs of Staff Minutes of Special Meeting," 29 April 1943, 4, folder Joint Chiefs of Staff Meetings, 71st–86th, RG 218, NA.

94. See Hansell to Lt. Col. David MacIsaac, 24 August 1975, and Hansell to Sorenson, 11 February 1943, MS 6, HSMC.

95. Anderson to Maj. Gen. George Stratemeyer, 21 July 1943, folder Central Decimal Files, October 1942–May 1944, file 312.1-E Operations Letters, RG 18, NA.

96. Anderson to "Ed" [likely, Col. Ed Sorenson], 31 August 1943, file 312.1-F Operations Letters, June–October 1943, box 194, RG 18, NA.

97. Roosevelt, "The Nine Hundred and Sixty-second Press Conference, Waikiki, Honolulu, July 29, 1944," in Rosenman, *Public Papers, 1944–45*, 210.

98. Harris to Eaker, 15 April 1943, folder Eighth Air Force Correspondence to RAF Officers, 31 December 1942–1 January 1944, box 19, Eaker Papers.

99. For elaboration on the separate nature of the British and American campaigns, see Biddle, *Rhetoric and Reality*, 216–17.

100. Martin Middlebrook, *The Battle of Hamburg: Allied Bomber Forces against a German City in 1943* (New York: Charles Scribner's Sons, 1981), 87, 151, 166, 190. Ninety B-17s bombed Hamburg on 25 July, and fifty-seven bombed the city on 26 July, dropping a total of three hundred tons of ordnance.

101. United States Strategic Bombing Survey, *A Detailed Study of the Effects of Area Bombing on Hamburg* (Washington DC: U.S. Government Printing Office, January 1947), 8, 10.

102. Quoted in Sherry, *American Air Power*, 156.

103. Anderson to Maj. Gen. Barney Giles, Headquarters AAF, 4 August 1943, folder Central Decimal Files, October 1942–May 1944, file 312.1-E Operations Letters, box 194, RG 18, NA.

104. Arnold to Spaatz, 11 August 1943, folder Central Decimal Files, October 1942–May 1944, file 312.1-E Operations Letters, box 194, RG 18, NA.

105. Arnold to Assistant Chief of Air Staff, Management Control, "Analysis of Strategic Targets in Italy," 23 March 1943, file 118.01, v.2, AFHRA.

106. Arnold to Assistant Chief of Air Staff, Materiel, Maintenance, and

Distribution, memorandum, "Incendiary Bombs," 26 April 1943, file 39 (Bombing), box 41, Arnold Papers.

107. H. H. Arnold to All Air Force Commanders in Combat Zones, memorandum, "Evaluation of Bombing Methods and Purposes," 10 June 1943, file 36 (Bombing), box 41, Arnold Papers; T. J. Hanley to Assistant Chief of Air Staff, Personnel et. al., 30 April 1943, quoted in Schaffer, *Wings of Judgment*, 62.

108. Arnold to Eaker, 29 June 1943, box 16, Eaker Papers.

109. Arnold to Eaker, 24 July 1943, folder Central Decimal Files, October 1942–May 1944, file 312.1-E Operations Letters, box 194, RG 18, NA.

110. Eaker to Arnold, 20 July 1943, folder Central Decimal Files, October 1942–May 1944, file 312.1-E Operations Letters, box 194, RG 18, NA.

111. Eaker to Arnold, 31 July 1943, box 16, Eaker Papers. American engineers would develop a radar bombing device similar to H2S, designated H2X, which Eighth Air Force would begin receiving in late fall 1943.

112. Craven and Cate, *Army Air Forces*, 2:483; Larrabee, *Commander in Chief*, 250–51.

113. Eaker suffered even greater deficiencies in crews than he did in heavy bombers—he averaged only 265 operational crews between 1 April and 30 September, compared to the 423-crew average called for in the CBO plan. Eighth Air Force thus had 78 percent of the bombers called for in the CBO plan during that period, compared to 63 percent of the mandated crews. See Parton, *Air Force Spoken Here*, 323.

114. Biddle, *Rhetoric and Reality*, 223.

115. "Joint Chiefs of Staff Minutes of Special Meeting," 29 April 1943, 14, folder Joint Chiefs of Staff Meetings, 71st–86th, RG 218, NA.

116. Eaker to Arnold, 30 August 1943, file 312.1-F Operations Letters, June–October 1943, box 194, RG 18, NA.

117. Eaker to Arnold, 30 August 1943, file 312.1-F Operations Letters, June–October 1943, box 194, RG 18, NA.

118. The main Luftwaffe flak gun, the 88 mm, required an average expenditure of sixteen thousand shells to down one aircraft flying at high altitude. See Williamson Murray, *Strategy for Defeat: The Luftwaffe 1933–1945* (Maxwell Air Force Base AL: Air University Press, 1983), 190.

119. Eaker to Major General Giles, Assistant Chief of Air Staff, 29 June 1943, folder Central Decimal Files, October 1942–May 1944, file 312.1-E Operations Letters, box 194, RG 18, NA.

120. Only one B-17 crew member in four could expect to survive twenty-five missions. A November 1943 study of four heavy bomber groups in Eighth Air Force arriving in theater between October 1942 and June 1943 showed that for 1,000 crewmen, an average of 255 remained flying after twenty-five missions. See Headquarters USAAF in the UK, Office of the Surgeon, "Flying availability of initial combat crew members," 17 November 1943, folder Personal—January 1944, box 14, Spaatz Papers. The Eighth Air Force had a 3.8 percent heavy bomber loss rate from July–November 1943, which meant that for every 100 crewmen in July, by December 64 would be dead, seriously wounded, or prisoners of war. See Perret, *Winged Victory*, 281–84; Parton, *Air Force Spoken Here*, 328.

121. Eaker to Arnold, 22 October 1943, file 312.1-F Operations Letters, June–October 1943, box 194, RG 18, NA.

122. "Aerial Gunner," folder Miscellaneous Personal Correspondence, February 1943–June 1944, box 81, LeMay Papers. For the definitive study of morale problems among bomber crews, see Mark K. Wells, *Courage and Air Warfare: The Allied Aircrew Experience in the Second World War* (London: Frank Cass, 1995).

123. Williamson Murray, "Ultra: Some Thoughts on Its Impact on the Second World War," *Air University Review* 35 (July–August 1984): 58. Eaker was not mistaken regarding the impact that aerial attrition had on the Luftwaffe fighter force; in fall 1943 twelve German pilots with 1,146 victories among them died in air combat in the West. See Stephen L. McFarland and Wesley Phillips Newton, *To Command the Sky: The Battle for Air Superiority over Germany, 1942–1944* (Washington DC: Smithsonian Institution Press, 1991), 136.

124. For a detailed look at the second great Schweinfurt raid, see Martin Caidin, *Black Thursday* (New York: Dell, 1960).

125. Biddle, *Rhetoric and Reality*, 225.

126. Parton, *Air Force Spoken Here*, 316.

127. Eaker to Anderson, "Press Reports on General Arnold's Statement Concerning Schweinfurt Raid," 22 October 1943, file 312.1-F Operations Letters, June–October 1943, box 194, RG 18, NA.

128. "Sixty Bombers Are Missing," *Time*, 25 October 1943, 23.

129. Actual German losses were thirty-one fighters destroyed, twelve written off, and thirty-four damaged. See Murray, *Strategy for Defeat*, 225.

130. Eaker to Arnold, cable, 15 October 1943, quoted in Parton, *Air Force Spoken Here*, 316.

131. Arnold to Eaker, cable, 15 October 1943, quoted in Parton, *Air Force Spoken Here*, 318.

132. Letter from Air Marshal Richard Peck to Eaker, 15 February 1943, Eighth Air Force File, vol. 1, box 17, Eaker Papers; Eaker to Arnold, folder Central Decimal Files, October 1942–May 1944, file 312.1-E Operations Letters, RG 18, NA.

133. Perera to Major General Fairchild, memorandum, "Timing of Economic Effect of Attacks Contemplated by Eighth Air Force Plan: Ball Bearings," 5 May 1943, file 118.01, v.2, AFHRA.

134. Memorandum of Conference with C. V. Whitney, 23 October 1943, tab B: Summary of Changes in German Oil Industry Since Adoption of Pointblank, file 118.01, v.2, AFHRA.

135. Eaker begged Arnold not to take his replacements and argued that the location of the Fifteenth would prevent it from attacking most of Germany's key industries, but Arnold insisted that the Fifteenth would spread thin German defenses and thus benefit the Eighth's effort. See Eaker to Arnold, 1 October 1943, file 312.1-F Operations Letters, June–October 1943, box 194, RG 18, NA; Arnold to Eaker, 22 October 1943, file 312.1-F Operations Letters, June–October 1943, box 194, RG 18, NA.

136. Portal to Arnold, 24 October 1943, file 312.1-F Operations Letters, June–October 1943, box 194, RG 18, NA. According to the April 1943 Combined Bomber Offensive plan, Eighth Air Force was supposed to have 1,192 heavy bombers by October; on 1 October Eaker actually possessed 750, of which 679 were operational. See "Status of Heavy and Medium Bombers and Fighters with Tactical Groups as of 2000 Hours, 1 October 1943," 1 October 1943, file 312.1-F Operations Letters, June–October 1943, box 194, RG 18, NA.

137. Charles W. McArthur, *Operations Analysis in the U.S. Army Eighth Air Force in World War II* (Providence RI: American Mathematical Society, 1990), 109.

138. Eaker to Arnold, 16 November 1943, folder Bombing—Overcast Operations, box 82, Spaatz Papers.

139. Eaker remarked that destroying cities through radar bombing gave the Germans "the greatest concern. Attacking them when they are under solid cloud cover undoubtedly lowers the morale of the people dangerously." See

Eaker to Giles, Chief of Air Staff, 13 December 1943, Giles File, box 17, Eaker Papers. He further observed regarding the radar bombing of Kiel in December: "To have bombs come raining down on the city under these conditions [complete overcast] must indeed have been a dismal prospect." See Eaker to Lovett, 15 December 1943, Robert A. Lovett File, box 17, Eaker Papers.

140. Eaker to Ronald Schaffer, 11 January 1979, MS 6, HSMC.

141. Portal to Arnold, 24 October 1943, file 312.1-F Operations Letters, June–October 1943, box 194, RG 18, NA.

142. Memorandum of Conference with C. V. Whitney, 23 October 1943, tab B: Summary of Changes in German Oil Industry Since Adoption of Pointblank, file 118.01, v.2, AFHRA.

143. Schaffer, *Wings of Judgment*, 67.

144. Eighth Air Force received three additional groups of heavy bombers in June, two each in July, August, and September, none in October, one in November, and five in December. See Parton, *Air Force Spoken Here*, 289–90.

145. Robin Neillands, *The Bomber War: The Allied Air Offensive against Nazi Germany* (New York: Overlook Press, 2001), 278.

146. Eaker summarized the bombing of Kiel: "There was a concentration [of bombs] over the aiming point, and great sections of Kiel have been absolutely burned out or blown out." See Eaker to Col. George A. Brownell, Executive Officer, Office of the Assistant Secretary for Air, 22 December 1943, box 17, Eaker Papers.

147. Eaker to Lovett, 15 December 1943, Lovett File, box 17, Eaker Papers.

148. Eaker to Giles, Chief of Air Staff, 13 December 1943, Giles File, box 17, Eaker Papers.

149. Eaker to Fechet, 22 December 1943, folder General Correspondence—December 1943, box 9, Eaker Papers.

5. Bludgeoning with Bombs

Robert A. Lovett, "The Growth of the U.S. Army Air Forces during the Last Two Years," speech, NYC University Club, 9 December 1943, Robert A. Lovett File, box 17, Ira C. Eaker Papers, Library of Congress. Original emphasis.

Doolittle to Spaatz, message, 1 February 1945, box 23, Carl A. Spaatz Papers, Library of Congress. At the bottom of Doolittle's message, Spaatz typed: "Replied by telephone conversation and told Doolittle to hit oil if visual assured; otherwise, Berlin—center of City. C. S."

1. "RAF Summary of Bomber Command Operations," 1 January 1945–28 February 1945, file 1, 4, 2N (3) (2), Record Group (hereafter RG) 243, National Archives (hereafter NA), Washington DC.

2. Air Force Historical Research Agency (hereafter AFHRA) Film Document No. 506.55A, Air Force Office of History, Bolling Air Force Base DC; Wesley Frank Craven and James Lea Cate, eds., *The Army Air Forces in World War II* (Chicago: University of Chicago Press, 1949; repr., Washington DC: Office of Air Force History, 1983), 3:732.

3. AFHRA Film Document No. 506.55A. See also Tami Davis Biddle, "Dresden 1945: Reality, History, and Memory," *Journal of Military History* 72 (April 2008): 424.

4. Spaatz to Arnold, memorandum UA 64471, 19 February 1945, folder Personal—February 1945, box 20, Spaatz Papers. Maj. Gen. Frederick Anderson, Spaatz's Deputy Commander for Operations, provided Arnold with the text of Grierson's statement and drafted this message while Spaatz was away in the Mediterranean.

5. Arnold to Spaatz, incoming message 39722, 18 February 1945, folder Personal—February 1945, box 20, Spaatz Papers.

6. Arnold to Spaatz, incoming message 39730, 18 February 1945, folder Personal—February 1945, box 20, Spaatz Papers.

7. Arnold to Spaatz, incoming message 39730, 18 February 1945, folder Personal—February 1945, box 20, Spaatz Papers.

8. Spaatz to Arnold, memorandum UA 64471, 19 February 1945, folder Personal—February 1945, box 20, Spaatz Papers. In addition to sending this message to Arnold on Spaatz's behalf, Anderson also sent a copy to Spaatz, and notified Spaatz of Cowan's accusation that "we have adopted a policy of terror raids." Anderson added: "I am discussing this matter with either Beetle Smith [*sic*] or General Eisenhower tomorrow morning, with a view to recommending that a statement be released clarifying the U.S. Strategic Air Forces' position in this matter. This embarrassing position for the U.S. Air Forces is a direct result of a R.A.F. officer, representing SHAEF, speaking for the Strategic Air Forces without authority." See Anderson to Spaatz, memorandum, 19 February 1945, folder Private Diary—February 1945, box 21, Spaatz Papers.

9. Spaatz to Arnold, UA 64462, 18 February 1945, folder Personal—February 1945, box 20, Spaatz Papers.

10. Transcript of USAAF press conference, 21 February 1945, quoted in

Tami Davis Biddle, *Rhetoric and Reality in Air Warfare: The Evolution of British and American Ideas about Strategic Bombing, 1914–1945* (Princeton: Princeton University Press, 2002), 259.

11. Field Order no. 629, Mission Reports of the Ninety-second Bombardment Group, mission no. 391, RG 18, NA. To prevent friendly fire accidents, Allied ground and air commanders marked front line positions on a map with a "bomb line" that prohibited air attacks inside its borders.

12. Thomas M. Coffey, *Hap: The Story of the U.S. Air Force and the Man Who Built It* (New York: Viking Press, 1982), 102–3.

13. Richard G. Davis, *Carl A. Spaatz and the Air War in Europe* (Washington DC: Center for Air Force History, 1993), 592.

14. Eaker to Arnold, 24 November 1944, file MAAF, vol. 3—Correspondence with Arnold, box 22, Eaker Papers.

15. See James Parton, *Air Force Spoken Here: General Ira Eaker and the Command of the Air* (Bethesda MD: Adler and Adler, 1986), 331–32.

16. Maj. Gen. Haywood Hansell's assertion regarding Spaatz, a fellow air commander that he knew well, comes from a letter that Hansell wrote to Dr. David MacIsaac on 8 January 1988. Hansell added that Spaatz "was almost alone among top-flight American air leaders in consistent support of decisive strategic air warfare." See Hansell Small Manuscript Collection, MS 6, Special Collections Branch, U.S. Air Force Academy Library CO (hereafter, HSMC).

17. Hansell to MacIsaac, 8 January 1988, MS 6, HSMC.

18. The bomb load that a B-17 or B-24 could carry depended on its distance to target. For raids deep into Germany, five thousand pounds of bombs per bomber were closer to the mark. The B-24 could carry slightly more ordnance than the B-17.

19. Craven and Cate, *Army Air Forces*, 3:18; Biddle, *Rhetoric and Reality*, 226; Parton, *Air Force Spoken Here*, 289–90; Michael S. Sherry, *The Rise of American Air Power: The Creation of Armageddon* (New Haven: Yale University Press, 1987), 161; Geoffrey Perret, *Winged Victory: The Army Air Forces in World War II* (New York: Random House, 1993), 362.

20. Perret, *Winged Victory*, 116–20, 284–85, 294. Strafing airfields was dangerous work, however, and five times as many Eighth Air Force fighter pilots were lost in those missions than were downed in air-to-air combat.

21. Davis, *Carl A. Spaatz*, 302–3.

22. Spaatz to Arnold, message K-3214, 21 January 1944, folder Personal Correspondence, January 1944, box 14, Spaatz Papers.

23. Spaatz to Arnold, 25 January 1944, file MAAF, vol. 1—Correspondence with Arnold, 26 December 1943–30 April 1944, box 22, Eaker Papers. Spaatz had similarly stated on 23 January: "The basic plan we visualize employing at the present time is a full-out effort against as many German fighter factories as possible, whenever weather conditions insure effective results. These attacks in Germany beyond fighter range may and probably will result in rather heavy losses." See Spaatz to Arnold, 23 January 1944, folder Personal Correspondence, January 1944, box 14, Spaatz Papers. Note that Spaatz referred to Berlin as "an area target" from the beginning of his tenure as USSTAF commander.

24. Craven and Cate, Army Air Forces, 3:20. Eighth Air Force used H2X on fifteen of the twenty-one heavy bomber missions flown between 4 January and 15 February.

25. Arnold to Spaatz, 5 January 1944, and Spaatz to Arnold, 10 January 1944, folder Personal Correspondence—January 1944, box 14, Spaatz Papers.

26. Craven and Cate, Army Air Forces, 3:13.

27. See supplement to "Suggested Bombardment Program in Preparation for Overlord, dated 25 October 1943," 19 January 1944, and COA to Assistant Chief of Air Staff, Plans, memorandum, "Comments on Operational Directive of 11 January 1944," 5 February 1944, in COA Records, file 118.01, v.2, AFHRA, Maxwell Air Force Base AL.

28. Craven and Cate, Army Air Forces, 3:35. See also Davis, Carl A. Spaatz, 321.

29. Craven and Cate, Army Air Forces, 3:33–34.

30. Kit C. Carter and Robert Mueller, comp., The Army Air Forces in World War II—Combat Chronology, 1941–1945 (Washington DC: Office of Air Force History, 1973), 276–80; Parton, Air Force Spoken Here, 365; Perret, Winged Victory, 287–88.

31. Williamson Murray, Strategy for Defeat: The Luftwaffe, 1933–1945 (Maxwell Air Force Base AL: Air University Press, 1983), 243.

32. Perret, Winged Victory, 289.

33. Craven and Cate, Army Air Forces, 3:33–43.

34. Perret, Winged Victory, 287.

35. Sherry, American Air Power, 192.

36. R. J. Overy, *The Air War 1939–1945* (London: Macmillan Papermac, 1987), 123.

37. Craven and Cate, *Army Air Forces*, 3:51. Of the attacking force, 660 bombers managed to bomb their targets, and 69 bombers were shot down. See also Perret, *Winged Victory*, 290–92.

38. Craven and Cate, *Army Air Forces*, 3:51–53; Perret, *Winged Victory*, 292.

39. Murray, *Strategy for Defeat*, 243.

40. Perret, *Winged Victory*, 294.

41. DeWitt S. Copp contends that Spaatz was "the Ulysses S. Grant of the air war, and The Big Week was the beginning of his Wilderness Campaign. In a partnership with Eaker—which not Arnold but Spaatz had insisted on—he drove for the Luftwaffe's jugular, [with] the attrition on both sides brutal." See *Forged in Fire: Strategy and Decisions in the Airwar over Europe, 1940–1945* (Garden City NY: Doubleday, 1982), 475.

42. Donald L. Miller, *Masters of the Air: America's Bomber Boys Who Fought the Air War against Nazi Germany* (New York: Simon and Schuster, 2007), 7. The total includes those killed in flying accidents and those who suffered disabling mental breakdowns.

43. Perret, *Winged Victory*, 295.

44. In addition to losing more than half of the six-thousand-man raiding force, Allied forces lost 106 aircraft to 48 for the Luftwaffe in the air battles over the beach. See John Terraine, *A Time for Courage: The Royal Air Force in the European War, 1939–1945* (New York: Macmillan, 1985), 561.

45. "Excerpts from CCS 166/1/D, The Bomber Offensive from the United Kingdom," attachment to Portal's letter to Arnold, 15 April 1943, box 16, Eaker Papers.

46. Quoted in Parton, *Air Force Spoken Here*, 263. See also Hansell to Lt. Col. David MacIsaac, 24 August 1975, MS 6, HSMC.

47. Roosevelt to Churchill, 11 April 1944, quoted in Winston S. Churchill, *The Second World War: Closing the Ring* (New York: Bantam Books, 1951, 1962), 453.

48. Davis, *Carl A. Spaatz*, 403.

49. Perret, *Winged Victory*, 305.

50. Eaker to Commanding General, cable, headquarters, Army Air Forces, 11 January 1944, box 16, Eaker Papers.

51. Arnold to Eaker, 3 March 1944, marked "Eaker's Eyes Only," file

MAAF, vol. 1, Correspondence with Arnold, 26 December 1943–30 April 1944, box 22, Eaker Papers.

52. Quoted in David MacIsaac, *Strategic Bombing in World War Two: The Story of the United States Strategic Bombing Survey* (New York: Garland, 1976), 78.

53. Craven and Cate, *Army Air Forces*, 3:232; Thomas Alexander Hughes, *Over Lord: General Pete Quesada and the Triumph of Tactical Air Power in World War II* (New York: Free Press, 1995), 216; David E. Johnson, *Fast Tanks and Heavy Bombers: Innovation in the U.S. Army, 1917–1945* (Ithaca NY: Cornell University Press, 2003), 216–17. "Cobra" was not a perfect rendition of close air support, however; forty-two heavy bombers mistakenly dropped their ordnance on friendly troops and killed 111 men, including Lt. Gen. Lesley McNair.

54. Spaatz believed that achieving air superiority would permit the Army Air Forces "to put the strategic bombing theory to its decisive test in the destruction of German industry." See David R. Mets, *Master of Airpower: General Carl A. Spaatz* (Novato CA: Presidio Press, 1988), 189.

55. See COA to Assistant Chief of Air Staff, Plans, memorandum, "Request Comment on JIC 106/02," 12 January 1944, and COA to Assistant Chief of Air Staff, Plans, memorandum, "Report on German Aviation Gasoline Position," 18 January 1944, both in file 118.01, v.2, AFHRA.

56. Spaatz asserted that rail lines were difficult to shut down completely and easy to repair, while the loss of oil would cause the Germans to conserve fuel and restrict their movement in the West. See Ronald Schaffer, *Wings of Judgment: American Bombing in World War II* (New York: Oxford University Press, 1985), 41; Biddle, *Rhetoric and Reality*, 234–36; and David Eisenhower, *Eisenhower at War 1943–1945* (New York: Vintage, 1987), 184–90.

57. Mets, *Master of Airpower*, 210–11.

58. By July 1944 Eighth Air Force possessed 3,492 heavy bombers, and Fifteenth Air Force had 1,407. See Davis, *Carl A. Spaatz*, 440.

59. Craven and Cate, *Army Air Forces*, 3:174. Richard Davis contends that "Spaatz took risks with his career by authorizing the clandestine bombing of the Ploesti refineries." See *Carl A. Spaatz*, 416.

60. COA to Assistant Chief of Air Staff, Plans, memorandum, "Report on German Aviation Gasoline Position," 18 January 1944, file 118.01, v.2, AFHRA.

61. Craven and Cate, *Army Air Forces*, 3:176–77; Perret, *Winged Victory*, 300.

62. Murray, *Strategy for Defeat*, 58–59.

63. Albert Speer, *Inside the Third Reich* (New York: Avon Books, 1971), 445–46.

64. Speer, *Inside the Third Reich*, 449.

65. Minutes of COA Meeting, 16 June 1944, file 118.01, v.2, AFHRA.

66. Craven and Cate, *Army Air Forces*, 3:296–98; Perret, *Winged Victory*, 340–43.

67. Davis, *Carl A. Spaatz*, 426.

68. Davis, *Carl A. Spaatz*, 429–30.

69. Spaatz to Arnold, 10 December 1944, folder Central Decimal Files, October 1942–44, file 373-2B Operations Reports and Flight Missions, box 562, RG 18, NA. Between 21 and 30 September 1944 Eighth Air Force B-24s flew 1,175 sorties carrying gasoline to battle areas on the continent. See Carter and Mueller, *Army Air Forces*, 456–63.

70. Anderson to LeMay, 9 October 1944, folder III 1 (A) 4, Special Correspondence with Maj. Gen. F. L. Anderson, box B11, Curtis E. LeMay Papers, Library of Congress.

71. Chief of Air Staff, memorandum, "Air Attack on German Civilian Morale," 1 August 1944, Operational Plans—Thunderclap, box 153, Spaatz Papers.

72. "Operation Thunderclap (Attack on German Morale)," 20 August 1944, Operation Thunderclap File, Annex I, box 153, Spaatz Papers.

73. Schaffer, *Wings of Judgment*, 57.

74. Spaatz to Eisenhower, memorandum, "Thunderclap," 24 August 1944, Operational Plans—Thunderclap, box 153, Spaatz Papers.

75. "Air Attack on German Civilian Morale," 7 August 1944, folder Operation Alert (1), White House Central Files—confidential series, box 47, Dwight D. Eisenhower Presidential Library, Abilene, Kansas.

76. Eisenhower to Spaatz, first endorsement, 28 August 1944, folder Official Correspondence—August 1944, box 18, Spaatz Papers. See also Schaffer, *Wings of Judgment*, 84.

77. Eisenhower to Spaatz, 9 September 1944, quoted in Schaffer, *Wings of Judgment*, 84.

78. Kuter to Anderson, 15 August 1944, and Kuter to Arnold, memorandum, 9 August 1944, both in Operational Plans—Thunderclap, box 153,

Spaatz Papers. See also Conrad C. Crane, *Bombs, Cities, and Civilians* (Lawrence: Kansas University Press, 1993), 102–3.

79. Col. Charles Williamson to Anderson, memorandum, "Attack on German Civilian Morale," 12 September 1944, Operational Plans—Thunderclap, box 153, Spaatz Papers.

80. Lieutenant Newell to Colonel Sutterlin, memorandum, "Plan for Systematically Attacking Morale within Germany," 19 September 1944, Operational Plans—Thunderclap, box 153, Spaatz Papers.

81. Carter and Mueller, *Army Air Forces*, 461–68.

82. These numbers come from a report on bombing accuracy completed by the Eighth Air Force Operational Analysis Section, which also noted that bombs dropped via H2X generally fell short of the aiming point by an average of half a mile. The larger the attacking force, the greater the miss distance. See Charles W. McArthur, *Operations Analysis in the U.S. Army Eighth Air Force in World War II* (Providence RI: American Mathematical Society, 1990), 287–98.

83. Perret, *Winged Victory*, 328.

84. Davis, *Carl A. Spaatz*, 504.

85. Spaatz to Arnold, message, 13 December 1944, folder Personal Correspondence—December 1944, box 16, Spaatz Papers.

86. Davis, *Carl A. Spaatz*, 536.

87. Charles B. MacDonald, *A Time for Trumpets: The Untold Story of the Battle of the Bulge* (New York: William Morrow, 1985), 618. This total included fifteen thousand men captured and nineteen thousand killed. Gerhard Weinberg lists a figure of seventy thousand Americans killed, wounded, or missing for the battle. See *A World at Arms: A Global History of World War II* (Cambridge: Cambridge University Press, 1994), 769.

88. Eisenhower, *Eisenhower*, 586. The executed deserter was Private Eddie Slovik, G Company, 109th Infantry Regiment, Twenty-eighth Division.

89. Eisenhower, *Eisenhower*, 607; "The Penalties," *Time*, 1 January 1945, 11.

90. Navy Capt. Harry C. Butcher, diary entry, 9 January 1945, quoted in Eisenhower, *Eisenhower*, 615. Butcher was Gen. Dwight Eisenhower's aide.

91. Arnold to Theodore von Karman, memorandum, 7 November 1944, "AAF Long Range Development Program," Deputy Chief of Staff, Operations, Director of Plans—General File, 1944–53, folder 67, box 16, RG 341, NA.

92. USSTAF MAIN-IN 15172, 1 February 1945, AFHRA Film Document No. 519.523.

93. Arnold wrote on 13 January 1945: "It's quite obvious that Marshal Stalin hasn't the faintest conception of the damage done to Germany and Japan by strategic bombing." He asked that General Lindsay create a "photographic album of strategic bombing—arranged in such a form that he will get a visual picture of what actually happened in localities—pictures taken before and after bombing of certain key points, critical positions and critical industries" for Arnold to present to Stalin at Yalta. See Arnold to Lindsay, 13 January 1945, official file 1932–46, folder Conferences (59), box 42, Henry H. Arnold Papers, Library of Congress.

94. Arnold to Spaatz, 14 January 1945, folder Personal Correspondence—January 1945, box 20, Spaatz Papers.

95. Craven and Cate, *Army Air Forces*, 3:725.

96. Nor was it significantly larger than the American raid against Berlin on 21 June 1944. On that date, 928 bombers dropped more than 2,000 tons of bombs on targets in the Berlin area in a massive daylight raid supported by twenty-three groups of escort fighters; 1,371 tons fell on the city center. See Craven and Cate, *Army Air Forces*, 3:284–85; Richard G. Davis, "Operation 'Thunderclap': The U.S. Army Air Forces and the Bombing of Berlin," *Journal of Strategic Studies* 14 (March 1991): 92.

97. Davis, "Operation 'Thunderclap,'" 106. Only 250 tons of this total were incendiaries; the remaining bombs were high explosives.

98. Craven and Cate, *Army Air Forces*, 3:725–26. Richard Davis questions this total, citing research in Berlin city and Federal Republic archives that indicates tolls of 2,895 dead, 729 injured, and 120,000 made homeless. Davis believes that accurate bombing combined with the meager number of incendiaries used on the mission may have produced fewer casualties than those claimed by Craven and Cate. See Davis, "Operation 'Thunderclap,'" 106.

99. Biddle, "Dresden 1945," 424; see also Mark Clodfelter, "Culmination: Dresden, 1945," *Aerospace Historian* 26 (Fall 1979): 136.

100. Spaatz to Arnold, 5 February 1945, file Personal Diary—February 1945, box 20, Spaatz Papers.

101. Doolittle to Spaatz, message, 1 February 1945, box 23, Spaatz Papers. Spaatz had his response to Doolittle typed at the bottom of the message.

102. Giles to Arnold, memorandum, 7 March 1945, file Diary of Events

and Decisions Made in Absence of Arnold, folder Diaries—Florida—22 January–21 March 1945, box 223, Arnold Papers.

103. Carter and Mueller, *Army Air Forces*, 377, 582.

104. On Spaatz's willingness to gamble that the 3 February 1945 attack would succeed in breaking German morale, see Davis, *Carl A. Spaatz*, 552; Mets, *Master of Airpower*, 270–71.

105. Notes Sherry: "The path to unconditional surrender lay through unconditional destruction." See *American Air Power*, 251.

106. H. H. Arnold to All Air Force Commanders in Combat Zones, memorandum, "Evaluation of Bombing Methods and Purposes," 10 June 1943, file 36 (Bombing), box 41, Arnold Papers.

107. Eaker to Spaatz, marked "General Spaatz' Eyes Only," 1 January 1945, file Personal Diary—January 1945, box 20, Spaatz Papers.

108. Craven and Cate, *Army Air Forces*, 3:733–35.

109. Davis, *Carl A. Spaatz*, 573.

110. Davis, *Carl A. Spaatz*, 573.

111. Radar bombing occurred on 75 percent of raids against thirty-eight marshalling yards attacked between 1 January and 30 April. See Biddle, *Rhetoric and Reality*, 254.

112. For the importance of coal to German industry, and the impact that destroying the German rail system had on industrial production, the definitive study is Alfred C. Mierjejewski, *The Collapse of the German War Economy, 1944–1945: Allied Air Power and the German National Railway* (Chapel Hill: University of North Carolina Press, 1988). See in particular 177–87. Robert A. Pape notes that the advance of Allied armies also contributed to the dearth of coal by capturing key transportation lines. See *Bombing to Win: Air Power and Coercion in War* (Ithaca: Cornell University Press, 1996), 312.

113. David MacIsaac, gen. ed., *The United States Strategic Bombing Survey* (hereafter USSBS), vol. 1, *Overall Report (European War)* (New York: Garland, 1976), 1, 71.

114. Charles Webster and Noble Frankland, *The Strategic Air Offensive against Germany, 1939–1945*, vol. 3, *Victory* (London: Her Majesty's Stationery Office, 1961), 4.

115. MacIsaac, USSBS, vol. 1, *Overall Report (European War)*, 37.

116. Sherry, *American Air Power*, 142.

117. MacIsaac, *USSBS*, vol. 1, *The Effects of Strategic Bombing on German Morale*, 7, and vol. 1, *Overall Report (European War)*, 37. Hans Rumpf, a German fire engineer before the war who commanded a regiment of "fire police" during the conflict, contended that Allied bombing killed six hundred thousand German civilians and seriously wounded eight hundred thousand. See Hans Rumpf, *The Bombing of Germany*, trans. Edward Fitzgerald (New York: Holt, Rinehart, and Winston, 1962), 164.

118. Miller, *Masters of the Air*, 7.

119. Davis, *Carl A. Spaatz*, 587.

120. Davis, *Carl A. Spaatz*, 587.

121. Webster and Frankland, *Strategic Air Offensive against Germany*, 3:286–87. The number includes those killed in combat and flying accidents.

122. MacIsaac, *USSBS*, vol. 1, *Overall Report (European War)*, 107. MacIsaac's *Strategic Bombing in World War Two: The Story of the United States Strategic Bombing Survey* is the classic account of the Survey, which had more than one thousand people assigned to it, including John Kenneth Galbraith, Paul Nitze, and George Ball, and produced a total of 321 reports, 212 on the European War and 109 on the Pacific War. Gian P. Gentile also provides a thorough analysis of the Survey in *How Effective is Strategic Bombing? Lessons Learned from World War II to Kosovo* (New York: New York University Press, 2001).

123. MacIsaac, *USSBS*, vol. 1, *Overall Report (European War)*, 38.

6. Fire from the Sky

Norstad to LeMay, 3 April 1945, folder Official Correspondence with General Norstad, box B11, Curtis E. LeMay Papers, Library of Congress.

LeMay to Norstad, TC NF-25-11, 25 April 1945, quoted in Wesley Frank Craven and James Lea Cate, eds., *The Army Air Forces in World War II* (Chicago: University of Chicago Press, 1949; repr., Washington DC: Office of Air Force History, 1983), 5:626.

1. E. Bartlett Kerr, *Flames over Tokyo: The U.S. Army Air Forces' Incendiary Campaign against Japan, 1944–1945* (New York: Donald I. Fine, 1991), 166.

2. Michael S. Sherry, *The Rise of American Air Power: The Creation of Armageddon* (New Haven: Yale University Press, 1987), 273.

3. St. Clair McKelway, "A Reporter with the B-29s: The Cigar, the Three Wings, and the Low-Level Attacks," *The New Yorker*, 23 June 1945, 36.

4. Curtis E. LeMay with MacKinlay Kantor, *Mission with LeMay* (Garden City NY: Doubleday, 1965), 352.

5. Norstad to LeMay, 3 April 1945, folder Official Correspondence with General Norstad, box B11, LeMay Papers.

6. LeMay with Kantor, *Mission*, 347.

7. Curtis LeMay, interview, March 1970, Air Force Historical Research Agency (hereafter AFHRA), Maxwell Air Force Base AL, microfilm roll 43824, quoted in William W. Ralph, "Improvised Destruction: Arnold, LeMay, and the Firebombing of Japan," *War in History* 13 (Winter 2006): 512.

8. LeMay to Norstad, 3 March 1945, folder Official Correspondence with General Norstad, box B11, LeMay Papers.

9. Ralph Nutter, who had served as a navigator for LeMay in the European theater and now was on the XXI Bomber Command staff, attended the briefing and noted that one crewman called out, "This is stupid. It's suicide," when hearing of planned low-level tactics. See Ralph H. Nutter, *With the Possum and the Eagle: The Memoir of a Navigator's War over Germany and Japan* (Novato CA: Presidio Press, 2002), 238. See also Kenneth P. Werrell, *Blankets of Fire: U.S. Bombers over Japan during World War II* (Washington DC: Smithsonian Institution Press, 1996), 159.

10. "Report of Operations, 10 March 1945," to Commanding General, Twentieth Air Force, 15 April 1945, folder Mission No. 40—Tokyo, Urban Area, 10 March 1945, Meetinghouse 2, file Headquarters Twentieth Air Force, XXI Bomber Command Mission Reports, 1944–45, box 45, Record Group (hereafter RG) 18, National Archives (hereafter NA), Washington DC.

11. Geoffrey Perret, *Winged Victory: The Army Air Forces in World War II* (New York: Random House, 1993), 454.

12. Craven and Cate, *Army Air Forces*, 5:617.

13. McKelway, "Reporter with the B-29s," 32. The Japanese had only four night fighter units, and only two of those were deployed in the home islands. See Werrell, *Blankets of Fire*, 155.

14. "Report of Operations, 10 March 1945," to Commanding General, Twentieth Air Force, 15 April 1945, folder Mission No. 40—Tokyo, Urban Area, 10 March 1945, Meetinghouse 2, file Headquarters Twentieth Air Force, XXI Bomber Command Mission Reports, 1944–45, box 45, RG 18, NA.

15. Quoted in Kerr, *Flames over Tokyo*, 242–43.

16. Norstad to CC AF20, teletype message, 11 March 1945, folder Mission No. 40—Tokyo, 10 March 1945, Meetinghouse 2, file Headquarters Twentieth Air Force XXI Bomber Command Mission Reports, 1944–45, box 45, RG 18, NA.

17. Arnold to LeMay, message, 10 March 1945, "Commendation on March 9th Attack upon Tokyo," folder 9–17 March Incendiary Missions XXI Bomber Command, file Headquarters Twentieth Air Force XXI Bomber Command Mission Reports, 1944–45, box 45, RG 18, NA.

18. Norstad to LeMay, 3 April 1945, folder Official Correspondence with General Norstad, box B11, LeMay Papers.

19. For insights on the desire for retribution possessed by some air commanders, see Ronald Schaffer, *Wings of Judgment: American Bombing in World War II* (New York: Oxford University Press, 1985), 152–53.

20. Haywood S. Hansell Jr., *The Strategic Air War against Germany and Japan: A Memoir* (Washington DC: Office of Air Force History, 1986), 228.

21. McKelway, "Reporter with the B-29s," 35.

22. "Target Information Sheet: Tokyo Urban Industrial Area," 9 March 1945, folder 9–17 March Incendiary Missions XXI Bomber Command, file Headquarters Twentieth Air Force XXI Bomber Command Mission Reports, 1944–45, box 45, RG 18, NA.

23. Marshall made his comments to a group of correspondents on 15 November 1941. The quotation comes from a memorandum by Robert Sherrod, one of the reporters attending the press conference, and is cited by Sherry, *American Air Power*, 109. Sherry points out that the AAF sent incendiary bombs to the Philippines on the eve of Pearl Harbor.

24. Perret, *Winged Victory*, 78, 161.

25. Quoted in Ralph, "Improvised Destruction," 500–501.

26. Arnold to Assistant Chief of Air Staff, Management Control, memorandum, "Analysis of Strategic Targets in Italy," 23 March 1943, file 118.01, v.2, AFHRA. Arnold's memo tasked the COA to determine what targets, if destroyed, "would knock Italy out of the war," and after completing that study, they were to prepare "a similar analysis of strategic targets located in Japan."

27. Colonel Perera to Brigadier General Hansell, memorandum, "Effect of Destruction of Coke Ovens upon Japan's War Effort," 1 December 1943, file 118.01, v.2, AFHRA.

28. COA to General Arnold, memorandum, "Report of Committee of Op-

erational Analysts on Economic Objectives in the Far East," 11 November 1943, quoted in Kerr, *Flames over Tokyo*, 46.

29. Kerr, *Flames over Tokyo*, 46.

30. The Assistant Chief of Air Staff, Intelligence (A-2), submitted the report, entitled "Japan, Incendiary Attack Data," on 15 October 1943. See Kerr, *Flames over Tokyo*, 40–45.

31. Kerr, *Flames over Tokyo*, 43.

32. Kerr, *Flames over Tokyo*, 31–32.

33. On B-29 capabilities and specifications, see Werrell, *Blankets of Fire*, 55–83; Keith Wheeler, *Bombers over Japan* (Alexandria VA: Time-Life Books, 1982), 20–33; and Perret, *Winged Victory*, 37, 102, 447–49.

34. Henry H. Arnold, *Global Mission* (New York: Harper and Brothers, 1949), 348.

35. Combined Chiefs of Staff Document 417, 2 December 1943, quoted in Haywood S. Hansell Jr., *Strategic Air War against Japan* (Washington DC: U.S. Government Printing Office, 1980), 19.

36. Hansell compared Arnold's potential control of the B-29 force to the unified control that Admiral King exerted over all U.S. Naval forces in the Pacific as "Commander in Chief, U.S. Fleet." King thought that the comparison was a good one and endorsed Arnold as Twentieth Air Force Commander. See Hansell, *The Strategic Air War against Germany and Japan: A Memoir*, 157–58.

37. "The Eight Hundred and Eighty-first Press Conference—Joint Conference of the President and Mme. Chiang Kai-shek, 19 February 1943," in Samuel I. Rosenman, comp., *The Public Papers and Addresses of Franklin D. Roosevelt, 1943* (New York: Harper and Brothers, 1950), 105.

38. Roosevelt to Marshall, memorandum, 15 October 1943, quoted in Craven and Cate, *Army Air Forces*, 5:21.

39. Arnold to Roosevelt, memorandum, 22 February 1944, quoted in Sherry, *American Air Power*, 171.

40. Arnold to Chief of the Air Staff, memorandum, 20 February 1944, folder 334 (case 63), Official Decimal Files, 1938–46, box 94, Henry H. Arnold Papers, Library of Congress. Arnold wrote, regarding Joint Chiefs of Staff conferences in the White House with the president on 11 and 19 February that focused on the B-29: "[I]t has been accepted that control of this strategic weapon will be retained in Washington and it was generally understood that executive direction of its development and control is vested with the Chief of the Army Air Forces."

41. Eric Larrabee, *Commander in Chief: Franklin Roosevelt, His Lieutenants, and Their War* (New York: Simon and Schuster, 1987), 610.

42. Perret, *Winged Victory*, 402; Larrabee, *Commander in Chief*, 610.

43. Thomas M. Coffey, *Hap: The Story of the U.S. Air Force and the Man Who Built It* (New York: Viking Press, 1982), 339–40; Larrabee, *Commander in Chief*, 612.

44. Sherry, *American Air Power*, 171.

45. LeMay continued: "It is true that I have taken other steps to increase our efficiency besides inaugurating a training program, however, they were taken on my arrival here, September 1st. The increase in our bombing accuracy and increase in load carrying capacity does not start until the last of October, after our training had taken hold." See LeMay to Arnold, 29 November 1944, folder Special Official Correspondence with General Arnold, box 11, LeMay Papers.

46. Arnold to Spaatz, 29 September 1944, quoted in Craven and Cate, *Army Air Forces*, 5:104.

47. See Arnold to LeMay, 22 September 1944, and Arnold to LeMay, 17 November 1944, folder Special Official Correspondence with General Arnold, box 11, LeMay Papers.

48. Arnold to LeMay, 17 December 1944, folder Special Official Correspondence with General Arnold, box 11, LeMay Papers.

49. Perera to Kuter, memorandum, 6 February 1944, file 118.01, v.2, AFHRA.

50. Perera to Colonel Lindsay, memorandum, "Comments on Chart of Proposed VLR Employment," 5 August 1944, file 118.01, v.2, AFHRA. Emphasis added.

51. Hansell to Col. Rollin C. Reineck, 9 January 1978, Hansell Small Manuscript Collection, MS 6, Special Collections Branch, U.S. Air Force Academy Library CO (hereafter HSMC).

52. Hansell to Robert F. Futrell, 5 July 1988, MS 6, HSMC.

53. Kerr, *Flames over Tokyo*, 92–93; Hansell, *Strategic Air War against Japan*, 36.

54. Hansell, *Strategic Air War against Japan*, 36.

55. Hansell to Colonel Reineck, 9 January 1978. See also Hansell to Kevin B. Herbert, 8 April 1983, MS 6, HSMC.

56. CCS 680/2, 16 September 1944, quoted in Craven and Cate, *Army Air Forces*, 5:677.

57. Arnold to Hansell, 22 September 1944, reprinted in Hansell, *Strategic Air War against Japan*, 129.

58. Kerr, *Flames over Tokyo*, 93.

59. Hansell to Colonel Reineck, 9 January 1978, MS 6, HSMC.

60. Craven and Cate, *Army Air Forces*, 5:558–59. See also Kit C. Carter and Robert Mueller, comp., *The Army Air Forces in World War II—Combat Chronology, 1941–1945* (Washington DC: Office of Air Force History, 1973), 505, which contends that thirty-five B-29s bombed the aircraft plant, and fifty bombed urban areas and docks.

61. Craven and Cate, *Army Air Forces*, 5:559. See also Perret, *Winged Victory*, 450–51.

62. Craven and Cate, *Army Air Forces*, 5:559.

63. Craven and Cate, *Army Air Forces*, 5:562. Post-strike photographs showed that 16 percent of the bombs dropped fell within one thousand feet of the aiming point, and that almost 20 percent of the plant's roofed area had been destroyed.

64. Kerr, *Flames over Tokyo*, 102.

65. Hansell to Colonel Reineck, 9 January 1978, MS 6, HSMC.

66. Hansell to Arnold, 16 December 1944, folder 201—Hansell, Haywood S., Jr., file Headquarters Twentieth Air Force Decimal File 1944–45, box 1, RG 18, NA.

67. Norstad to Hansell, 7 December 1944, folder 201—Hansell, Haywood S., Jr., file Headquarters Twentieth Air Force Decimal File 1944–45, box 1, RG 18, NA.

68. Minutes of the COA, 14 September 1944, file 118.15, AFHRA, quoted in Kerr, *Flames over Tokyo*, 80.

69. Kerr, *Flames over Tokyo*, 81.

70. Kerr, *Flames over Tokyo*, 82.

71. "Revised Report of the COA on Economic Targets in the Far East," 10 October 1944, 2–3, file 118.01, v.2, AFHRA.

72. "Revised Report of the COA on Economic Targets in the Far East," 10 October 1944, 4, file 118.01, v.2, AFHRA. The report added: "The direct loss that they [area attacks] impose on war production is not inconsiderable. . . . This production loss results from two elements: (a) direct damage to industrial facilities and housing; [and] (b) the diversion of Japanese industry from its normal activities to the repair and replacement of this dam-

age. The direct production loss results mainly from the interruption of production in damaged factories; partly from absenteeism induced by bombing and general damage" (51).

73. "Revised Report of the COA on Economic Targets in the Far East," 10 October 1944, 51, file 118.01, v.2, AFHRA. The report further stated: "The loss imposed by the burden of repair and replacement of incendiary damage would fall chiefly on the construction industry and producers of industrial equipment. Since these industries lie deep in the productive process, the effect on front-line strength would be delayed and diffuse. Most seriously affected will be the machine tool industry, it being estimated that over 15 per cent of all machine tools (almost one year's output of the industry) will be destroyed or heavily damaged. It appears likely that machine tool replacement will be the limiting factor in recuperation; it should not, however, delay recuperation in any high priority industry beyond the limits assumed in this study" (52).

74. "Revised Report of the COA on Economic Targets in the Far East," 10 October 1944, 4, file 118.01, v.2, AFHRA.

75. "Revised Report of the COA on Economic Targets in the Far East," 10 October 1944, 3, file 118.01, v.2, AFHRA.

76. Hansell, *Strategic Air War against Japan*, 50.

77. Norstad to Assistant Chief of Air Staff, Plans, memorandum, "Report of Committee of Operations Analysts," 17 November 1944, file 118.01, v.2, AFHRA.

78. Hansell to Norstad, telecommunication, "Incendiary Attack of City of Nogoya," quoted in Kerr, *Flames over Tokyo*, 118.

79. Norstad to Hansell, telecommunication, quoted in Kerr, *Flames over Tokyo*, 118.

80. Carter and Mueller, *Army Air Forces*, 532; Kerr, *Flames over Tokyo*, 118, 235; Werrell, *Blankets of Fire*, 47–49.

81. Arnold to Hansell, 27 December 1944, folder 201—Hansell, Haywood S., Jr., file Headquarters Twentieth Air Force Decimal File 1944–45, box 1, RG 18, NA. The U.S. government had recently released information regarding the Bataan Death March, and the U.S. Navy had experienced several Kamikaze attacks in concert with the October 1944 invasion of the Philippines. See Sherry, *American Air Power*, 242.

82. Quoted in Kerr, *Flames over Tokyo*, 119.

83. General Kuter to Brigadier General Lindsay, memorandum, "Con-

ference in General Arnold's Office," 29 September 1944, file 118.01, v.2, AFHRA.

84. Arnold to LeMay, 10 November 1944, folder 201—Hansell, Haywood S., Jr., file Headquarters Twentieth Air Force Decimal File 1944–45, box 1, RG 18, NA. This same letter is also found in folder Special Correspondence with General Arnold, box 11, LeMay Papers, with a date of 13 November 1944.

85. LeMay later stated that since he outranked Hansell, and a consolidation of the XX and XXI Bomber Commands was imminent, he was the logical choice to take command. That explanation may have been a polite way to avoid saying that Arnold was dissatisfied with Hansell's performance. See Thomas M. Coffey, *Iron Eagle: The Turbulent Life of General Curtis LeMay* (New York: Crown, 1986), 133–34.

86. Hansell to Arnold, 14 January 1945, folder 201—Hansell, Haywood S., Jr., file Headquarters Twentieth Air Force Decimal File 1944–45, box 1, RG 18, NA.

87. Hansell, *The Strategic Air War against Germany and Japan: A Memoir*, 213.

88. Brig. Gen. H. M. McClelland to Commanding General, Twentieth Air Force, memorandum, "Analysis of the First Ten Missions of the XX Bomber Command," 14 December 1944, folder Central Decimal Files, October 1942–44, file 373.2-B Operations Reports and Flight Missions, box 562, RG 18, NA.

89. On the Hankow raid, see Craven and Cate, *Army Air Forces*, 5:142–44; Kerr, *Flames over Tokyo*, 114–16; Perret, *Winged Victory*, 399; and Sherry, *American Air Power*, 256.

90. Arnold to Stimson, 13 February 1945, quoted in Sherry, *American Air Power*, 256.

91. Hansell, *The Strategic Air War against Germany and Japan: A Memoir*, 213.

92. Arnold to Norstad, 14 January 1945, reprinted in Coffey, *Hap*, 348.

93. LeMay to Norstad, 16 November 1944, folder III 1 (A) 3, Official Correspondence with General Norstad, box B11, LeMay Papers.

94. Norstad to LeMay, 3 April 1945, folder Official Correspondence with General Norstad, box B11, LeMay Papers.

95. LeMay with Kantor, *Mission*, 338.

96. LeMay to Norstad, 31 January 1945, folder Official Correspondence with General Norstad, box B11, LeMay Papers.

97. Kerr, *Flames over Tokyo*, 129–32; Carter and Mueller, *Army Air Forces*, 557.

98. LeMay to Anderson, 16 January 1945, folder III 1 (A) 4, Special Official Correspondence with Maj. Gen. F. L. Anderson, box B11, LeMay Papers.

99. Giles to Arnold, memorandum, 30 January 1945, file Diary of Events and Decisions Made in Absence of Arnold, folder Diaries—Florida—22 January–21 March 1945, box 223, Arnold Papers.

100. Norstad to Arnold, memorandum, quoted in Schaffer, *Wings of Judgment*, 123.

101. Richard G. Davis, "Operation 'Thunderclap': The U.S. Army Air Forces and the Bombing of Berlin," *Journal of Strategic Studies* 14 (March 1991): 106; Kerr, *Flames over Tokyo*, 133. Berlin received 250 tons of incendiaries.

102. Kerr, *Flames over Tokyo*, 133.

103. Norstad to LeMay, telecommunication, 12 February 1945, quoted in Kerr, *Flames over Tokyo*, 134.

104. Norstad to LeMay and others, telecommunication, 19 February 1945, quoted in Sherry, *American Air Power*, 266.

105. Kerr, *Flames over Tokyo*, 135–36.

106. Quoted in Wheeler, *Bombers over Japan*, 113.

107. Arnold to Giles, 16 February 1945, quoted in Coffey, *Hap*, 350.

108. Ralph, "Improvised Destruction," 511–12; Carter and Mueller, *Army Air Forces*, 576.

109. Kerr, *Flames over Tokyo*, 141; Carter and Mueller, *Army Air Forces*, 582.

110. Werrell, *Blankets of Fire*, 152.

111. Carter and Mueller, *Army Air Forces*, 589.

112. Wheeler, *Bombers over Japan*, 115. O'Donnell requested clarification of the altitude and then protested when LeMay confirmed fifty feet. The mission went as LeMay intended, and all bombers returned safely.

113. LeMay to Norstad, 3 March 1945, folder Official Correspondence with General Norstad, box B11, LeMay Papers.

114. Giles to Arnold, 2 March 1945, file Diary of Events and Decisions Made in Absence of Arnold, folder Diaries—Florida—22 January–21 March 1945, box 223, Arnold Papers.

115. LeMay with Kantor, *Mission*, 347.

116. "If we accomplished the job in any given battle without exterminating too many of our own folks, we considered that we'd had a pretty good day," LeMay later observed. See LeMay with Kantor, *Mission*, 383.

117. LeMay with Kantor, *Mission*, 382.

118. Sherry, *American Air Power*, 283.

119. Arnold to LeMay, 21 March 1945, folder Special Official Correspondence with General Arnold, box 11, LeMay Papers.

120. Carter and Mueller, *Army Air Forces*, 595–602; Ralph, "Improvised Destruction," 513–14.

121. COMAF 20 to COMGENBOMBCOM 21, teletype message, "Osaka Coverage," 14 March 1945, folder Mission No. 42 Osaka PEACHBOWL 1 13 March 1945, file Headquarters Twentieth AF XXI Bomber Command Mission Reports, 1944–45, box 45, RG 18, NA.

122. Norstad press conference, verbatim transcript, 23 March 1945, quoted in Sherry, *American Air Power*, 289.

123. Sherry, *American Air Power*, 258–59.

124. The 10 October 1944 report of the COA had warned that incendiary attacks would have a minimal impact on Japan's frontline fighting capability. See "Revised Report of the COA on Economic Targets in the Far East," 10 October 1944, 51–52, file 118.01, v.2, AFHRA. See also Ralph, "Improvised Destruction," 522; Sherry, *American Air Power*, 286–87.

125. COMAF 20 to COMGENBOMBCOM 21 INFO DEPCOMAF 20, message, 12 March 1945, folder Mission No. 41 Nagoya—Microscope 2, 11 March 1945, file Headquarters Twentieth Air Force, XXI Bomber Command Mission Reports, 1944–45, box 45, RG 18, NA; LeMay to Commanding General, Twentieth Air Force, "Report of Operations, 11–12 March 1945," 16 April 1945, folder Mission No. 41 Urban Area—Microscope 3, Nagoya, 11/12 March 1945, file Headquarters Twentieth Air Force, XXI Bomber Command Mission Reports, 1944–45, box 45, RG 18, NA.

126. "Tactical Mission Report, Mission No. 40, 10 March 1945," folder Mission No. 40—Tokyo, Urban Area, 10 March 1945, Meetinghouse 2, file Headquarters Twentieth Air Force, XXI Bomber Command Mission Reports, 1944–45, box 45, RG 18, NA. Original emphasis.

127. Colonel Combs to Brigadier General Hansell, 28 March 1945, folder 201—Hansell, Haywood S., Jr., file Headquarters Twentieth Air Force Decimal File 1944–45, box 1, RG 18, NA. Combs also noted the unique way that

the Joint Target Group, a targeting intelligence organization comprising many of the same military and civilian analysts as the COA, thought about Japan. Brig. Gen. John A. "Sammy" Samford, director of the JTG, had decided "that there are no single strategic bottlenecks in Japan (except for aircraft engine and assembly plants), and that our further activity must be aimed at destroying Japanese industry as a whole."

128. Gen. Curtis E. LeMay, USAF, Ret., "The Command Realities," in *Impact: The Army Air Forces' Confidential Picture History of World War II* (Harrisburg PA: Historical Times, 1982), 5:xvi.

129. Norstad to LeMay, 3 April 1945, folder Official Correspondence with General Norstad, box B11, LeMay Papers.

130. Norstad to LeMay, 17 April 1945, folder III 1 (A) 3, Official Correspondence with General Norstad, box B11, LeMay Papers.

131. "Practically all Germans deny the fact that they surrendered in the last war, but this time they are going to know it. And so are the Japs," Roosevelt told journalists in July 1944. See "The Nine Hundred and Sixty-second Press Conference, Waikiki, Honolulu, July 29, 1944," in Rosenman, *Public Papers, 1944–45*, 210. See also Richard B. Frank, *Downfall: The End of the Imperial Japanese Empire* (New York: Penguin, 2001), 336–37; Sherry, *American Air Power*, 246–51.

132. Spaatz stated after the war: "We had not the same urge, or the same feeling as far as bombing Germany is concerned, as we had for the Japs who had first attacked at Pearl Harbor. . . . We didn't hear any complaints from the American people about [the] mass bombing of Japan; as a matter of fact, I think they felt the more we did the better. That was our feeling towards the Japanese at the time." See Spaatz, interview by Mr. Arthur Goldberg, 19 May 1965, file K239.0512-755, AFHRA. For accounts of American wartime attitudes toward the Japanese, see John W. Dower, *War without Mercy: Race and Power in the Pacific War* (New York: Pantheon Books, 1986); Gerald F. Linderman, *The World within War: America's Combat Experience in World War II* (New York: Free Press, 1997), 143–84.

133. Arnold, diary entry, 16 June 1945, in John W. Huston, ed., *American Airpower Comes of Age: General Henry H. "Hap" Arnold's World War II Diaries* (Maxwell Air Force Base AL: Air University Press, 2002), 2:332.

134. O'Donnell to LeMay, folder Special Official Correspondence with General Officers, O'Donnell File, box B11, LeMay Papers.

135. As reported in the official Army account, American casualties at Ok-

inawa numbered 12,520 killed or missing and 36,613 wounded. Another accounting lists ground forces casualties as 6,319 killed, 32,943 wounded, and 33,096 "non-battle" casualties that included psychiatric cases, injuries, illnesses, and deaths, for a total of 72,358. See Frank, *Downfall*, 71. See also Ronald H. Spector, *Eagle against the Sun: The American War with Japan* (New York: Free Press, 1985), 540; Max Hastings, *Retribution: The Battle for Japan, 1944–45* (New York: Alfred A. Knopf, 2008), 402.

136. From 17 April to 11 May, XXI Bomber Command devoted 75 percent of its effort to support the Okinawa invasion force that endured Japanese air attacks—including Kamikazes—from Kyushu and Shikoku islands. B-29s flew more than 2,100 sorties against seventeen Japanese airfields. See Carter and Mueller, *Army Air Forces*, 631.

137. B-29s dropped more than twelve thousand mines in Japanese home waters and effectively ended travel across the Shimonoseki Strait between Kyushu and Honshu. Mines dropped by the 313th Wing sank or disabled 163,000 tons of shipping, with more than half of the losses occurring in the Shimonoseki Strait. See Craven and Cate, *Army Air Forces*, 5:662–74; Werrell, *Blankets of Fire*, 170–76.

138. Arnold to LeMay, 21 March 1945, folder Special Official Correspondence with General Arnold, box 11, LeMay Papers.

139. Perret, *Winged Victory*, 457.

140. Craven and Cate, *Army Air Forces*, 5:643; Kerr, *Flames over Tokyo*, 261. The planned target area of those six cities comprised a total of 112.7 square miles; the total urban area of those cities was 257.2 square miles.

141. Perret, *Winged Victory*, 457. More than two thousand stricken B-29s landed on Iwo Jima in 1945.

142. Arnold, diary entry, 15 June 1945, in Huston, *American Airpower*, 2:330.

143. Frank, *Downfall*, 146. See also Sherry, *American Air Power*, 306.

144. Quoted in Huston, *American Airpower*, 2:352n90.

145. Huston speculates that Arnold's fragile health prevented him from attending the Washington DC meeting. Arnold was on Guam when he received word of it and dispatched LeMay. LeMay's trip took thirty-six flying hours to get to Washington DC in a stripped B-29, and he arrived a day and a half before the JCS meeting, though Ira Eaker, then serving as Arnold's deputy, attended the meeting with the president. LeMay attended a JCS meet-

ing the following day where Truman was not present. See Huston, *American Airpower*, 2:316–19.

146. Sherry, *American Air Power*, 307–8; Arnold, diary entry, 13 June 1945, in Huston, *American Airpower*, 2:326.

147. "My briefing didn't have much effect," LeMay remembered. See LeMay, interview by Max Rosenberg, 12 January 1965, file K239.0512-714, AFHRA.

148. Arnold to LeMay, 5 July 1945, folder III 1 (A) 1, Official Correspondence with General Arnold, box B11, LeMay Papers.

149. Sherry, *American Air Power*, 310.

150. Craven and Cate, *Army Air Forces*, 5:656–57.

151. The Joint Chiefs created the Joint Target Group (originally known as the Joint Target Analysis Group) in September 1944 to integrate and coordinate intelligence analyses of air targets in the Pacific War. Directed by Army Air Forces Brig. Gen. John A. Samford, the JTG reported to Arnold and was also part of the Army Air Forces' A-2 (intelligence) office, but it included Navy representatives, as well as a special panel of consultants, many of whom were civilians and former members of the Committee of Operations Analysts. See John F. Kreis, ed., *Piercing the Fog: Intelligence and Army Air Forces Operations in World War II* (Washington DC: Air Force History and Museums Program, 1996), 368–69.

152. David MacIsaac, *Strategic Bombing in World War Two: The Story of the United States Strategic Bombing Survey* (New York: Garland, 1976), 99–102. See also Frank, *Downfall*, 303–4.

153. Spaatz, interview by Mr. Arthur Goldberg, 19 May 1965.

154. Gen. Curtis LeMay, interview by Dr. Edgar F. Puryear Jr., 17 November 1976, file K239.0512-1450, AFHRA.

155. Bob Greene, "Life After Wartime," *New York Times*, 12 November 2007. The article appeared following the death of Tibbets at age ninety-two.

156. David MacIsaac, gen. ed., *The United States Strategic Bombing Survey* (hereafter USSBS), vol. 7, *The Effects of Atomic Bombs on Hiroshima and Nagasaki* (New York: Garland, 1976), 15.

157. Norstad to Spaatz, telecon message Nr 9-1, 8 August 1945, folder Personal Correspondence—August 1945, box 21, Spaatz Papers.

158. Spaatz stated after the war: "I thought that if we were going to drop the atomic bomb, drop it on the outskirts—say in Tokyo Bay—so that the

effects would not be as devastating to the city and the people. I made this suggestion over the phone between the Hiroshima and Nagasaki bombings and I was told to go ahead with our targets." See Spaatz, interview by Brig. Gen. Noel F. Parrish and Dr. Alfred Goldberg, 21 February 1962, file K239.0512-754, AFHRA.

159. MacIsaac, USSBS, vol. 7, *The Effects of Atomic Bombs on Hiroshima and Nagasaki*, 15.

160. Sherry, *American Air Power*, 310; Craven and Cate, *Army Air Forces*, 5:732–33. Along with 186 fighter escorts, the B-29s on 14 August surpassed Arnold's goal of putting 1,000 aircraft over Japan in a single day.

161. Craven and Cate, *Army Air Forces*, 5:732. Spaatz later stated: "After Nagasaki I called off any further raids but was ordered by Washington to resume them as the Japanese had not surrendered as yet. We then ran two more raids which I did not consider necessary—they surrendered two days later." See Spaatz, interview by Parrish and Goldberg, 21 February 1962, file K239.0512-754, AFHRA.

162. Marshall, eyes only for Spaatz, War Dept. to CG U.S. Army Strategic Air Forces, Guam, 8 August 1945; and Spaatz, eyes only for General Marshall, Headquarters, U.S. Army Strategic Air Forces, Guam, to War Dept., 9 August 1945; both contained in folder War Dept. Special Staff Public Relations Division Gen Records, Top-Secret Correspondence, 1944–46, file II 1945, Records of the War Dept. Gen and Special Staffs, box 3, RG 165, NA.

163. Craven and Cate, *Army Air Forces*, 5:732. Components for a third bomb were available, but Marshall decided to save it for the invasion if the Japanese did not surrender after Nagasaki. See Perret, *Winged Victory*, 461; Frank, *Downfall*, 312.

164. Fred Anderson's view was typical. After the Japanese agreed to surrender, he wrote Spaatz: "I wish to congratulate you upon proving to the world that a nation can be defeated by air power alone." See Anderson to Spaatz, 17 August 1945, folder Personal Correspondence—August 1945, box 21, Spaatz Papers.

165. Harry S. Truman, *Memoirs* (Garden City NY: Doubleday, 1955), 1:417. See also Truman's letter to Prof. James L. Cate, 12 January 1953, reprinted in Craven and Cate, *Army Air Forces*, 5:712–13. In part, the letter stated: "Dropping the [atomic] bombs ended the war, saved lives, and gave the free nations a chance to face the facts."

166. Frank, *Downfall*, 136–48. See also Thomas B. Allen and Norman Polmar, *Code-Name Downfall: The Secret Plan To Invade Japan—and Why Truman Dropped the Bomb* (New York: Simon and Schuster, 1995), 203–15.

167. Frank, *Downfall*, 202–3, 245–46.

168. Harry S. Truman, *Public Papers of the Presidents of the United States: Harry S. Truman, 1945* (Washington DC: U.S. Government Printing Office, 1961), 212. Truman had expressed similar sentiments in a diary entry while at Potsdam on 25 July 1945, writing: "Even if the Japs are savages, ruthless, merciless and fanatic, we as the leader of the world for the common welfare can not drop this terrible bomb on the old capital or new. . . . The target will be a purely military one and we will issue a warning statement asking the Japs to surrender and save lives. I'm sure they will not do that, but we will have given them the chance." See Robert H. Ferrell, ed., *Off the Record: The Private Papers of Harry S. Truman* (New York: Harper and Row, 1980), 55–56. Truman likely considered Hiroshima a military target because it contained a naval base and the headquarters of the Japanese Second General Army.

169. Winston S. Churchill, *The Second World War: Triumph and Tragedy* (New York: Bantam Books, 1953, 1962), 545–46.

170. MacIsaac, USSBS, vol. 7, *Summary Report (Pacific War)*, 26.

171. Frank, *Downfall*, 288–96, 308–21, outlines how those factors persuaded the Emperor to accept surrender and contributed to an acceptance of the Emperor's decision by the members of Japan's Supreme War Council. See also Hastings, *Retribution*, 504–15. Hastings maintains that the atomic bombs and the Soviet entry into the war were the key factors that induced surrender. He writes: "Those who seek to argue that Japan was ready to surrender before Hiroshima are peddlers of fantasies" (513).

172. The Survey stated: "By August 1945, even without direct air attack on her cities and industries, the over-all level of Japanese war production would have declined below the peak levels of 1944 by 40 to 50 percent solely as a result of the interdiction of overseas imports." MacIsaac, USSBS, vol. 7, *Summary Report (Pacific War)*, 15. See also Craven and Cate, *Army Air Forces*, 5:753–54.

173. R. J. Overy, *The Air War 1939–1945* (London: Macmillan Papermac, 1987), 125.

174. MacIsaac, USSBS, vol. 7, *Summary Report (Pacific War)*, 21.

175. MacIsaac, USSBS, vol. 7, *Summary Report (Pacific War)*, 92. See also

Robert A. Pape, *Bombing to Win: Air Power and Coercion in War* (Ithaca NY: Cornell University Press, 1996), 104.

176. Ralph, "Improvised Destruction," 517; Pape, *Bombing to Win*, 104.

177. Craven and Cate, *Army Air Forces*, 5:751. The B-29 death toll is the total number of battle deaths for airmen in the Pacific theater's U.S. Army Strategic Air Forces. See U.S. Department of the Army, *Army Battle Casualties and Nonbattle Deaths in World War II—Final Report, 7 December 1941–31 December 1946*, 90. For Eighth Air Force losses, see Donald L. Miller, *Masters of the Air: America's Bomber Boys Who Fought the Air War against Nazi Germany* (New York: Simon and Schuster, 2007), 7.

178. LeMay, interview by Rosenberg, 12 January 1965, file K239.0512-714, AFHRA.

179. LeMay to Anderson, 25 August 1945, folder III 1 (A) 4, Special Official Correspondence with Maj. Gen. Frederick L. Anderson, box B11, LeMay Papers.

7. Progressive Legacies

Arnold to Theodore von Karman, memorandum, 7 November 1944, "AAF Long Range Development Program," Deputy Chief of Staff, Operations, Director of Plans—General File, 1944–53, folder 67, box 16, Record Group 341, National Archives, Washington DC.

John A. Warden III, "Employing Air Power in the Twenty-first Century," in *The Future of Air Power in the Aftermath of the Gulf War*, ed. Richard H. Shultz Jr. and Robert L. Pfaltzgraff Jr. (Maxwell Air Force Base AL: Air University Press, 1992), 61.

1. German Field Marshal Eric von Manstein noted after the war that the unconditional surrender policy helped persuade him to shun the 20 July 1944 plot against Hitler and continue fighting. "It was already clear by that time that not even a *coup d'état* would make any difference to the Allied demand for unconditional surrender," he remarked. See *Lost Victories*, ed. and trans. Anthony G. Powell (Novato CA: Presidio Press, 1982), 288. See also Johannes Steinhoff, Peter Pechel, and Dennis Showalter, eds., *Voices from the Third Reich: An Oral History* (Washington DC: Regnery Gateway, 1989), 387.

2. The nineteenth-century Prussian military philosopher Carl von Clausewitz referred to those elements that "distinguish real war from war on paper" and make "the apparently easy so difficult" as "friction." Those elements

are danger, exertion, uncertainty, and chance. See Carl von Clausewitz, *On War*, ed. and trans. Michael Howard and Peter Paret (Princeton: Princeton University Press, 1976), 104, 119, 121.

3. Arnold, diary entry, 13 June 1945, in John W. Huston, ed., *American Airpower Comes of Age: General Henry H. "Hap" Arnold's World War II Diaries* (Maxwell Air Force Base AL: Air University Press, 2002), 2:326. See also Michael S. Sherry, *The Rise of American Air Power: The Creation of Armageddon* (New Haven: Yale University Press, 1987), 307–8.

4. Carl Spaatz, "Strategic Air Power: Fulfillment of a Concept," *Foreign Affairs* 24 (April 1946): 385. In 1947 Spaatz became the first chief of staff of the newly formed U.S. Air Force.

5. Curtis E. LeMay with MacKinlay Kantor, *Mission with LeMay* (Garden City NY: Doubleday, 1965), 388.

6. LeMay with Kantor, *Mission*, 381. LeMay said that he mentioned at a postwar press conference in Japan that "if a nuclear weapon shortened the war by only a week, probably it saved more lives than were taken by that single glare of heat and radiation." "The Japanese reaction was all to the good," LeMay claimed. "They believed along with me that it was a question of military expediency and not a moral issue."

7. Eaker to Ronald Schaffer, 11 January 1979, Hansell Small Manuscript Collection, MS 6, Special Collections Branch, U.S. Air Force Academy Library CO (hereafter HSMC).

8. Hansell to Lt. Col. David MacIsaac, 24 August 1975, MS 6, HSMC.

9. Gen. Curtis E. LeMay, USAF, Ret., "The Command Realities," in *Impact: The Army Air Forces' Confidential Picture History of World War II* (Harrisburg PA: Historical Times, 1982), 5:xvii.

10. Hansell to Dr. David MacIsaac, 8 January 1988, MS 6, HSMC.

11. Anderson to Spaatz, 17 August 1945, folder Personal Correspondence—August 1945, box 21, Carl A. Spaatz Papers, Library of Congress.

12. Air Force Manual 1-2, *United States Air Force Basic Doctrine*, 1 April 1955, 10.

13. Air Force Manual 1-2, *United States Air Force Basic Doctrine*, 1 April 1955, 10.

14. Air Force Manual 1-1, *Basic Aerospace Doctrine*, 16 March 1984, 2–6.

15. Air Force Manual 1-1, *Basic Aerospace Doctrine*, 16 March 1984, 3–2.

16. Air Force Manual 1-1, *Basic Aerospace Doctrine*, 16 March 1984, 3–2.

17. Curtis LeMay, interview by Mary-Ann Bendel, printed in *USA Today*, 23 July 1986, 9A.

18. See Mark Clodfelter, *The Limits of Air Power: The American Bombing of North Vietnam* (New York: Free Press, 1989), 134–46, 175–76, 194–210.

19. Air Force Doctrine Document 1, *Basic Doctrine*, 17 November 2003, 40.

20. Air Force Doctrine Document 1, *Basic Doctrine*, 17 November 2003, 41. The manual notes that "strategic attack is not an argument for replacing ground combat with airpower; the ground battle will often still be necessary." Yet the sentence that follows implies that a savvy commander, seeking a decisive outcome, would be foolish not to rely on strategic attack: "Strategic attack simply offers JFCs [Joint Force Commanders] another option, a flexible one that can go to the heart of an enemy and attain a variety of effects directly at the strategic level."

21. For an excellent analysis of Warden and his ideas, see John Andreas Olsen, *John Warden and the Renaissance of American Air Power* (Dulles VA: Potomac Books, 2007). See also David S. Fadok, "John Boyd and John Warden: Airpower's Quest for Strategic Paralysis," in *The Paths of Heaven: The Evolution of Airpower Theory*, ed. Phillip S. Meilinger (Maxwell Air Force Base AL: Air University Press, 1997): 357–98.

22. Warden, "Employing Air Power," 61.

23. Warden, "Employing Air Power," 65; John A. Warden III, *The Air Campaign: Planning for Combat* (Washington DC: National Defense University Press, 1988), 139.

24. Warden, "Employing Air Power," 67–68.

25. Warden, "Employing Air Power," 66.

26. George H. W. Bush, "Address Before a Joint Session of Congress on the State of the Union," in *Public Papers of the Presidents: George Bush—1991* (Washington DC: U.S. Government Printing Office, 1992), 1:79.

27. On American war aims in the 1991 Persian Gulf War, see Ilana Kass and Bard O'Neill, "The Persian Gulf War: A Political-Military Assessment," *Comparative Strategy* 11 (April–June 1992): 214–16.

28. U.S. Department of Defense, "Operation Desert Shield/Desert

Storm Timeline." Accessed at http://www.defenselink.mil/news/newsarticle
.aspx?id=45404.

29. Eliot A. Cohen, "The Mystique of U.S. Airpower," *Foreign Affairs*
73 (January–February 1994): 122.

30. Robert C. Owen, "The Balkans Air Campaign Study: Part 2," *Air-power Journal* 11 (Fall 1997): 12.

31. William J. Clinton, "Statement on the Decision to End Airstrikes in
Bosnia," 20 September 1995, in *Public Papers of the Presidents: William J.
Clinton—1995* (Washington DC: U.S. Government Printing Office, 1996),
2:1410.

32. Owen, "Balkans Air Campaign Study," 15.

33. Owen, "Balkans Air Campaign Study," 26n112.

34. Clinton, "Commencement Address at the United States Air Force
Academy in Colorado Springs," 2 June 1999, in *Public Papers of the Pres-idents: William J. Clinton—1999* (Washington DC: U.S. Government Print-ing Office, 2000), 1:871.

35. Clinton, *Public Papers, 1999*, 1:868.

36. Benjamin S. Lambeth, "Lessons from the War in Kosovo," *Joint Force
Quarterly* (Spring 2002): 12.

37. See Robert A. Pape, "The True Worth of Air Power," *Foreign Affairs*
83 (March–April 2004): 116–30; Benjamin S. Lambeth, NATO's *Air War for
Kosovo: A Strategic and Operational Assessment* (Santa Monica CA: RAND,
2001); and Daniel L. Byman and Matthew C. Waxman, "Kosovo and the
Great Air Power Debate," *International Security* 24 (Spring 2000): 5–38.

38. Byman and Waxman, "Kosovo." See also William M. Arkin, "Civil-ian Casualties and the Air War," washingtonpost.com, 21 October 2001.
Human Rights Watch estimated that ninety incidents occurred involving ci-vilian deaths, in which between 488 and 527 civilians may have died, while
Serbs claimed 1,200–5,700 non-combatant deaths. See Lord Robertson of
Port Ellen, Secretary General of NATO, "Kosovo One Year On: Achievement
and Challenge," 15. Undated manuscript, accessed at http://www.nato.int
/kosovo/repo2000/report-en.pdf.

39. John Keegan, "Please Mr Blair, never take such a risk again," *Daily
Telegraph*, 6 June 1999; Andrew L. Stigler, "A Clear Victory for Airpower:
NATO's Empty Threat to Invade Kosovo," *International Security* 27 (Win-ter 2002–3): 124–57.

40. John Keegan, "Please Mr Blair," *Daily Telegraph*, 6 June 1999.

41. Pape, "True Worth," 126–27.

42. For a month-by-month listing of U.S. and Coalition Forces casualties in Afghanistan, see http://icasualties.org/oef/.

43. George W. Bush, "President Speaks on War Effort to Citadel Cadets," Charleston SC, 11 December 2001. Accessed at http://www.whitehouse.gov /news/releases/2001/12/20011211-6.html.

44. One report called the "shock and awe" attack on Baghdad targets "the most devastating air raid since Dresden." See John T. Correll, "What Happened to Shock and Awe?" *Air Force Magazine*, November 2003, 57.

45. Bob Woodward, *Plan of Attack* (New York: Simon and Schuster, 2004), 405.

46. See Iraq Body Count, accessed at http://www.iraqbodycount.org/anal ysis/numbers/surge-2008/. The death toll climbed with the "surge" of U.S. combat activity in spring 2007. In 2006 air strikes killed 252 Iraqi civilians; in 2007 aerial bombing killed 943; and in 2008, through November, aerial bombing killed 365 civilians.

47. See Human Rights Watch, accessed at http://www.hrw.org/en /node/75157/section/3, for data from 2006 and 2007. Data for 2008 comes from a February 2009 United Nations report. See UN News Service, "Number of Afghan civilian deaths in 2008 highest since Taliban ouster, says UN," 17 February 2009, accessed at http://www.un.org/apps//news/story.asp?Ne wsID=29918&Cr=Afghan&Cr1=civilian+rights.

48. In Afghanistan, 3,572 American and NATO airstrikes occurred in 2007, more than double the total for 2006 and twenty times the number for 2005. See Josh White, "U.S. Boosts Its Use of Airstrikes in Iraq," *Washington Post*, 17 January 2008. The article compared the increases in bombing associated with the surge in Iraq to bombing in Afghanistan. In terms of ordnance dropped in Afghanistan, U.S. and NATO forces expended 2,644 aerial munitions in 2006, 5,198 in 2007, 5,051 in 2008, and 4,184 in 2009, according to Combined Forces Air Component Commander statistics. See "Airpower Operations in Afghanistan (as of December 31, 2009)," accessed at http://www.airforce -magazine.com/datapoints/2010/Pages/dp021810_OEFsorties.aspx. By 1 October 2009 the United States had conducted eighty-seven airstrikes inside Pakistan, with seventy-six of those occurring since January 2008. The number of strikes in 2009 eclipsed the total for 2008. See Bill Roggio and Alexander Mayer, "Analysis: A look at U.S. airstrikes in Pakistan through September

2009," *Long War Journal*, 1 October 2009, accessed at http://www.longwarjour
nal.org/archives/2009/10/analysis_us_airstrik.php.

49. See, for example, Helene Cooper, "Afghan Leader Says Civilian Deaths Strain Ties with U.S.," *New York Times*, 9 May 2009.

50. David Kilcullen and Andrew McDonald Exum, "Death from Above, Outrage from Below," *New York Times*, 17 May 2009. See also Ismail Khan and Pir Zubair Shah, "U.S. Airstrike Kills 20 People in Pakistan," *New York Times*, 28 October 2008.

51. Robert F. Futrell, *The United States Air Force in Korea 1950–1953* (New York: Duell, Sloan, and Pearce, 1961; rev. ed., Washington DC: U.S. Government Printing Office, 1983), 504.

52. Cohen, "Mystique of U.S. Airpower," 109. British historian and defense analyst Colin S. Gray makes a similar claim. "When politicians want to 'do something' . . . it is a great temptation to reach for one's airpower 'gun,'" he observes. "Because American airpower, necessarily and advantageously, is all but ubiquitously available to lead or support military action, it cannot help but invite and produce addiction." See "Understanding Airpower: Bonfire of the Fallacies," *Strategic Studies Quarterly* 2 (Winter 2008): 71.

53. See, for example, Mark Mazzetti and David E. Sanger, "Obama Expands Missile Strikes inside Pakistan," *New York Times*, 21 February 2009; Scott Shane, "C.I.A. to Expand Use of Drones in Pakistan," *New York Times*, 4 December 2009; and Bill Roggio, "U.S. launches cruise missile strikes against al Qaeda in Yemen," *Long War Journal*, 19 December 2009, accessed at http://www.longwarjournal.org/archives/2009/12/us_launches _cruise_m.php.

54. David Halberstam, *War in a Time of Peace: Bush, Clinton, and the Generals* (New York: Scribner, 2001), 460.

55. Quoted in William Drozdiak, "NATO General Predicts Victory in Two Months," *Washington Post*, 24 May 1999.

56. Clausewitz, *On War*, 89.

57. Clausewitz, *On War*, 75.

BIBLIOGRAPHY

Archival Sources

Air Force Historical Research Agency, Maxwell Air Force Base AL

AWPD-I
Oral History Interviews
Records of the Air Corps Tactical School
Records of the Committee of Operations Analysts
Records of the Eighth Air Force
Records of the Fifteenth Air Force
Records of the Twentieth Air Force

Dwight D. Eisenhower Presidential Library, Abilene KS

Various documents pertaining to World War II

Library of Congress, Manuscript Collection, Washington DC

Papers of Frank M. Andrews
Papers of Henry H. Arnold
Papers of Ira C. Eaker
Papers of Curtis E. LeMay
Papers of William Mitchell
Papers of Carl A. Spaatz

National Archives and Records Administration, Washington DC

Record Group 18, Records of the Army Air Forces
Record Group 218, Records of the Joint Chiefs of Staff
Record Group 243, Records of the U.S. Strategic Bombing Survey
Record Group 319, Records of the Army Staff
Record Group 341, Records of Headquarters United States Air Force
    Air Staff)
Record Group 407, Records of the Adjutant General's Office, 1917–58

Office of Air Force History, Bolling Air Force Base, Washington DC

Microfilm of various documents on file at the Air Force Historical
    Research Agency

Special Collections Branch, U.S. Air Force Academy Library, USAFA CO

Papers of Haywood S. Hansell Jr.

Papers of Laurence S. Kuter

Published Sources

Adams, Henry H. *Harry Hopkins.* New York: G. P. Putnam's Sons, 1977.

Allen, Thomas B., and Norman Polmar. *Code-Name Downfall: The Secret Plan To Invade Japan—and Why Truman Dropped the Bomb.* New York: Simon and Schuster, 1995.

Armstrong, Anne. *Unconditional Surrender: The Impact of the Casablanca Policy on World War II.* New Brunswick NJ: Rutgers University Press, 1961.

Arnold, Henry H. *Global Mission.* New York: Harper and Brothers, 1949.

Atkinson, J. L. Boone. "Italian Influence on the Origins of the American Concept of Strategic Bombardment." *Air Power Historian* 4 (July 1957): 141–49.

"Battle of Japan." *Time,* 13 August 1945.

Biddle, Tami Davis. "Dresden 1945: Reality, History, and Memory." *Journal of Military History* 72 (April 2008): 413–39.

———. *Rhetoric and Reality in Air Warfare: The Evolution of British and American Ideas about Strategic Bombing, 1914–1945.* Princeton: Princeton University Press, 2002.

"A Bomb on Norden." *Time,* 1 January 1945.

Boyle, Andrew. *Trenchard.* London: Collins, 1962.

Brodie, Bernard. *War and Politics.* New York: Macmillan, 1973.

Bush, George. *Public Papers of the Presidents of the United States: George Bush, 1991.* Washington DC: U.S. Government Printing Office, 1992.

Byman, Daniel L., and Matthew C. Waxman. "Kosovo and the Great Air Power Debate." *International Security* 24 (Spring 2000): 5–38.

Caidin, Martin. *Black Thursday.* New York: Dell, 1960.

Carter, Kit C., and Robert Mueller, comp. *The Army Air Forces in World War II—Combat Chronology, 1941–1945.* Washington DC: Office of Air Force History, 1973.

Churchill, Winston S. *The Second World War*. 6 vols. New York: Bantam Books, 1951, 1962.

Clausewitz, Carl von. *On War*. Edited and translated by Michael Howard and Peter Paret. Princeton: Princeton University Press, 1976.

Clinton, William J. *Public Papers of the Presidents of the United States: William J. Clinton, 1995*. Washington DC: U.S. Government Printing Office, 1996.

———. *Public Papers of the Presidents of the United States: William J. Clinton, 1999*. Washington DC: U.S. Government Printing Office, 2000.

Clodfelter, Mark. "Culmination: Dresden, 1945." *Aerospace Historian* 26 (Fall 1979): 134–47.

———. *The Limits of Air Power: The American Bombing of North Vietnam*. New York: Free Press, 1989.

Coffey, Thomas M. *Decision over Schweinfurt*. New York: David MacKay, 1977.

———. *Hap: The Story of the U.S. Air Force and the Man Who Built It*. New York: Viking Press, 1982.

———. *Iron Eagle: The Turbulent Life of General Curtis LeMay*. New York: Crown, 1986.

Coffman, Edward M. *The War to End All Wars: The American Military Experience in World War I*. Madison: University of Wisconsin Press, 1986.

Cohen, Eliot A. "The Mystique of U.S. Airpower." *Foreign Affairs* 73 (January–February 1994): 109–24.

Copp, DeWitt S. *A Few Great Captains*. Garden City NY: Doubleday, 1980.

———. *Forged in Fire: Strategy and Decisions in the Airwar over Europe, 1940–1945*. Garden City NY: Doubleday, 1982.

Correll, John T. "Rendezvous With the *Rex*." *Air Force Magazine*, December 2008, 54–57.

———. "What Happened to Shock and Awe?" *Air Force Magazine*, November 2003, 52–57.

Crane, Conrad C. *Bombs, Cities, and Civilians*. Lawrence: Kansas University Press, 1993.

———. "'Contrary to Our National Ideals': American Strategic Bombing of Civilians in World War II." In *Civilians in the Path of War*, edited by Mark Grimsley and Clifford J. Rogers, 219–49. Lincoln: University of Nebraska Press, 2002.

Craven, Wesley Frank, and James Lea Cate. *The Army Air Forces in World War II*. 7 vols. Washington DC: Office of Air Force History, 1983. First published 1948–58 by University of Chicago Press.

Davis, Richard G. *Carl A. Spaatz and the Air War in Europe*. Washington DC: Center for Air Force History, 1993.

———. "Operation 'Thunderclap': The U.S. Army Air Forces and the Bombing of Berlin." *Journal of Strategic Studies* 14 (March 1991): 90–111.

Douhet, Giulio. *The Command of the Air*. New York: Coward-McCann, 1942; repr., Washington DC: Office of Air Force History, 1983.

Dower, John W. *War without Mercy: Race and Power in the Pacific War*. New York: Pantheon Books, 1986.

Eaker, Ira C. "Maj. Gen. James E. Fechet: Chief of the Air Corps, 1927–1931." *Air Force Magazine*, September 1978, 95–98.

———. "Some Memories of Winston Churchill." *Aerospace Historian* 19 (Fall 1972): 121–24.

Eisenhower, David. *Eisenhower at War 1943–1945*. New York: Vintage, 1987.

Emme, Eugene M., ed. *The Impact of Air Power: National Security and World Politics*. New York: D. Van Nostrand, 1959.

Faber, Peter R. "Interwar U.S. Army Aviation and the Air Corps Tactical School: Incubators of American Airpower." In *The Paths of Heaven: The Evolution of Airpower Theory*, edited by Phillip S. Meilinger, 183–238. Maxwell Air Force Base AL: Air University Press, 1997.

Fabyanic, Thomas. *Strategic Air Attack in the United States Air Force: A Case Study*. Manhattan: Kansas State University/Aerospace Historian, 1976.

Fadok, David S. "John Boyd and John Warden: Airpower's Quest for Strategic Paralysis." In *The Paths of Heaven: The Evolution of Airpower Theory*, edited by Phillip S. Meilinger, 357–98. Maxwell Air Force Base AL: Air University Press, 1997.

Felice, Carman P. "The Men and the Machines: Air Operations in World War I." *Aerospace Historian* 5 (January 1958): 41–46.

Ferrell, Robert H., ed. *Off the Record: The Private Papers of Harry S. Truman*. New York: Harper and Row, 1980.

Finney, Robert T. *History of the Air Corps Tactical School, 1920–1940*. Maxwell Air Force Base AL: Air University Press, 1955; repr., Washington DC: Office of Air Force History, 1992.

Flugel, Raymond. "United States Air Power Doctrine: A Study of the Influence of William Mitchell and Giulio Douhet at the Air Corps Tactical School, 1921–1935." PhD diss., University of Oklahoma, 1965.

Frank, Richard B. *Downfall: The End of the Imperial Japanese Empire*. New York: Penguin Books, 2001.

Fredette, Raymond H. *The Sky on Fire: The First Battle of Britain 1917–1918 and the Birth of the Royal Air Force*. New York: Holt, Rinehart, and Winston, 1966.

Frisbee, John L., ed. *Makers of the United States Air Force*. Washington DC: Office of Air Force History, 1987.

Futrell, Robert F. *Ideas, Concepts, Doctrine: Basic Thinking in the United States Air Force, 1907–1984*. 2 vols. Maxwell Air Force Base AL: Air University Press, 1989.

———. *The United States Air Force in Korea 1950–1953*. New York: Duell, Sloan, and Pearce, 1961; rev. ed., Washington DC: U.S. Government Printing Office, 1983.

Gaston, James C. *Planning the American Air War: Four Men and Nine Days in 1941*. Washington DC: National Defense University Press, 1983.

Gentile, Gian P. *How Effective Is Strategic Bombing? Lessons Learned from World War II to Kosovo*. New York: New York University Press, 2001.

Goldberg, Alfred, ed. *A History of the United States Air Force, 1907–1957*. Princeton NJ: Van Nostrand, 1957.

Gorrell, Edgar S. *The Measure of America's World War Aeronautical Effort*. Northfield VT: Norwich University, 1940.

Gray, Colin S. "Understanding Airpower: Bonfire of the Fallacies." *Strategic Studies Quarterly* 2 (Winter 2008): 43–83.

Greer, Thomas H. *The Development of Air Doctrine in the Army Air Arm, 1917–1941*. Washington DC: Office of Air Force History, 1955, 1985.

Halberstam, David. *War in a Time of Peace: Bush, Clinton, and the Generals*. New York: Scribner, 2001.

Hansell, Haywood S., Jr. *The Air Plan That Defeated Hitler.* Atlanta: Higgins-McArthur/Logino and Porter, 1972.

———. *The Strategic Air War against Germany and Japan: A Memoir.* Washington DC: Office of Air Force History, 1986.

———. *Strategic Air War against Japan.* Washington DC: U.S. Government Printing Office, 1980.

———. "USAAF Plans and Strategic Effects." In *Impact: The Army Air Forces' Confidential Picture History of World War II,* 4:iv–xiii. Harrisburg PA: Historical Times, 1982.

Hastings, Max. *Retribution: The Battle for Japan, 1944–45.* New York: Alfred A. Knopf, 2008.

Hennessy, Juliette A. *The United States Army Air Arm: April 1861 to April 1917.* Washington DC: Office of Air Force History, 1958, 1985.

Higham, Robin. *Air Power: A Concise History.* New York: St. Martin's Press, 1972.

Hofstadter, Richard. *The Age of Reform: From Bryan to F.D.R.* New York: Alfred A. Knopf, 1955, 1968.

Holley, I. B., Jr. *Ideas and Weapons.* New Haven: Yale University Press, 1953; repr., Washington DC: Office of Air Force History, 1983.

Hopper, Bruce C. "American Day Bombardment in World War I." *Aerospace Historian* 4 (April 1957): 88–91.

The Howitzer: The Yearbook of the United States Corps of Cadets— 1912. New York: Charles L. Willard, 1912.

Hudson, James J. *Hostile Skies: A Combat History of the American Air Service in World War I.* Syracuse: Syracuse University Press, 1968.

Hughes, Thomas Alexander. *Over Lord: General Pete Quesada and the Triumph of Tactical Air Power in World War II.* New York: Free Press, 1995.

Hurley, Alfred F. *Billy Mitchell: Crusader for Air Power.* New York: Franklin Watts, 1964; new ed., Bloomington: Indiana University Press, 1975.

Hurley, Alfred F., and Robert C. Ehrhart, eds. *Air Power and Warfare: Proceedings of the Eighth Military History Symposium, USAF Academy, 1978.* Washington DC: U.S. Government Printing Office, 1979.

Huston, John W., ed. *American Airpower Comes of Age: General Henry H. "Hap" Arnold's World War II Diaries.* 2 vols. Maxwell Air Force Base AL: Air University Press, 2002.

Jablonski, Edward. *Double Strike: The Epic Air Raids on Regensburg/ Schweinfurt*. Garden City NY: Doubleday, 1974.

Johnson, David E. *Fast Tanks and Heavy Bombers: Innovation in the U.S. Army, 1917–1945*. Ithaca NY: Cornell University Press, 2003.

Kass, Ilana, and Bard O'Neill. "The Persian Gulf War: A Political-Military Assessment." *Comparative Strategy* 11 (April–June 1992): 213–40.

Kennett, Lee. *A History of Strategic Bombing*. New York: Charles Scribner's Sons, 1982.

Kerr, E. Bartlett. *Flames over Tokyo: The U.S. Army Air Forces' Incendiary Campaign against Japan, 1944–1945*. New York: Donald I. Fine, 1991.

Kozak, Warren. *LeMay: The Life and Wars of General Curtis LeMay*. Washington DC: Regnery, 2009.

Kreis, John F., ed. *Piercing the Fog: Intelligence and Army Air Forces Operations in World War II*. Washington DC: Air Force History and Museums Program, 1996.

Lambeth, Benjamin S. "Lessons from the War in Kosovo." *Joint Force Quarterly* (Spring 2002): 126–33.

———. *NATO's Air War for Kosovo: A Strategic and Operational Assessment*. Santa Monica CA: RAND, 2001.

Larrabee, Eric. *Commander in Chief: Franklin Delano Roosevelt, His Lieutenants, and Their War*. New York: Simon and Schuster, 1987.

LeMay, Curtis E. "The Command Realities." In *Impact: The Army Air Forces' Confidential Picture History of World War II*, 5:x–xvii. Harrisburg PA: Historical Times, 1982.

LeMay, Curtis E., with MacKinlay Kantor. *Mission with LeMay*. Garden City NY: Doubleday, 1965.

Levine, Alan J. *The Strategic Bombing of Germany, 1940–1945*. Westport CT: Praeger, 1992.

Levine, Isaac Don. *Mitchell: Pioneer of Air Power*. New York: Duell, Sloan and Pearce, 1943, 1958.

Linderman, Gerald F. *The War within War: America's Combat Experience in World War II*. New York: Free Press, 1995.

Link, Arthur S. "Not So Tired." In *The Progressive Era: Liberal Renaissance or Liberal Failure*, edited by Arthur Mann, 105–19. New York: Holt, Rinehart, and Winston, 1963.

MacDonald, Charles B. *A Time for Trumpets: The Untold Story of the Battle of the Bulge*. New York: William Morrow, 1985.

MacIsaac, David. "Eisenhower: A Reputation in Transition." *Air University Review* 33 (September–October 1982): 86–99.

———. "Europe in the Throes of Total War." *Air University Review* 20 (September–October 1969): 90–93.

———. "A New Look at Old Lessons." *Air Force Magazine*, September 1970, 121–25.

———. *Strategic Bombing in World War Two: The Story of the United States Strategic Bombing Survey*. New York: Garland, 1976.

———, gen. ed. *The United States Strategic Bombing Survey*. 10 vols. New York: Garland, 1976.

———. "Voices from the Central Blue: The Air Power Theorists." In *Makers of Modern Strategy from Machiavelli to the Nuclear Age*, edited by Peter Paret, 624–47. Princeton: Princeton University Press, 1986.

———. "What the Bombing Survey Really Says." *Air Force Magazine*, June 1973, 60–63.

Malloy, Sean L. "'The Rules of Civilized Warfare': Scientists, Soldiers, Civilians, and American Nuclear Targeting, 1940–1945." *Journal of Strategic Studies* 30 (June 2007): 475–512.

Manstein, Erich von. *Lost Victories*. Edited and translated by Anthony G. Powell. Novato CA: Presidio Press, 1982.

Maurer, Maurer. "Flying with Fiorello: The U.S. Air Service in Italy." *Aerospace Historian* 11 (October 1964): 113–18.

———, ed. *The U.S. Air Service in World War I*. 4 vols. Washington DC: U.S. Government Printing Office, 1979.

McArthur, Charles W. *Operations Analysis in the U.S. Army Eighth Air Force in World War II*. Providence RI: American Mathematical Society, 1990.

McFarland, Stephen L., and Wesley Phillips Newton. *To Command the Sky: The Battle for Air Superiority over Germany, 1942–1944*. Washington DC: Smithsonian Institution Press, 1991.

McKelway, St. Clair. "A Reporter with the B-29s: The Cigar, the Three Wings, and the Low-Level Attacks." *New Yorker*, 23 June 1945, 26–39.

Meilinger, Phillip. "Giulio Douhet and the Origins of Airpower Theory."

In *The Paths of Heaven: The Evolution of Airpower Theory*, edited by Phillip S. Meilinger, 1–40. Maxwell Air Force Base AL: Air University Press, 1997.

———, ed. *The Paths of Heaven: The Evolution of Airpower Theory*. Maxwell Air Force Base AL: Air University Press, 1997.

Mets, David R. *Master of Airpower: General Carl A. Spaatz*. Novato CA: Presidio Press, 1988.

Middlebrook, Martin. *The Battle of Hamburg: Allied Bomber Forces against a German City in 1943*. New York: Charles Scribner's Sons, 1981.

———. *The Schweinfurt-Regensburg Mission*. New York: Charles Scribner's Sons, 1983.

Mierjejewski, Alfred C. *The Collapse of the German War Economy, 1944–1945: Allied Air Power and the German National Railway*. Chapel Hill: University of North Carolina Press, 1988.

Miller, Donald L. *Masters of the Air: America's Bomber Boys Who Fought the Air War against Nazi Germany*. New York: Simon and Schuster, 2007.

Mitchell, William. "Aeronautical Era." *Saturday Evening Post*, 20 December 1924, 3–4, 99–103.

———. *Memoirs of World War I*. New York: Random House, 1960.

———. *Skyways*. Philadelphia: J. B. Lippincott, 1930.

———. *Winged Defense*. New York: G. P. Putnam's Sons, 1925; repr., New York: Dover, 1988.

Morrow, John H., Jr. *The Great War in the Air: Military Aviation from 1909 to 1921*. Washington DC: Smithsonian Institution Press, 1993.

Murray, Williamson. *Strategy for Defeat: The Luftwaffe, 1933–1945*. Maxwell Air Force Base AL: Air University Press, 1983.

———. "Ultra: Some Thoughts on Its Impact on the Second World War." *Air University Review* 35 (July–August 1984): 52–64.

Neillands, Robin. *The Bomber War: The Allied Air Offensive against Nazi Germany*. New York: Overlook Press, 2001.

Nevin, David. *Architects of Air Power*. Alexandria VA: Time-Life Books, 1981.

Nisos, Michael J. "The Bombardier and His Bombsight." *Air Force Magazine*, September 1981, 106–13.

Nutter, Ralph H. *With the Possum and the Eagle: The Memoir of a Nav-*

igator's War over Germany and Japan. Novato CA: Presidio Press, 2002.

O'Connor, Raymond G. *Diplomacy for Victory: FDR and Unconditional Surrender*. New York: W. W. Norton, 1971.

Olsen, John Andreas. *John Warden and the Renaissance of American Air Power*. Dulles VA: Potomac Books, 2007.

Overy, R. J. *The Air War 1939–1945*. London: Macmillan Papermac, 1987.

Owen, Robert C. "The Balkans Air Campaign Study: Part 2." *Airpower Journal* 11 (Fall 1997): 6–27.

Pape, Robert A. *Bombing to Win: Air Power and Coercion in War*. Ithaca: Cornell University Press, 1996.

———. "The True Worth of Air Power." *Foreign Affairs* 83 (March–April 2004): 116–30.

Parton, James. *Air Force Spoken Here: General Ira Eaker and the Command of the Air*. Bethesda MD: Adler and Adler, 1986.

———. "The Thirty-One Year Gestation of the Independent Air Force." *Aerospace Historian* 34 (September 1987): 150–57.

"The Penalties." *Time*, 1 January 1945.

Perret, Geoffrey. *Winged Victory: The Army Air Forces in World War II*. New York: Random House, 1993.

Pershing, John J. *My Experiences in the World War*. 2 vols. New York: Frederick A. Stokes, 1931.

Ralph, William W. "Improvised Destruction: Arnold, LeMay, and the Firebombing of Japan." *War in History* 13 (Winter 2006): 495–522.

Rice, Rondall R. *The Politics of Air Power: From Confrontation to Cooperation in Army Aviation Civil-Military Relations*. Lincoln: University of Nebraska Press, 2004.

Rosenman, Samuel I., comp. *The Public Papers and Addresses of Franklin D. Roosevelt*. 10 vols. New York: Harper and Brothers, 1950.

Rumpf, Hans. *The Bombing of Germany*. Translated by Edward Fitzgerald. New York: Holt, Rinehart, and Winston, 1962.

Salveneschi, Nino. *Let us Kill the War; Let Us Aim at the Heart of the Enemy*. Milan: Milesi and Nicola, 1917.

Schaffer, Ronald. *Wings of Judgment: American Bombing in World War II*. New York: Oxford University Press, 1985.

Schlesinger, Arthur M., Jr. *The Age of Roosevelt: The Crisis of the Old Order.* Boston: Houghton Mifflin, 1957.

Sherry, Michael S. *The Rise of American Air Power: The Creation of Armageddon.* New Haven: Yale University Press, 1987.

Sherwood, Robert E. *Roosevelt and Hopkins: An Intimate History.* New York: Harper and Brothers, 1948.

Shiner, John F. *Foulois and the U.S. Army Air Corps 1931–1935.* Washington DC: Office of Air Force History, 1983.

"Sixty Bombers Are Missing." *Time,* 25 October 1943.

Spaatz, Carl. "Leaves from My Battle of Britain Diary." *Air Power Historian* 4 (April 1957): 66–75.

———. "Strategic Air Power: Fulfillment of a Concept." *Foreign Affairs* 24 (April 1946): 385–96.

Spector, Ronald H. *Eagle against the Sun: The American War with Japan.* New York: Free Press, 1985.

Speer, Albert. *Inside the Third Reich.* New York: Avon Books, 1970.

Steinhoff, Johannes, Peter Pechel, and Dennis Showalter, eds. *Voices from the Third Reich: An Oral History.* Washington DC: Regnery Gateway, 1989.

Stigler, Andrew L. "A Clear Victory for Airpower: NATO's Empty Threat to Invade Kosovo." *International Security* 27 (Winter 2002–3): 124–57.

Tanaka, Yuki, and Marilyn B. Young, eds. *Bombing Civilians: A Twentieth-Century History.* New York: New Press, 2009.

Terraine, John. *A Time for Courage: The Royal Air Force in the European War, 1939–1945.* New York: Macmillan, 1985.

Traxel, David. *Crusader Nation: The United States in Peace and the Great War, 1898–1920.* New York: Alfred A. Knopf, 2006.

Truman, Harry S. *Memoirs.* Vol. 1, *Year of Decisions: 1945.* Garden City NY: Doubleday, 1955.

———. *Public Papers of the Presidents of the United States: Harry Truman, 1945.* Washington DC: U.S. Government Printing Office, 1997.

Underwood, Jeffery S. *The Wings of Democracy: The Influence of Air Power on the Roosevelt Administration 1933–1941.* College Station: Texas A&M University Press, 1991.

U.S. Air Force Doctrine Document 1, *Air Force Basic Doctrine,* 17 November 2003.

U.S. Air Force Manual 1-1, *United States Air Force Basic Aerospace Doctrine*, 16 March 1984.

U.S. Air Force Manual 1-2, *United States Air Force Basic Doctrine*, 1 April 1955.

U.S. Air Force Manual 1-2, *United States Air Force Basic Doctrine*, 1 December 1959.

U.S. Army Air Forces. ULTRA *and the History of the United States Strategic Air Force in Europe vs. the German Air Force*. Edited by Paul L. Kesaris. Frederick MD: University Publications of America, 1980.

U.S. Department of the Army. *Army Battle Casualties and Nonbattle Deaths in World War II—Final Report, 7 December 1941–31 December 1946*. Prepared by Statistical and Accounting Branch, Office of the Adjutant General, Washington DC.

"Victory Is in the Air." *Time*, 30 August 1943.

Warden, John A., III. *The Air Campaign: Planning for Combat*. Washington DC: National Defense University Press, 1988.

———. "Employing Air Power in the Twenty-first Century." In *The Future of Air Power in the Aftermath of the Gulf War*, edited by Richard H. Shultz Jr. and Robert L. Pfaltzgraff Jr., 57–82. Maxwell Air Force Base AL: Air University Press, 1992.

Watts, Barry D. *The Foundation of U.S. Air Doctrine: The Problem of Friction in War*. Maxwell Air Force Base AL: Air University Press, 1984.

Webster, Charles, and Noble Frankland. *The Strategic Air Offensive against Germany, 1939–1945*. 3 vols. London: Her Majesty's Stationery Office, 1961.

Weinberg, Gerhard L. *A World at Arms: A Global History of World War II*. Cambridge: Cambridge University Press, 1994.

Wells, Mark K. *Courage and Air Warfare: The Allied Aircrew Experience in the Second World War*. London: Frank Cass, 1995.

Werrell, Kenneth P. *Blankets of Fire: U.S. Bombers over Japan during World War II*. Washington DC: Smithsonian, 1998.

———. *Death from the Heavens: A History of Strategic Bombing*. Annapolis: Naval Institute Press, 2009.

Wheeler, Keith. *Bombers over Japan*. Alexandria VA: Time-Life Books, 1982.

Wiebe, Robert H. *The Search for Order.* New York: Hill and Wang, 1967.

Williams, George K. "'The Shank of the Drill': Americans and Strategical Aviation in the Great War." *Journal of Strategic Studies* 19 (September 1996): 381–431.

Wilson, Donald. "Origin of a Theory for Air Strategy." *Aerospace Historian* 18 (March 1971): 19–25.

Wilson, Woodrow. *The Public Papers of Woodrow Wilson: War and Peace.* 2 vols. New York: Harper and Brothers, 1927.

Woodward, Bob. *Plan of Attack.* New York: Simon and Schuster, 2004.

INDEX

Afghanistan, 250, 251–52, 318n48

Air Corps: and Army control, 72, 88; expansion of, 49, 84–85, 92, 275n86; and General Headquarters Air Force, 49–50, 76, 81, 88; name change to, 49; organization of, 49–50, 76. *See also* Air Corps Tactical School (ACTS); Air Force; Air Service; Army Air Forces (AAF); Signal Corps

Air Corps Tactical School (ACTS), 96; and Air Force autonomy, 54; curriculum of, 52–66, 72, 73; and enemy will, 59–61, 63; and industrial web theory, 57–64, 66, 72, 73; and international students, 62; and precision bombing, 64; and progressive air power beliefs, 4–5, 63–64, 73, 94, 101–2, 139, 147; and strategic bombing, 5, 57, 73, 90. *See also* Air Corps

aircraft: B-17 ("Flying Fortress"), 68–70, 72–74, 75, 76–79, 80, 82–83, 85, 87, 112–13, 114, 120–21, 140–41, 148–49, 154, 158, 162, 164, 175, 191, 195, 205, 217, 291n18; B-24 ("Liberator"), 113, 120–21, 128, 136–37, 154, 156, 158, 162, 164–66, 167, 195, 205, 291n18, 295n69; B-29 ("Superfortress"), 184, 187, 188, 194–96, 197, 198–99, 200, 201, 203–6, 211, 213, 214–15, 216, 218–19, 226, 227, 238, 240; and escort fighters, 44, 65, 124, 138, 153; and

loss rates, 106–7, 118, 120, 121, 124, 137–38, 157, 159, 164, 166, 171, 182, 188, 213, 216, 222, 227, 240, 293n44; P-47 ("Thunderbolt"), 138, 154, 158; P-51 ("Mustang"), 138, 154, 158; production of, in 1930s, 70–72, 76, 79, 80, 84–85; production of, in World War I, 10–14, 30–32; production of, in World War II, 87, 99, 115, 116, 153, 237

aircraft factory targets, 95, 144–45, 156–58, 160, 204, 205–6, 208–10, 218–19. *See also* industrial targets

Air Force: and Allied Force campaign (Kosovo), 248–50, 254–55; and Basic Doctrine Manual, 243–45; creation of, 236; and Operation Deliberate Force (Bosnia), 247–48; and Operation Enduring Freedom (Afghanistan), 250, 251–52; and Operation Iraqi Freedom (Iraq), 250–51; and Persian Gulf War, 246–47; and progressive air power beliefs, 5, 242–45, 246, 251, 252–56. *See also* Air Corps; Air Service; Army Air Forces (AAF); Signal Corps

Air Force autonomy. *See* autonomy, Air Force

Air Service, 23, 25–26; and Army ground support, 23, 27–28, 30, 45; autonomy of, 34, 45–46; name change from, 49; and strategic bombing plans, 16–17, 23–24,

Studies in War, Society, and the Military

To order or obtain more information
on these or other University of
Nebraska Press titles, visit www
.nebraskapress.unl.edu.